THE CANADIAN NAVAL CHRONICLE

THE CANADIAN NAVAL CHRONICLE

1939 - 1945

The Successes and Losses of the Canadian Navy in World War II.

REVISED EDITION

Captain Robert A. Darlington and

Commander Fraser M. McKee

Vanwell Publishing Limited

St. Catharines ON

First published in Canada by Vanwell Publishing Limited
St. Catharines, Ontario.

Design: Linda L. Moroz-Irvine

Cover: The sinking of ***U 257*** by HMCS ***Waskesiu,***
by Bo Hermanson, Victoria.

Vanwell Publishing Limited
1 Northrup Crescent
P.O. Box 2131
St. Catharines, Ontario L2R 7S2

First Edition 1996
Printed in Canada.

Canadian Cataloguing in Publication Data
Darlington, Robert A.
The Canadian Naval Chronicle 1939-1945: the successes and losses of the Canadian Navy in World War II

Includes bibliographical references and index.
ISBN 1-55125-017-9
ISBN 1-55125-032-2 hardcover edition

1. Canada. Royal Canadian Navy - History - World War, 1939-1945.
2. World War, 1939-1945 - Naval operations, Canadian. 3. Canada. Royal Canadian Navy - Lists of vessels . 4. Warships - Canada - History - 20th century. I. McKee, Fraser M. 1925 - . II. Title.

D779.C2D37 1998 940.54'5971 C98-931303-4

This register of successes and losses is dedicated, firstly, to our great wives, Wendy and Rosalind, who have so amiably put up with our researches for so long, not for the first–or last–time, and made many suggestions for improvement; and to those seamen who served in these ships and in too many cases–over 1,300–gave their lives for their country and for the freedom of the seas, "...for such as pass on the seas upon their lawful occasions."

CONTENTS

Dedication iv
Foreword vii
Preface viii

1940

1. ***Revenge*** on Little HMCS ***Ypres*** 15
2. The Loss of HMCS ***Fraser***: A Controversial Collision 18
3. Overwhelmed by the Ice: HMCS ***Bras D'Or*** 21
4. The Short Life of HMCS ***Margaree*** 23
5. The First HMCS ***Ottawa***: A Late Success 27

1941

6. HMCS ***Otter***: Lost By Fire 30
7. HMCS ***Chambly, Moose Jaw*** and the RCN's First U-boat Success 33
8. HMCS ***Lévis***: First Corvette Lost 37
9. HMCS ***Windflower*** in Collision in Heavy Fog 40
10. The Loss of the Forgotten Patrol Ship: HMCS ***Adversus*** 43

1942

11. ***Spikenard's*** Spike: Lost in Mid-Atlantic 46
12. HMCS ***St. Croix*** Proves that Old Can Still Be Good 50
13. A Successful Attack by C-3 Ships: HMCS ***Skeena*** and ***Wetaskiwin*** 53
14. HMCS ***Assiniboine:*** "Bones" Bags a Boat 56
15. Ramming and Boarding: HMCS ***Oakville's*** Successful Tactics 60
16. HMCS ***Morden*** and ***U 756***: Another Late Credit 63
17. The Yacht HMCS ***Raccoon*** Disappears 65
18. HMCS ***Charlottetown***: A St. Lawrence River Casualty 68
19. The Loss of HMCS ***Ottawa*** and 114 Naval Men 71
20. HMCS ***St. Laurent*** and Five Corvettes Sink ***U 356***: A Turning Point 75

1943

21. HMCS ***Ville De Québec*** Acts Quickly 80
22. HMCS ***Port Arthur*** Sinks ***Tritone*** 83
23. HMCS ***Louisburg***: Canada's Only Naval Loss to Enemy Aircraft 85
24. HMCS ***Regina***: A Well Conducted Attack Sinks ***Avorio*** 88
25. The Mining Of HMCS ***Weyburn*** 91
26. The Silk Stocking Run: HMCS ***Shediac*** and ***St. Croix*** with Convoy KMS-10 . . 94
27. A Skilful Attack by HMCS ***Prescott*** 97
28. HMCS ***Drumheller***: Success at Long Last 100
29. The Loss of HMCS ***St Croix:*** A New Weapon Sinks an Old but Successful Ship 102
30. The Loss of HMCS ***Chedabucto***: Inexperience and a Moment's Confusion . . . 106
31. ***U 536*** Sunk by Joint Action of Royal Navy and RCN 110

1944

32. HMCS ***Camrose*** and HMS ***Bayntun*** Get ***U 757*** 114
33. HMCS ***Waskesiu*** Sinks ***U 257***, and is Rarely Mentioned 117
34. The Hunt to Exhaustion of ***U 744***. C-2 Support Group Shows Veteran's Skills . 121
35. Escort Groups C-1 and EG-9 Combine to Sink ***U 845*** 126
36. HMCS ***Prince Rupert***, the USN and ***U 575*** 131
37. HMCS ***Swansea*** and HMS ***Pelican*** Share in the End of ***U 448*** 134

38. HMCS ***Matane, Swansea*** and ***U 311***: A Change in the Records 137
39. HMCS ***Haida, Huron*** and ***Athabaskan*** Help Sink the German Destroyer ***T 29*** . 139
40. Tragedy in the Channel: The Loss of HMCS ***Athabaskan*** 142
41. HMCS ***Valleyfield***: The Only Frigate Sunk 147
42. HMCS ***Haida*** and HMCS ***Huron*** Help Sink Two Large German Destroyers . . 151
43. Sinking German Coastal Forces: A Series of Stories 154
44. HMCS ***Haida*** and HMS ***Eskimo*** of 10 DF Sink ***U 971*** 158
45. HMCS ***Huron*** and HMS ***Eskimo*** in a Gun Battle that Sinks...Someone 161
46. Too Often Forgotten: ***MTBs 460*** and ***463*** 163
47. HMCS ***Ottawa, Kootenay*** and the Sinking of ***U 678***: Innovative Tactics 166
48. A Casualty of the Invasion: HMCS ***Regina*** 169
49. Escort Group 11 Scores Two Kills 172
50. HMCS ***Alberni*** Sinks in Thirty Seconds 175
51. A Long Hunt: HMCS ***Saint John*** and ***Swansea*** 178
52. HMCS ***Dunver*** and ***Hespeler*** Sink ***U 484*** Using All Three A/S Weapons 182
53. An Alert Radar Watch: HMCS ***Annan*** and ***Loch Achanalt*** Sink ***U 1006*** 185
54. HMCS ***Skeena*** Aground in a Gale 189
55. HMCS ***Shawinigan***: Lost with No Survivors 193
56. HMCS ***Clayoquot***: A Christmas Eve Loss 196
57. HMCS ***St Thomas*** and ***Sea Cliff***: A Second Squid Success 200

1945

58. The Destruction of the 29th MTB Flotilla 204
59. HMCS ***Saint John*** Sinks ***U 309,*** her Second Success 206
60. The Loss of HMCS ***Trentonian*** 208
61. The Frigates of EG-25 Combine to Sink ***U 1302*** 210
62. HMCS ***Guysborough***: Our Last Overseas Loss 214
63. Sunk "By Other Means": HMCS ***New Glasgow*** and ***U 1003*** 217
64. HMCS ***Esquimalt***: A Late and Last Loss 220
65. Canadian Merchant Ships Lost in World War II 224

Photo Credits 245

TABLES

TABLE 1: RCN Losses in World War II 246
TABLE 2: RCN Successes over Enemy Warships 246
TABLE 3: Cooperative Methods of Destruction 247
TABLE 4: U-boat Survivor Rates 247
TABLE 5: Successes and Losses: A Chronological Table 248
TABLE 6: Ships Removed from RCN Service for Other Reasons 250
TABLE 7: Merchant Ships Sunk: Non-Canadian Prewar and Fishing Vessels 251
TABLE 8: RCAF Successes Against U-boats 253

Glossary and Abbreviations 255
Bibliography 258
Index of Persons 262
Index of Persons for Chapter 65 265
Index of Ships 266
Index of U-boats and Italian Submarines 271

FOREWORD

It is an era that must not be forgotten in Canadian history... Canadians at war. A war that started far away beyond the borders of this vast, scarcely populated and peaceful land. It revealed how our young men and women coped with the enormous and deadly series of events with which they were faced.

The grey, rust-streaked, salt-encrusted ships from the hastily constructed navy are long gone. They live today only in fading photographs and in the memories of aging men from every walk of life, many who had never seen salt water, who cheerfully and bravely manned them across the storm-battered, war-torn North Atlantic.

This book records every episode of losses and most of the successes which engaged our ships, our Air Force and our Merchant Navy; the triumphs and the tragedies. After months of painstaking work researching many sources, including Boards of Inquiry, Reports of Proceedings and government archives, our two authors have brought the events together in easy access readable form.

A volume that will serve as a valuable reference to remind present and future generations of events that shaped the Canadian character, and which might be forgotten under the impact of modern development, that has a tendency to blur memories with the passage of time.

Howard L. Quinn, DSC CD
Commodore, RCN (Ret'd)

Commodore Howard Quinn was a pre-war RCNVR *in Prince Rupert, BC. During the war he commanded the corvette* HMCS ***Eyebright*** *and the frigates* ***Strathadam*** *and* ***Beacon Hill.*** *He was awarded a Mention in Despatches, and a* DSC *for sinking* ***U 1302*** *in March, 1945, and transferred to the* RCN *at the war's end.*

PREFACE

CHRONICLE - An especially historical account of facts or events that are arranged in order of time and usually continuous and detailed but without analysis or interpretation.

Webster's Third International Dictionary

When this jointly authored volume was initially proposed by Bob Darlington, it was simply to be an accurate narration of the stories of the RCN ships lost in the Second War. But on several occasions, usually at church services for Battle of the Atlantic Sunday, ex-naval people have commented that while we should and must honour those that gave their lives and the ships lost, why is it we pay so little heed to the notable successes achieved? After all, we did win the war, and we sank more U-boats, destroyers and other enemy warships than we lost. We are too reticent about these successes; they are mentioned too rarely. We were, and have, a darned good Navy, a Navy of which all Canadians can be proud.

So it was expanded to tell the stories of the successful ships as well. Those that won the day's battle.

This led to the question "What is success?" For the convoy escorts, corvettes, armed yachts, destroyers, *Bangors* and so forth it was, as the Convoy Escort Instructions told them, "The safe and timely arrival of the convoy". For the MTBs, it was driving off E-boats determined to mine the swept channels along the British east coast or harass the merchant ships. For the D-Day minesweepers it was opening the mine-filled lanes to the beaches whereon landed safely 95% of the troops despatched for the re-invasion of Europe. What about the German supply ships captured or scuttled when confronted by the armed merchant cruiser HMCS ***Prince Robert***?

All of these were successes. But including their stories would have meant encompassing almost every ship of the Navy, and many of the RCAF's coastal squadrons. Altogether too large a net. So we regretfully resolved to include only the losses, and the stories of enemy warship defeats attributable in the main to RCN ships. A not entirely satisfactory line drawn, but of necessity. The authors chose the title because it best fits the nature of this book. Joseph Schull, Michael Hadley, Marc Milner and a few others should be read for analysis, interpretation and for placing the events into historical context and understanding them.

We then decided to include very brief histories of the forty-four Canadian-owned and registered merchant vessels lost, found in Chapter 65. This was done as much because the Merchant Navy was as embroiled in the naval war at sea as the "regular" Navy and because that full listing is very hard to find in any volume and should be available. Table 7 is a list of European ships taken over by Canada when their home countries were overrun, and of fishing vessels sunk, although this listing is not necessarily complete. This in turn led to Table 8, a brief summary of RCAF Squadron successes against U-boats. Their successes against surface warships needs further research and would be valuable.

For the histories, two volumes were the basic foundation upon which all else was constructed: Joseph Schull's *Far Distant Ships* (Queen's Printer, 1950) and Ken Macpherson and John Burgess's *The Ships of Canada's Naval Forces* (Collins, 1981). While both have recently been reprinted, these editions were matchless for our purpose. Then the verification and fleshing out of the stories came firstly from the excellent files of the DND Directorate of History, with the unstinting help of the then-Director Dr. Alec Douglas and Drs. Carl Christie and Roger Sarty and Rob Fisher of that staff. What they do not hold was easily supplemented by the voluminous Record Group 24 files of the National Archives. Practically every RCN ship's story was developed in these files, but as they are not easily available as a reference to the readers of this volume, their file numbers are not listed in the bibliographies. We only refer to books that are, or could be, procurable by readers.

We should mention here the ridiculous subsequent cut-backs in the very small staff at DHist, for practically no saving that would be measurable in the DND budget, but which creates a major problem for all maritime researchers. This has nothing to do with defence - it is a blow to the study of Canadian history.

A multitude of very useful volumes have been consulted to augment and cross-check the stories, and are listed in the sources and in the bibliography. Several were both reliable and fairly complete; others had some inaccuracies, often carried forward from wartime assessments, repeating errors in previous volumes, or omitting deserving histories of successes or losses, which even occurs in Schull.

Of much help in telling the stories accurately, and more specifically up to date, we have drawn on the carefully researched reports of Mr. R.M. Coppock of the British Ministry of Defence, Foreign Documents Section. In these he has been reassessing all unproven U-boat kills. His studies shed new light on the RCN's efforts, especially in the gloomy earlier days of the war, and in reappraisals of air attacks, usually unprovable at the time. Also of very great assistance in carrying out research for us in the Public Records Office in Kew was Mr. Frank Redfern of Hampton, England, particularly for merchant ship loss details. In the same way Jack Muir's Naval Network files in Toronto have been of much help in verifying names and contacting participants. It is a completely hand-maintained huge file, of great value. Ms. Marylin Gurney's records at Admiralty House in Halifax were also an aid in locating personnel.

A major share in the credit for this volume must go to the late Captain R.L. Donaldson, OMM, CD, RCN (Ret'd) who read every chapter, every table, several times over. He corrected our spelling, punctuation, syntax and seamanship details and made a multitude of valuable suggestions for improvement. We didn't take them all, but they caused us to consider carefully. His name should really appear on the cover hereof, but that sort of expansion annoys librarians and cataloguers, so we acknowledge his great contribution here. His contemporaries who also held him in high regard, called him "Donaldson the Good" to distinguish him from any other Donaldsons, and for reason! It is sad that he died before seeing these results.

The photos of the RCN ships came very largely from the outstanding collection of Ken Macpherson, although in most cases their original source is shown as the National Archives of Canada. Ken's several detailed books on ship classes were also consulted frequently. Ken read the volume during preparation and his suggested corrections and changes were of the greatest value. His photos were supplemented on occasion by those loaned by individuals (or their family descendants) who had been involved fifty years ago. Since one U-boat or Italian *sommergibile* of a class looks largely the same as another, we did not try to provide actual photos of all thirty-three sunk. Photo credits are given at the end of the text.

The original cover painting was especially commissioned for this volume from Bo Hermanson, a west coast marine artist. It shows the frigate ***Waskesiu*** firing at ***U 257*** as HMS ***Nene*** hurries up to join in the finale. It is, we felt, an evocative painting of an RCN success that all too typically has received scant credit. Mr. Hermanson is well known in naval circles and receives numerous commissions for paintings of Canadian warships. A number of ***Waskesiu's*** ship's company answered our letters asking for a description of this event and Mr. Hermanson has incorporated these as well as his own expert knowledge in the painting.

Another reading of the earlier chapters by LCdr Colin Darlington, CD, was of much help in the overall aim of "getting it right."

There was an enthusiastic response to letters in Service magazines and newsletters. Also from the authors' direct approaches to many participants in these actions, asking for personal memories of the events to make the history a little more human, and to ensure accuracy by checking their recollections against official reports in the files. Practically all stories could have been doubled in length. This would have made the volume prohibitive in size and cost. Many responded with pages of details, and should be mentioned specifically. However this would be a poor measure of value, as sometimes even a brief response solved a major conundrum. So we acknowledge that we owe much to our correspondents. Each letter added to the tone of the tales and we trust that those who went to considerable trouble to contribute will be in part rewarded by "their ship's" story, even if their actual words are not included.

Cdr E.R. Paquette and Lt C.G. Bainbridges' *Honours & Awards, Canadian Naval Forces, World War II* has been particularly useful, and Ed Paquette also provided a ship-by-ship analysis of awards. However, not all awards were associated with particular successes. Some were noted as for long and valiant service, and the sinking of a U-boat was just the culminating factor. So no doubt some awards are not noted for particular actions, and for this we apologize.

In the same way, the lists of those seamen who were lost in sinkings were developed from records held in DND's Department of History. It is believed that the originals were prepared by M. Emile Beaudoin when researching his *Unlucky Lady*, the history of ***Athabaskan's*** loss. It has not been possible to re-check these lists for accuracy, so again we apologise for any errors that appear. For instance it seems that some names are included of seamen who had died previously in the ships named but not in the actual sinkings. In the same way other seamen were killed in actions when their ship was not sunk and so do not appear in the lists herein.

We also thank most warmly Ben Kooter, President of Vanwell Publishing who so readily accepted this volume for publication as part of that firm's continuing involvement with and promotion of naval history, and Angela Dobler for her publishing and editorial advice and skills in the production stages.

Times given are local whenever possible, and in the Service twenty-four-hour clock system, unless otherwise noted. A glossary is included as Table 9 for those not familiar with naval terms. Ranks are those held at the time of the event, but sometimes with added notes re future careers. In most cases we have elected to not indicate "acting" ranks as different from confirmed ranks.

We trust that this volume will serve as a ready reference to the 180 Canadian naval ships referred to, some of whom disappeared in the cold Atlantic, alone and yet herein memorialised; some of whom returned covered in honours, real or at least acknowledged. The Navy has a brief two-letter signal or flag hoist used to convey the appreciation by a senior of a job "Well Done". To these ships, and their crews, we also say

BRAVO ZULU

Battle of Atlantic Sunday
May 5, 1996
Robert A. Darlington, Victoria, BC and
Fraser M. McKee, Markdale, ON

THE CANADIAN NAVAL CHRONICLE

1940

A year of hard lessons and losses, and one unrealized success

While some of the ships and personnel in the RCN were involved in the war in 1939, the events which are the subject of this book began in 1940.

CHAPTER 1

REVENGE ON LITTLE HMCS YPRES

A collision at sea can ruin your entire day

Attributed to Thucydides, 5th Century BC

Ypres: Battle class A/S trawler
Builder: Polson Iron Works, Toronto, 16 Jun 17
1st Comm: 13 Nov 17
2nd Comm: 1938

Fate: Rammed by HMS *Revenge*, Halifax harbour, 12 May 40
Casualties: None

HMCS *Ypres* in 1926.

HMCS ***Ypres*** was one of twelve Battle class anti-submarine trawlers built to meet the growing U-boat menace of 1916-17. She was retained as a training ship until 1932, then placed in reserve. Recommissioned in 1938, she, like five sisters, was employed as a gate vessel for handling the harbour defence gates, in her case off Maugher's Beach, Halifax.

There was one vessel on each side of the gate with sufficient room between for the largest vessel to pass through in single file when the gate was opened. The defence consisted of a vertical double line of heavy wire rope net, reaching to the shore at either end, held at the surface by large steel and wood barrel-shaped buoys and anchored to the bottom. There was a gate of similar material and support, more or less in mid-channel, that could be pulled open like a farm gate when ordered by shore authorities. The two gate vessels faced seaward, Ypres (designated ***Gate Vessel No.1*** and commanded by Lieutenant Antoine Herbert Cassivi, RCNR) and HMCS ***Festubert (G.V. No. 2).***

In the early days of World War II, important convoys were provided with an elderly British battleship for protection against German surface raiders and battle cruisers that were roaming the sea lanes in the hope of finding unprotected convoys. The 33,500-ton battleship HMS ***Revenge,*** 624 feet long, and 88½ feet on the beam (compared to ***Ypres'*** 350 tons, 130 by 23 foot size) was one of these, a frequent visitor to Halifax.

In the late afternoon of Sunday, 12 May 1940 troop convoy TC-4A, consisting of two large liners, the CPR's 20,000-ton ***Duchess of Bedford*** and the 14,000-ton Cunard White Star's ***Antonia***, was preparing to leave Halifax for the Clyde, to be accompanied by ***Revenge***. At 1352 ***Revenge*** requested the gate be opened at 1830 for her departure. The battleship planned on sailing half an hour ahead of the convoy so she could get out her minesweeping paravanes, fitted to her bows, once clear of the gate. Then matters began to go astray.

The naval signal station atop the Federal Building in downtown Halifax advised the gate vessels that ***Revenge*** was moving at 1810. By 1826 the gate was opened as planned. But the huge battleship slowed and then stopped inside the gate, evidently awaiting her two charges.

Due to some difficulties in their departure arrangements, the liners' sailing was postponed, although the Extended Defence Officer (XDO) responsible for gate operations and the gate vessels were not advised. ***Revenge*** then backed up the harbour again, to anchor near George's Island in mid-harbour, about two and a half miles above the gate.

By this time it was cold at 46°F, raining, and sunset was at 2029. Visibility was not good, and in those early days, there was no radar. Being about two hours after low water, the channel was not much wider than the gate itself. At 1919, with nothing happening as far as the gate vessels could see, the gate was closed again to await further developments. At night a red light was shown in one of the gate vessels to indicate the gate itself was closed, a green light indicating the gate was fully opened.

Subsequently, although unknown to the XDO, sailing was set for 2015. And as it would be nightfall by the time the convoy reached the outer approaches, ***Revenge's*** paravanes would not be needed, and she could sail directly ahead of the liners. At 2039 the XDO watchkeeper was advised by the signal station that ***Antonia*** was moving from her berth. There was no reference to ***Revenge***. He advised ***Festubert*** by telephone line to watch for her and open the gate in time for her passage. At 2045 the signal station reported that ***Revenge*** was dropping into line *ahead* of ***Antonia*** and ***Duchess of Bedford*** and promptly at 2046 the XDO ordered the gate opened. While ***Ypres*** reported the gate fully open at 2055, at exactly 2051 by her report ***Revenge*** hit the starboard-hand gate vessel HMCS ***Ypr****es* a glancing blow, rolling her almost on her side, and flooding her through upper deck openings. The times of messages in the XDO and the gate vessels agree.

But a quotation from ***Revenge's*** log book tells a somewhat different sequence of events as far as timing is concerned, and as seen from the battleship's bridge:

2048 Middle Ground buoy abeam, port.
2049 Boom gate shut. Full astern.
2051 Struck stbd. GV
2054 Stopped
2057 P'sed thro' gate
2105 Stopped outside boom.
2126 Proc'd, Courses & Speeds as reqis. Halifax approaches.
2159 Neverfail [buoy] abeam starboard

She had, of course, with a momentum of over 33,000 tons at eight knots, been unable to stop in time. In a recent book by a paymaster midshipman[1] on board, he says the CO decided that hitting the gate vessel would do the least damage to ***Revenge*** and be less likely to delay the ship and thus the convoy. Interestingly, ***Revenge's*** captain, Capt E.R. Archer, RN, was known by the nickname "Rammer", as he had advised his ship's company he would ram any German battleship encountered if necessary.

Thundering on, although slowing, the battleship scooped up the gate on her stem. ***Ypres***, secured to the gate's cables, caromed off the battleship's bow, then crashed against her again, now listing forty to fifty degrees. ***Revenge*** drove the little ship some 500 yards south-eastward and to seaward, dragging both net and gate vessel with her before they both came to a stop clear of the channel. Although ***Festubert*** could see little of what was happening to her companion, the CO, Skipper S.K. Creaser, ordered his tiny skiff launched under Petty Officer Phillips to go to the assistance of the stricken vessel.

Fortunately ***Ypres*** did not sink at once and her crew were able to abandon her in some haste but in good order. Thirteen were hauled aboard ***Revenge*** herself at the forecastle, and her crew threw life rings to some men now in the water. ***Festubert's*** skiff picked up five ratings, two from the water and three off the slowly foundering ***Ypres.*** One of these was a ***Revenge*** rating, AB Black, who had jumped overboard to save a Canadian seaman. ***Ypres*** sank at about 2125, settling on part of the net and its moorings. With ***Revenge*** and her captive off to one side, ***Antonia*** and ***Duchess of Bedford*** passed out of the harbour. After ascertaining there was no loss of life, at 2126 ***Revenge*** continued with her convoy. ***Ypres'*** eighteen-man crew had three slightly injured and all were taken ashore by various harbour craft, the three being checked at a hospital and released. She was replaced the next day by the tug ***Pugwash***, and on the 16th by another Battle class trawler HMCS ***Arleux.*** The gate, buoys and net were recovered, the displaced moorings relaid. The gate was back in operation that day.

After consideration of the cost of recovering ***Ypres***, her age and the damage probably done to the ship, it was decided to demolish her where

1. Robert Clarkson, *Headlong Into the Sea*, pp. 40-41.

HMS *Revenge* in August, 1939

she lay. Recently divers reported no signs of her now remain.

The Board of Inquiry (presided over by Cmdre G.C. Jones, RCN) and notes in the files make for an interesting social study. A hand-written note by Commodore Leonard Murray notes: "The *Revenge* class are the worst in the world to handle under such circumstances, but I feel ***R*** was slack in not looking for the gate vessels' signals before they got too close."

In testimony, the CO of ***Revenge,*** Captain Archer, advised that he expected the gate to remain open, and when it was seen this was not so, it was too late to take full avoiding action, with the two troopers close astern of her and in a restricted channel. Anyway, Captain Archer commented that he felt his responsibilities as escort only started when he took over the convoy at sea, and its sailing arrangements were not his responsibility. This despite the initial 1352 signal for the gate opening having been originated by ***Revenge.*** His Officer of the Watch (OOW), Lieutenant Barber, RN, first noticed at four and a half cables that the gate appeared closed. On the bridge were the captain, the navigating officer and the principal weapons control officer. At first the engines were stopped, and "ships astern warned by siren and signal". Then the captain at first put on port and then starboard wheel, making it appear from the gate vessels she was heading for the eastern section of the barrier, between ***Festubert*** and Maugher's Beach. She then slewed to starboard and with engines again going astern, in her CO's comments, he "tried to skirt around the eastern limit of the opening gate" but hit ***Ypres*** a glancing blow, as described above. He was afraid that if he hit the gate itself the wire mesh would become wrapped around his screws, his ship immobilised and the gate blocked for traffic.

The XDO commander, in a separate report, was incensed that the Board implied it might be their fault for not having the gate fully opened in time. He reported a simple telephone conversation in the late afternoon with the staff officer of the Rear Admiral 3rd Battle Squadron, to which ***Revenge*** belonged.

"If this was intended to be taken as a request for the gate, it was transmitted in the wrong form, by the wrong authority and to the wrong address. Furthermore it had no Time of Origin, and no acknowledgement was asked for or transmitted."

The Board only assessed the sinking as due to errors in communication, and, one suspects, hesitated to allocate blame to an RN captain.

The next time HMS ***Revenge*** entered Halifax harbour, the crews of the two gate vessels ostentatiously manned their upper decks and donned lifejackets as she passed. And ***Ypres'*** replacement, HMCS ***Arleux*** was also hit in the same fashion somewhat later but not sunk by RMS ***Queen Mary,*** although again the little ship was partially flooded. War at sea may have been dangerous, but so was life in a gate vessel. ***Revenge*** herself survived the war and was scrapped in Scotland in 1948.

SOURCES:

Note: Oddly, for the loss of a Canadian "warship" to another force's vessel, there is little in the literature or even DND files except a brief paragraph. The National Archives produced the only report of the Board of Inquiry. A search in Britain has not even produced a Report of Collision and Grounding by ***Revenge.***

Clarkson, *Headlong Into The Sea,* pp. 30, 40-41.

Macpherson & Burgess, *Ships of Canada's Naval Forces*, pp. 11, 25, 207.

Tucker, *Naval Service of Canada*, Vol. II, p. 112.

CHAPTER 2

THE LOSS OF HMCS FRASER: A CONTROVERSIAL COLLISION

Fraser: River class destroyer
Builder: Vickers-Armstrong Ltd, Barrow UK,
1st Comm: as HMS *Crescent,* 1931
2nd Comm: 17 Feb 37
Crew: 14 officers, 158 crew

Fate: Collision with HMS *Calcutta,* 25 Jun 40, near Pointe de Courbre light
Casualties: 47 crew, 13 RN

Eternal Father, strong to save,
Whose arm hath bound the restless wave,
Who bidd'st the mighty ocean deep
Its own appointed limits keep;
O hear us when we cry to Thee
For those in peril on the sea.

William Whiting, *The Naval Hymn*

HMCS *Fraser* transiting the Panama Canal in the balmy peacetime days of April 1937.

HMCS ***Fraser*** was in Vancouver, BC for the Canadian Pacific Exhibition on 31 August 1939 when orders were received to proceed to Halifax. In company with HMCS ***St. Laurent*** the two sailed without returning to their home port at Esquimalt. As one of her ship's company remarked many years later, "We left clothing ashore, rented rooms, family and unpaid bills."[1] And so ***Fraser*** rushed to enter the Atlantic war.

After eight months of east coast and Caribbean patrol and escort duties, at the Admiralty's urgent request ***Fraser*** was ordered to England, arriving 3 June 1940. By 11 June, with newly-fitted anti-aircraft armament in lieu of one of her torpedo mounts, she joined the other Canadian destroyers in what Schull described as "salvaging the melancholy remnants of defeat."[2]

On 21 June ***Fraser*** was ordered to proceed to St. Jean de Luz, a small French port near the Spanish border, where thousands of troops had retreated from the advancing German army. On the evening of 25 June, with forty-four members of the British, French and Polish forces on board, ***Fraser*** joined her sister ship HMCS ***Restigouche*** and the RN cruiser HMS ***Calcutta to*** return to Plymouth.

Calcutta was a 4,290-ton light cruiser, built at the end of the First World War. On this occasion Vice Admiral A.T.B. Curteis, Flag Officer Commanding Second Cruiser Squadron, was on board and in command of this small force.

Due to the deteriorating situation ashore and the pressures on the ships, almost none of the crew had had sufficient sleep in weeks. The disposition of the ships at the time, just after 2200, was on a course of 006° at a brisk twenty-five knots. The Admiral then ordered speed for twenty knots and an alteration to a course to the westward of 250°, which put ***Fraser*** bearing 34° on ***Calcutta's*** starboard bow and ***Restigouche*** on the cruiser's port quarter.[3]

1. Interview with LCdr P.E. Palmer.
2. Joseph Schull, *The Far Distant Ships*, p.18.
3. In *The Sea Is At Our Gates,* p.78, German incorrectly locates ***Fraser*** on ***Calcutta's*** port bow, but this may just be as a result of a difference in his assessment of timing due to considerable manoeuvering that took place as darkness fell.

The Admiral then ordered "Form single line ahead in sequence of fleet numbers" and reduced the speed of the formation to fourteen knots. The resulting formation would have been with ***Calcutta*** leading, followed by ***Fraser*** then ***Restigouche***. The latter destroyer temporarily increased speed to close the cruiser and altered to starboard but allowed sufficient room for ***Fraser*** to take station between herself and ***Calcutta***. Lieutenant Commander H.N. Lay, CO of ***Restigouche***, states this situation clearly in his report. Some narratives have suggested that without a record of the ships' sequence numbers assigned at that time there was some confusion over the order the two destroyers should take in line astern of ***Calcutta***. Apparently Lay was not in any doubt.

The commanding officer of ***Fraser*** was Commander Wallace B. Creery. On the bridge at the time of the order to form line ahead, he told the Officer of the Watch, Lieutenant H.V.W. Groos, to carry on with the manoeuvre. Creery's intention was to turn sharply to port and pass down the starboard side of ***Calcutta*** to take station astern of her. Groos gave the order "Port 10". Creery told the OOW to increase speed to twenty knots.

In his subsequent report, written the day after the collision, Commander Creery stated that he soon realised the OOW had insufficient wheel on to turn short of ***Calcutta***. Creery then took over conning the ship and ordered "Port 20" and then "Hard-a-port".

He immediately appreciated that the additional port helm would still not turn him short of the cruiser's line of advance, so he decided to turn sharply to starboard and pass across the bows of the larger ship, and thus down her port side. He ordered "Hard-a-starboard" and "One short blast" (on the ship's siren).

Before that order could take effect, it was evident that the two ships were facing a head-on collision, so Creery ordered "Hard-a-port, full speed astern both engines."

All the above orders, from the first "Port 10" by the OOW to full astern by the CO took place over a period of only two and a half minutes.

Captain D.M. Lees was the commanding officer of HMS ***Calcutta***. He too rendered a report on 26 June. From his position on his bridge he observed the initial modest turn to port by ***Fraser*** and concluded that Creery's intention was at that time to cross his bows and proceed down his port side. He reported "I estimate that ***Fraser*** crossed my line of advance about two and a half cables (500 yds) ahead of me..."

He further stated that he felt that ***Fraser*** would pass dangerously close down his port side, so ordered starboard wheel and one short blast. When he saw ***Fraser*** turn more sharply to port he realised that collision was imminent and ordered "Full astern" to lessen the impact.

Calcutta's bow struck ***Fraser*** on the port side abreast B gun, penetrating to the centre line of the destroyer. The forward part of the ship broke away, still floating upright. The wheelhouse and bridge structure were scooped onto ***Calcutta's*** forecastle. Creery led the few bridge personnel to safety by jumping to the forecastle deck of the cruiser. He returned briefly to the wrecked wheelhouse to rescue Able Seaman Todeus whose feet had been badly crushed.

Restigouche at first thought ***Fraser*** had collided with a submerged wreck. On sighting the floating after end of the ship, Lay closed it so that his quarterdeck was alongside the stern of ***Fraser*** for about ten minutes. All of the survivors from the after end of ***Fraser*** were taken aboard ***Restigouche***. Lay then lowered his whaler under command of Lt D.W. Groos and including Leading Signalman P.E. Palmer with a hand-held night light for communications. Many years later retired LCdr "Paddy" Palmer recalls that Groos filled the whaler to its maximum with exhausted survivors plucked from the very cold water. When the boat pulled back to ***Restigouche's*** starboard quarter, and just prior to reaching her rescue ladder, the ship's screws began turning. The stern came down on the whaler throwing everyone into the water. All were able to swim to the ladder except one ordinary seaman from ***Restigouche*** who was lost. Later, on closing ***Fraser's*** sinking bow portion it capsized and another group of men were rescued with the aid of Carley floats. Lay was extremely proud of his ship's company for their actions during these rescue operations.

Calcutta also assisted in the rescue work. But years later Lay wrote that the Admiral in ***Calcutta*** had not stayed to help pick up survivors and in fact had gone off without even picking up his own whaler. There is, not surprisingly, some confusion as to the number of men lost and the number of survivors. If it is taken that ***Fraser's*** total complement would have been about 172 officers and men, all fourteen officers were rescued (eleven by ***Restigouche*** and three by ***Calcutta***), and forty-five men are listed by name as lost (DND records) plus another thirteen RN ratings lost. Those rescued amounted to about

Probably the last photo of *Fraser*, off St. Jean de Luz, taking aboard troops and others from the evacuation of France, 25 June. She was lost that night.

100 men, which conforms fairly closely with Nelson Lay's memory of rescuing about ninety-six, plus two or three men in ***Calcutta*** of the bridge party. In the day's confusion, it is nowhere noted if any of the evacuated soldiers were killed in the collision.

Restigouche's David Groos' brother was 1st Lieutenant of ***Fraser***. This younger Groos was not aware until much later that his brother had stepped from the destroyer's bridge to the forecastle of ***Calcutta***.

LCdr Lay was ordered to sink the after portion of ***Fraser***. A small party, led by ***Fraser's*** engineer officer went aboard the wreck, looking for other survivors, recovering some money from the captain's safe, and undertaking scuttling preparations, using several explosive charges fitted with time fuses. With daylight approaching and the threat of German aircraft, ***Restigouche*** departed the area as the remains of ***Fraser*** sank rapidly.

A Board of Inquiry was held in Plymouth on 29 June 1940. It is not surprising that ***Fraser's*** commanding officer was held to blame for "an error in judgement", in that he had turned toward ***Calcutta*** with too little wheel. Creery himself had reported that, when he observed there was insufficient wheel, he made an error in judgement in thinking it would still be possible to turn short of ***Calcutta***. He also noted in extenuation that he may have been affected by too little sleep, having had only one complete night's sleep since leaving the West Indies in May. But he was also critical of the report of the commanding officer of ***Calcutta***. He said that ***Fraser*** never did cross ***Calcutta's*** bow and that the collision would not have occurred if ***Calcutta*** had not altered to starboard.

The loss of forty-six Canadian sailors (including the one from ***Restigouche***) was a tragic blow to the small Navy with which Canada had entered the war. The sadness felt by the families of those lost was soon to be reinforced by the next loss, when many of ***Fraser's*** survivors were lost as well four months later in HMCS ***Margaree*** (see Chapter 4). And one of ***Calcutta's*** able seamen stated years later that, in Devonport where the survivors were taken, "There was understandably a terrible feeling of outright hatred and animosity toward us by the Canadians."

Restigouche continued in operations throughout the war. HMS ***Calcutta*** had extensive damage to her bows. She was repaired and transferred to the Mediterranean Fleet. On 1 June 1941 she was bombed and sunk by German and Italian aircraft northwest of Alexandria.

LOST:

Archer, Arther E., LS
Barrett, Osborne G., CVA
Baxter, Richard A., PO
Bisson, George P., Sto
Bodger, Richard R., PO
Brown, Hugh S., Shipwt
Call, George, Sto PO
Carlton, Douglas A., AB
Carolan, Robert E., Sto
Clark, John R., OS
Clarke, William, OS
Conway, Archibald H.W., LS
Cook, John E., Sto
Fecteau, Ernest, C.Ord.Art
Ford, Malgwyn C., AB
Gagnon, William M., Sto
Hicks, Earl C., PO Cook
Johnston, James M., AB
Kelly, John R., AB
Kennedy, Archibald, AB
Kennedy, Robert M., AB
Logan, Clifford M., AB
McDowell, Andrew V., Sto
McGibmey, Frank, Elec.Art
Macklin, Franklin G., L.Sig
McLaughlan, George H., Sto
Marcotte, Joseph L.P., AB
Marr, David, PO Tel
Miller, Lloyd G., AB
Mitchell, Donald W., OS
Moore, Arthur J., Yeo.Sig
More, Andrew, AB
Paddon, James W., AB
Paul, Gordon M., AB
Pratt, William R., AB
Price, John R., CPO
Ross, William G., Sto.PO
Saunders, Arthur R., AB
Sciban, Henry A., AB
Senyk, Steven, Sto
Smith, Charles D., OS
Swindlehurst, John C., O.Sig
Wagar, Donald F., AB
Watt, Thomas, Sto.PO
White, Donald H., OS
Wright, Richard C.F., Sto

Plus 13 RN ratings serving in HMCS ***Fraser*** were lost, and the one OS from ***Restigouche***.

SOURCES:

German, *The Sea is at Our Gates*, pp. 78-79.
Lay, *Memoirs of a Mariner,* pp. 109-113.
Lenton & Colledge, *Warships of World War II.*
Macpherson, *River Class Destroyers*, pp. 26-29.
Macpherson & Burgess, *Ships of Canada's Naval Forces 1910-1993.*
Schull, *Far Distant Ships*, pp. 33-38.

CHAPTER 3

OVERWHELMED BY THE ICE: HMCS BRAS D'OR

Bras D'Or: trawler auxiliary
Builder: Sorel, PQ, 1919
Requisitioned: 15 Sep 39
Crew: 4 officers, 20 crew

Fate: foundered, Gulf of St. Lawrence, 19 Oct 40
Casualties: 5 officers, 25 crew

He casteth forth his ice like morsels;
who can stand before his cold?

Psalm 147, v. 17

HMCS *Bras D'Or* in 1940.

The little auxiliary minesweeper ***Bras D'Or*** was a holdover from the 1st War period. She was a 124-foot trawler of 265 tons ordered by a New York ship owner who went bankrupt, and she was not completed until 1926 for the Canadian Government's Department of Marine and Fisheries as ***Lightship No. 25***. Requisitioned as an "auxiliary minesweeper" on 15 September 1939 to augment the Navy's meagre resources in minesweepers and patrol vessels, she was part of the Halifax local patrol force during the fall and winter of 1939 - 1940. On 14 November she was in a collision with the destroyer HMCS ***Fraser,*** the latter valuable ship having to be repaired in the dockyard for three weeks.

In June 1940 ***Bras D'Or*** was stationed at Rimouski, Quebec "to carry out shallow water searching sweeps to ensure no mining (by U-boats) took place undetected" although, in fact, no U-boats were to penetrate the Gulf until 1942. However, she became a maritime rarity at the beginning of June by taking control "at sea" in the Gulf of St. Lawrence of the Italian 4,000-ton, 370-foot freighter ***Capo Noli,*** trying to escape on the eve of Italy's declaration of war on 10 June. Actually, the freighter ran herself aground and her crew set her afire. She was then boarded by ***Bras D'Or*** seamen who extinguished the flames. Taken into Canadian government service as the freighter ***Bic Island***, this capture was paradoxically sunk two years later, on 29 October 1942 by ***U 224*** in mid-Atlantic.

Bras D'Or spent much of the summer in a general refit to repair defects resulting from her abnormal continuous use for ten months.

In mid-October, commanded by Lt. Charles A. Hornsby, RCNR, she was despatched from Clark City on Quebec's North Shore to shadow a suspicious vessel, the Rumanian steamship ***Ingener N. Vlassopol,*** preparing to sail from the newsprint-shipping port of Baie Comeau, further up the St. Lawrence North Shore. Because ***Bras D'Or*** followed her instructions closely, the captain of the freighter had to use his steam whistle to get ***Bras D'Or*** out of his way when he slipped. The two sailed in company bound for Sydney, the small warship keeping close company on the notion that the ***Vlassopol*** might keep going to enemy occupied Europe, and require stopping. On the night of 18 October the weather was very cold and foul, the seas rough. There was nothing to tell authorities that ***Bras D'Or*** was missing until ***Ingener N. Vlassopol*** arrived in Sydney alone. Her master was interviewed by A/Cdr J.D. Prentice. The master reported that ***Bras D'Or*** had been in company when he sailed, and was at different times astern, ahead or abeam until he went to bed on the night of the 18th. He reported that at dusk ***Vlassopol*** had switched on navigation lights and despite the war, in view of the weather conditions ***Bras D'Or*** had done the same. The merchant ship's 1st officer reported that at 0350 on the 19th the lights of ***Bras D'Or*** had suddenly disappeared.

Bras D'Or did not respond to signals the next day, and it was presumed by the Board of Enquiry that she foundered during the night "due to stress of weather." It was commented that a contributing factor might have been her grounding at Rimouski the night of 17 October 1940. There was a possibility that the ship had suffered strain not evident at the time which led to flooding of some compartments in the very heavy weather prevailing on 18 October.

There were no survivors, nor was any trace ever found of the valiant little vessel. She lies still at the bottom of the Gulf of St. Lawrence. The same violent storm caused the loss of the fishing schooner ***Bluebird***, operating out of Glace Bay, Cape Breton and her Newfoundland crew of five.

In the late 1950s the experimental high speed naval hydrofoil HMCS ***Bras D'Or*** was named in part in the small trawler's honour, as well as after Graham Bell's home at Bras D'Or, Cape Breton where he had carried out hydrofoil experiments in the early years of this century.

LOST:

Armes, Walter G., OS
Brenton, George W., Tel
Brown, Walter J., AB
Burton, Joseph P.L., Skpr
Chaddock, Harold G., Sto
Clancy, Harold G., AB
Conrad, Elward R., Skpr
Cumming, Malcolm, Lt(E)
D'Entremont, Joseph F., LS
Doherty, William J., AB
Ellis, Gerald K., Cook
Gordon, Gilbert B., Stwd
Hacker, John W., Sto.PO
Hill, Leonard, Engnmn
Hillier, Walter M., AB
Hornsby, Charles A., Lt
Jones, Hugh J.F., PO
Keating, William D., AB
Korning, Isben, Tel
May, Clarence L., AB
Murphy, Harry, Enginmn
Pelletier, Joseph E.R., AB
Pettipas, Guy D., Sto
Ruel, Herman, Skpr
Stasin, John J., O.Sig
Stewart, Joseph E., Sto
Walters, Gordon W., AB
Watson, Matthew, ERA
Webb, Miles, L., Sig
Young, James L., Sto

SOURCES:

Macpherson & Burgess, *Ships of Canada's Naval Forces,* p. 144.

Schull, *Far Distant Ships*, p. 42.

Tucker, *Naval Service of Canada,* Vol. II, pp. 148-9.

CHAPTER 4

THE SHORT LIFE OF HMCS MARGAREE

Margaree: River class destroyer
Builder: Palmer's Shipbuilding, Hebburn-on-Tyne
1st Comm: as HMS *Diana*, 16 Jun 32
2nd Comm: 6 Sep 40
Crew: 10 officers, 166 crew

Fate: Collision with MV *Port Fairy*, Atlantic, 22 Oct 40
Casualties: 4 officers, 138 crew

For fog and fate no charm is found to lighten or amend.
I, hurrying to my bride, was drowned - cut down by my best friend.

Rudyard Kipling, *Epitaph of the War: Destroyers in Collision*

A 1933 photo of HMS *Diana* later to become HMCS *Margaree*, replacing the lost *Fraser*.

When HMCS ***Fraser*** was lost in June of 1940 arrangements were immediately made by the Canadian government to purchase a replacement from the Royal Navy. HMS ***Diana*** had served in the Mediterranean and Home Fleets, and was of a very similar class to the other RCN British-built destroyers acquired. When selected for transfer to the Royal Canadian Navy she returned to Albert Docks, London to be refitted.

The refit was carried out during some of the worst raids by German aircraft and the ship received some damage from bombs.

The majority of the ship's company was made up of survivors from the ***Fraser***. A few of those survivors were sent on courses in England. Even thirteen of the wounded had recovered sufficiently to be assigned to the new ship.

On completion of the refit, ***Margaree***, commanded by Cdr J.W.R. Roy, RCN went to Londonderry. She was to return to Canada and for passage was assigned as the sole escort for a small convoy of five ships, designated OL-8. It was one of a small series of convoys of generally larger and faster ships outbound from the Mersey and Clyde rivers.

The convoy sailed on 20 October. The ships were disposed in four columns, with the 8,300-ton MV ***Port Fairy*** leading the port column, followed by the SS ***Jamaica Planter***. The other three ships were in single columns to starboard of ***Port Fairy*** at 1,200 yard intervals. Speed of the convoy was unusually high at fourteen and a half knots and the ships were proceeding on a steady course and without zig-zagging. The first day passed without incident.

On 21 October ***Margaree*** was stationed approximately one to one and a half miles ahead of the convoy during the first watch (2000 to 2359). The 1st lieutenant, just prior to going off watch, had observed that a fine rain was reducing his visibility and had ordered a small reduction in engine revolutions in order to drop back closer to the convoy. At midnight he turned over the watch and advised his relief of the fact that the ship was slowly closing with the convoy by allowing it to catch up with her.

Aboard ***Port Fairy*** the first indication of trouble was in the early morning of the 22nd at about 0100, when her chief officer observed a vessel fine on his starboard bow and on a converging track with his own ship. He stopped his engines and, when he saw that the warship was moving rapidly to port, ordered full speed astern, put his wheel hard-a-port and sounded three short blasts to warn the destroyer as well as ***Jamaica Planter*** astern of him. He could not move to starboard due to the other convoy ships.

trapped. As Landymore said to a reporter in Bermuda a few days later "There was no noise at all. No shouts even in the after part. Not even the sound of escaping steam. There was just the slapping of the sea and us wallowing. I guess I barked a few noises out. I don't remember what I shouted."

SLt R.W. Timbrell, who also came off watch at midnight was, at the time of the collision, asleep in his cabin beneath the after torpedo tubes. With SurgLt T.B. McLean who had been asleep in an adjoining cabin, and AB V.H. Holman who was the duty watchkeeper at the low power switchboard, they had to force open a deck hatch jammed shut in the collision. Once on deck Timbrell and Holman, on orders from Lt Russell, went to the four throwers and two rails to reset the depth charges to "safe".

HMCS *Margaree*, her bows sheared off, taken from *Port Fairy* the morning after their collision.
Photo from the *Toronto Daily Star* paper, three weeks later.

It was only seconds later that ***Port Fairy's*** stem cut through ***Margaree's*** bridge area with sufficient force to break away the forward portion of the ship. The whole bow section of ***Margaree*** sank immediately, carrying to their deaths most of the off-watch personnel, still in their bunks and hammocks, as well as the officers and men on the bridge.

Lieutenant P.F.X. Russell, the 1st lieutenant, was the senior surviving officer in the stern section. With no bow it was not clear how long the forward bulkheads would withstand the sea and wave pressures and the order to abandon ship was given. Another surviving officer was Lieutenant W.M. Landymore who had been aboard ***Fraser*** when she was cut in two by HMS ***Calcutta***. He and Russell went forward to see if any men were

Operational procedures at the time were to set five charges to "shallow" and five to "deep", ready for an urgent attack on any U-boat detected. ***Margaree*** and ***Port Fairy*** were still scraping alongside each other, adding to the clamour and difficulties.

McLean went looking for any killed or injured. But, unlike in ***Fraser***, there were no injuries. Men either died or escaped with some shock but no physical damage. Timbrell then dove into the boiler room to ensure everyone was out. The decks were slippery and thick with oil from the destroyer's ruptured fuel tanks.

Meanwhile the freighter was lying alongside the damaged destroyer, crashing up and down against her with the swell. Of the six officers and twenty-eight men who survived aboard the after section, three officers and twenty-five men were able to scramble up ladders and ropes to the safety of the ***Port Fairy's*** decks. Two unfortunates lost their grip on the oily ladders, fell and were crushed between the two ships. Russell, Landymore, Timbrell and AB Holman remained on board the destroyer as the freighter then backed clear. They released a Carley float that had been secured on top of the torpedo mounting and with much effort heaved it over the side. But Lt Russell had thrown a rope from it to Bill Landymore, telling him to hang on tight so the float would not drift away when it hit the water. Unfortunately they had not noticed the rope was only four feet long, so when the heavy float at last slid overboard, it pulled Landymore with it. Even in these dire straits, the aplomb of those remaining is illustrated in the 1st lieutenant's shout down to Landymore in the sea: "Landymore, did I give you permission to leave the ship?" The others then leapt after him, and after fighting across the seas with paddles for an hour were finally picked up by ***Port Fairy*** as well.

Although it had seemed that the after section was in imminent danger of sinking it was still afloat. Not only was the hulk a danger to navigation, but the confidential books remained on board. The suggestion of reboarding was rejected by the Master of ***Port Fairy***. That ship was armed with a 4-inch gun and it was decided to try sinking the remains of ***Margaree*** by gunfire. By 1000 ***Port Fairy*** had expended all her 4-inch ammunition. At one point in daylight hours an attempt was made to put a party back on board under Russell but there was concern over the fires that had been started and the possibility of exploding ammunition, so they returned to the freighter. When last seen ***Margaree*** was listing heavily to starboard and sinking by the stern.

With the loss of all the personnel on watch on the bridge it was difficult for a Board of Inquiry to determine the events from the time that the 1st lieutenant had gone off watch at midnight. The turn to port which brought the ship across ***Port Fairy's*** course was the action which precipitated the collision. The Board could only speculate on why the turn was made. They concluded that four possible causes existed:

- gyro compass wander;
- breakdown in steering gear;
- misunderstood helm order;
- error in judgement by the officer conning the ship.

Whatever blame that could be assessed was directed at ***Margaree*** since it was her responsibility as an escort to keep clear of the convoy. ***Port Fairy*** was praised for her efficient rescue of the survivors.

HMS ***Laconia***, an armed merchant cruiser, searched the area of the collision twenty-four hours later. The commanding officer of that ship found nothing, and it was assumed that the after section of the ship had sunk.

Port Fairy delivered the survivors to Bermuda. Landymore had married in London just two months earlier and just two months after being a survivor of ***Fraser***. And eighty-six of the 142 who went down with ***Margaree*** had also survived ***Fraser's*** collision. The loss of the two destroyers by collision in four months was a bitter blow to the Canadian Navy and the large loss of lives was a shock to all at home.

The Canadian survivors were home by 13 November. The *Toronto Telegram* interviewed some of them and obtained first hand accounts of the last moments on board. As usual, luck or chance played a role. One young gunner had been on watch in B gun just forward of the bridge. When the gun's crew was told to leave only two men at the mounting and let the others find more shelter, he was told by the captain of the gun to go aft to a gun shield that was out of the weather. He survived, but the captain of the gun had remained and went down with the bow section.

For R.W. Timbrell it was his second collision involving a D class destroyer: in 1939, serving as a midshipman in the battleship ***Barham***, when entering the Clyde in thick fog she had run down the destroyer HMS ***Duchess***, a sister of ***Diana/Margaree***. The destroyer was rolled right over and there were only twenty-three survivors. Admiral Timbrell notes that this was the first time he had seen an asdic dome, projecting from the bottom of the destroyer's hull, for he was later to become an asdic specialist.

Port Fairy survived the war, although damaged by air attack on 12 July 1943 west of Gibraltar. And of the surviving officers of ***Margaree***, Landymore, Russell, Timbrell and McLean all eventually made commodore or rear admiral.

LOST:

Akram, Thomas, CERA
Amyes, Alf. W.B., Elec.Art
Archer, George, CPO
Armstrong, Arthur W., Tel
Arnott, Robert S., LS
Aulenback, George V., AB
Baker, Owen C., AB
Baker, Thomas M., AB
Barrow, Israel, SPO
Beattie, William I., AB
Beaucamp, Gerald J.C., AB
Bingham, Edward J.B., CPO
Boileau, Joseph P.L., OS
Boutet, Charles H., OS
Brebber, John G., L.Sto
Burnett, John H., Sto
Calder, William A., LS
Campbell, Donald L., AB
Candy, Alexander A., LS
Cann, Malcolm A., AB
Carse, James G., Sto
Carter, Victor E., LS
Chedister, Ward D., LS
Clarke, Ralph L., Tel
Cole, John W., Sig
Conway, Leo C., AB
Corbin, William H., PO
Coxon, Thomas, AB
Crane, Alan C., ERA
Cunningham, Edward A., AB
Day, Stanley G., LVA
Dickens, Alex J.W., OS
Domeier, Eric C., AB
Donaldson, William, LS
Edwards, Norman W., OS
Estabrooks, Vernon W., AB
Fearey, Charles E., OS
Fenerty, Morris St.G., PO
Ferguson, Robert S., OS
Fleming, Ronald J., VA
Francis, James A., Cook
Frankham, David G., AB
Frayer, Donald L., AB
Frost, Lawrence V., AB
Fuller, Raymond H., AB
Gill, John H., Ord.Art
Goldsmith, William E., AB
Gray, Harold F., Sto
Gutteridge, Neville H., Sto.PO
Hancock, Sydney C., PO
Harrington, Edgar, Sto
Hartley, Ernest O., Sto
Harvey, William J., AB
Heale, Renfred C., AB
Hean, John D., L.Sig
Henderson, James M., Sig
Heycock, Selwyn R., AB
Holland, James R., Sig
Holloway, Arthur G., Cook
Hopper, Jack H., Sto
Jones, Ackland H., OS
Jones, Alfred E., OS
Keeping, Robert, AB
Kelly, James G., ERA
Kirkwood, Thomas A., OS
Kyle, Kenneth H., AB
Laak, Mike, LS
Lamb, Thomas H., ERA
Legault, Marcel, Sto
Lemieux, Joseph E., Sto.PO
Lewis, Bernard A., Cmd.Gnr
Lindsay, James, Sto.PO
McAlister, William J., AB
McConnell, James C., SBA
MacDougall, Gord. W., Shpwt
McIldoon, Edward, LS
Mackie, Ronald, AB
McKinnon, Desmond S., C.Sto
McLuskie, William R., VA
McMurtry, Alexander E., Lt
McTaggart, David A., Tel
Mara, John J., PO
Martin, Jean M., L.Sto
Martin, Merle G., Cook
Martin, Sidney F., PO Cook
Matthews, Thomas H., AB
Maynard, William H., Stwd
Meadows, Charles B., Tel
Millar, James R., OS
Miller, James B., AB
Mills, Frederick J., OS
Moore, Ronald J., AB
Munro, Gordon W., LS
Murray, Wallace H., Sto
Mylrea, Russell E., Sto
Norris, Cyril A., Tel
Olson, Clarence J., OS
Olson, Ole A., Sto
Overy, Ernest K., Sto.PO
Pegnem, John C., PO Instr
Penney, Selby J., AB
Petts, Clifford, LS
Ponder, Harold R., AB
Pope, Rufus C., Lt
Powell, Stephen B., OS
Reading, William J.., Sig
Reid, Robert B., Ord.Art
Robertson, William D., Sto
Rowe, Frederick E., LS
Rowse, Edward G., LS
Roy, Joseph W.R., Cdr
Sanders, Leslie, AB
Simpkin, Donald H., LVA
Skinner, Edward L., AB
Smith, Cedric de H., L.Sig
Smith, George B., Elec. Art
Smith, Gordon E., AB
Smith, Robert, AB
Smith, Robert B., OS
Smithson, David B., AB
Snowsell, Ernest W., AB
Standing, Thomas, LS
Stark, Horace C., Tel
Stephens, Richard H., Sto
Todos, William, AB
Underwood, John C., AB
Venne, Joseph R.G., VA
Walker, William, L.Sto
Watkins, Harry, Sig
Webb, Horace M., LS
Webb, Valentine G., Sto.PO
Weiser, Lincoln E., Sto
Wheeler, Victor S., AB
Wight, Alan E., Sto
Williams, Robert, AB
Willis, Daniel C., AB
Wilson, Charles M., PO
Wilson, George R., ERA
Wood, Stanley E., AB
Young, Alfred, AB

Plus 2 RN ratings.

SOURCES:

German, *The Sea Is At Our Gates,* pp. 81-82.

HMSO, *British Vessels Lost at Sea 1939-45,* p. 82.

Lenton & Colledge, *Warships of World War II,* p. 27.

Macpherson, *River Class Destroyers of the RCN,* p. 62.

Schull, *Far Distant Ships*, pp. 49-50.

Van der Vat, *The Atlantic Campaign,* pp. 136-137.

CHAPTER 5

THE FIRST HMCS OTTAWA: A LATE SUCCESS

It cannot be too often repeated that in modern war, and especially in modern naval war, the chief factor in achieving triumph is what has been done in the way of thorough preparation and training before the beginning of the war.

Theodore Roosevelt, to US Naval Academy, 1902

Ottawa: River class destroyer
Builder: Portsmouth Naval Dockyard
1st Comm: as HMS *Crusader*, 1932
2nd Comm: 15 Jun 38
Crew: 10 officers, 170 crew

Action: Sank Italian submarine *Commandante Faa' Di Bruno*, Atlantic, 6 Nov 40
Casualties: About 57
No survivors

HMCS *Ottawa*, H 60, in September, 1942. Note the few depth charges and the stern fitting for the TSDS - Two Speed Destoyer Sweep.

The first HMCS ***Ottawa*** was one of only six destroyers with which Canada embarked on a five-year anti-submarine war. She was on the west coast at the time, coming around to Halifax in November of 1939.

She escorted the first troop convoy to the United Kingdom in December, carrying troops of the First Canadian Division. She continued with this escorting role until April, when ***Ottawa*** was damaged in a collision. By August 1940 the destroyer was again in the UK, now commanded by Cdr Rollo Mainguy, RCN. In September she rescued 118 survivors of torpedoed merchantmen from Convoy OB-217, landing them at Greenock.

While back at sea the first week of November, 1940, ***Ottawa*** and the RN destroyer ***Harvester*** were ordered to the assistance of the 2,500-ton merchant ship ***Melrose Abbey,*** which had reported being pursued by a submarine 500 miles southwest of Ireland. On the afternoon of 6 November, as the two drew near they saw the submarine on the surface astern of the freighter and firing at her. Both destroyers immediately opened fire with their forward guns as they hastened to the rescue. ***Ottawa*** got off five salvos before the submarine dived.

An anti-submarine sweep was commenced at modest speeds at once but it was some considerable time before an asdic contact was gained. ***Ottawa*** then made four separate attacks, dropping twenty-one depth charges, and ***Harvester*** five attacks, reportedly dropping sixty-two charges, although this seems rather high. The ships circled, and it was noted that after two of ***Harvester's*** attacks underwater explosions were heard that did not seem to be related to depth charges themselves.

At first light the next morning a large patch of oil was found but no other surface evidence. After a careful search, the two left the area. ***Ottawa's*** CO, Cdr Mainguy, was certain they had been successful, but there was no visible proof.

Captain (D) Liverpool and Admiral Sir Percy Noble, C-in-C Western Approaches, were also both convinced, as was the CO of ***Harvester,*** that a submarine had been sunk. The U-boat Assessment Committee, on the other hand, while agreeing a submarine had been present, felt there was insufficient evidence of destruction and assessed it as a "probably damaged" submarine. This Committee was, quite correctly, very hard-nosed about claimed "kills", to avoid over-confidence against the tough U-boats, and took much convincing. This led to ships sometimes going to considerable trouble, even at hazard to themselves on occasion, to retrieve evidence of sinkings to prove their successes.

While it eventually became known to British intelligence that ***Faa' di Bruno*** had disappeared, her loss was ascribed to various causes until long after the war. In end-of-the-war assessments, the loss of the Italian submarine was credited to HMS ***Havelock,*** who had carried out a good attack on 8 November in a position 300 miles north of ***Ottawa*** and ***Harvester*** two days later. To those on the Assessment Committee, her attack was judged as the more likely to have been successful, and certainly ***Faa' Di Bruno*** had disappeared about then.

Faa' Di Bruno, only commissioned on 23 October 1939, had sailed on 31 October from the French port of Bordeaux to patrol west of 20°W, north of 57°. Recent postwar analysis of her patrol orders and dead reckoning showed her route would have been well to the west of ***Havelock's*** attack, but almost on track for ***Ottawa*** and ***Harvester's,*** although somewhat behind schedule. This could have been caused by bad weather or a mechanical problem. Then in a postwar examination of Italian submarine logs, it was noted that their submarine ***Marconi***, the Italian's only successful submarine so far in 1940, had been attacked on 8 November, although not seriously damaged. This would have been ***Havelock's*** attack. Also by the 8th ***Faa' Di Bruno*** had made no signals for over a week, a bit unusual. Unless she was lost as a result of an unlikely marine casualty, then she must have been sunk by ***Ottawa*** and ***Harvester***, since their target could not have been a German U-boat, as none were operating then in that area. To add more confusion, one Italian history credits HMS ***Hero*** with her destruction, probably a confusion of names only; otherwise they report her as an unknown loss. Recent Italian histories now agree it was ***Harvester,*** although Ottawa is often not mentioned. To add to the story, HMS ***Harvester*** had sunk ***U 32*** only a week before, with ***Highlander.***

Thus the credit goes to these two, the very first anti-submarine success of the RCN in the war, but some forty-two years after the event (the re-assessment was made in 1982 by the RN's Naval Historical Branch). It is regrettable that Vice Admiral Rollo Mainguy, who retired as Chief of the Naval Staff, died before he knew of this success. His son, Vice Admiral Dan Mainguy noted that "My father would have been delighted to know that all his peace-time years of preparation paid off."

SOURCES:

German, *The Sea Is At Our Gates,* pp. 82-83.

Macpherson, *River Class Destroyers,* pp. 37-46.

Pollina & Bertini, *I Sommergibili Italiani,* pp. 245 & 248.

Research notes, R.M. Coppock, MoD, London.

1941

More losses, mostly from the dangers of the sea, offset by a first known success.

CHAPTER 6

HMCS OTTER: LOST BY FIRE

Otter: Animal class yacht
Builder: Robt Jacob, New York, 1921, as *Nourmahal*
Comm: 4 Oct 40
Crew: 4 officers, 37 crew

Fate: Took fire and sank off Halifax, 26 Mar 41
Casualties: 2 officers, 17 crew

The Theory: Article 1073, King's Regulations and Admiralty Instructions on the subject of fire should be known by every officer.

1932 Seamanship Manual

The yacht *Conseco* on arrival at Halifax, flying the Canadian red ensign of her new owners and still in her handsome pre-war paint job. The after boat-deck house and the saloon forward were cut off when she was converted as HMCS *Otter*.

HMCS ***Otter*** was one of the armed yachts bought secretly in the United States in the early spring of 1940 to provide some semblance of anti-submarine protection off the Nova Scotia coast until new-construction warships could be commissioned from the builders.

She had started life as the elegant 160-foot private yacht of Vincent Astor of New York. In the 1920's he sold her to John W. Hubbard of Pittsburg and purchased a larger ***Nourmahal,*** sometimes confused with this smaller yacht. Hubbard used her for coastal cruising, often on extended trips. Her designed civilian crew was nineteen. The Navy required forty-one to man her equipment, so mess decks were pretty crowded. But the Canadian Navy was desperately determined to acquire some semblance of a patrol force, and these small but sturdy vessels were the only ones available, for the time being.

Ostensibly bought by Montreal business executive Philip S. Ross in March of 1940, he, and others, had been prompted by the Canadian government to go looking in the US for surplus motor yachts, "able to keep the sea", 130 feet or more, capable of a minimum speed of twelve knots and decks strong enough to take a 4-inch gun and depth charges. Mr. Ross was given an excuse when his own fifty-four-foot schooner yacht was "requisitioned" by the Navy on 26 February. This subterfuge was set up by C.D. Howe's Ministry of Munitions and Supply after Cdr J.W.R. Roy, RCN, had secretly scouted around American boat yards and dealers in December 1939 to identify potential patrol yachts. The thirteen Canadian yachtsmen who went south to buy these yachts had to be cautious. American criminal law provided that *anyone* concerned with the provision or purchase of just such vessels for war purposes risked a $10,000 fine, a prison term and confiscation of the vessel. The US was determinedly neutral in stance, although the president was firmly cooperative.

In all fourteen yachts eventually reached Canada and most of the new owners had their own yachts returned, "found to be unsuitable for naval requirements." ***Conseco***, as she was by now named, arrived at Halifax in late May of 1940, where Lt D.S. Mossman, RCNR was appointed in command and took her to Quebec for fitting out as an armed yacht. Delayed by other urgent naval requirements, it was 4 October before she could be equipped with a 12-pounder 3-inch gun forward, a simple Type 123 (magnetic compass) asdic set and eight depth charges. She returned to Halifax and was commissioned as HMCS ***Otter.*** All the yachts bought in the US were given new animal names to disguise their origins somewhat. While they all differed considerably, and two of them did not even need name changes ***(Sans Peur*** because she was British-owned, ***Ambler*** because she was a Canadian yacht), they are referred to in many records as the Animal Class yachts. ***Otter*** had cost $72,374 to buy and deliver and another $68,415 to fit out as a warship.

Otter at once was sent on patrols off Halifax to provide visible defence for four HX "fast" (9 knots and over) and five SC "slow" convoys. She suffered during the harsh winter to follow. Built as a pleasure yacht, much of her wiring was canvas-covered and short-circuited occasionally, precipitating minor fires when inundated with salt water. Some wiring was replaced in the dockyard at Halifax in January, 1941. As one crewman of those days, T.C. Carey, commented: "One stormy night heading for Newfoundland... due to short circuits we were one blue flashing light, so the senior officer chased us home! Old wires no longer required were just cut, so when wet, shorted." There were those who felt she was not built robustly enough to serve in the boisterous North Atlantic in winter; probably true enough. Although steel-hulled, most of her upper works and decks were of wood.

On 26 March 1941, ***Otter*** was despatched to wait in the vicinity of the Sambro Light Vessel, about twenty miles out of Halifax, to meet a scheduled in-bound British submarine, HMS ***Talisman.*** This was a precaution taken at most ports when an Allied submarine was expected, to prevent over-eager defenders attacking her in mistake for a U-boat. ***Otter*** slipped from the dockyard at 0500 and by 0730 was idling a mile or so from Sambro. It was cold, with intermittent rain, a heavy sea was running and a Force 6 strong wind was blowing spume off the wave-tops, causing ***Otter*** to roll and pound uncomfortably in ten-foot waves. Lt Mossman left the bridge to an officer of the watch and went to his cabin.

At 0845 there was a loud shout of "FIRE, FIRE!" The alarm bells sounded and the pounding of running feet was heard. Within five minutes flames and black smoke had burst through ***Otter's*** wooden upper deck above the engine room. While there were sand buckets, the sand had no effect, and the fire extinguishers that worked–some were either frozen or defective–made no impression on the conflagration that soon enveloped the W/T office and cabins. As the generator itself was afire the pumps could not be operated. Mossman, considering it hopeless, ordered the magazine flooded, a distress message sent, threw overboard the weighted confidential books, and ordered "Abandon ship" at 0855. ***Otter*** had two small dinghies and one Carley float life raft. By 0911 all of the crew had leapt over the side into them or been pulled from the water. The wind and sea tended to blow the dinghies and raft away from the now blazing ship. Then it was seen that Lt Mossman was still on board, near the stern. He had evidently gone below to ensure no-one was still on board in true nautical tradition, and had been left behind in the confusion.

The port lifeboat put about and its crew began pulling back toward the vessel to rescue Mossman. But it was difficult to row with the crowd already packed into the little boat and the heaving seas. So, as it struggled past the life raft, one rating volunteered to take his chance with those clinging to the float up to their shoulders in the sea to relieve the over-crowding. Two others followed him and the lifeboat was able to reach the ship and take Mossman aboard. The three who gave up their places were AB Thomas K. Guilford, OS John H. Slavin and OS Ian Wallace O'Hara of Westmount, Quebec. O'Hara was to lose his life during rescue operations. These three, and three others, were later awarded Mentions in Despatches for their devotion to their comrades. O'Hara's citation simply noted that it was "For gallantry and devotion to duty when HMCS ***Otter*** was lost." It was a modest award for someone who truly "laid down his life for his friends."

In near-freezing water, heavy waves continually swept over the men in the raft until most died of exposure. By this time ***Talisman*** had appeared, plus a large Eagle Oil tanker, and the in-bound Polish merchantman ***Wisla***, Capt Pawel Traczewski, Master, coming up from New York to join an eastbound convoy. The latter and ***Talisman*** made strenuous efforts to rescue the men in the water. In the words of ***Talisman's*** navigator, Lt Louis Sheppard, RNR, it was "filthy weather, blowing half a SW gale and temperature freezing." The tanker pumped oil over the side in an effort to flatten the seas somewhat to make rescue easier.

However the two other ships were ill suited as rescue ships in the prevailing weather. The submarine had broad saddle tanks extending along most of her sides over which the seas surged and retreated. The 3,100-ton ***Wisla*** had a high freeboard, with rough towering sides, making it very dangerous to try to lift men or boats from water level. The small starboard lifeboat capsized alongside her throwing the occupants into the sea, where all but three were carried beyond reach. The three were hauled aboard by life lines, one of the ship's seamen also losing his life in the sea when he slipped trying to rescue the others. The captain attempted to lower his own boats but these were battered against her sides in the rolling. It was twenty minutes before he could manoeuvre the ungainly ship to try rescuing some of those who had swum back to the water-filled little lifeboat, but most of these perished as well. Two of those rescued died later aboard ***Wisla***, who also recovered several bodies. Efforts were made in vain to resuscitate these men in the ship's saloon. One of those who kept trying to rescue his mates was Chief Motor Mechanic Daniel E. Gillis who also gave his life for his efforts and was mentioned in despatches.

Aboard ***Talisman***, her 1st Lieutenant, K.W.M. Meyrick, RN, was later to be singled out for high commendation in attempting to rescue those alongside, although only four were plucked from the sea onto her casing. On first sighting the men in the rafts, the submarine had thrown them a heaving line, which broke. Lt Sheppard recalls: "Lt Meyrick then asked his CO's permission to jump over the side and help. Owing to the weather conditions, this was refused. However Meyrick jumped from the conning tower into the sea anyway, and got to the raft... Glad to say we got him back, together with survivors from that raft. In my opinion, the bravest man I had the pleasure of meeting." Lt Meyrick was later awarded the Royal Humane Society's Bronze Medal for this bravery. However only six months later he was to be lost when the submarine HMS ***Tetrarch*** was mined with no survivors off Sicily on 27 October 1941. He had drawn lots with Lt Sheppard to determine who would leave ***Talisman*** first when they were both appointed to other submarines and had "won" the draw.

At 1115 ***Otter*** sank, and rescue efforts ended by 1120. Some of her crew had been in the freezing water for almost two and a half hours. ***Otter's*** emergency message had not been completed as the batteries in the engine room had caught fire, ***Wisla's*** W/T was out of action, and while a message from the Sambro Light Vessel might have made a difference, her crew presumed others had sent one and did nothing. At the Board of Inquiry, there was criticism of the level of training of the newly-joined seamen in fire fighting and in familiarity with other parts of the ship than their own. It recommended that hand pumps should be provided in future. The probable cause of the fire was attributed to a sudden overload of the starboard generator caused when an air compressor was started. Since none of the on-watch engine room staff were saved, the definite cause was never established. It was a sad end for a gallant, ill-equipped small naval vessel and her crew, the only one to be lost by fire.

Lt Mossman survived, as did one other officer and twenty of ***Otter's*** crew.

LOST:

Armstrong, Irvine C., Tel
Blyth, John, OS
Darrach, Ronald M., MM
Day, Earle A., Tel
D'Eon, Gerald V., VA
Drew, John G., MM
Gillis, Daniel E., CMM
Graham, John A., AB
Johnston, Beverly, EM
Laurin, J.A., OS
Mabey, Elmer A., Tel
Mason, Dudley H., Sto.1
O'Hara, Wallace, OS
Parker, Andrew S., Ch.Skpr
Stuart, Lionel E., Sto.1
Thibadeau, Leonard P., OS
Walker, Alan M., Lt
Wall, Edward T., Sto.1
Woods, Norman G., O.Sig

SOURCES:

Chatterton Dickson, *Seedie's Submarine List*, p. 39.

McKee, *Armed Yachts of Canada*, pp. 73, 93, 137-139.

Paquette & Bainbridge, *Honours & Awards*, 137, 202, 223, 414.

CHAPTER 8

HMCS LÉVIS: FIRST CORVETTE LOST

We aren't no thin red 'eros, nor aren't no blackguards too,
But single men in barricks, most remarkable like you.

Rudyard Kipling, "Tommy"

Lévis: Flower class corvette
Builder: George T. Davie & Sons, Lauzon PQ
Comm: 16 May 41
Crew: 5 officers, 53 Crew

Fate: Torpedoed by *U 74*, off Greenland, 19 Sep 41
Casualties: 18 crew

Lévis sinking, September, 1941. An unusual photo, as corvettes normally sank too fast to have photos taken.

Lévis was one of the earliest corvettes commissioned and when sunk still had no AA armament aft, nor even a canvas dodger around her bridge. In a critical report after her loss, a Board of Inquiry also noted she had no damage control equipment which might have helped save her. It was a sign, as one crew member now comments, "How rushed and ill prepared our ships were." After only a few weeks of work-ups, ***Lévis*** was assigned to the 19th Escort Group of the Newfoundland Escort Force, and was commanded by Lt C.W. Gilding, RCNR. Already she had been accidentally hit by a Quebec ferry and, in her first eastward crossing with a convoy, became separated in heavy weather from her charges. Her fatal convoy was only her second.

It was an evil time for the newly commissioned escorts, thrown into the fray, as Canadian Rear Admiral Murray commented, "With their safety dependant on the commanding officer's ability to stay awake" for days on end. Group senior officers (SOs) often had no more than just met their ships' COs. With almost no group training, and tactics against U-boats operating in "wolf-packs" not yet developed, let alone practised, confusion and doubt frequently occurred. Shortly before, Convoy SC-42 had taken a severe beating from *Gruppe Markgraf* U-boats, losing fifteen ships sunk and two damaged of the sixty-four that set out, although HMCS ***Chambly*** and ***Moose Jaw*** had sunk ***U 501*** (see Chapter 7). A sixteenth was sunk later.

Convoy SC-44, fifty-one ships in twelve columns, had been reduced by drop-outs to forty-eight by the time ***Lévis*** joined. It had, for those days, an unusually strong escort, due to the harsh experiences of SC-42. The SO was in the elderly Town class destroyer HMS ***Chesterfield*** and there was a close escort of four corvettes with three more in support. On 18 September, ***Lévis*** reported her asdic as defective–one crew member recalls it being due to hitting a floating balk of timber which struck the underwater dome as ***Lévis*** reared up on a sea. Thereafter she could only keep a listening watch for the hydrophone effect of any U-boat's motors. She was zig-zagging on the convoy's port side in the dark not far astern of her sister corvette ***Mayflower*** when, at 0410 local time, she was hit by a torpedo on her port side just before the bridge. Detonating about forty feet from her bow, it almost severed it, opening a huge gash through which daylight later could be seen across the mess decks to her starboard side. At first her CO thought they had been mined, but LCdr George Stephen, RCNR, in ***Mayflower,*** an ebullient and consummate seaman who will appear in many of these tales, reported seeing another torpedo pass just astern of his own ship.

Mayflower turned back immediately and with the corvette ***Agassiz*** swept down the convoy's port side. ***Mayflower*** got a suspicious underwater contact and dropped a pattern of nine charges with no visible result. The RN corvette ***Honeysuckle*** swept across the stern as the convoy forged ahead, and ***Chesterfield*** swept back toward them as well, all without further contact with the quiet-lying U-boats.

Thereupon Stephen turned back to help ***Lévis*** and signalled the senior officer "***Lévis*** torpedoed 0410Q/19. Not sinking. ***Mayflower*** standing by to take in tow for Iceland. Request a tug may be sent."

U 74, commanded by KK Eitel-Friedrich Kentrat, of VII U-Flottille based at St. Nazaire on the French Biscay coast, had fired a four-torpedo spread, claiming a hit on a convoy merchantman and on ***Lévis***. She was one of five U-boats of *Gruppe Markgraf* remaining in the area from the attacks on SC-42. They sank three merchantmen the next day as well, with 100 survivors, and a tanker was hit and exploded with no survivors. ***Lévis'*** torpedoing was just one day's disaster. No one really found or even seriously attacked ***U 74***.

In the initial explosion, seventeen had been killed outright, one an RN rating, only two surviving of the off-watch stokers immediately above the torpedo hit. One more was to die later in ***Mayflower.*** The CO had just left the bridge fifteen minutes before the torpedo hit. He was shocked and dazed when he staggered back on deck in the confusion. Seeing the damaged bow, partly submerged in the relatively calm seas, he ordered "Abandon ship". This was quite strongly criticised later, although he legitimately feared another torpedo fired at his now stopped ship. Men were clambering through holes in the fore upper seamen's mess deck-head, some helping rescue injured mates in the darkness. The surviving engine room stokers shut down the boilers to prevent an explosion if the cold sea water were to reach them, but left the diesel generator running for power and light.

Soon her two sea boats and Carley floats were launched, one boat under Lt Gilding's command, both of which boats pulled away from the stricken vessel. The 1st lieutenant, Lt Fraser, was still aboard, ensuring every survivor was preparing to leave. ***Mayflower*** came alongside and began picking up survivors in the water. ***Lévis'*** SLt R.G. Hatrick entered the seamen's mess, a shambles of twisted steel plates, tumbled lockers and equipment, hissing steam from broken pipes, sea water sloshing about, a smell of cordite from the explosion, all pitch black still. He found bodies, obviously dead. "I hailed at the top of my voice and then kept silent and listened. I received no reply." He also was directing the rescue of men from elsewhere below, ensured the depth charges on the quarterdeck were all set to safe. Other ships of the convoy were warned of the torpedoing. For his efforts Hatrick received the DSC, although this was not gazetted until January of 1946.

Everyone was off ***Lévis*** in about fifteen minutes. At least one of ***Agassiz's*** seamen ended in the frigid North Atlantic waters when she too returned to help and he fell from her scramble net trying to haul in oil-slippery and injured ***Lévis*** survivors. Then, at Stephen's urging, the 1st lieutenants of ***Lévis*** and ***Mayflower*** re-boarded to examine the bulkhead aft of the explosion to see if it would likely hold and she could be saved, and to ensure the depth charges were indeed safe. Their report was encouraging so ten of ***Mayflower's*** crew boarded and arranged to take ***Lévis*** in tow, which they did at 0540. The towing hawser parted at 0700, but she was under way again for Iceland by 0830 with a heavier one. At one stage, checking the mess decks again, they very fortunately found the injured telegraphist Emile Beaudoin (now known in naval circles as the co-author of HMCS ***Athabaskan's*** history *Unlucky Lady*.) He was to spend nearly six months in hospital as a result of his ***Lévis*** injuries.

The towing went slowly and the working party was withdrawn at 1130 when ***Lévis'*** stability seemed to be getting more dubious. At about 1700 ***Lévis*** abruptly settled lower in the water, the line was cut, and at 1710 she slowly rolled on her side and sank.

The survivors were landed in Iceland, spending ten days awaiting return passage to

Canada, and some such as Beaudoin remaining in hospital there for a time.

A Board of Inquiry was held on ***Lévis'*** loss in the destroyer depot ship HMS ***Greenwich*** at St. John's on 10 October 1941, chaired by Acting Commander Hugh F. Pullen of HMCS ***Ottawa,*** with an RN officer and an engineer lieutenant commander. They found the abandonment of ***Lévis*** too precipitate but understandable in the circumstances, and Lt Gilding was not charged. George Stephen was commended for his efforts to salvage ***Lévis*** by re-boarding her and twice getting her under tow, typical of that ex-merchant seaman. The report was bitterly critical of the lack of any organization or material for damage control. As a result new ship-building contracts specified that the builder was responsible for its supply in the future. Those at sea were just beginning to appreciate the minutiae of wartime battles. It was for all, the RCN, the RCNVRs and the RCNRs a "learn as you go" type of war.

The report added "We consider it deplorable that such attempts at salvage as were made... were left in the hands of comparatively inexperienced RCNVR officers... but they are worthy of commendation." Hence Hatrick's DSC. The Board had no suggestions how officers, chiefs or petty officers experienced in damage control under war conditions were to be found for assignment to each ship likely to be damaged. That experience came, but it was hard won. There were several letters of commendation recorded in the files, to ***Mayflower*** and ***Lévis*** personnel.

U 74 herself was to be sunk only seven months later on 2 May, 1942 by HMS ***Wishart*** and ***Wrestler*** and aircraft of RAF 202 Squadron in the Bay of Biscay off Spain, under another CO. Of her crew of forty-six there were no survivors.

LOST:

Ashley, Orville W., AB
Broughton, Arthur W., O.Sig
Craig, Daniel A., Tel
Davieaux, Joseph A., Sto
Eadie, Jack J., OS
Edwards, William J., OS
Gagne, Joseph A.A., OS
Grant, Garfoeld, S., LS
Jaynes, George E., Sto
Kneeland, Melvin L., Sto
McCarthy, John M., AB
Mansfield, William E., OS
Meurant, Andrew L., Sto
Page, Orville S., Sto
Sheckleton, Robert J., AB
Smyth, Angus D., Sto
White, Robert B., Sto.
Plus 1 RN rating.

SOURCES:

German, *The Sea Is At Our Gates*, p. 108.

Goodeve, A.G., survivor, unpublished memoir.

Gröner, *German Warships, 1815-1945,* p. 48.

Johnston, *Corvettes Canada,* pp. 53-59.

Lenton, *German Submarines*, Vol. 1, p.29.

Macpherson & Burgess, *Ships of Canada's Naval Forces.*

Milner, *North Atlantic Run*, pp. 44-45.

Schull, *Far Distant Ships*, p. 86.

Tarrant, *The U-Boat Offensive*, p. 143.

CHAPTER 9

HMCS WINDFLOWER IN COLLISION IN HEAVY FOG

The Zephyranthes Candida (windflower) must have sun and shelter.

Complete Indoor Gardener

Windflower: Flower class corvette
Builder: Davie Shipbuilding Co, Lauzon, PQ
Comm: as HMS *Windflower,* 20 Oct 40
2nd Comm: 15 May 41

Fate: Collision with SS *Zypenberg,* off St. John's NF, 7 Dec 41
Casualties: 4 officers, 19 crew

Windflower on builder's trials, 1940. She has no armament and flies a rather elegant builder's flag aft.

As one of the ten corvettes built in Canada for the Royal Navy (and one of two of this group lost), ***Windflower*** was the first Canadian built corvette to be commissioned. She sailed from Quebec City to Halifax and, in order to get her to the UK as quickly as possible, sailed with a scratch crew and only partly armed, in company with HMCS ***Trail*** as escort to Convoy HX-94.

After fitting-out with her proper armament and work-ups at Tobermory in western Scotland, still as HMS ***Windflower*** she served with her Canadian crew out of Greenock with the Western Approaches Command EG-4, commissioning as HMCS in mid-May with the rest of the Canadian-built flower-named corvettes. In June she returned to Canadian waters, serving with various groups in the Newfoundland Escort Force, completing four convoy escorts to Iceland. In October, 1941, Lt John Price, RCNR took over command from A/LCdr J.H.S. MacDonald, RCNR.

In November ***Windflower*** rescued twenty-seven survivors from a merchant ship torpedoed in Convoy SC-52. On 4 December 1941 Convoy SC-58 sailed from Sydney, Nova Scotia, with ***Drumheller*** (SO), ***Thunder, Kamsack, Shawinigan*** and ***Summerside*** as local escort. The convoy consisted of forty-nine vessels in ten columns. On the morning of the 6th the local escort force passed the convoy over to the mid-ocean escort of ***St. Laurent*** (SO, Lt H.S. Rayner, RCN), ***Hepatica, Moose Jaw, Pictou, Buctouche, Windflower*** and HMS ***Nasturtium.***

Much of what transpired on the morning of 7 December is taken from the Board of Inquiry that was held on 9 and 11 December at St. John's. Four of the five officers, including the commanding officer of ***Windflower*** and the officer of the watch were lost in the collision, so evidence was largely second hand. The Board consisted of Captain Rollo Mainguy as president, A/Cdr Alfred Wurtele and LCdr Guy Windeyer as members, all experienced pre-war RCN officers and, in the case of Guy Windeyer, an ex-RN officer.

The most important factor leading to the collision was the weather, typical for the Grand Banks. The sea was relatively calm but the convoy was in dense fog which had prevailed since noon the previous day. At 0740 on the 7th, ***Windflower's*** position had been fixed by radar two and a half miles, 20° on the starboard bow of the leading ship of the starboard wing column. Her allotted station was referred to as position "C, NE 7" in WACI (Western Approaches Convoy Instructions) Night Escort Diagram 7. But the Board concluded that the ship had erroneously kept station in position "C, DE 7" in the *day* escort diagram during the morning watch, 0400 to 0800. The escorts were not zig-zagging.

The Board recorded that the officer taking over the forenoon watch at 0800 then attempted to do one of two things. Either he had lost touch with the convoy and was turning to port toward its presumed location to regain it, or he was turning to take up his proper station abeam of the leading ship of the starboard column of the convoy. ***Windflower's*** movements between 0800 and 0920 when the collision took place are not recorded. One of the survivors later posed the question why the captain, or the OOW, turned his ship around in order to close the convoy rather than simply decreasing speed and easing to port, given the fog. The Board voiced similar criticism.

SS ***Zypenberg*** was the fourth ship in the starboard column, a 5,000-ton freighter of Dutch registry. Just prior to the collision she was steering 062° at a speed of seven knots. ***Windflower*** and ***Zypenberg*** sighted each other looming suddenly out of the fog when the two ships were less than two cables (400 yards) apart. ***Windflower*** was crossing the larger ship's bow from starboard to port. Reaction by both was immediate. ***Windflower*** went full ahead and turned sharply to starboard, while Captain Jan Bakker of ***Zypenberg*** went full astern, sounded three short blasts on her whistle and also turned to starboard. She could hardly have turned to port because of other ships in the convoy, as well as ***Windflower*** still swinging that way. But the distance was too close for the time needed to pass clear. ***Zypenberg's*** bow sliced into the port quarter of the small corvette at a forty-five degree angle, cutting off twenty-five feet of her stern.

The initial appreciation aboard the corvette by the CO and the 1st lieutenant, Lt G.G. Fraser, RCNVR, was that the ship could be saved and preparations were made to have her taken in tow. If the after bulkhead held, the flooding could be controlled. Depth charges were set to safe and the magazines flooded.

But within ten minutes the bulkhead gave way and number one boiler exploded. A surviving stoker reported that the boiler fires had been drawn but presumably the heat and pressure had not subsided sufficiently when the 34°F sea water flooded in. The majority of casualties were caused by this explosion. Within another ten minutes, at 0950, the ship had sunk stern first.

The boiler explosion had also severely damaged ***Windflower's*** lifeboats. The starboard whaler was blown over the side, carrying with it several seamen who were attempting to launch it. The port boat was launched but was soon capsized due to a jammed boat's fall. The CO was observed to leap into the sea from the port bridge wing, but was not seen again. Those in the water were clinging to a variety of debris including the sinking skiff. ***Zypenberg*** had meanwhile stopped engines and then gone astern, lowered two lifeboats and was blowing her whistle so those in the water would not lose her in the continuing heavy fog. Even so she was narrowly missed by her next astern, the 3,300-ton ***Baltara.*** That ship had already sunk another freighter in a convoy collision on 27 November.

The weather was cold but fortunately there was only a slight swell. ***Zypenberg*** rescued forty-seven survivors, three of whom died before she could land them at St. John's.

When the boiler exploded, ***Nasturtium*** concluded that a ship had been torpedoed. She was in position "G", astern and to starboard of the convoy. Rushing up in the fog she obtained a contact on her asdic and dropped depth charges on what later proved to be the sinking ***Windflower.*** One depth charge detonated prematurely and other charges, probably ***Windflower's***, also exploded, damaging ***Nasturtium*** herself. With no asdic, all wireless aerials down and leaking oil fuel lines, she accompanied ***Zypenberg*** to St. John's. The commanding officer of ***Nasturtium*** was deemed by the Board to have taken the correct action, presuming the convoy was under attack, and the depth charge explosions had no bearing on the subsequent loss of life.

The Board fully exonerated the master of ***Zypenberg***. His conduct in promptly rescuing survivors was acknowledged; his boats had all forty-seven survivors aboard only forty-five minutes after the collision. The principal cause of the collision was attributed to ***Windflower*** turning back to rejoin the convoy, having presumably misjudged her position relative to its nearest ships.

There was much bravery aboard the corvette between the collision and the rescue. The Board noted the conditions on board, explosions, escaping steam, damaged life saving equipment and the water temperature. They recommended that the behaviour of some of the more noteworthy be recognised, and as a result Mentions in Despatches were awarded to Lt Fraser, CPO Julien Duchesne, Stoker P.O. Wallace Chandler, LS Joseph Charrier, LSig Fred Morgan and AB James Sharpe.

The convoy continued with a much reduced escort and was fortunate not to be attacked. Four days later it was completely scattered by a gale wherein one Norwegian ship foundered on the night of 15 December. Although ***Pictou*** in some records is shown as accompanying ***Nasturtium*** and ***Zypenberg*** to St. John's, she is also recorded as rescuing all twenty-five men of the Norwegian crew and taking them safely into Reykjavik. The other ships all eventually reached port.

Zypenberg's owners initially made a claim for damage to her bow which flooded her forepeak but did not press the issue when the Canadian government refused to accept liability. She appears to have survived the war.

LOST:

Ayers, Ernest W., Sig
Bartlett, Frederick E., OS
Bright, Jerome D., OS
Collin, Alfred J.K., Mate
Duddles, Stanley E., ERA
Farewell, Elmo R., OS
Fiddler, Roderick, C.ERA
Gautier, Leonard E., Sto
Hare, Alphonse L., Tel
Livingstone, John F., Sto.PO
McDougall, William H.B., OS
Martin, Kenneth W., ERA
Mills, Murray, K., OS
Morris, Wilbur L., L.Sto
Patterson, Cecil C., O.Tel
Peck, James P.C., SLt
Price, John, Lt
Shields, Walter E., SLt
Spear, Wilfred D., AB
Todd, James W., O.Coder
Webber, Bernard, OS
Witney, Alfred E., OS
Woodcock, Richard A., AB

SOURCES:

German, *The Sea Is At Our Gates,* p. 110.

Johnston, *Corvettes Canada,* pp. 63-67.

Lloyd's *Register, 1941-42.*

Macpherson & Burgess, *Ships of Canada's Naval Forces.*

Macpherson & Milner, *Corvettes of the RCN,* pp. 22, 122.

Paquette & Bainbridge, *Honours & Awards.*

Schull, *Far Distant Ships*, pp. 90-91.

CHAPTER 10

THE LOSS OF THE FORGOTTEN PATROL SHIP: HMCS ADVERSUS

I am forgotten as a dead man, out of mind:
I am like a broken vessel.

Psalm 31, v. 12

Adversus: Auxiliary patrol vessel
Builder: Ditchburn Boats Ltd, ON, 1931
Comm: Sep 39
Crew: 3 officers, 13 crew

Fate: Stranded and sank off Shelburne, NS, 20 Dec 41
Casualties: None

HMCS *Adversus* in 1940.

The loss of the small patrol ship HMCS ***Adversus*** has received scant mention in any of the records. Although a small and not very significant warship, she was lost in circumstances little different from those of HMCS ***Skeena*** three years later, but without loss of life. She deserves memorial as much as that destroyer, or other ships such as ***Bras d'Or***, lost due to the dangers of the sea.

Adversus was employed within a few days of the war's outbreak as a coastal patrol vessel when taken over from the RCMP.

NOIC Sydney reported to NSHQ: "The only suitable vessels available for A/S patrols are ***Adversus*** and ***Alachasse*** (a sister ship, also ex-RCMP). Am fitting these with locally made D/Cs as emergency arrangements. Report follows. 1503/7 SEP 39"

LCdr J.D. "Chummy" Prentice, RCN, the staff A/S defence officer was forced by a shortage of even simple depth charges to improvise his own, out of farmers' large bulk-milk cans packed with coal mine Forcite explosive, detonated by fuses lit with matches.

But even by 6 September Prentice had noted that ***Adversus*** "was not suitable as an A/S vessel and not strong enough for a gun." The little vessel was evidently a very good sea boat, as she had travelled from Halifax to Vancouver alone via the Panama Canal in 1933 in RCMP service and back in 1938, gales and all.

Employed at first on patrols off Sydney and then based on Canso, NS, when more suitable and larger vessels became available she was relegated to guard ship at the Halifax Narrows, to control traffic between the inner harbour and Bedford

Basin. Relieved on 15 November, 1941 by the motor-schooner HMCS ***Venture***, ***Adversus*** was sent to Lunenburg for a brief refit, then assigned both as guard-ship examination-vessel and for patrols off Shelburne on Nova Scotia's south shore. The ship was now commanded by Skipper William R. Chandler, RCNR. Chandler, forty-nine years old, had been a chief petty officer of the RCMP's marine section, having previously been an officer in CN Steamships in 1933. Additionally he had served in the RNCVR during World War I from January 1915 to December 1918. Chandler was thus an officer with considerable small ship experience.

On 20 December 1941 ***Adversus*** was serving as examination vessel off Shelburne, checking inbound shipping. The St. John, NB tug ***Ocean Eagle*** was proceeding into Shelburne in a full gale and almost nil visibility due to heavy snow. Skipper Chandler decided to accompany her to the harbour entrance. Passing close to McNutt Island which lies in the harbour mouth, the tug touched ground but was able to back clear. ***Adversus*** in her turn went solidly aground on the island at 1902 within view of ***Ocean Eagle*** which made no attempt to assist but carried on into the harbour. There is an indication from some present on the island that night that ***Adversus'*** skipper tried to turn at the last moment but was driven ashore almost stern first.

By 1915 that evening the naval staff officer in Shelburne had been notified, perhaps by the lightkeeper on the island, that a vessel was aground. While he still did not know the exact location of the incident, he signalled the armed yacht HMCS ***Lynx*** and the small local vessel ***Aquharaza*** to make ready for sea. He sailed in Lynx at 2030 with some sailors from the base at Shelburne. Despite the gale and blizzard producing nil visibility, he eventually found ***Adversus*** in a cove just around from the northeast bluff of the island, where she had been driven by the storm after grounding. The ship was stern to the shore, bows submerged. She had been abandoned, her crew having landed on the island.

Skipper Chandler, in his report of the incident, stated that when he grounded his pumps were not useable. Fortunately ***Adversus*** grounded on one of the very few sandy areas, and the heavy seas drove the vessel well up the beach. The crew abandoned the vessel at 1945 and were all ashore over her stern, uninjured, by 2100. Given the weather and the remoteness of her grounding, it would seem a competent feat of seamanship that Chandler was able to save his crew. Somehow the small army garrison on the other side of the island also heard there was a ship ashore and set off across the island to see if help was needed. They met Chandler's wet but safe crew walking toward their barracks.

A Board of Inquiry was held on 27 December 1941, where the failure of Chandler to accurately fix his position was noted. But the Board also took into consideration the weather and the paucity of aids to navigation in the area. In particular it was observed that the foghorn on Cape Roseway could not be heard at the point of land where the grounding took place.

While Chandler was recorded as incurring the displeasure of the Department for failing to ascertain his position (a relatively mild rebuke for losing one's ship), the file was closed. Chandler was promoted to Skipper Lieutenant in September 1943, but was not given another command. He returned to the RCMP's marine section in 1945 and retired in 1949. He died at Chester in 1966. In the late 1940s divers descended to the wreck, which had been washed out into Shelburne Bay near the island, and recovered some parts of the ship including a bronze propellor.

But the Navy was very critical of ***Ocean Eagle*** for its "lack of interest" in not coming to the assistance of ***Adversus***, which was "not in keeping with the traditions of the sea." The captain of ***Ocean Eagle*** stated that he had a green crew and his rescue gun wouldn't work.

This small loss in the Navy's list of ships deserves remembrance as much as any other.

SOURCE:

Only in Macpherson & Burgess's *Ships of Canada's Naval Forces, 1910-1993*, p. 143, is ***Adversus*** even listed as a naval vessel. The above details were obtained in RG 24 of the National Archives of Canada, from the RCMP's Historical Branch, courtesy Glen Gordon, and in correspondence with Eugene Rennehan of Gunner Cove, NS

Navy List, 1940; Apr. 1945.

1942

The seamen learn their trades and successes begin to mount, offsetting four losses

CHAPTER 11

SPIKENARD'S SPIKE: LOST IN MID-ATLANTIC

My sledge and anvil lie declined,
My bellows too have lost their wind;
My fire's extinct, my forge decayed,
And in the dust my vice is laid.
My coals are spent, my iron's gone
My spike is drove, my work is done.

Anonymous, Nettlebed Churchyard

Spikenard: Flower class corvette
Builder: Davie Shipbuilding & Repairing, Lauzon PQ
Comm: 6 Dec 40
Crew: 5 officers, 60 crew

Fate: Torpedoed by *U 136*, mid-Atlantic, 10 Feb 42
Casualties: 5 officers, 52 crew

Spikenard hastening down Halifax harbour, fall 1941.

When the war began, Canada and the UK started a series of discussions concerning the building of destroyers for the RCN in the UK and of smaller escort ships in Canada. One of the results was the decision to build an initial order of sixty-four corvettes in Canada, with ten of them to meet an Admiralty order. ***Spikenard*** was one of these original ten and thus given a "flower" name as opposed to a city or town name.

When completed these ten vessels were simply manned by Canadian steaming crews for delivery to UK ports in January, 1941. By the time they arrived the decision had been made not to man them with RN personnel due to a shortage of available British sailors. So ***Spikenard*** remained in Canadian hands, and her steaming crew became her operational crew, with almost no further training, certainly with no serious experience as a cohesive ship's company. She worked out of Greenock, Scotland after alterations to prepare her for escort duty and work-ups, and then with the 4th Escort Group out of Reykjavik, Iceland.

Her commanding officer was LCdr H.G."Bert" Shadforth, RCNR, an experienced west coast marine pilot before the war. His initial navigator was SLt Joe C. Marston, RCNR who had been on convoy runs as a Merchant Navy officer but wanted to serve in warships. He describes Shadforth as "a most popular officer, highly regarded by both subordinates and superiors. His sense of humour was legend, and the little stage acts he was capable of delivering were always in demand at parties." Fortunately Joe Marston left ***Spikenard*** before her last convoy run.

The ship was invariably called ***Spike*** by those who sailed in her. After three convoy runs to Iceland she was transferred to the Newfoundland Escort Force, had a boiler clean in Halifax and then was employed on the "Newfie-Derry" convoy run from off Newfoundland to mid-ocean. The escorts then handed their convoy over to British groups and proceeded to Londonderry for fuel, short leave, repairs, and another convoy run back.

The first of these new escort arrangements was with SC-67 which sailed from Sydney, NS on 2 February 1942. It was a slow convoy–five to eight and a half knots in good weather–of twenty-two merchant vessels. They had almost reached MOMP (the Mid-Ocean Meeting Point) without any attacks but with winter fogs and heavy weather that were often considered enemies equal to the U-boat threat. The escorts anticipated meeting the British group that would take over the next morning. Their radars were not of sufficient range or quality to pick up the British ships before daylight.

The Canadian escort consisted of six of the more experienced corvettes, designated N15 or Task Unit 4.1.15, a precursor to Escort Group C-15. LCdr Shadforth in ***Spikenard*** was senior officer, with the others being ***Louisburg, Dauphin, Chilliwack, Shediac*** and ***Lethbridge.*** The ships' positions relative to the convoy were an important factor in their COs' interpretation of what they saw and how they reacted when the U-boat attacks began. In attempting to reconstruct the events of the night of 10 February the Reports of Proceedings give a picture of five corvettes trying to respond to an uncertain situation. It was still early days in escort work, before intelligible convoy defence doctrine had been firmly worked out and passed down to the lowly corvette groups.

The twenty-two merchantmen were disposed in a rectangle of seven columns three or four ships deep, spread across almost a mile and a half frontage, in fairly heavy seas, on a very dark night. ***Spikenard*** was zig-zagging ahead of the starboard column, her radar not working at the time, a not unusual occurrence. ***Louisburg*** was 2,000 yards to starboard of the lead ship in that starboard column, more than a mile off ***Spikenard's*** starboard quarter. ***Dauphin*** was about a mile astern of the starboard column or almost three miles from ***Spikenard. Chilliwack*** was off the port beam of the leading ship of the port column, ***Shediac*** off the port quarter of the last ship in that column. ***Lethbridge*** was further astern and to port of ***Shediac.*** It was an almost completely black night, and all ships' positions were approximate, varying with their zig-zagging and their OOW's estimates of where they were relative to the nearest convoy ship.

The first of the U-boat attacks was made at 2230 by at least two boats firing torpedoes from off the starboard bow of the convoy at almost precisely the same time.[1] One torpedo struck the Norwegian ship ***Heina***, which burst into flames. Within seconds a torpedo from ***U 136***, commanded by KL Heinrich Zimmermann, struck ***Spikenard*** between the bridge and the forecastle, opening a huge gap in the hull, evidently on her port side, and destroying almost everything above, including the bridge. It is of vital significance that both torpedoes struck within seconds of each other and that it was the senior officer's ship that disappeared.

The most critical factor for ***Spikenard*** was that, although some heard two closely spaced explosions, none of the other escorts realized that she had been torpedoed, or that in five minutes she was utterly gone. The reasons for this vary according to the distance separating each ship, and their duties relative to the convoy. Aboard ***Spikenard*** the initial explosion created such extensive damage that the ship sank within five minutes without being able to transmit an emergency signal. In that brief time fires also made it difficult for the crew to abandon ship using the life-saving equipment. A second underwater explosion as the ship sank caused additional casualties.

About this time ***Chilliwack***, on the opposite side of the convoy, had sighted a faint shadow of a surfaced U-boat, lost it, obtained and then lost a submarine asdic contact and was again searching. ***Dauphin***, astern, saw the explosions, then the blazing ***Heina***, and after a brief asdic sweep, picked up all the survivors from the

---

1. Rohwer identifies the first submarine as ***U 591***, crediting her with the hit on ***Heina.*** Macpherson and Milner in *Corvettes of the RCN* say ***U 136*** fired both torpedoes.

Norwegian ship by 0015 of the 11th, presuming that was all there were. ***Shediac*** rushed over from her position on the port quarter of the convoy, then moved up its flank conducting a search for the attacking submarine. She closed ***Dauphin***, busy with her rescue job. In the absence of any orders from the senior officer in ***Spikenard***, but obviously somewhat concerned, ***Dauphin's*** commanding officer LCdr R.A.S. MacNeil, RCNR, an officer with considerable convoy experience already, ordered ***Shediac*** to search for a possible second ship torpedoed. She swept aft down the side of the convoy but those aboard saw nothing of ***Spikenard*** or her survivors.

Louisburg actually sighted the wake of one of the torpedoes close by her own port side and had moved out to starboard along their track. She obtained an asdic contact and was busy attacking for an hour and a half, without visible results. ***Lethbridge*** moved forward to take up a defensive position on the port side of the convoy.

It was not until daylight, some eight or more hours after the attack, that any of the remaining five corvettes realized that ***Spikenard*** was actually missing and that the problem was not just radio failure. The subsequent Board of Inquiry addressed this question but exonerated the commanding officers of the remaining ships. Undoubtedly there was much confusion as, although no more ships in the convoy were sunk, several torpedoes were fired which were set to explode at the end of their runs. Although Schull says attempts were made to reach ***Spikenard*** by radio, these sets were not normally to be used except in emergency. ***Spikenard's*** was presumably destroyed in the torpedoing, and the Canadian corvettes' radars were very unreliable. As a priority in convoy protection, escorts were expected to search for and attack U-boats without orders if none were received. The areas of convoy coverage were large, ships showed no lights, and night and weather often determined what could be seen and how the tactical situation was understood in each ship.

Dauphin closed the convoy commodore's ship at dawn and asked how many ships had been torpedoed. "One" was the reply. Bob MacNeil then began to feel more certain that one of the two close-spaced explosions could have been ***Spikenard***.

The British group arrived to take over as the ocean escort mid-morning of the 11th. When the senior officer, in the destroyer ***St. Albans***, was told ***Spikenard*** seemed to be missing he sent the RN corvette ***Gentian*** (Lt F.V. Osborne, RAN) to search in the wake of the convoy. There, many miles astern in the late afternoon, she found and recovered just eight survivors from one of ***Spikenard's*** rescue rafts, almost nineteen hours after they abandoned their sinking corvette. Neither Shadforth nor any of his four officers were among them.

The ship had not been at Action Stations when the torpedo struck almost below the bridge (although official records show they were; in fact, the Action Stations alarm had just rung), so some of those in seamen's mess decks survived. A drum of gasoline stored on the upper deck was ignited and destroyed one of the ship's boats. The second was demolished as the ship sank. Those who managed to reach the surviving floats and rafts in the bitter water saw the dark shape of ***Shediac*** sweep past them but they had no flares or lights and were not seen. The Carley float, with ten aboard, was abandoned for a merchant service-type raft because it floated higher in the water. During the long cold night two of the injured survivors died and were committed to the sea with a prayer, their clothes retained for the frozen survivors.

The survivors were landed from ***Gentian*** at Gladstone Dock, Liverpool, and four taken to hospital at Seaforth.

This was the second corvette sinking by ***U 136***, of VI U-Flottille out of St. Nazaire, France. Just five days earlier she had torpedoed HMS ***Arbutus*** when attacking outbound convoy ONS-63. In the next few months Zimmermann was credited with sinking three more merchantmen, and possibly the Canadian fishing schooner ***Mildred Pauline*** off Nova Scotia, where the U-boat was detected by the *Bangor* escort ***Clayoquot*** but lost amidst ice pack off Halifax. But her own end came in July, 1942, when the RN sloop ***Pelican***, the frigate ***Spey*** and the French destroyer ***Léopard*** destroyed her with depth charges off the Canary Islands, with no survivors.

A memento of ***Spikenard*** exists still in the famous Crow's Nest Club in St. John's, Newfoundland. In January 1942 Commodore Murray had agreed to assist in establishing the Seagoing Officers Club on the fourth floor of a warehouse in the city. On an evening just before ***Spikenard's*** group sailed, the officers gathered in the club, still being renovated. After a few drinks at the makeshift bar set up on builder's planks, a competition was held to see who could drive large 6-inch nails into the hard pine floor with the least number of blows of hammers still lying about. Bert Shadforth was one of the competitors, reportedly the winner. When he failed to return, a brass ring was cast to surround his "spike" in the floor, engraved "SPIKENARD - HIS SPIKE". At the end of the war, when the club temporarily closed, it was cut out of the flooring and hangs on the wall to this day. Another of the competitors had been "Liverlips" McNeil, the COs in that group all adopting names for radio communications of Damon Runyan's characters, Shadforth's "Hot Horse Herbie" and others.

LOST:

Anderson, John, Stwd
Bate, Leonard, L.Tel
Blouin, Joseph A.Y., AB
Boudreau, John R., AB
Boutin, Conrad W., AB
Campbell, Alan D., AB
Canavan, Lloyd F., Sto
Condie, James R., Sig
Connor, John W., Sto
Cove, Gilbert L., ERA
Cowan, Murray A., L.Sto
Curr, Stanley R., AB
Dearlove, Kenneth H., Sig
Donnet, Daniel H., AB
Dunn, Rupert M., Cook
Edwards, Norman J., Sto
Fawcett, Charles C., Lt
Fisher, Edmund J., AB
Galbraith, Stuart, L.Sto
Gamble, John M., ERA
Gilboe, Arthur F., AB
Greenblatt, Moses, Tel
Griffin, Patrick B., Sig
Hall, John R., AB
Hounsell, Lionel R., OS
Hughes, Robert A., Lt
Jamieson, Robert D., LS
Jordon, Donald, AB
Kennedy, Thomas R., L.Sto
Kettle, Alfred S., CPO
Kitchen, Cyril F., L.Sto
Lamoureux, Romeo J., LS
Legendre, Jean-Marie, Sto.PO
MacLean, John A., C.ERA
Markham, Gerald A., S/Lt
Meacoe, William A., Coder
Milthorp, Patrick R.F., Lt
Morley, William, AB
Oxborough, George W., LS
Pryor, Albert L., OS
Real, Clare A., AB
Regalbuto, Charles C., OS
Rennie, William A., SBA
Richards, Donald P., VA
Ring, Norman E., AB
Seaman, William J., Sto
Sennett, John P., Sto
Shadforth, Hubert C., LCdr
Smith, Harold W., AB
Stephens, William D., AB
Stewart, Albert M., AB
Upton, Charles M.A., O.Coder
Walker, Samuel C., Tel
Watts, Dan J., Stwd
Webb, William L.A., AB
Whittemore, Edwin G., Cook
Wilcox, Russell H., Sto

SOURCES:

Bishop, *Courage At Sea,* pp. 34-35.

Johnston, *Corvettes Canada*, p. 73.

Lenton, *German Submarines of WW II,* p. 39.

Macpherson & Burgess, *Ships of Canada's Naval Forces.*

Macpherson & Milner, *Corvettes of the RCN,* pp. 40, 121.

Rohwer, *Axis Submarine Successes 1939-1945*, pp. 78, 316.

Schull, *Far Distant Ships*, pp. 101-104.

Tarrant, *The U-Boat Offensive 1914-1945*, p. 143.

Tucker, *The Naval Service of Canada,* Vol. II, pp. 10, 38.

CHAPTER 12

HMCS ST. CROIX PROVES THAT OLD CAN STILL BE GOOD

St. Croix: Town class destroyer
Builder: Bethlehem Steel, Quincy Mass
1st Comm: as USS *McCook*, 30 Apr 19
2nd Comm: 24 Sep 40
Crew: 10 officers, 143 crew

Action: Sank *U 90*, North Atlantic, 24 Jul 42
Casualties: 44
No survivors

The 50 American destroyers are rapidly coming into service just when they are most needed.

Winston Churchill, 5 November, 1940

During the spring of 1940 Britain lost twelve destroyers in actions off Norway, the Low Countries and France. So when it became known through diplomatic channels that President Roosevelt would either sell surplus warships or transfer them in return for lease of base rights in British colonial territories, Churchill quickly responded. When the Royal Navy did not have sufficient personnel available to man all fifty destroyers offered, Canada undertook to provide crews for six of them. In the end Canada took over two more, HMCS ***Hamilton*** in 1941, and later in 1943 ***Buxton*** when her boilers gave out, to be used as a stationary training vessel.

These destroyers were what remained of 273 flush-deckers built for the USN as World War I was ending. Those still available by 1940, approximately 113, had been in and out of service with the USN for twenty years. So it was not surprising that those which Canada manned provided service that was limited by the condition of their equipment. Of the Canadian-manned ships only ***St. Croix*** was to be sunk on active service, but her record before that melancholy day was significant.

As the USS ***McCook*** she was placed in reserve in 1922 and remained thus until 1939. When she commissioned as HMCS ***St. Croix*** the ship's company were surprised to find her completely equipped with every possible requirement, indeed luxury. The USN contributed paint and cordage, binoculars and sextants, mess traps and silverware, typewriters and pencils, books and magazines, plus fully stocked store rooms. Not all Americans were isolationists.

But the ships were old[1] and the defects of age included problems relating to their role as anti-submarine vessels. For that task they were not sufficiently manoeuverable, and although relatively fast, were narrow and of shallow draft. Added depth charges and other top hamper rendered them somewhat unstable and very "wet" ships, both on the upper deck and below in the mess decks. All of this made them miserable for the crews in the rough Atlantic. By 1940 with the addition of new equipment such as asdic they were over-crowded and difficult to maintain.

Because of early storm damage ***St. Croix*** did not become operational until March 1941. After a short period in the Halifax Local Escort Force and more repairs, she joined the Newfoundland Escort Force in August. Another lengthy refit followed before she joined C-1 Escort Group. She was briefly assigned to C-2 and was with that group whwn the following events took place. From January 1942 until September 1943 her third commanding officer was LCdr A.H. Dobson, RCNR.

In January 1942 C-2 was led by the RN destroyer HMS ***Burnham***, another of the flush-deckers, with the senior officer A/Cdr T. Taylor, RN. The others of the group were the RCN corvettes ***Brandon, Dauphin*** and ***Drumheller*** and the RN corvette ***Polyanthus.***

ON-113 was a west-bound convoy of thirty-three ships which had sailed from the UK in mid-July, 1942. During most of the crossing the convoy was in heavy fog which was of dubious value to the escorts since none of them were fitted with the more reliable British 271 radar or with HF/DF equipment. On 24 July both

1. "Old" is relative. ***St. Croix*** was twenty years old. Canada sent HMCS ***Terra Nova*** to the Persian Gulf War for Operation Friction, a destroyer that had been launched thirty-seven years before.

HMCS *St. Croix* in December, 1940, returning to port after aborted crossing to the U.K. It illustrates these ships' very narrow beam, provoking severe rolling in heavy weather.

sides in the forthcoming battle were assisted by intelligence. ***U 552*** reported the convoy's presence to their B-Dienst and C-2 was advised by the Admiralty that U-boats could be expected in their vicinity. Cdr Taylor's response was to send his two destroyers to screening stations ten miles ahead on the convoy's course. This move soon paid off when about 1330 an alert masthead lookout in ***St. Croix*** sighted two surfaced submarines. Burnham took off after one, without success when it dived and could not be detected.

St. Croix concentrated on the other. When first seen the U-boat was at 6,000 yards and a more experienced or luckier captain might have evaded the destroyer. The U-boat quickly dived, thus restricting its speed and making it at least an asdic target. Dobson estimated the U-boat's probable diving course and his asdic 1st operator soon had a solid contact. ***St. Croix*** made three attacks in quick succession (some sources say four), dropping depth charges and regaining contact each time. After the third attack there were signs that the U-boat was damaged, with some oil and debris coming to the surface. But Dobson felt that one more attack was required to be certain. This one produced unmistakable proof of a kill. Among the litter of personal items such as cigarettes and food were human remains.

It was later discovered they had sunk ***U 90.*** German U-boat headquarters, BdU, were not satisfied with the results of attacks on ON-113 that day or later. They partly blamed the inexperience of the U-boat captains. ***U 90***, KK Oldörp, of IX U-Flottille, launched in October, 1941 and operating out of Brest as part of their *Gruppe Wolf,* had not made a single attack on Allied shipping before its career was ended by a 23-year-old veteran of another war.

The balance in favour of the escorts in this convoy passage did not last much longer. The convoy was poorly directed from ashore as it passed from Admiralty to American control. One factor was the "blackout" at Bletchley Park's (the British Code and Cypher School) intelligence section, caused when the German BdU changed its cypher code. The new one was not broken until late in 1942. Another was that the track assigned allowed the ten U-boats of *Gruppe Steinbrinck* to make contact and sink three merchantmen and heavily damage another between 25 and 30 July. There was an average of seventy U-boats operationally at sea in July and the total of boats available was rising by eleven per month–a worrying prospect, although the USN was now fully committed to the anti-submarine war, and support aircraft were arriving.

As a result of the destruction of ***U 90*** LCdr Dobson was gazetted for a DSC in November, 1942 but lost his life when ***St. Croix*** was sunk in September, 1943 (See Chapter 29). The contribution of this veteran to the Battle of the Atlantic was a significant one, and for another success see Chapter 26. At the time, ***U 90*** was only the second U-boat credited as sunk by the RCN in the Atlantic battle. ***Ottawa*** had sunk the Italian ***Faa' di Bruno*** in 1940, but this was not discovered until the mid-1980s.

SOURCES:

Alden, *Flush Decks And Four Pipes,* p. 23.

Hague, *The Towns,* pp. 9-10.

Lenton, *German Submarines*, Vol. I, p. 32.

Macpherson & Burgess, *Ships of Canada's Naval Forces.*

Milner, *North Atlantic Run,* pp. 125-127.

Paquette & Bainbridge, *Honours & Awards,* p. 147.

Rohwer, *Axis Submarine Successes,* p. 111.

Schull, *Far Distant Ships,* pp. 56, 131.

Showell, *U-Boat Command and the Battle of the Atlantic,* p. 114.

Tarrant, *The U-Boat Offensive, 1914-1945,* p. 106.

Terraine, *U-Boat Wars, 1916-1945*, pp. 461-462.

CHAPTER 13

A SUCCESSFUL ATTACK BY C-3 SHIPS HMCS SKEENA AND WETASKIWIN

'Tis not in mortals to command success,
But we'll do more Sempronius; we'll deserve it.

Joseph Addison, *Cato*

Skeena: River class destroyer
Builder: John I. Thornycroft & Co, Southampton
Comm: 10 Jun 31
Crew: 10 officers, 171 crew

Wetaskiwin: Flower class corvette
Builder: Burrard Dry Dock Co, Vancouver
Comm: 17 Dec 40
Crew: 6 officers, 79 crew

Action: Sank *U 588*, mid-Atlantic, 31 Jul 42
Casualties: 46
No survivors

HMCS *Skeena* in January, 1942, with a new 'I' pendant number, cut-down after funnel, and Y gun replaced by depth charge rails for her new A/S role.

By mid-1942, when Canadian Escort Group C-3 was assigned the task of bringing Convoy ON-115 from Londonderry to North America, it was a relatively experienced and seasoned team. The senior officer was Acting Commander D.C. Wallace, RCNR, in the destroyer ***Saguenay.*** A/LCdr Kenneth L. Dyer, RCN, commanded ***Skeena*** and LCdr Guy Windeyer, RCN commanded ***Wetaskiwin.*** The others of the group were the corvettes ***Galt*** (Lt A.D. Landles, RCNR), ***Louisburg*** (LCdr W.F. Campbell, RCNVR) and ***Sackville*** (Lt A.H. Easton, RCNR).

Skeena was one of six destroyers in the pre-war RCN. By 1942, now eleven years old, she was under her sixth captain since the war began. She had taken the second wartime convoy out of Halifax in September, 1939, had served in UK waters in 1940, and rescued 230 survivors of the armed merchant cruiser HMS ***Cheshire*** when she was torpedoed, although not sunk, in October, 1940. Skeena then served in the Newfoundland Escort Force in 1941. She was an escort to the ill-starred Convoy SC-42 in September, 1941 which lost sixteen ships to a pack of U-boats. By July 1942 she was part of C-3 of the Mid-Ocean Escort Force (MOEF).

Wetaskiwin was an early corvette, a veteran of the Newfoundland Escort Force with many convoys to Iceland on her record. She had joined C-3 in May, 1942 in Londonderry.

ON-115 sailed late in July, 1942. Although the escort was competent and experienced, it suffered from equipment shortages that prevented it from being a much more proficient

Wetaskiwin, known by friends as "Wet-Ass-Queen", not inappropriate for a corvette with its tendency to "roll on wet grass." In 1943, still with her short forecastle and mast before the bridge.

adversary to the U-boats. Specifically the ships lacked 271M radar and HF/DF. Once in the open Atlantic westbound, ***Saguenay*** chased a couple of echoes and radio reports that were possibly U-boats on the 27th, and ***Wetaskiwin*** tried unsuccessfully to close a radar contact the same day. The 28th and 29th produced more indications that the Germans were gathering, as medium-frequency radio transmissions were intercepted by the convoy commodore's ship, although these gave no clear direction of the transmitting U-boats except that they were astern of the convoy, then on the starboard beam. The convoy had been sighted by chance and reported by ***U 210*** on her way to the US coast on the 29th and six U-boats were directed by BdU to attack.

On the 30th ***Skeena*** gained some possible asdic contacts and attacked them without any indication of success. Meanwhile the convoy's course had been altered with the hope of throwing off the shadowers or finding a less dangerous route around them. Cdr Wallace sent the destroyers out thirty miles to hunt potential U-boats and give the impression the convoy would stay on its original course. He appreciated that the greatest threat to the convoy would probably come from its starboard side. Thus, on the evening of 30 July, he placed his two most experienced commanding officers, Dyer in ***Skeena*** and Windeyer in ***Wetaskiwin***, on that side as escort protection. They had cooperated before in coordinated U-boat attacks and Wallace thought their professionalism might come in handy.

During the early morning hours on the 31st, ***Skeena*** had a dubious asdic contact and steamed in a diamond-shaped pattern, dropping single charges at the corners in hopes of causing the U-boat to reveal herself by some more definite action. Then at 0636 she sighted a submarine on the surface. ***Wetaskiwin*** was ordered to her assistance by the senior officer, so ***Skeena*** sent a signal to the corvette: *"ACTS 16, V.9"*.[1]

The two ships altered toward the target and, although Windeyer was the senior of the two, he asked that ***Skeena*** direct the hunt as she was better equipped and with more staff. The U-boat dived and ***Skeena*** had made two attacks before ***Wetaskiwin*** arrived on the scene at 0800. ***Skeena*** then directed her to take station on her beam at one mile, and gave her courses to steer so that they could alternate with directed attacks.

An attack was made by ***Wetaskiwin*** followed by another by ***Skeena***, without visible results. The contact was lost for an hour. Then, as a result of a careful plot maintained in ***Wetaskiwin***, asdic contact was regained just

1. "And a vision appeared to Paul in the night; there stood a man of Macedonia and prayed him saying, 'Come over into Macedonia and help us.' "

after 1030 by that ship which made two more attacks. The COs then assessed that their target was quite deep, and set up a series of controlled attacks with one ship directing from the sidelines while the other dropped depth charges set to 550 feet when over by plot or by asdic range and bearing. The last was by ***Skeena*** at 1118, directed by ***Wetaskiwin***. It was a series of well coordinated attacks, but this last effort had reportedly used ***Skeena's*** last depth charges.

There were no results immediately noted and further attacks were being set up when they were rewarded with two closely-spaced underwater explosions. A series of inter-ship signals tells the story:

Skeena:	DID YOU HEAR THAT UNDERWATER EXPLOSION?
Wetaskiwin:	YES. DEFINITELY
Skeena:	YOUR TURN
Wetaskiwin:	PLENTY OF WRECKAGE OVER THIS WAY. REVELATIONS 13, V.1[2]

The ships put boats in the water and collected the evidence, including human remains brought back to Canada and assessed as "largely internals" by Surgeon Captain Archie McCallum, RCNVR. It was an outstanding example of teamwork and patience by the Canadians, lasting over four hours.

The two headed back to rejoin ON-115 but the two destroyers ***Skeena*** and ***Saguenay,*** and ***Wetaskiwin*** (who never did locate the convoy again) had to depart for St. John's because of fuel shortages due to the long U-boat hunts. This success was offset by the loss of three merchantmen to another U-boat group, *Pirat,* on 3 and 4 August just as the escort was re-strengthened by the arrival of the corvette ***Agassiz*** and the destroyers HMCS ***Hamilton*** and HMS ***Witch.*** Although there was considerable staff criticism about fuel expenditure of the escorts, the destruction of the U-boat was at least a positive contribution to the battle.

Their victim was ***U 588***, commanded by KL Victor Vogel. Launched in July 1941, she had achieved seven sinkings since her first attack in January, 1942 in American waters. She was part of VI U-Flottille based on St. Nazaire.

In November awards were gazetted of DSCs to Dyer, Windeyer and SLt D.L. Hanington of ***Wetaskiwin*** and of DSMs to P.O. HSD A.A. Butchart, RCN, of ***Skeena*** who had controlled the asdic search and ERAs R. Renaud of ***Wetaskiwin*** and L. Mills of ***Skeena*** for their reliable work in the engine rooms that day. Additionally there were ten Mentions in Despatches awarded to members of the asdic teams, the depth charge parties and others of the two ships.

Skeena remained with MOEF for almost two more years, participating in eighteen convoys. She then moved on to EG-11 and EG-12 in 1944, but ended on the rocks off Iceland. (See Chapter 54).

In May, 1943 ***Wetaskiwin*** became part of C-5 in the MOEF. In 1944 she had a refit to extend her forecastle and make other improvements, then joined the Western Local Escort Force where she finished the war. In 1946 she was sold to the Venezuelan Navy as ***Victoria*** until discarded in 1962.

Kenneth Dyer went on to command ***Kootenay*** and had a distinguished postwar career, retiring as a Vice Admiral. Guy Windeyer had joined the Royal Navy during World War I, transferred to the RCN after he was released by the RN, and after ***Wetaskiwin,*** commanded the destroyer ***St. Laurent***. He ended the war in command of the Combined Operations depot ***Givenchy III*** on the west coast.

SOURCES:

German, *The Sea Is At Our Gates*, p. 124.

Hadley, *U-Boats Against Canada,* pp. 83-84.

Herzog, *Deutsche U-Boote*, p. 277.

Johnston, *Corvettes Canada,* pp. 165-166.

Lenton, *German Submarines* Vol 1, p. 116.

MacFarlane, Maritime Museum of BC *Notes,* No. 4.

Macpherson, *River Class Destroyers of the RCN,* pp. 18-25.

Macpherson & Burgess, *Ships of Canada's Naval Forces.*

Macpherson & Milner, *Corvettes of the RCN,* p.116.

Milner, *North Atlantic Run*, pp. 130-140.

Milner, "Participation in the Battle of the Atlantic", p. 158.

Paquette & Bainbridge, *Honours & Awards.*

Rohwer, *Axis Submarine Successes,* pp. 83-84.

Schull, *Far Distant Ships,* pp. 19, 131-134.

Terraine, *The U-Boat Wars, 1916-1945,* pp. 462-466.

2. "And I stood upon the sand of the sea and saw a beast rise up out of the sea having seven heads and ten horns, and upon his horns ten crowns, and upon his head the name of blasphemy."

CHAPTER 14

HMCS ASSINIBOINE: 'BONES' BAGS A BOAT

I can hear, underground, that sucking and sobbing
In my veins, in my bones I feel it -
The small waters creeping upwards,
The tight grains parting at last.

Theodore Roethe, *Cuttings Later*

Assiniboine: River class destroyer
Builder: J. Samuel White & Co., Isle of Wight
1st Comm: as HMS *Kempenfelt*, 1932
2nd Comm: 19 Oct 39
Crew: 10 officers, 171 men

Action: Sank *U 210*, Atlantic, 6 Aug 42
Casualties: 6

Canada entered the Second World War with just thirteen ships in its navy. Of these, six were destroyers of two Royal Navy classes but in the RCN they all were named after Canadian rivers and thus known as River class destroyers. The remaining few small ships were minesweepers or small training tenders.

A seventh destroyer was acquired on 19 October, 1939 when HMS ***Kempenfelt*** was commissioned as HMCS ***Assiniboine***. Canadian sailors soon dubbed their ship ***Bones*** and the nickname stuck. She arrived in Halifax on 17 November and within twenty-four hours had started duties in convoy protection.

Assiniboine made the news in March, 1940 when she and the RN cruiser HMS ***Dunedin*** intercepted the German prize ***Hannover,*** a merchant ship striving to run for home from the West Indies. The German crew attempted to scuttle the ship, setting her on fire. ***Dunedin*** was trying to put out the fires and asked ***Assiniboine*** for help. With one warship on either side, the Germans were anxious to abandon their stopped and burning vessel. Vice Admiral Ralph Hennessy, then a watch-keeping lieutenant in ***Assiniboine***, describes the encounter: "We, in effect, said to them: 'You set her on fire, you put the fire out or you don't get rescued!' We both passed fire hoses as their pumps were kaput, and they succeeded in putting it out."

In four days they towed this valuable capture to Kingston, Jamaica. By 1941 she had been converted into the Royal Navy's first escort carrier, HMS ***Audacity,*** with a flight deck over the existing hull and with six Martlet fighters. Assigned to the important Gibraltar convoy run, the ship gave brief but valuable service providing air cover in the Bay of Biscay.

Assiniboine arrives at St. John's Newfoundland on 9 August 1942, just after sinking *U 210*. Her bent forefoot from ramming the U-boat can be seen.

She was sunk by ***U 751*** on 21 December 1941 during a major convoy battle, when the famous Captain "Johnny" Walker's 36th Escort Group sank four U-boats in retaliation.

One of ***Assiniboine's*** significant assignments in 1941 was in screening the battleship HMS ***Prince of Wales*** which brought Winston Churchill to Placentia Bay, Newfoundland for his meeting with President Roosevelt for the famous Atlantic Charter declaration.

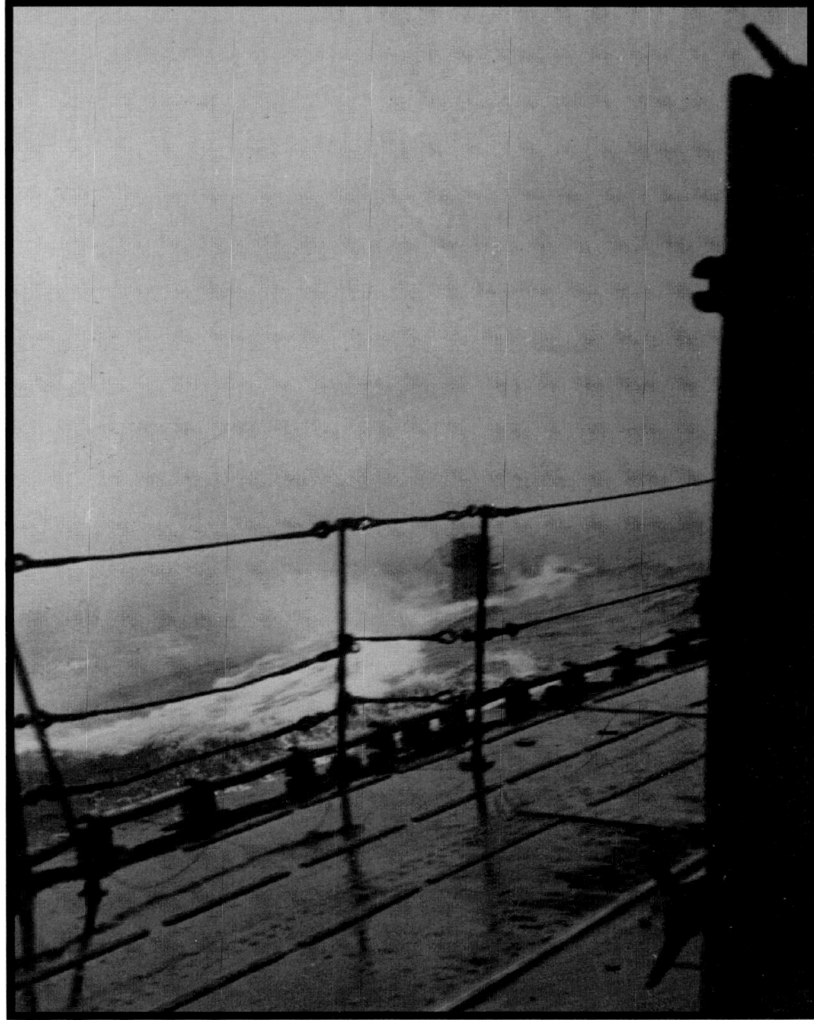

The last moments of *U 210,* close alongside *Assiniboine* and still running at considerable speed.

Assiniboine had ten different commanding officers during six years of war, three of them twice, including Ralph Hennessy. The longest tenure was that of A/LCdr John H. Stubbs, who was CO from February 1941 to October 1942. He was but 30 years old. Stubbs commanded the ship during the action against ***U 210.***

Convoy SC-94 was an eastbound group of thirty-three slow merchantmen (one source says there were initially thirty-six) that had sailed from Sydney, Cape Breton on 31 July 1942. The convoy escort was C-1 group consisting of ***Assiniboine*** and six corvettes, the Canadians ***Chilliwack, Orillia*** and ***Battleford*** plus the RN corvettes ***Primrose, Dianthus*** and ***Nasturtium,*** some of these only lent for this escort job. Although Stubbs had the largest and fastest ship, due to his relatively junior rank the senior officer was LCdr A. Ayre, RNR, commanding ***Primrose.***

Weather played an important role in the events of the 5th and 6th of August. The convoy was outbound in the Grand Banks area, the ships moving in and out of fog banks. The British corvettes were the only ships of the escort fitted with the more efficient Type 271 radar. The fog also limited the amount and effectiveness of air cover from Newfoundland.

First enemy contact with the convoy was by ***U 593*** under KL Gerd Kelbling who torpedoed the straggling Dutch ship ***Spar*** at 1848 on the 5th. She had been part of a small group of ships that had become separated from the main body in the fog the day before. Kelbling was able to determine the convoy course and speed without being detected himself. Soon eighteen submarines, designated as *Gruppe Steinbrinck* by BdU, were running hard on the surface to form an intercepting patrol line ahead of the convoy. One of the first to arrive was the Type VIIC ***U 210***. This boat had been launched at Kiel on 23 December 1941. With no successes so far, she sailed from Kiel on 18 July 1942. By August, commanded by KL Rudolph Lemcke, she had not been credited even with any attacks on Allied shipping, according to German records now available.

At 1125, in misty and variable fog patches, ***U 210*** was sighted a few miles away on the convoy's starboard bow by an ***Assiniboine*** lookout, the ship's British-fitted 286M radar having detected nothing. ***Assiniboine*** reported the sighting, increased speed to twenty-two knots toward it, soon identifying a conning tower and firing at it as she hastened toward the surfaced boat. ***Dianthus*** was despatched to help at her best speed of some seventeen knots. Stubbs steered slightly to starboard of his target, both to allow all guns to bear and so that if the boat dived she would be inclined to alter to port and away, thus narrowing the search area. The submarine dived after only three salvoes from ***Bones*** and three depth charge attacks were made. When no wreckage was found and contact by asdic was lost it was feared the submarine had escaped. Stubbs altered to the northeast to rejoin the convoy, now twenty-one miles ahead, with ***Dianthus*** five miles on her port beam. In fact insufficient damage had been done to force the U-boat's CO to abandon his attacks so, after an hour's silence, he surfaced and headed again for the convoy now many miles ahead.

Assiniboine's yeoman of signals again sighted the surfaced boat at 1712 about half a mile away, still in shifting and sometimes dense fog patches. A wild chase in and out of the fog began that went on for an hour. Whenever the destroyer's 4.7-inch guns were "on target" the target disappeared in fog. Finally Stubbs was so close that only the secondary armament was able to depress sufficiently to bear on the twisting U-boat. ***Bones*** was firing her half-inch calibre machine guns while the aggressive ***U 210*** was returning fire with her 37mm and 20mm guns.

The ship's company of ***Assiniboine*** was impressed with the calm confidence of Stubbs as he conned his ship. But KL Lemcke kept altering toward the destroyer, using his smaller turning circle to advantage, standing on his small bridge and shouting orders down the voice pipe to his control-room crew. Hits were being made on both sides. German sailors were swept from the boat's casing when they came up to man the guns, in particular their deck gun forward. German shells were striking ***Assiniboine's*** bridge and forward gun positions. One Canadian gunner, OS Kenneth W. Watson, was killed. Serving as an ammunition number he was wounded but carried on supplying ammunition to his gun's crew until hit again and killed. Thirteen others were wounded in the hail of fire. Ultimately a fire was started from motor cutter gasoline stored on ***Assiniboine's*** upper deck to starboard of the wheelhouse.

Acting Chief Petty Officer M.L. Bernays, RCNR, was the ship's coxswain and he manned the wheel through all the turns and twists. With a fire burning just outside his wheelhouse, he ordered the two other members of his team to go out and fight the fire, carrying on alone at the wheel. Chief ERA Don Portree, who had taken charge of the fire party, was holding the nozzle of a fire hose when the pressure suddenly came on, and he was neatly flipped over the rails, holding onto the hose for dear life. Other members of the party hauled him aboard again. Lt Ralph Hennessy, now ***Assiniboine's*** 1st lieutenant, sent to take charge of the fire fighting, was forced to reach the upper deck by climbing down the lower mast as the bridge ladders were enveloped in flames. On arrival he found that Chief Portree and Chief Torpedoman Burgess already had a fire-fighting team in action. Stubbs continued his battle with the U-boat and depth charges were dropped without seriously damaging her.

Finally Stubbs was able to move off so that his 4.7-inch guns could obtain a major hit on the submarine's bridge which killed the German captain, although he may have already been hit by machine gun fire. Her 1st watch officer assumed command and although wounded himself, kept the A/A armament firing at the destroyer and, despite the wrecked bridge, decided to dive. Stubbs was then able at last to ram the U-boat just behind the conning tower when the boat held to a steady course for diving. The submarine surfaced again and even resumed 20mm fire at ***Assiniboine***, which was able to respond with her 4.7-inch Y gun. Stubbs then circled and rammed her again and this time ***U 210*** was finished. The order was given by the engineer officer to "Abandon ship" and ***U 210*** sank in about two minutes. ***Dianthus*** arrived in time to pick twenty-eight German survivors from the water and ***Assiniboine*** took on the remaining ten including the 1st watch officer. She also rescued another later found in the water as well as six transferred from the over-crowded ***Dianthus***. Six men had been killed during the fight or in abandoning the submarine. An interested spectator on Stubbs' bridge had been Dr. Gilbert Tucker, the Navy's official historian.

Bones had done so much damage to her bow that she had to withdraw to Newfoundland and then Halifax for repairs. The German pack had now gathered. Not only was the escort reduced, but the Germans were employing simultaneous submerged daylight attacks from ahead of the convoy, a new tactic which introduced an element of uncertainty into defensive measures of the escort force. On the 17th ***U 176*** sank three ships, while ***U 379*** sank two more but ***Dianthus*** sighted ***U 379*** and, after depth charge attacks and four rammings, was able to claim a kill. A nice touch for the corvette that had been helpful in the ***U 210*** affair.

For Convoy SC-94 the troubles were not yet over. Even though two destroyers joined the escort force, it was to lose four more ships before arriving in the UK. The final tally was the loss of eleven merchantmen totalling 53,000 tons for the destruction of two U-boats.

Assiniboine could not be repaired and returned to duty until January, 1943. Stubbs received the DSO, but was to lose his life in the torpedoing of HMCS ***Athabaskan*** (see Chapter 40). Hennessy received a DSC, Bernays the rarely awarded Conspicuous Gallantry Medal (the only other CGM awarded was to AB M.R. Kerwin of ***Haida*** for rescuing members of a gun's crew caught in a fire during a battle with German destroyers). Chief ERA Donald Portree and three others, P.O. Cook C.F. Daly, an ammunition supply number; L/S P. Smith of A gun; L/S E. Costello who manned a .5-inch machine gun all received DSMs, and there were fourteen mentions in despatches.

Bones returned to serve in the 3rd and 1st Escort Groups, then the 12th, 11th and 14th Support Groups until the end of the war. In February, 1945 she collided with S.S. ***Empire Bond*** in the Channel, and was paid off from naval service on 8 August 1945. Sold for scrapping, in tow for Baltimore she broke her tow-line and went aground on the eastern tip of Prince Edward Island, where she was eventually broken up.

The successful U-boats that operated against SC-94 were not to see many more months of active service. ***U 660*** was depth charged and sunk by RN ships on 12 November, 1942, ***U 438 by*** HMS ***Pelican i***n May of 1943. ***U 176*** was also destroyed that month by a Cuban sub-chaser and USN aircraft. ***U 593*** lasted until December 1943 when she was depth charged by USS ***Wainwright*** and HMS ***Calpe.***

SOURCES:

Note: This list illustrates the typical potential sources that contributed to this chapter alone, but omits the files in DHist and National Archives Record Group 24. Some are mere mentions of the action, often setting its place in the over-all battle. Others are detailed, sometimes dramatic. In addition there are many newspaper articles of the day, complete with photographs and extensive quotations by participants. It seemed to catch various authors' fancy. In addition to these references, this story's accuracy has been much helped by a careful review by Vice Admiral R.L. Hennessy, DSC, CD.

German, *The Sea Is At Our Gates,* pp. 124-5.

Hadley, *U-Boats Against Canada,* p. 202.

Hoyt, *Death of the U-Boats,* pp. 162-6.

Lawrence, *Tales of the North Atlantic*, pp. 165-9.

Lenton, *Navies of the Second World War.*

Lenton & Colledge, *Warships of World War II,* Part II, p. 26.

Lynch, *Salty Dips*, Vol. 2, pp. 11-12.

MacIntyre, *Battle of the Atlantic*, pp. 150-156

Macpherson, *The River Class Destroyers*, pp.53-61.

Macpherson & Burgess, *Ships of Canada's Naval Forces.*

Milner, *North Atlantic Run*, pp. 142-7.

Milner, *The U-Boat Hunters,* p. 12.

Paquette & Bainbridge, *Honours & Awards.*

Roberts, *Canada's War At Sea*, Vol. II, Part I, pp. 45-46.

Robertson, *Walker, RN,* p. 51.

Rohwer, *Axis Submarine Successes*, 1939-1945.

Roskill, *The War At Sea*, Vol 1, p. 276.

Schull, *Far Distant Ships*, pp. 135-7.

Terraine, *The U-Boat Wars*, pp. 476-7.

Tucker, *Naval Service of Canada*, pp. 8 & 22.

Van der Vat, *The Atlantic Campaign*, p. 291.

Y'Blood, *Hunter Killer*, p. 5.

CHAPTER 15

RAMMING and BOARDING: HMCS OAKVILLE'S SUCCESSFUL TACTICS

The new moon night is black as ink.
Off Hatteras the tankers sink,
While sadly Roosevelt counts the score
Some fifty thousand tons - by Mohr.

KK Johann Mohr, *U 124*

Oakville: Flower class corvette
Builder: Port Arthur Shipbuilding, ON
Comm: 18 Nov 41
Crew: 5 officers, 70-75 crew

Action: Sank *U 94*, North Caribbean, 28 Aug 42
Casualties: 19 lost

Winston Churchill said at the war's end that the only thing that really frightened him during the war was the U-boat peril. The success of one of the protagonists in this chapter provides a solid basis for the concern felt by Churchill.

U 94 was another of the ubiquitous Type VIIC submarines that are found in so many of these accounts, but a most successful one. Launched in June 1940, between December and May 1941 she accounted for thirteen Allied ships totalling almost 75,000 tons. Under her second captain, KL Otto Ites, from September 1941 until June 1942 she sank another fourteen ships, another 75,000 tons. This submarine had been involved in most of the early convoy attacks (such as those on HX-90 and -126, SC-19 and -26, OB-318 and ONS-92) when the escorts were few, there was but little air cover and many of the warships were manned by crews with very inadequate equipment or experience.

Now, in August 1942, still commanded by Ites, one of VII U-Flottille out of St. Nazaire, France, she was assigned to the Caribbean to strike at the tanker convoys which yielded so many kills. The United States, responsible for the defence in the area, learned hard lessons through their reluctance–or shortage of escorts–to adopt the convoy system.

Convoy TAW-15 (Trinidad-Aruba-Key West) sailed from Port of Spain, Trinidad, in late August and consisted of twenty-nine ships, mostly tankers. The escort comprised three Canadian corvettes, ***Oakville, Snowberry*** and ***Halifax***, the 1936-built Dutch minelayer ***Jan van Brakel*** converted to an escort ship, the 1918-built four-stack, flush deck destroyer USS ***Lea*** (DD 118) plus three small US Coast Guard patrol craft. They were northbound, about to enter the Jamaican Channel and Windward Passage between Haiti and Cuba.

Oakville was commanded by LCdr Clarence A. King, DSC, RCNR, who had been credited with sinking a U-boat in the first war when commanding a sailing Q-Ship. At fifty-six years of age he was considerably older than most corvette commanders, some of whom were RCNVRs in their mid-twenties.

U 94 was not the only submarine in the area. On 25 August the convoy lost the ***Amakura*** to ***U 558*** and the ***Stad Amsterdam*** to ***U 164.*** By late evening,

HMCS *Oakville* in 1942, with short forecastle and looking typically care-worn for a corvette of the early war.

about 2300 of the 27th, ***U 94*** was approaching from the north on a course of 180° in hazy moonlight. Ites and his 1st watch officer were both on the bridge when they sighted the convoy. His boat was surfaced, but trimmed down so only the conning tower was above the surface. Ites estimated the convoy was on a course of 340° at a speed of ten knots, a reasonably accurate estimate at his distance of about four miles, as its actual course and speed were 351°, eight knots.

Snowberry was screening directly ahead of the convoy, weaving back and forth to keep her speed-of-advance at about convoy speed. ***Oakville*** was 5,000 yards, 30° to port of the lead ship of the port column, moving at twelve knots. Ites watched ***Snowberry*** until she made a turn away from him, for he planned to turn toward the targets as soon as he felt that he was beyond the range of ***Snowberry's*** asdic sweep.

Ites had had a very successful career so far but now his luck was affected by a twist of fate and a pilot's hunch. That day a US *Catalina* PBY-5A pilot at the USN's base at Guantanamo Bay, Cuba, who had been flying protective patrols in the Caribbean but had not been scheduled to fly, had a feeling that submarines were refuelling south of the Windward Passage. So he asked his commanding officer for permission to make an extra flight. Once airborne, he was redirected to provide air cover for TAW-15. One of the aircraft that had been part of its air cover developed mechanical problems and *Catalina* 92-P-6 of VP-92 was the replacement.

It was a clear night, although ***Oakville's*** 1st lieutenant, K.B. Culley, recalls it as a black night, with wind force four, and there were some surface whitecaps in a heavy swell from a storm during the day. At 0257 on the 28th, from an altitude of 500 feet, ***U 94*** was sighted by the *Catalina* in the light of the moon's path. The PBY made an immediate run and from a height of about seventy-five feet dropped four MK XXIX depth bombs. Ites had been watching the convoy and became aware of the air attack too late to take avoiding action. The bombs exploded on both sides of the conning tower and blew ***U 94's*** stern into the air, wrecking her after diving planes. The aircraft also dropped marker flares as the U-boat appeared to dive.

When the attack on ***U 94*** developed, SLt Graham Scott was OOW on ***Oakville's*** bridge. King was a stickler for practice and as usual had exercised action station routines in the dog watches, from four to eight p.m., so the ship was prepared for any eventuality. Scott heard an explosion, saw a white column of water at a distance and sounded "Action Stations". LCdr King immediately ordered full speed ahead and altered toward the flares. On reaching the spot where the flare was by now extinguished he dropped five depth charges set to 100 feet. At this point he did not have asdic contact and only estimated the time to fire.

Almost immediately after the explosions, as ***Oakville*** was turning sharply around, a surface contact was gained at 600 yards, 10° on the ship's starboard bow. King altered toward it and, within a minute and a half, the U-boat was sighted on the surface about 100 yards ahead, moving left. Two white rockets were fired by ***Oakville*** to warn the convoy of a surfaced submarine. King altered course to ram and told his 1st lieutenant to prepare to shore up bulkheads if they were damaged themselves. When it appeared the submarine would pass close under the ship's bow, "hard-a-port" was ordered and ***U 94*** crashed down the port side of the corvette.

Those on board could see only the bow of the submarine at this point and were firing .5-inch machine guns at what they could see. King then altered to starboard to open the range and allow his 4-inch gun to bear. At 400 yards one round was fired at the bow for a near miss, two more rounds were fired at the conning tower. By now the Oerlikons, machine guns and small arms were all firing at the U-boat which effectively prevented the Germans from manning any of their guns.

Ites had increased speed and was dodging the corvette's movements. He passed to starboard of ***Oakville*** but his 88mm deck gun had been destroyed by a 4-inch shell. King wheeled and again rammed the U-boat, striking her another glancing blow on the starboard side, as upper deck stokers hurled soda bottles from a storage locker at the no doubt startled people on the U-boat's bridge. With all the firing, shouting of orders to the various guns, there was an air of organized uproar.

A further depth charge was fired, this one exploding right under the submarine which at least caused her to decrease speed. Again King opened the range, turned and this time truly rammed the U-boat squarely abaft the conning tower. Although this provided the *coup de grâce* for ***U 94*** it also smashed ***Oakville's*** asdic dome and oscillator and flooded the lower asdic equipment compartment. One of her crashes against the submarine had severely gashed ***Oakville's*** hull, causing serious flooding in No. 2 boiler room.

King intended to capture the U-boat by putting SLt H.E.T. Lawrence, his gunnery officer, on board by boat in charge of a boarding party of twelve. With the now-stopped submarine close by, however, King ordered the boarding party to jump from the forecastle. As the ship swung toward the wallowing boat, Hal Lawrence was almost wiped out by ***Oakville's*** 4-inch gun firing a last round. There had been a misfire which Lt Culley was dealing with, and Scott, on the bridge and separated from the gun platform in these short-forecastle corvettes, was also shouting to the gun's crew. The gun captain reloaded and fired another round, unaware in the turmoil of Lawrence preparing to board the U-boat close alongside. At last "Cease fire!" was ordered. Only Lawrence and Stoker Petty Officer A.J. Powell of the boarding party were able to make the leap to the U-boat's casing. The rest of their party were stunned by the gun's blast and ***Oakville*** rebounded before they could recover.

Once aboard the partly submerged and rolling submarine affairs were still in a wild state. Lawrence lost his tropical shorts when his belt broke and he was washed over the side in a wave surging across the casing. Helped to the deck again by Powell, they were now in danger of being hit by small arms fire from ***Oakville***, still directed at the U-boat. Then the two were met by Germans emerging from the conning tower. After a brief struggle in which two Germans were shot by Lawrence and Powell, they controlled at least the upper deck. At this point it was decided to let the remaining U-boat crew come on deck where Powell gathered them on the after anti-aircraft gun platform.

Lawrence descended into the boat's control room, searching for the most valuable prizes sought in all submarine engagements, the secret signal books and machines. But he could do nothing as the submarine was already filling with water and obviously sinking. Powell called down for him to come up and Lawrence was obliged to swim back to the ladder to climb back out of the conning tower. He quickly ordered everyone into the water. As he swam away he looked back and saw the U-boat sink.

USS ***Lea*** had closed the area to look for survivors and was asked by King to rescue his own boarding party as well, as he was now temporarily stopped by ***Oakville's*** engine room flooding. The Chief ERA organized damage control efficiently, while ***Lea*** collected twenty-one Germans and SLt Lawrence. With no uniform on of any kind, Lawrence had to resort to some un-German salty language to convince his American rescuers that he was Canadian, not part of the U-boat's crew. ***Oakville*** picked up Petty Officer Powell and five Germans in her own dinghy. Lawrence had cut his hand in the leap to the submarine's deck and this was the only Canadian injury. Otto Ites was wounded by three bullets but was rescued. Nineteen of his crew were killed by gunfire or went down with ***U 94.***

Unfortunately, while all this action was taking place, three more ships of the convoy were torpedoed by ***U 511*** although one, the valuable tanker ***Esso Aruba***, made port on her own. The victorious corvette was soon able to get under way again but ***Oakville's*** damage was too great to allow her to continue as a useful escort. She was detached at 0705 and arrived at Guantanamo Bay at 1700 on 28 August. After temporary repairs, she steamed on one boiler to New York and Halifax for a refit.

For the rest of the war ***Oakville*** served in a number of escort groups including W-7 and W-8 of Western Local, finishing with W-6. She was paid off into reserve in 1945 and sold to the Venezuelan Navy in 1946. Renamed ***Patria***, she served until 1962.

LCdr King was awarded the DSO and the United States Legion of Merit for his destruction of ***U 94.*** He went on to assist in the sinking of three more U-boats when CO of the frigate ***Swansea,*** earning a second DSC and two Mentions in Despatches. He eventually commanded an escort group and retired as a captain. Hal Lawrence was awarded a DSC to add to his M.i.D earned earlier in ***Moose Jaw's*** destruction of ***U 501***. He was later to write several books about this and other actions in the Atlantic battle. Stoker Petty Officers Powell and David Wilson both received DSMs, the latter for his quick reaction in ***Oakville's*** boiler and engine rooms when flooding occurred due to the multiple rammings. Lt Culley was awarded a Mention in Despatches.

SOURCES:

Borrett, *East Coast Port.*

Conway's *All the Worlds' Fighting Ships,* p. 393.

Johnston, *Corvettes Canada*, pp. 151-152.

Lawrence, *A Bloody War,* pp. 95-106.

Lawrence, *Victory at Sea*, pp. 152-160

Macpherson & Burgess, *Ships of Canada's Naval Forces*, p. 82 & 232.

Macpherson & Milner, *Corvettes of the RCN,* p. 107.

McKee, *HMCS Swansea, The Life & Times of a Frigate*, pp. 37-42

Paquette & Bainbridge, *Honours & Awards Canadian Naval Forces.*

Rohwer, *Axis Submarine Successes 1939-1945*, p. 119 and var, pp.

Roscoe & Wattles, *US Destroyer Operations in WW II,* p. 134.

Tarrant, *The U-Boat Offensive 1914-1945*, p. 143.

Schull, *Far Distant Ships,* pp. 137-138

United States Fleet, Headquarters of the C-in-C, *Information Bulletin No. 19, Anti-Submarine Warfare.*

CHAPTER 16

HMCS MORDEN AND U 756: ANOTHER LATE CREDIT

A very good piece of work, I assure you

Wm. Shakespeare, *A Midsummer Nigth's Dream*

Morden: Flower class corvette
Builder: Port Arthur Shipbuilding, ON
Comm: 6 Sep 41
Crew: 6 officers, 71 men

Action: Sank *U 756*, mid-Atlantic, 1 Sep 42
Casualties: 43
No survivors

HMCS *Morden* on builder's trials in Lake Ontario in 1941 with the original short forecastle, no radar or HF/DF, an open bridge and gun mount, and minesweeping davits aft.

The disappearance of ***U 756*** was credited after the war to USN Patrol Squadron 73's *Catalina* B on 1 September 1942 at 1632 local time. However a detailed cross-check in the Admiralty Historical Section in 1987 proved that attack had been on ***U 91*** as revealed by her war diary. ***U 91*** was only slightly damaged and survived. ***U 756*** under KL Klaus Harney had left Kiel in north Germany for Atlantic patrol on 15 August, and made her last signal on 1 September at 1115. She reported to BdU that she had been driven off earlier by an escort when executing a daylight attack (on Convoy SC-97). She had been counter-attacked but was undamaged. She was then astern of the convoy but in pursuit and gave the convoy position. This was the normal routine to allow for BdU's U-boat control. Thus, when BdU heard no more, on 3 September ***U 756*** was asked to report her position. There was no response. So BdU posted her as missing from that date. All other U-boats operating against SC-97 returned safely and their diaries have since been examined.

On 1 September ***Morden*** assuredly attacked a surfaced submarine, based on her CO's report (Lt J.J. Hodgkinson, RCNR of Verdun, Quebec). Attacks at the time on all the other returning U-boats have all been attributed to other aircraft or ships, on boats that suffered only superficial damage, so ***Morden*** gets the credit for sinking ***U 756.***

HMCS ***Morden,*** under Hodgkinson, initially arrived in Halifax from her builders in mid-September, 1941. After work-ups she joined the Newfoundland Escort Force, taking a slow convoy to the UK. Already she was in need of a brief refit at Southampton, and then left the Clyde in March with west-bound Convoy ON-73, remaining continuously on this service as a member of EG C-2 until the fall of 1943.

At this stage RN senior officers were becoming somewhat disillusioned with the capabilities and training levels of the RCN groups and ships, and even Canadian commanders were dissatisfied with the lack of group training and our inability to develop a strong base of anti-submarine skills. This was not without some reason, as our ships were being continuously thrown into the harsh fray with little group experience or even brief opportunities to work together. Too often as soon as a crew or officers gained seasoning they were split up to provide a minimum of competence for the host of new ships arriving on the scene faster than crews could be trained to man them. Additionally, these ships were fitted with outdated radar, and usually had no HF/DF. ***Morden*** and Jack Hodgkinson were to prove that the RCN was better than its detractors felt.

On the evening of 31 August 1942, at 2250 she was zig-zagging two miles astern of SC-97 in the dark, watching for exactly the sort of attack that ***U 756*** would have been trying to set up, as evidenced by her message to BdU. When on the port leg of a zig-zag, ***Morden's*** alert radar operator detected a surfaced target close by. Shortly the vague wash and outline of a U-boat was sighted. ***Morden*** altered course to ram it but was foiled when the submarine belatedly saw the charging corvette and dived. Hodgkinson then made a series of three depth charge attacks, the first an urgent attack by eye, the next two in a more carefully calculated manner on reasonable asdic contacts. Contact was then lost. Given the black night and the requirement to catch up with the convoy that was pulling away from him, after a careful but quick look around the area, Hodgkinson departed.

He later reported that he felt "it was difficult to imagine the U-boat could have avoided being hit by depth charges." But the hard-nosed Admiralty Assessment Committee recorded that on the evidence then available to it, it was impossible to determine the result of the attack and thus assessed it as "insufficient evidence of damage."

If ***U 756*** had survived the attack, she would on surfacing later most certainly have made a signal, whether damaged or not, since she would have once more lost a vital contact with the convoy. Other attacks on the U-boat group, on ***U 91, 92, 211*** and ***609*** are all accounted for. Thus, some forty-five years after the event, the official records have been adjusted to credit Hodgkinson, ***Morden*** and her crew with destroying ***U 756.***

Morden, under J.J. Hodgkinson, became known as an outstanding rescue ship, perhaps aided by his experience as a pre-war merchant ship captain with Saguenay Terminals Shipping. They picked up several hundred survivors of merchant ship sinkings from Atlantic waters on several occasions. One lot of 197 included many women and children from the French passenger liner ***Winnipeg***, a real achievement for a ship with a complement of only seventy-one. On another occasion she rescued the 102 crew of the bombed freighter ***City of Christchurch*** and a seventy-foot motor launch carried as deck cargo which floated free when the ship sank, and which ***Morden's*** 1st lieutenant took on a 300 mile passage to Gibraltar.

After a brief refit in Lunenburg, ***Morden*** joined the new 9th Escort Group, mostly working out of the UK. She reinforced the unfortunate Convoy ONS-18/ON-202 when the Germans introduced their GNAT acoustic homing torpedo, sinking six merchantmen, the corvette HMS ***Polyanthus,*** the frigate ***Itchen*** and HMCS ***St Croix*** (see Chapter 29). The U-boats were then concentrating on sinking escorts rather than just merchant ships. Later, in Londonderry, ***Morden*** had a long refit to extend her forecastle, rejoined the C-2 close escort group, and finished the war in Western Local Escort out of Halifax, appropriately escorting the last HX convoy eastward. She was paid off in June, 1945 and broken up in Hamilton in 1946. Jack Hodgkinson went back to his job as a master with Saguenay Terminals Limited.

SOURCES:

Johnston, *Corvettes Canada*, pp. 168-170, 198, 219.

Macpherson & Burgess, *Ships of Canada's Naval Forces*, p. 81.

CHAPTER 17

THE YACHT HMCS RACCOON DISAPPEARS

Raccoon: Animal class yacht
Builder: Bath Iron Works, Maine, 1931, as *Halonia*
Comm: 22 Jun 40
Crew: 4 officers, 33 crew

Fate: Torpedoed by *U 165*, Gulf of St. Lawrence, 7 Sep 42
Casualties: 4 officers, 33 crew

How sleep the brave who sink to rest
By all their country's wishes blest!

William Collins, "Ode Written in the Beginning of 1746"

The yacht *Halonia* in 1940 when delivered by yachtsman Montye MacRae at Halifax, with a red ensign.

HMCS ***Raccoon*** was one of fourteen large American motor yachts acquired in early 1940 to provide a minimal anti-submarine protection off the Nova Scotia coast in the earliest war years, until regular warships arrived from the builders' yards. She was originally owned by Charles Thorne of Chicago as ***Halonia***. In March 1940 she was secretly bought by Torontonian Montye MacRae from New York jeweller Ray van Clief on behalf of the Canadian government for $207,100. In late August, just painted grey, unarmed, and manned by ex-merchant seamen and green-as-grass volunteer reservists, she was sent on patrols off Halifax to lend the appearance of a naval presence to the merchantmen.

Fitted later in the fall, when she could be spared, with a 3-inch gun and simple asdic, she undertook patrols as did several similar ex-yachts and other miscellaneous Canadian vessels taken up from government departments such as the RCMP and Mines and Resources. She also took training classes to sea and, in July 1941, was assigned to the Gulf of St. Lawrence Gaspé Force, alternating between there and Halifax. ***Raccoon*** returned permanently to the Gaspé patrols in the St. Lawrence in the spring of 1942. U-boats had penetrated Gulf waters in May, sinking three merchant ships to the vocal dismay of locals, one ship within fifty miles of Gaspé itself. The Navy resisted withdrawing any significant number of their too-few ocean escort corvettes and destroyers from the critical Battle of the Atlantic arena. To augment the warships in the Gulf, however, ***Raccoon*** (commanded by LCdr J.N. Smith, RCNR, an ex-1st officer of the CNR's *Lady* boats that took tours to the West Indies) joined the force of five *Bangor* escorts, three new wooden Fairmile B motor launches and three corvettes. Assigned to protect up-and down-bound convoys from Quebec to Sydney, Newfoundland and Halifax, it was a mixed bag operating in notoriously bad asdic conditions, due to the mix of fresh and salt water. None of them detected any U-boats, although six ships had been sunk that spring and summer.

On 1 September ***Raccoon*** lay at Baie Comeau on the north shore of the St. Lawrence where a dance was held for the ship's company. The next day, out in the Gulf escorting an up-bound convoy, she was fired on by ***U 517*** or ***U 165***, reporting that torpedoes "had passed ahead of me and under me forward of the bridge... tracks clearly visible due to phosphorescence. Ran up the track 600 yards dropping depth charges but no contact. Resumed station." She had been fortunate that the torpedoes' running depth had been set deep for a merchantman target.

Patrolling ahead, either just awash or maybe even submerged, was ***U 165***, KL Eberhard Hoffman searching through binoculars or his periscope for the approaching convoy, six torpedoes ready. He had left his base at Lorient in July, assigned to the Canadian coast or the Gulf depending on available targets. He and Paul Hartwig of ***U 517*** were operating as a team, with Hartwig further down the Gulf.

At 2110 the 4,700-ton Greek freighter ***Aeas*** was torpedoed with no warning contact whatsoever and sank quickly. ***Arrowhead*** at once altered back down the seaward side of the

HMCS *Raccoon* in her wartime colours, April, 1941.

convoy, illuminating the area with starshell to see if a U-boat could be caught on the surface. Although she saw no enemy, she did faintly see the shadowy grey profile of ***Raccoon*** in her expected station astern, also searching. ***Arrowhead*** slowed to pick up twenty-nine survivors of ***Aeas*** from the water and from lifeboats. She returned to her station near the front of the convoy. ***U 165***, having torpedoed ***Aeas***, also altered to keep up with the convoy, moving quietly, undetected and unobserved.

At 1130 on 6 September Convoy QS-33 bound for Sydney, Nova Scotia passed the reporting station at Father Point following a south shore route. There were eight merchant ships in two columns, with an escort of the corvette ***Arrowhead*** and the *Bangor* escort ***Truro*** on the port and starboard bows, Fairmiles ***Q 083*** right ahead and ***Q 065*** right astern. ***Raccoon*** was astern and out to port in the main river channel from whence an attack might be expected. The day passed quietly although trouble was anticipated. Little more could be done than keep a careful watch, with the dubious asdic and, as the lookouts said, "by Mark 1 eyeball." The night was very dark with visibility not over half a mile in haze, with a slight breeze and swell. None of these ships had radar and most not even voice radio; certainly not ***Raccoon***.

Then at twelve minutes after midnight, two resonant explosions in rapid succession were heard astern of the ships and to port. ***Q 065*** was later to report that her bridge watch had vaguely seen two columns of white water out in the Gulf, and heard a short blast on a siren. It was considered this was probably ***Raccoon*** carrying out a depth charge attack on a possible contact.

Since she didn't ask the Fairmile for help either by shaded light or W/T, it did not warrant the latter deserting her post to see what was afoot.

Again ***Arrowhead*** put about and swept aft and astern, but nothing was seen or heard. She returned to her station, her CO very frustrated and only slightly puzzled at not seeing ***Raccoon*** on this sweep. He presumed she had been farther out in the river than the last time he saw her. Cdr E.G. Skinner, RCNR was an experienced sailor and his assumptions were reasonable under the circumstances. The convoy and its escorts steamed valiantly on northeastward, unable to do more.

By 0727 the next morning ***Arrowhead's*** CO, now becoming more concerned, and still required to stay with his remaining charges, reported by W/T to Gaspé that he "had not seen ***Raccoon*** and that she was not in sight." The base signalled ***Raccoon*** to report her present position. Ominously, there was no response.

In fact KL Hoffman had fired three torpedoes at what he reported as two merchant ships, getting two hits. He had actually hit ***Raccoon*** with three-quarters of a ton of explosive, obliterating her in two closely spaced thunderous blasts. Her entire complement of thirty-seven were evidently killed at once. No details of this attack of Hoffmann's are available, for his boat was sunk with no survivors in the Bay of Biscay by a patrolling RAF aircraft on 27 September on his way home. He simply reported by radio as hitting two ships that night in the Gulf. One of his torpedoes evidently missed.

An all-out search for the missing ***Raccoon*** was prevented on the 7th for, between 0330 and 0400, three more merchantmen of the same ill-fated convoy were torpedoed near Cap des Rosiers. Corvettes HMCS ***Hepatica*** and ***Weyburn*** and the *Bangors* ***Chedabucto*** and ***Vegreville*** and some RCAF aircraft were sent to try to help, and to search for the missing yacht. Nothing was seen of either U-boats or ***Raccoon.***

But the ordeal was not over. On the 11th the corvette ***Charlottetown*** was torpedoed and sunk (see Chapter 18). On the 15th and 16th three more merchantmen were sunk and two damaged in an up-bound (Sydney to Quebec) convoy, also by Hoffman and Hartwig.

The severity of the attacks and their location in the Gulf was not made public, to avoid a hue and cry for more protection. However, those living all along that coast were well aware of the sinkings, and even local newspapers form a more reliable source than usual for descriptions of the events, as many surviving crew members of the merchant ships reached shore in their own boats or rafts.

All that was ever found of little ***Raccoon***, some weeks later, was the body of SLt Russ McConnell, an outstanding McGill University athlete before the war; a corner of the wooden bridge structure; some loose signal messages; and a life preserver with the words ***Halonia*** still partly visible. In early October, Russ McConnell was buried at sea off Gaspé.

LOST:

Adams, George M., MM
Allen, John M., MM
Anderson, James C., Stwd
Ashmall, Royden G., Tel
Belanger, Roger, AB
Boudreau, John J., LS
Champion, Charles R., AB
Cherpeta, John E., AB
Cook, John F., Lt
Dillabough, Guy, L.Sto
Duncan, William, OS
Fowler, George, C.MM
Fralic, Owen W., MM
Gallant, Frank J., Tel
Hamilton, William C., OS
Harvie, William A., Cook
Henderson, Robert H., Sig
Holmes, Arthur G., AB
Howe, Ernest F., Sto
Hughes, John J., LS
LaFlamme, Joseph W.G., O.Sig
Lucas, Henry B., AB
McConnell, Russell H., S/Lt
McDonald, John H., AB
Martindale, Ralph O., OS
Monkley, Harry F., AB
Muller, Howard J., L.Sto
Parsons, John G., OS
Payne, Albert J., AB
Prowse, Louis H., Sto
Sheflin, John E., SA
Smith, John N., LCdr
Stewart, Beverly G., AB
Sweeney, Michael, Tel
Taylor, Glenwood L., OS
Thomas, James E., S/Lt
Thomas, Percy J., O.Sig

SOURCES:

Essex, *Victory in the St. Lawrence,* pp.109-117.
German, *The Sea is at Our Gates*, p. 119.
Hadley, *U-Boats Against Canada,* pp. 82, 112-118.
McKee, *Armed Yachts of Canada,* pp. 139-143.
Rohwer, *Axis Submarine Successes*, pp. 120-123.
Schull, *Far Distant Ships,* 117-8.

CHAPTER 18

HMCS CHARLOTTETOWN: A ST. LAWRENCE RIVER CASUALTY

Fame is like a river, that beareth up things light and swollen, and drowns things weighty and solid.

Francis Bacon , *Essays, 1625*

Charlottetown:
Revised Flower class corvette
Builder: Kingston Shipbuilding Co, ON
Comm: 13 Dec 41
Crew: 6 officers, 58 crew

Fate: Torpedoed by *U 517*, St. Lawrence River, 11 Sep 42
Casualties: 1 officer, 9 crew

HMCS *Charlottetown* in 1942. As she only lasted for nine months, photos of this ship are scarce.

HMCS ***Charlottetown*** was one of the ten corvettes approved in 1940 as an urgent requirement to supplement the already overworked ships of the 1939-1940 building program. They were the first RCN corvettes built with extended forecastles and water-tube boilers. When she commissioned in Quebec City her commanding officer was Lt J. Willard Bonner, RCNR who was with her to the end.

For the first seven months she was assigned to the Western Local Escort Force, but the increased threat from U-boats which had moved into the Gulf of St. Lawrence in 1942 required escorts for the Quebec-Sydney convoy runs. ***Charlottetown*** was transferred to the Gulf Escort Force in July. Michael Hadley in his book *U-Boats Against Canada* credits her with eleven convoys on this run between July and 11 September. She was a very busy ship.

Her last convoy was SQ-35, Sydney to Quebec. This convoy had been taken as far up-river as was considered necessary. Near the mouth of the Saguenay River the depth was deemed to be insufficient for U-boat operations. On the morning of 11 September ***Charlottetown***, accompanied by the *Bangor* minesweeper ***Clayoquot*** were returning to their operating base at Gaspé. They were steaming at an economical speed of about eleven knots because they had not refuelled at Rimouski. ***Clayoquot*** was one mile on the port beam of ***Charlottetown*** and the ships were not zig-zagging.

The weather was generally calm but there was low lying fog. At 0800 in any warship there is a change of watchkeepers in all parts of the ship. Those coming off the morning watch are going for breakfast and those going on the forenoon watch are conducting a number of routines associated with the duties they are taking over. So there was a good deal of activity at approximately 0800 when the first torpedo struck the ship on the starboard quarter. Seconds later the second one struck, again on the starboard side but further forward. There had been no warning whatsoever of the presence of a U-boat. Asdic conditions in the fresh-and-salt water mix of the St. Lawrence were notoriously poor at any time.

Although the ship sank in three or four minutes, the starboard lifeboat was able to clear the ship. The ship had almost at once taken an extreme list to starboard as sea flooded into her and those who went to their lifeboat stations on the port side could not lower that boat. Bonner was on the port side and Tel Gerald Martin and AB Joe Montgomery and Ray MacAulay all remember him giving the "Abandon ship" order. Sto Bill McFadyen was also at the port boat and when Bonner gave the order to jump for it, saw one sailor, Fred Rush, take off his boots, line them up neatly on the deck and then execute a beautiful swan dive into the St. Lawrence. Montgomery had gone directly from his hammock into the water clad only in jockey shorts.[1]

Some of the Carley floats had also been released. Seaman Bill Coates threw a ten-foot two-inch-thick staging plank over the side and on it was able to paddle away from the ship as she sank. He was later pulled into the starboard lifeboat. Some of the survivors remember the heroism of one of the crew, seaman John "Judy" Garland, who stood by the lifejacket locker passing out jackets to those who passed him including MacAulay who had just gone on watch as helmsman. Garland went down with the ship when he ran back to the messdeck to rescue the ship's pet dog, Screech. In fact the dog had already been thrown into the water and survived, to be given some weeks later to "Judy" Garland's mother. But there were comparatively few casualties as a result of the torpedoes (evidently one ERA was killed) and the ship sinking. She went down stern-first.

It was the ship's own depth charges that killed six of the nine lost.[2] A number of others sustained injuries from these explosions.

G.M. Moors, the ship's first lieutenant, was in the starboard lifeboat, collecting the Carley floats and organizing the survivors. His boat was damaged and leaking. He placed the injured on the Carley floats because of the overcrowding in his lifeboat. The captain's dead body was encountered floating in the river and was lashed to the rudder, but both rudder and body were torn away from the boat as the crew tried to pull for the shore and they drifted away. Evidently the captain had been killed by the subsequent depth charge explosions. His body was never recovered.

When ***Clayoquot*** saw that ***Charlottetown*** was struck she immediately began an asdic search to locate the submarine. Conditions were not good but a number of depth charges were dropped on vague possible contacts. Her CO, Lt H.E. Lade, RCNR decided to break off the attack because of the possibility of his charges killing the survivors in the water. Finally she set about taking the survivors aboard. Survivors, stunned and numbed by the cold water, recall the rescue taking from three and a half to six hours. Records vary slightly as to the number taken aboard; fifty-seven or fifty-eight. Some died later in hospital in Gaspé where they were taken by ***Clayoquot.***

One area of total agreement among survivors was the support and attention given to the wounded by ***Charlottetown's*** sick berth attendant Cecil Bateman. Although himself a survivor and hurt, he performed his duty to his shipmates during the passage in ***Clayoquot*** until his medical supplies were exhausted. He was later awarded a Mention in Despatches. Some of the injured were taken first to the home of Cdr Barry German, the base commander, where they were tended by his wife before being moved to the village hospital.

The submarine that sank ***Charlottetown*** was the Type IXC ***U 517*** commanded by KL Paul Hartwig of the X U-Flottille out of Lorient, France, operating in company with ***U 165***. They had been sent to exploit the traffic leaving the St. Lawrence River. On 27 August ***U 517*** had sunk the American troopship ***Chatham***. The next day he delivered the *coup de grâce* to the American freighter ***Arlyn*** which had previously been torpedoed by KK Eberhard Hoffmann in

1. When the charges went off they flattened his Bulova wrist watch. While on survivor's leave he sent the watch to Bulova and told them what had happened. They sent him a new watch which he still has.

2. Hadley suggests a number of explosions; Essex, *Victory In The St. Lawrence*, says "about six". McFadyen and Coates remember only "two or three". Most agree that the first torpedo may have jarred the charges from their racks and damaged their safety settings.

U 165. He may also have delivered another *coup de grâce* to an American tanker, but records do not agree.

On 3 September Hartwig struck again, this time attacking convoy LN-7 to Newfoundland, sinking the Canadian laker ***Donald Stewart*** (See Chapter 65). The corvette ***Weyburn*** saw him at the time of this torpedoing and turned to ram. Shots were fired by ***Weyburn*** without success and Hartwig escaped detection by her asdic after he dived.

On 6 and 7 September, ***U 517*** joined ***U 165*** in an attack on Convoy QS-33 (Quebec to Sydney). Hoffmann sank the Greek ship ***Aeas*** and the armed yacht ***Raccoon*** (See Chapter 17). Hartwig fired one torpedo salvo that sank the Greek ships ***Mount Pindus*** and ***Mount Taygetus***, and the Canadian pulpwood carrier ***Oakton*** in a fifteen-minute debacle. After torpedoing ***Charlottetown*** on the 11th, Hartwig completed his attacks on Gulf shipping on the 15th when he sank two ships from Convoy SQ-36, ***Saturnus*** and ***Inger Elisabeth***. In none of these battles were either U-boat detected and held by the warships' asdic, nor by aircraft sent in support.

Hartwig himself survived the war to become a senior officer in the postwar Bundesmarine, but ***U 517*** had only two more months of life. On 21 November, 1942 off Iceland she was depth charged and sunk by aircraft of Royal Navy 417 Squadron operating from the carrier HMS ***Victorious.*** In this case most of the crew survived.

The investigation into the sinking of ***Charlottetown*** was critical of the fact that she and ***Clayoquot*** were steaming on a steady course rather than on a zig-zag. There certainly was fog which might have made the latter manoeuvering more dangerous, but the ships were one mile apart. There was also some question as to whether the depth charges had been set to safe. And senior officers commented on the need to enforce the wearing of lifejackets when ships were at sea, but this would not be the last sinking where lives were lost because lifejackets were not worn or were inadequate in design to protect the wearers from underwater explosions.

The survivors were sent off on the usual thirty days' survivor's leave with orders to keep the sinking secret. But a loss so close to Canadian shores could not long be kept from the Canadian public. When the official announcement was released on 18 September there was no indication of the actual circumstances and the public understood that she went down in a battle with submarines attacking an Atlantic convoy. The fact was suppressed that it had been much closer to home. In April, 1944 a new River class frigate was named HMCS ***Charlottetown*** to commemorate the lost corvette. She survived the war, but was expended as a breakwater at Oyster Bay, BC in 1948. Again, the name has re-entered naval service with the commissioning of another HMCS ***Charlottetown*** in the 1990s, a City or Halifax class frigate.

LOST:

Bonner, John W., LCdr
Bowser, D.St.C., AB
Garland, John C., OS
Grant, John A., Sto.PO
Lovat, Peter K., ERA
Lundrigan, John, Sto
MacDonald, Thomas A., ERA
Robinson, Edmund C., L.Tel
Todd, David, ERA
Wharton, Leonard A., AB

SOURCES:

Bishop, *Courage At Sea,* pp. 41-42 (Caution: several names are incorrect or incorrectly spelled in this account)

Essex, *Victory in the St. Lawrence,* pp. 119-128.

German, *The Sea Is At Our Gates,* pp. 118-120.

Hadley, *U-Boats Against Canada*, pp. 121-125.

Johnston, *Corvettes Canada,* pp. 155-160.

Lamb, *On The Triangle Run,* pp. 112-123.

Lenton, *German Submarines of WW II,* p. 101.

Macpherson & Burgess, *Ships of Canada's Naval Forces.*

Macpherson & Milner, *Corvettes of the RCN.,* pp. 41, 127-128.

Paquette & Bainbridge, *Honours & Awards,* p. 33.

Richards, *Operation Sick Bay,* p. 98.

Schull, *Far Distant Ships,* pp. 118-9.

CHAPTER 19

THE LOSS OF HMCS OTTAWA AND 119 NAVAL MEN

Still true to the ideals when as men
They sailed to meet the foe again;
Their names enroled in Honour's Court
They're riding anchor in Home Port.

From *Messdeck News*, author unknowon

Ottawa:
(See Chapter 5)

Fate: Torpedoed by *U 91*, mid-Atlantic, 13 Sep 42
Casualties: 5 officers, 108 crew, 6 RN seamen, 22 merchant seamen

HMCS *Ottawa* on September 5,1942, a handsome last photo taken only a week before her loss.

Ottawa returned to her convoy escort role after her unknowingly successful attack on the Italian submarine ***Faa' di Bruno*** (see Chapter 5). Again, as she had done before, she rescued survivors of sunken merchantmen on two occasions. In June 1941 she and the other RCN River class destroyers were sent back from the UK to bolster the recently established Newfoundland Escort Force. She supported several hard-pressed convoys in which ships were lost to U-boats. In May, 1942, her then CO, Cdr C.D. Donald, RCN, became senior officer of C-4 Escort Group, and the ship made several crossings to Londonderry in that role.

On 5 September 1942, she left Londonderry to join Convoy ON-127 from Lough Foyle, ***Ottawa*** now commanded by LCdr C.A. "Larry" Rutherford, RCN, an experienced young officer who on occasions before had taken over as senior officer of the escort. The group now comprised two RCN destroyers with the senior officer in HMCS ***St. Croix,*** and four corvettes. Only the one RN corvette HMS ***Celandine*** had the newer Type 271 radar, and even that was unserviceable. It later developed that thirteen U-boats lay across their path. Seven ships were sunk over the next three days and four more hit but survived. ***Ottawa*** rescued survivors once again, this time twenty-four from a lifeboat from the tanker ***Empire Oil***, one a badly injured DEMS gunner. ***Ottawa's*** medical officer operated on the lad but was not able to save him, and he was buried by his mates the next day.

The destroyer also attacked U-boat contacts around and astern of the convoy, without success this time, assisted by the venerable ***St. Croix*** and the corvettes. It was a desperate time of thrust, parry and counter-thrust, by both sides. The U-boats attacked trimmed down on the surface, and a good radar set such as the newer Type 271M could have detected them in time to take measures to thwart at least some attacks. ***Ottawa*** had only an early British 281 set.

Just before 2300 on 13 September, when south of Greenland in mid-Atlantic, screening her convoy and about ten miles ahead of it to meet an incoming RN destroyer from Newfoundland, ***Ottawa*** picked up two surface radar contacts, possibly U-boats. She altered to investigate, encountering her in-coming relief, HMS ***Witch*** and HMCS ***Annapolis.*** The officer of the watch was Lt L.B. "Yogi" Jenson, RCN, the ship's gunnery officer. As ***Ottawa*** was altering to port away from ***Witch*** at 2306 she was torpedoed near the port bow, just forward of A gun. As Norman Wilson, the seaman QR 2 rating on B gun just above and behind A gun, recalls "I remember clearly even today the sudden smash, noise and water cascading down on us. My first words were 'Christ, we've been fished!' We could see the forecastle deck torn up like a sardine can and the barrel of the [B gun] 4.7-inch bent upwards."

The fish, one of two aimed at her target, had been fired by ***U 91***, KL Heinz Walkerling. His was a Type VIIC boat operating out of Kiel, although she returned to Brest in October. ***U 91*** was to sink five more ships, but not until a patrol in March of 1943, and was herself sunk by RN frigates in February, 1944, with a few survivors.

At first it seemed possible ***Ottawa*** could be saved although her bow was entirely gone. Her 1st lieutenant, Tom Pullen, went forward and reported that the forward mess decks were "scenes of carnage and a shambles... wreckage, and you could see the sea straight ahead where the bow used to be, with men trapped in compartments I couldn't reach or open." A good part of the ship's bow section had disappeared in the explosion. However she remained afloat and on an even keel, although somewhat down by the bows. ***St. Croix*** closed her to render assistance, but on seeing her in no obvious danger of sinking, although stopped, turned away to assist a torpedoed and sinking merchantman whose crew were already in the water and seemed in more immediate need.

Although the Carley floats were cleared away, the order came not to abandon ship–yet. After this initial explosion and in the confusion, or even anticipating orders to abandon ship, some ratings had already leapt overboard. One of the radar operators, Terry Terrebassi asked the bridge if he should throw the still very secret radar set overboard, but was told "Not yet", as there were hopes ***Ottawa*** might be able to proceed stern-first toward Newfoundland. SLt Donald Wilson went below to get secret documents and confidential books out of their locked steel case and put them in weighted bags and throw them over, despite the fact that if the ship sank they would go down safely with her. He was not seen again. Two Kisbie-float life rings had been blown or thrown into the water to starboard and their brilliant calcium flares had ignited, silhouetting the stopped ship.

Fifteen minutes later, as anticipated by many of the ship's company, another torpedo

HMCS *Ottawa's* bridge in 1941 as seen by one of her officers, Lt L.B. 'Yogi' Jenson, RCN, who himself was one of the survivors of her torpedoing in 1942.

struck ***Ottawa*** almost amidships in Number 2 boiler room on the starboard side, evidently from the same U-boat that had circled around to ensure that the target of her first attack was sinking.

After the crash, suddenly there was quiet. This one proved fatal, breaking her back, and she rolled onto her starboard side and sank quickly in two parts, the foreward section first and then the stern section. Several men were trapped below in offices and cabins jammed by debris. To offset the string of calamities, all the depth charges had been set to "safe" by the gunner(T), Mr. L.I. Jones, so did not explode when they fell into the sea from the sinking stern section.

While the larger part of her surviving complement was able to abandon ship into the cold waters, and the wounded were pushed onto Carley floats, other ships, even their sister escort ***St. Croix***, had to dash past those in the water in pursuit of a surfaced U-boat that had been reported. A signalman in ***St. Croix***, herself to be sunk almost exactly a year later, still recalls the men in the water calling out "***Saint Croix!... Saint Croix!..***" as they sped past.

Yogi Jenson floated with the aid of his Mae West-style life belt and a dan buoy. By the time salvation arrived some four hours later in the shape of the corvettes ***Celandine*** (Lt Collings, aged only twenty-four) and HMCS ***Arvida***, they were only able to rescue sixty-nine men. Survivors in the water were plagued by masses of stinging jelly fish, whose tentacles caused almost unbearable itching later when the injured were in hospital. In all 141 souls were lost, officers, men and already-rescued survivors. One seaman was to die shortly from his injuries.

Rough seas complicated the rescue, and several men in the water lost their lives when the lurching corvette, scramble-nets hung over her side, came down on top of them. Included in the missing was LCdr Rutherford, who had given his life belt to a rating who did not have his. Most of the rescued merchant ship survivors who had been aboard ***Ottawa*** were lost as well. Of the ***Empire Oil*** survivors the only ones to be rescued from this second disaster were a gunner from the Marine Regiment Royal Artillery, E. Douglas, and a galley boy. Many, in shock and unprepared for this disaster, just gave up and drifted off into the night from the bobbing Carley floats. ***Celandine*** carried no medical officer, so her sick berth attendant, the "tiffy", did the best he could with the injured. Ed Fox, a seaman in ***Ottawa*** recalls: "I was found to have one leg and the side of my chest laid open. The tiffy had no experience in stitching and when he jabbed the cat-gutted needle into my side it hit a rib and broke. He said, in his Midlands accent, 'Ee, ba goom lad, tha's got an 'ide like a rhinoceros!' "

But then for others, life just moved on normally: when Jenson arrived eventually in ***Celandine's*** wardroom, wet and oil-soaked, he was greeted by ***Ottawa's*** Leading Steward Barriault, also rescued: "Good evening Sir, would you like a cup of tea?" "Good evening, Barriault, that would be very nice, thank you" Jenson responded.

Survivors were taken to hospital in St. John's. Again, their unquenchable spirit in the face of extreme adversity is illustrated in another Ed Fox story: AB Rod Skillen had a badly mangled leg which doctors hoped to save, but it was not to be. A doctor came into the ward a few days later and said "I'm sorry to have to tell you, Able Seaman Skillen, but we will have to remove your right leg." "That's all right, Doc" was the reply. "My sister's got a cedar chest; why shouldn't I have a wooden leg?"

Of the thirty-three ships in the convoy when attacked, seven were sunk, plus one of their escort, ***Ottawa***, and four damaged but able to reach port. No U-boat was even damaged more than incidentally. The German BdU at the time assessed nineteen ships as sunk and another six damaged, based on U-boat reports.

It was a low point in the Battle of the Atlantic for the Allies, and there was considerable criticism by RN staff of the competence of the Canadian staff to manage their scarce resources. More ships (which would further have diluted availability of the RCN's few professionals) was not necessarily the whole answer. But at least if the ones on duty had had better radar, ahead-throwing weapons and HF/DF it would have helped immeasurably. Canada's inferior radars, for instance, contributed to the shortcomings, and in the battle, ***Ottawa*** paid a very high price. But as LCdr Larry Rutherford said to Tom Pullen as they stood briefly on the bilge keel before jumping into the sea, "She was a good ship!"

Another ***Ottawa*** was soon named in her stead and a third after the war. Now yet another ***Ottawa*** is in the fleet in the 1990s as a City class frigate.

Lt Pullen went on to become a captain and a notable Arctic navigator. Lt Jenson is a well regarded Nova Scotia artist, after a long naval career.

LOST:

Adlington, Howard H. SA
Ashley, Robert P., AB
Baird, John A., Sto
Baker, Elgy E., Sto
Beddes, Samuel, ERA
Bell, David, O, OS
Bowen, Stephen D., Sto
Bowman, Eric J., AB
Brown, Robert D., LS
Bucheski, William, AB
Burn, Albert E., OS
Burroughs, Walter P., AB
Campbell, Gordon K., AB
Campbell, Woodrow, OS
Chandler, Harry M., AB
Chisholm, Robert D., AB
Clemo, Frederick J., AB
Collier, Chesley, AB
Collin, Joseph A.J.L., Sto
Connolly, Richard, LS
Coomer, Frederick, AB
Cooper, Edward B., LS
Cousineau, Lionel, Sto
Crane, Walter J., Sig
Crawford, Gordon R., PO
Creaney, Thomas, AB
Cressey, H. Frederick, Sig
Cudmore, Alfred, AB
Culliford, Doyle I., Sto
Davies, William T., AB
Deeves, Arthur J., L.Tel
Don, John P., Tel
Doran, Patrick D., Sto
Douglas, Albert, AB
Dugay, Henri R., Cook
Emerslund, Arnold G., Tel *
Fisher, John A., AB
Froats, Donald M., Cook
Gallagher, Howard J., LS
Gerland, Melvin, AB
Gibb, James A., AB
Glasgow, Charles E., AB
Harker, James S., L.Tel
Harris, Carl, OS
Heiberg, Kenneth G., PO
Hendry, George A., Surg Lt
Henry, Robert, AB
Hickey, John C., AB
Hobbis, William H., Elec.Art
Hockley, John W., Stwd
Holmes, Earl I., AB
Houghton, David H., O.Sig
Howard, Frederick C., Tel
Hunt, William E.D., Sto
King, Arthur, OS
Kostenko, Nicholas, Tel
Labonte, Ernest, Sto
Leroy, Charles E., AB
Leslie, Kenneth L., Sto
MacDonald, Arthur A., L.SA
MacDonald, Herbert, C., C.Sto
MacKenzie, Charles, A., LS
MacMillan, Alexander, SBA
Masson, André, OS
McKechnie, Morton H., OS
McLeod, Ian, S/Lt
Milburn, John R., Ord.Art
Miller, Earl, Sto
Moore, Albert A., L.Sto
Morrison, Francis A., Sto.PO
Morrison, Harry, Sto
Muchmore, John V., Sto
Murphy, Gerald W., OS
Neath, John F., AB
Neil, Percy T., AB
Palmer, Ralph B., AB
Paradis, Paul V., AB
Peppler, Stanley, AB
Pettit, John B., Sto
Piontek, Jack W., AB
Pooles, Donald H., Tel
Porter, Hartold S., OS
Purcell, Herbert A., ERA
Quigley, Lloyd P.W., AB
Rasmussen, Clifford J., OS
Riches, Clifford, AB
Robertson, Earl J., Coder
Robinson, Walter V.D., AB
Robshaw, George A., AB
Roop, Roy M., AB
Rutherford, Clark A., LCdr
Secord, Gerard F., AB
Sheppard, David G., L.Sig
Shillito, John G., AB
Simons, Clinton L., O.Sig
Slaunwhite, Harry M., AB
Smith, Alexander, AB
Smith, Arthur, AB
Smith, Kenneth G., Cook
Smith, Roseville St.C., Sto
Southall, Harry K., AB
Stephens, Oswald B., Sto
Taylor, Earnest F., AB
Taylor, Frederick F., OS
Trainor, Alfred N., PO.Stwd
Tremblay, Joseph A.S., AB
Trudel, Camile G., Sto
Whiting, Basil E., AB
Wilson, Archibald W., Sto
Wilson, Donald A., S/Lt
Wright, Keith F., S/Lt
Young, Thomas W., AB
Zink, Cyril M., SA

Plus 6 RN crew and about 22 merchant seamen survivors.

* Subsequently died of injuries.

SOURCES:

German, *The Sea Is At Our Gates,* pp. 125-6.

Lawrence, *Tales of the North Atlantic,* pp. 181-183.

Macpherson, *River Class Destroyers,* pp. 37-46.

Milner, *North Atlantic Run,* pp. 159-164

Rohwer, *Axis Submarine Successes,* p. 123.

Roskill, *The War At Sea,* Vols. I and II.

Schull, *Far Distant Ships,* p. 138.

T.C. Pullen, *Northern Mariner/Le Marin du Nord,* Vol II, No. 2, April 1992.

CHAPTER 20

HMCS ST. LAURENT AND FIVE CORVETTES SINK U 356: A TURNING POINT

He which hath no stomach to this fight
Let him depart; his passport shall be made,
And crowns for convoy put into his purse;
We would not die in that man's company
That fears his fellowship to die with us.

Wm. Shakespeare, *Henry V*

St. Laurent: River class destroyer
Builder: Vickers-Armstrong Ltd, Barrow UK
1st Comm: as HMS *Cygnet*, 1931
2nd Comm: 17 Feb 37
Crew: 10 officers, 171 crew

Action: With 5 corvettes, sank *U 356*, NW of Azores, 27 Dec 42
Casualties: 46
No survivors

St. Laurent in August, 1941 with initial wartime modifications such as cut down after funnel, removal of her main mast and a British mast-head radar.

In this chapter all ships comprising the escort for Convoy ONS-154 are listed as participants and in some references all but ***Shediac*** are given some credit for the kill. However the balance of evidence suggests that ***St. Laurent*** may have achieved the success on her own. The sinking of ***U 356*** was not confirmed until after the war. It is not the purpose of this record to allocate credit or resolve the question of which ship was the specific victor. They all were, in one way or another.

St. Laurent was one of six destroyers with which Canada had entered the war. Acquired from the Royal Navy in 1937, she had had a busy war to date with many convoy escorts on her record.

The five corvettes were already veterans of Atlantic convoys. ONS-154 was a convoy of forty-five merchantmen that gathered on 18-19 December 1942 north of Ireland from the ports of Loch Ewe, Mersey and the Clyde. Some of the ships were returning to North America in ballast and others were fully loaded for destinations in Africa, the Caribbean and South America. When formed, the convoy comprised twelve columns of three or four ships each. In addition to the merchantmen there was one rescue ship, the little 1,571-ton British passenger vessel ***Toward*** and the special service vessel HMS ***Fidelity*** carrying a motor torpedo boat (MTB) and two Kingfisher patrol aircraft. The convoy commodore was Vice Admiral Wion de Malpas Egerton, DSO, RN, in ***Empire Shackleton***. In World War I as CO of a destroyer, Egerton had invented his own depth charge in frustration at having no weapon with which to attack submerged U-boats, so was sympathetic with the escorts' problems in the new struggle. In a destroyer on the first day of the First World War he had helped sink the German minelayer ***Konigin Luise***.

Because some of the ships were bound for African destinations the convoy route was further to the south than normal, which extended the convoy track over which air cover could not be provided. A participant in one of the corvettes, who went on to a full career in the RCN postwar, still wonders about this track selection. It put the convoy directly in the path of a submarine pack. He wonders if there were other "target" convoys, possibly troop carriers for the North African Operation Torch, that may have been at sea and from which ONS-154 drew away the U-boats.

The close escort was the Canadian C-1 group comprised of ***St. Laurent*** (LCdr Guy Windeyer, DSC, RCN), ***Battleford*** (Lt F.A. Beck, RCNVR), ***Chilliwack*** (A/LCdr L.L. Foxall, RCNR), ***Kenogami*** (Lt J.L. Percy, RCNVR), ***Napanee*** (Lt S. Henderson, RCNR) and ***Shediac*** (Lt J.E. Clayton, RCNR). An additional member of the group, the ex-USN four-stacker HMS ***Burwell,*** was unable to sail due to mechanical problems of the sort that plagued these elderly ships. This was not the only problem that the escorts encountered prior to sailing. ***St. Laurent*** had a new HF/DF set but it had not been calibrated. And a pre-sailing anti-submarine exercise had been cancelled due to weather and target submarine unavailability. The ships had been newly fitted with Type 271 radar but as yet had little operator experience. Windeyer and Percy had commanded their ships for little more than a month, thus could hardly know the capabilities, strengths and weaknesses of their officers, petty officers and men. Yet this was not untypical of this period. The captain of ***Shediac*** had a premonition of what was to come. He told his chief engineer prior to sailing "This is going to be a tough one, Chief."

For the first week the enemy was the weather, not the German Navy. Gales and heavy seas dispersed the ships and forced them to look only to their own safety. By 24 December the escorts were able to start reassembling the convoy but they had been located by a U-boat, which reported this to BdU. In all, nineteen submarines were directed by BdU into the path of the convoy with orders to commence their attacks after darkness fell on 26 December. By late evening both sides were in contact with each other, as the escorts detected U-boat radio transmissions and the U-boats shadowed the convoy, waiting for nightfall. Then sightings of surfaced U-boats produced starshell from the warships and "snowflake" rocket flares from the merchantmen.

OL Gunther Ruppelt, commanding ***U 356,*** was the first of the pack to press home an attack with success. Early on the 27th he struck on the starboard side of the convoy and torpedoed the leading ships in two columns. ***Melrose Abbey*** and ***Empire Union*** both sank. Ruppelt reloaded his torpedo tubes and moved into the columns of ships and over the space of another few minutes sank ***King Edward*** and damaged the Dutch ***Soekaboemi***. The latter was abandoned by her crew and later sunk by ***U 441***.

It is at this point in the melee that ***U 356*** may have been lost. After the first ships were torpedoed, Guy Windeyer knew there were survivors in boats and rafts, and ordered ***Toward*** to rescue them if possible and ***Napanee*** to screen that operation. ***St. Laurent*** moved to fill the escort station on the starboard quarter of the convoy. From there she obtained a radar contact, then sighted a U-boat moving into the convoy lanes. Windeyer increased speed and opened fire with his Oerlikons at about 700 yards. As the 20mm rounds began hitting the submarine, his 4.7-inch B gun was able to fire and observers on the bridge felt sure a hit was made.

As the submarine passed from starboard to port she dived and the destroyer dropped one shallow pattern of depth charges as she passed over. Asdic contact was regained astern and ***St. Laurent*** wheeled to make a second attack of ten charges, which seemed to produce an eleventh underwater explosion. Before contact was lost another pattern of charges was dropped when passing over the position of a surface oil slick.

Although it is tempting to consider that these attacks were the *coup de grâce* for ***U 356***,

Typical of all five corvettes, *Battleford* is still with the short forecastle, mast before the bridge, and minesweeping davits at her stern. This is one of the most familiar of the early corvette photos.

it is not at all certain. There were other occasions that night when the kill might have been made. ***Napanee, Chilliwack*** and ***Battleford*** all had sightings and all three dropped depth charges on submarines seen diving but, without physical evidence of a destroyed submarine, no positive assessment was awarded. It has generally been concluded that ***U 356*** was destroyed on the 27th because there is no indication that she played a further role in the battle that followed.

The following day, the 28th, was a partial respite for the escorts as the Germans lost contact with the convoy. But the worst was yet to come and now fuel shortages in C-1 were an additional problem for the SOE. The tanker assigned to fuel the escorts, ***Scottish Heather,*** was damaged by a torpedo on the evening of the 27th after refuelling ***Chilliwack.*** In the early hours of the 28th this corvette attacked a submarine sighted only 500 feet off her bow, first firing her 4-inch which some claimed hit the U-boat, which dived. The corvette attacked at once, dropping a ten-charge pattern by eye, three of which, her report later claimed "were right on top of her." An additional underwater explosion was satisfying but inconclusive.

In the evening of the 28th ***Battleford*** sighted four U-boats and gave chase. Unfortunately her radar was put out of commission by her own gun fire and she lost contact with the enemy, whose speed on the surface was greater than a corvette's. She also lost the convoy when it altered course while she was away and could not rejoin until the following morning. In the meantime the pack struck again. Within the space of just over two hours, nine ships were hit with torpedoes; two sank immediately, others were finished off in additional attacks as they fell behind the convoy and were picked off by searching submarines. One of those lost was ***Empire Shackleton*** with the convoy commodore on board.[1]

For those present it was a scene that they had difficulty describing. The merchantmen were firing snowflake to illuminate the marauding submarines travelling rapidly on the surface around and within the convoy. The escorts were firing starshell and all ships were shooting, with the night lit by tracer flying in all directions. And among this scene of chaos were sinking and burning ships, lifeboats, rafts and swimming survivors with the red lights on their survival gear adding to the confusion. For the corvettes' COs there was the added terrible decision of whether to stay hunting a possible U-boat and so fall astern of the convoy which would take hours to catch up, pause however briefly to rescue survivors seen in the water, or stay with their convoy protection job driving off attackers.

1. There is a memorial to him in the cathedral at Chester in England.

HMS ***Fidelity*** fell astern of the convoy when her main engine broke down. Windeyer ordered ***Shediac*** to screen this valuable ship. Meanwhile ***Toward*** had taken in as many survivors as she could, 164 in all, and so the SOE directed the ships at the rear of the convoy columns to pick up survivors. But with the coming of daylight on the 29th the main battle was over. Two RN fleet destroyers, ***Milne*** and ***Meteor*** arrived in the afternoon and what was left of the convoy remained intact even though Windeyer had told the faster ships with passengers on board to proceed alone if they wished.

Again fuel for the escorts became a critical consideration. ***Shediac*** was the last escort sent for refuelling. Her chief ERA Bill Maxwell says that the tanker did not have the correct fuelling hose couplers and the operation commenced with a fire hose. With only about one ton taken ***Shediac*** obtained an asdic contact and broke away. As a result ***Battleford*** had to tow ***Shediac*** to the Azores, and Maxwell said his ship entered Ponta Delgada harbour steaming on galley fuel and the scrapings from his tanks.

Although there were no more attacks on the convoy, HMS ***Fidelity,*** having managed to restart her engines, became the fourteenth victim on the 30th when she was torpedoed by ***U 435*** while slowly steaming on her still-defective engine. This sinking was a disaster in itself since this ship had rescued Vice Admiral Egerton and survivors from ***Empire Shackleton***. There were almost no survivors from ***Fidelity***; an estimated 374 were thus lost in this ship alone. The only exceptions were from MTB ***105*** which had been launched prior to the ship being struck. The MTB, out of fuel, tried to sail to the UK with makeshift canvas sails. She was found by HMCS ***Woodstock***, her crew rescued and the MTB sunk by gunfire.

For LCdr Windeyer there had been no respite for two weeks. He had been in command of the corvette ***Wetaskiwin*** for almost two years in the heart of the Atlantic battle and earlier won a DSC for a U-boat kill (Chapter 13). Shortly after the remains of this convoy reached port, he was transferred to shore duties. There were no DSCs for those that sank ***U 356***. Three commanding officers of the corvettes, Foxall, Percy and Beck, were mentioned in despatches before the war ended for "service in command of HMC corvettes."

For the Canadian authorities ONS-154 was an issue that forced them to accept that their ships and the men needed specialized anti-submarine training. As Marc Milner says in *North Atlantic Run*, (p.4), "The battle for ONS-154 marked the end of the beginning for Canada's wartime Navy." Individual ships and groups were withdrawn from the battle while training was conducted.

U 356, of II U-Flottille operating out of Lorient, had no sinkings to her credit before the attack on ONS-154. In September, 1942, she had reported hitting and damaging a ship but records do not show the name of her target. She had unsuccessfully fired torpedoes at ON-153 just ten days before she was sunk.

All the escort ships of C-1 survived the war, four being scrapped in the late 1940s. ***Shediac*** lasted until 1966 as the Dutch whaler ***Jooske W. Winke***, and ***Battleford*** was transferred to the Venezuelan Navy as ***Libertad***, but was wrecked in 1949. Of the nineteen U-boats that had operated against ONS-154, eighteen were destroyed before the war's end. One was scuttled in 1944 but salvaged and later served in the French Navy.

SOURCES:

Bishop, *Courage At Sea,* pp. 55-59.

German, *The Sea Is At Our Gates,* pp. 129-131.

Johnston, *Corvettes Canada,* pp. 173-174, 197.

Lenton, *German Submarines WW II*, Vols. I & II.

Lenton & Colledge, *Warships of WW II,* pp. 309, 548.

Macpherson, *River Class Destroyers of the RCN,* pp. 30-36.

Macpherson & Milner, *Corvettes of the RCN.*

Milner, *North Atlantic Run*, pp. 4, 206-212.

Paquette & Bainbridge, *Honours & Awards,* pp. 38,186, 430.

Revely, *The Convoy That Nearly Died.*

Rohwer, *Axis Submarine Successes*, pp. 142-144.

Schull, *Far Distant Ships,* pp. 139-142.

Tarrant, *The U-Boat Offensive,* p. 142.

Tucker, *The Naval Service of Canada*, Vol. I, p. 355.

1943

A turning
point
in the
battle

CHAPTER 21

HMCS VILLE DE QUÉBEC ACTS QUICKLY

Act quickly now, this is the test to see
If you can quite complete -
A bite with me.

Admiralty House Supper Song

Ville de Québec: Revised Flower class corvette
Builder: Morton Engineering & Drydock, Quebec City
Comm: 24 May 42
Crew: 6 officers, 79 men

Action: Sank *U 224*, off Oran, Mediterranean, 13 Jan 43
Casualties: 45
1 survivor

HMCS *Ville de Québec,* 1942-1943, fitted out for the Mediterranean.

Although the new ship was to be named HMCS ***Québec***, HMS ***Québec*** was already in use in Scotland by a British combined operations base. So Cmdre Lord Louis Mountbatten arranged through Canada's High Commissioner Vincent Massey to avoid the conflict by naming the ship after the city of Quebec. She began operations with the Western Local Escort Force in June 1942 between Halifax, Boston and St. John's until assigned to protect Operation Torch convoys for the invasion of North Africa, crossing with Convoy HX-212. She was commanded by LCdr A.R.E. Coleman, RCNR, a Bell Canada manager before the war. He had joined the RNR as a midshipman in 1913, moving to Canada and joining the RCNVR in 1937.

On the way, as ***Ville de Québec*** was not part of the normal close escort group, the corvette picked up 172 survivors from six torpedoed ships, whom she landed at Liverpool. There she received new radar, as the British were prepared to provide these sets for escorts that would be working in their escort groups. She accompanied an assault convoy to Algiers, then was based at Gibraltar for support convoys.

On 13 January 1943, ninety miles west of Algiers at 1558, as ***Ville de Québec*** zig-zagged ahead and to starboard of the fifteen-ship convoy TE-13, Gibraltar to Bône, the alert asdic rating, AB Stan Miller picked up an underwater contact right ahead on ***Ville de Québec's*** starboard bow at 900 yards range–dangerously close. The weather was clear, with superior visibility, a strong breeze and excellent asdic conditions. In a matter of seconds LCdr Coleman recommended to the convoy commodore in SS ***Lycaon*** that he order an emergency turn to port to clear the area, sounded "A/S Action Stations" and increased to full speed for an urgent attack on the threatening submarine. Her echo was now reported as moving rapidly right.

A full pattern of ten depth charges from throwers and rails, set to between 150 and 300 feet, was fired by the asdic recorder trace at 1604 as the corvette crossed the U-boat's position. There had not been enough time to set up the careful track for a deliberate attack. ***Ville de Québec*** then altered sharply to starboard to repeat her attack if need be.

A minute and a half later, in the disturbed water where the charges had exploded, the bow of a U-boat suddenly appeared, emergency-surfacing and at full surface speed close ahead. ***Ville de Québec's*** Oerlikon gunners opened fire at once, the starboard gun firing over 200 rounds, hitting the conning tower and the hull with their explosive rounds. ***Ville de Québec's*** "main armament" of her forecastle 4-inch gun could not be depressed enough to fire at the target, moving quickly across from port to starboard.

To ensure the surfaced submarine's destruction, LCdr Coleman altered slightly to ram her. Despite possible damage to one's own ship, this was one of the preferred–and certain–methods of the day. The CO only stopped his engines moments before the impact to lessen the strain on his own ship. ***Ville de Québec*** hit the U-boat between the conning tower and the forward gun, which was thrown from its mounting. One person in the conning tower, who had been sent up to see what external damage had been done by ***Ville de Québec's*** depth charges, was thrown into the sea by the impact as the U-boat rolled nearly onto her side. Her bows dropped, exposing her after planes and propellers at a 45° angle and she disappeared. A minute later there was a muffled heavy underwater explosion. The corvette's attack had happened so swiftly, in sight of the convoy that the sailors in the merchantmen lined the rails and cheered as they watched ***Ville de Québec*** ram and sink their adversary–***U 224.***

With the U-boat obviously eliminated, LCdr Coleman asked fellow-corvette HMCS ***Port Arthur*** to pick up the swimming survivor as he checked on his own damage forward. This was not extensive, with the peak tank flooded, the anchor-chain locker leaking and the asdic dome smashed. Pumps were put on the flooding compartments and a collision mat ordered to be rigged over the somewhat crumpled bow to reduce the strain, although some crew members don't recall it being needed. Now with no asdic, ***Ville de Québec*** rejoined the convoy as an additional escort at a cautious eight knots. She was later repaired and provided with a new asdic dome at Gibraltar.

Port Arthur lowered a sea boat and rescued Leutnant-zur-See Wolf Dietrich Danckworth, suffering from shock. ***Ville de Québec*** asked ***Port Arthur*** by signal light: "Was he Italian or German?" The initial reply was "I think Italian", then shortly, "Survivor is a German Officer."

The survivor was the 1st watch officer and had graduated in the officer class of 1938 from their Academy. The CO of ***U 224***, OL Hans-Carl Kosbadt, in his first command, perished with the rest of the crew of forty-three. Oddly, he had the previous 29 October 1942, sunk the steamer ***Bic Island*** in Convoy HX-212 which was the former Italian ***Capo Noli,*** captured by HMCS ***Bras D'Or*** in 1940 in the St. Lawrence. He had sunk another 5,600-tonner in November.

Ville de Québec had sunk reportedly one of the most efficient U-boats in the German fleet,[1] as she had required only half of the normal work-up time before going on operations. Built at Germaniawerft, Kiel and commissioned in June 1942, she had left St. Nazaire, France on the morning of 3 January 1943. The crew thought they were bound for North American patrol as they were issued with fur coats. But on the 6th they passed Gibraltar at 2100 on the surface, to avoid the strong underwater outbound current, in the last of the moonlight. They were challenged by what was taken to be an MTB so they submerged, and were not attacked. Later, along the south shore, ***U 224*** passed across the bows of two ships, guessed to be destroyers, at 700 yards, dead slow on one engine. Again they were not sighted. She joined the XXIX U-Flottille at La Spezia. On the 13th on patrol they were warned to expect Convoy TE-13, went deep, and picked it up by hydrophone effect. ***U 224*** came to sixty-five feet, setting up for a torpedo attack. ***Ville de Québec*** managed to foil her intentions with finality.

Port Arthur's Report of Proceedings described her captive as "very close-mouthed; an experienced submarine officer, and typical

1. Intelligence reports.

Nazi." ***U 224*** had been approaching the convoy from an ideal attack position, selecting a tanker at two and a half miles range at periscope depth and at dead slow in her planned three-torpedo attack. After the initial depth charge attack damaged the U-boat, Kosbadt surfaced and sent Danckworth up to see what visible damage had been done, not appreciating that the corvette was about to ram her.

Ville de Québec's offensive was exemplary, taking only ten minutes from detection to sinking. Later in Algiers the ship was visited by the 1st Sea Lord, by Admiral Cunningham the C-in-C Mediterranean, Field Marshall Sir John Dill and others. Afterwards, Vice Admiral Mountbatten commented to the CIGS: "They're a bloody tough looking bunch of bastards!" Admiral Cunningham signalled: "The speed of the kill reflected credit on ***Ville de Québec's*** training and alertness." In early 1943 this was unusual praise for Canadians, who were generally regarded as not very competent by some of their RN counterparts.

LCdr Coleman received a DSO, Lt D.L. Miller, the ASCO, a DSC, and DSMs went to A/CERA J. Mitchel, the coxswain A/CPO D.A. Kent, AB J. Reid, the leading torpedo operator, with Mentions in Despatches for Lt R.G. Hatrick and AB 1st Operator S.F. Miller.

Ville de Québec returned to Canada for assignment to the Western Local Escort Force again and the Gulf Force, had a long refit, and returned once more to England where she finished the war with EG C-4. Paid off at Sorel in July, 1945, and sold in 1946, she lasted under four names until 1952 in mercantile service. One of the Navy's new City class frigates perpetuates the name of the wartime ***Ville de Québec.***

A well known painting by LCdr Harold Beament, RCNVR, in the Canadian War Museum's collection of ***Ville de Québec*** ramming ***U 224*** is said by participants to be accurate.

SOURCES:

Bishop, *Courage At Sea*, pp. 66-67.

Cunningham, *A Sailor's Odyssey,* pp. 520-521.

Johnston, *Corvettes Canada,* pp. 181-82.

Leslie Roberts, *Canada's War At Sea*, Vol II, pp. 53-54.

MacBeth, *Ready, Aye, Ready,* pp. 92-93.

Schull, *Far Distant Ships*, pp. 152-3.

CHAPTER 22

HMCS PORT ARTHUR SINKS TRITONE

Port Arthur: Flower class corvette

Builder: Port Arthur Shipbuilding ON

Comm: 26 May 42

Crew: 6 officers, 79 crew

Action: Sank Italian submarine *Tritone*, off N. Africa, 19 Jan 43

Casualties: About 23

26 survivors

Il Tritone ando perduto durante la sua prima missione di guerra al largo di Bougie, il 19 Gennaio 1943.

Paolo Pollina and Aldo Cocchia, *I Sommergibili, Italiani*

HMCS ***Port Arthur*** was one of a small group of late-commissioned corvettes, other than the twenty-seven "Increased Endurance" corvettes, that were built with the extended forecastle from the start. Sailed from her lakehead builders with only a steaming crew and doing trials in Toronto, she commissioned in Montreal, did work-ups at Halifax and joined the Western Local Force. After only two months, she was assigned for Operation Torch North African landings, escorting SC-105 to Londonderry, which lost no ships to U-boats, unlike the previous SC-104 which had lost eight. In Britain due to her planned role ***Port Arthur*** was fitted with increased A/A protection in the form of six Oerlikons. From 1 November to early March she was involved with escorting UK-Gibraltar-North Africa convoys out and back.

On 13 January when ***Port Arthur*** was one of the escorts for Convoy TE-13, Gibraltar to Bône, her sister corvette HMCS ***Ville de Québec*** detected and quickly sank ***U 224*** that was setting up to attack. When ***Ville de Québec*** rammed ***U 224***, the only survivor was LzS Danckworth, thrown from the conning tower into the sea (See Chapter 21). Due to ***Ville de Québec's*** damaged bow, ***Port Arthur*** was asked to pick up the swimming German which she did, delivering him to captivity in Bône.

Then on 19 January, at 1413 while escorting the slow North Africa to UK Convoy MKS-6, ***Port Arthur's*** alert asdic 1st operator picked up an echo, classified as possible submarine. He was replaced by a more experienced 1st operator when "Action Stations" was sounded, and it was then classed as a certain submarine. At 1,400 yards the target was moving left and increasing speed. Within five minutes ***Port Arthur's*** veteran CO, Lt Ted Simmons, RCNVR had altered towards it and applied the necessary "throw-off" course to lead the target to allow for the depth charge sinking time. He put in an excellent deliberate ten-charge attack. However the depth charges, set quite shallow, knocked out ***Port Arthur's*** asdic, so the RN destroyer

HMCS *Port Arthur* in 1942-1943, as built, with her extended forecastle, mast behind the bridge, and augmented A/A armament for Torch. These corvettes with the Mediterranean modification can be identified by the added support pillars under the after Oerlikon sponsons.

Antelope, which had moved to join the corvette's attack, then took over the hunt. The corvette opened out to 1,100 yards and was turning, as she tried to sort out her asdic problems.

Below the surface there was considerable chaos aboard the submarine, the Italian ***Tritone,*** with damage to motors and air pressure lines. The boat settled to 400 feet, but was in a bad way and the CO and his engineer agreed they must surface before air pressure was exhausted. Before ***Antelope*** could attack, the submarine surfaced not 700 yards ahead of her. The destroyer at once opened fire with her 4.7-inch A and B guns, pom-pom and Oerlikons. After only six rounds fire was checked as the submarine was now displaying a white cloth and apparently sinking, with the crew leaping overboard. Several had been killed by shellfire in the conning tower, including the 1st watch officer. She sank at 1425, twelve minutes after surfacing. Meanwhile, asdics repaired, ***Port Arthur*** went off after another possible submarine echo, which proved on careful tracking to be "non-sub." ***Antelope*** rescued the swimming survivors.

Port Arthur had sunk the submarine on her first wartime patrol. Commissioned only on the previous 10 October, 1942, ***Tritone*** was commanded by the aggressive Capitano di Corvetta Paolo Monechi, who survived. Of her crew of seven officers and forty-five men the two ships rescued four officers and twenty-two men. The first of her class of *sommergibili*, on sailing from her home base of Cagliari she was attacked by aircraft. The submarine's engineer officer had found sufficient faults in ***Tritone's*** quick-diving tank to recommend putting back to have them repaired. Monechi wouldn't hear of this and pressed on. Sighting Convoy MKS-6 and preparing for the attack, on flooding up her forward tubes ***Tritone*** had lost trim and dove to sixty feet. As she recovered, she was detected by ***Port Arthur***. The attack broke several high pressure air pipes, blew her main fuses and threw off the motor switches, as well as causing fuel tank leaks. Although Monechi ordered torpedoes fired, communications had also broken down, and ***Tritone*** surfaced in some confusion. When "Abandon ship" was ordered, apparently several crew were trapped in her forward torpedo room.

Ted Simmons received a DSO, the ASCO Lt Peter Cowan a DSC, and two of the ship's company DSMs, including AB HSD Gerald Boyer, the 1st operator. In addition, ***Port Arthur's*** crew shared an award of $1,000, put up at the time of her adoption by the city of Port Arthur for distribution if the ship should indeed sink a U-boat.

And a nice signal was received from Captain(D) at her home base of Gibraltar:

"Particular credit goes to the CO for skill and judgement and for the high state of asdic efficiency displayed by his ship. I consider the SD rating on watch who initially detected the contact (OS SD Donald McLean) to be as much responsible for this success as the HSD."

McLean, born in Scotland but an RCNVR, received the other DSM. These two successes, ***Ville de Québec's*** and ***Port Arthur's***, were followed on 8 February by HMCS ***Regina's*** sinking of another Italian submarine, ***Avorio.***

Port Arthur returned to Canada and Western Local for the rest of 1943 and part of 1944, even participating in the making of a dramatic movie for the National Film Board, *Corvette Port Arthur*, utilising a Dutch training submarine for her target. LTO Jack Skinner says "It was probably one of the worst movies I ever saw." She was assigned to Group EG-5 for mid-ocean again, then, after a refit, to W-9 in Western Local. Thence to St. John's and Londonderry for support escorting for the "Neptune" phase of the Normandy invasion, repelling German E-boats, Junkers aircraft and even glider bombs between 7 and 13 June. She returned to Canada in February of 1945 for a leisurely refit, on completion went to Sydney, and was paid off 11 July 1945. Sold to International Iron and Metal in Hamilton, she was broken up there in 1948.

Lt Ted Simmons' DSO was the only one of that order awarded to an RCNVR during the war. He had already been awarded a DSC in the action of September, 1941 when ***Chambly and Moose Jaw*** sank ***U 501*** (See Chapter 7). He went on to other commands and to be senior officer of EG-26 as an acting commander.

SOURCES:

Bishop, *Courage At Sea,* pp. 67-68.

Johnston, *Corvettes Canada*, pp. 181-183.

Macpherson, *Ships of Canada's Naval Forces,* pp. 93, 233.

Paquette & Bainbridge, *Honours & Awards,* pp. 62, 121, 347, 495.

Pollina & Bertini, *I Sommergibili Italiani,* pp. 186, 194.

Schull, *Far Distant Ships,* pp. 153-155.

CHAPTER 23

HMCS LOUISBURG: CANADA'S ONLY NAVAL LOSS TO ENEMY AIRCRAFT

Louisburg: Flower class corvette
Builder: Morton Engineering & Dry Dock, Quebec City
Comm: 2 Oct 41
Crew: 6 officers, 84 crew
Fate: Torpedoed by Italian aircraft, off Oran, Mediterranean, 6 Feb 43
Casualties: 2 officers, 35 crew, 3 RN crew

And that inverted bowl we call the Sky,
Whereunder crawling cooped we live and die,
Lift not thy hands to it for help - for It
Rolls impotently on as Thou or I.

Edward Fitzgerald, *The Rubaiyat of Omar Khayyam*

Louisburg in October 1942, as she went to the Mediterranean, with short forecastle, mast still before the bridge, but with additional AA armament aft and the newer 271 radar.

The importance of the build-up of supplies in the Mediterranean theatre during and after the Torch landings in North Africa is emphasized by the escort strength to Convoy KMS-8, Great Britain to Gibraltar and Mediterranean ports. ***Louisburg*** was one of the seventeen Canadian corvettes withdrawn from home waters and the Atlantic battle to ensure safe passage of this build-up.

She had already participated in several very difficult U-boat battles, at first working out of Sydney, NS then Newfoundland in support of slow convoys. After a four-month refit in Halifax she was assigned to C-3 Group, and as one of the escorts for Convoy ON-115 participated in a memorable battle with the wolf packs. Sent to the UK for Mediterranean duties she was refitted in Londonderry in December, 1942 to prepare her for the different conditions in the Mediterranean, one being an increased threat of air attacks.

Still under the command of her original CO, LCdr W.F. Campbell, RCNVR, she left Londonderry on 23 January 1943 for the Clyde to pick up the fifty-six ship Convoy KMS-8, escorted by the remarkable total of thirteen escorts, RCN and RN corvettes with the senior officer in the ex-US Coast Guard cutter HMS ***Landguard.*** After a very stormy passage in which one RN trawler in the convoy foundered with all hands in heavy seas, but otherwise safely passing Gibraltar, the escort force was reduced to eight Canadian corvettes with the senior officer in ***Louisburg.*** The corvettes ***Louisburg, Algoma, Prescott*** and ***Woodstock*** were ordered into Gibraltar for fuel. The escort was now augmented by two RN destroyers, ***Laforey*** and ***Lookout*** of the 19th DF and two smaller *Hunt* class destroyers, ***Lamerton*** and ***Wheatland***, of the 57th Destroyer Division, available for support. The captain of ***Laforey*** took over as senior officer for the Mediterranean passage; the primary danger would be air attack, not U-boats.

Lt John Charles, RCN was on loan to the RN in ***Laforey*** for fleet experience after completing his signals qualifying course and visited ***Louisburg*** on the 5th of February to discuss communications with LCdr Campbell. There was to be no direct person-to-person turn-over between the senior officers. The Canadian corvettes did not have VHF voice radio which the destroyers used to control air cover, so would only know from ***Laforey*** what was happening in that sphere. Thus the RCN ships would be controlled by ***Laforey*** directing them via ***Louisburg*** once they sailed. This was not a convenient or efficient arrangement. ***Louisburg*** was placed in Station A ahead of the centre of the convoy, with ***Laforey*** on her starboard beam to facilitate communications.

When they sailed from Gibraltar on the 6th, Lt Charles remembers ***Laforey*** dashing about from ship to ship reorganising the convoy so those ships with supplies for the air component of the North African forces and bound for Algiers could break off without disrupting those carrying First Army supplies to their advanced base at Bône.

Gibraltar was not a port in which secrets could be kept from the Germans. Convoy sailings were seen by watchers on the Spanish side of the border and quickly reported. Although there were some fifteen or more submarines in the Mediterranean at this point, the danger would come from enemy aircraft operating out of Sardinia and Sicily, beyond the range of Allied fighter protection from Gibraltar. So it is not surprising that the first air attacks took place by sunset on the 6th when the convoy was about sixty miles northeast of Oran. The sources are inconclusive as to whether the aircraft were Italian or German, and whether there were both bombers and torpedo aircraft. The convoy was in nine columns, about ten miles off the coast of North Africa, on a course of 068° at a speed of nine knots in a slight NE breeze. In the evening twilight it was noticed by others that ***Louisburg*** was still painted in light North Atlantic camouflage which made her rather conspicuous.

DND records say that at about 1900 Italian low level bombers swept in from the convoy's starboard bow and scattered near misses just clear of HMS ***Laforey*** and ***Lookout*** to starboard of ***Louisburg.*** About five minutes later up to five Italian torpedo bombers came over the coast broad on the convoy's bow. Charles reports much firing by all escorts at both bombers and torpedo aircraft, and air-dropped torpedoes approaching his ship which she was able to avoid, although a merchantman was hit, later being towed to Oran. ***Louisburg*** survivors reported an aircraft crossing the convoy's front from starboard to port, passing up the corvette's starboard side, then dropping from about 700 feet to very low over the sea, wheeling to drop a torpedo at them from up-sun. The masthead lookout reported its approach to the bridge but the drop was so close there was no time for the ship to avoid it. Charles also says the torpedo fired at his destroyer, which she had side-stepped, could have been the one to run on and hit ***Louisburg.***

At any rate, a torpedo hit her amidships at 1910, on the port side in the engine room with a flash and a roar and the ship heeled sharply to port. Most of those in the engine and boiler rooms perished in that explosion. Some narratives indicate that her gunners were still firing at their attacker and may even have hit it, since the aircraft was reported smoking as it flew away. But ***Louisburg*** was doomed and sank, stern first, within three minutes.

Apart from the stokers and ERAs, most of the remainder of the ship's company got away by simply jumping over the side before she sank as they had been at action stations on or near the weather decks. Fortunately the water was calm and relatively warm–about 60°F. At least the three starboard Carley floats got away and possibly the starboard dinghy. Reports are conflicting due to the confusion and, shortly after, the dark of night. But there had been no time to ensure that all the depth charges had been set to safe or withdraw their primers, and they detonated shortly after ***Louisburg*** foundered, causing the greater part of the casualties of those both killed and injured. Some survivors recall at least two deep underwater explosions.

One who did not survive was LCdr Campbell. As soon as he saw the condition of his ship, settling on her side to port, he ordered "Abandon ship!", which was carried out without delay. When last seen a few seconds before the ship went under LCdr

Campbell was entering the forward mess decks to ensure no one was left behind. Men had jumped overboard without lifejackets, which at least made it easier to swim away from the suction of the sinking ship, but provided no protection when her depth charges and boilers exploded. It was not for another year that the RCN provided vest-style lifejackets with a sturdy crotch flap to protect against just such eventualities. One man, Stoker James Hawes swam away for at least half an hour, and was then thrown a float from a passing merchantman who dared not stop for his rescue. Lt Hall W.F. Tingley, RCNVR, swam about helping others reach Carley floats and encouraging the survivors. It was only when he was later pulled aboard the rescuing destroyer, completely exhausted, that he was found to have a broken leg and ankle.

Woodstock having seen the sinking asked permission to pick up survivors. Her XO, Lt Dobson, recalls that at the time he was upset when permission was refused. The corvettes were not aware that HMS ***Lookout,*** with a doctor, space and speed had been ordered via VHS to recover survivors when the convoy had passed clear of them. Fortunately one of the survivors had uncapped a calcium flare to indicate their position, saving lives.

Thirty-seven RCN officers and men had lost their lives as well as three RN seamen who were merely taking passage in ***Louisburg*** to North Africa. Forty-seven RCN officers and men survived, as well as one RN rating. ***Lookout*** picked up most of the survivors by 2130, rejoined the convoy and, over the next two hours helped fend off air and U-boat attacks. One RCN rating died of his injuries after being plucked from the water. The survivors were treated sympathetically in the destroyer and landed eventually at Algiers,

Additionally an air reconnaissance of the area of the sinking at first light by a *Catalina* aircraft from Gibraltar yielded the rescue of four more survivors from their eleven-hour ordeal on a Carley float. However, sadly, three of these died on the way in to Algiers. Only LSto J.A. Willett survived, the other three being buried at that port.

The convoy's troubles were not over with the departure of the attacking aircraft. At about 0200 on the 7th ***U 77*** struck, torpedoing two merchantmen. The trawler HMS ***Tervani*** was sunk (with only two survivors) by the Italian submarine ***Acciaio*** later that evening. All this destruction was at least off-set on the 8th when the RCN corvette ***Regina*** sank the Italian submarine ***Avorio*** not far away (See Chapter 24).

In *Corvettes of the* RCN Milner reports that the loss of so many ***Louisburg*** seamen from depth charges exploding prompted the naval staff in Ottawa to make changes to the life saving equipment aboard corvettes. Two sixteen-foot dinghies were removed and a twenty-seven-foot whaler provided. Also the number of Carley floats was increased to be sufficient for 150% of the ships' companies in case some could not be freed if a ship rolled onto her side.

U 77, earlier in her wartime career in 1941 and 1942, had sunk four merchantmen in the Atlantic, and the *Hunt* class destroyer HMS ***Grove*** in the Mediterranean, and had damaged two other warships. But she did not long survive, being bombed and sunk by the RAF north of Cartagena on 28 March 1943, with thirty-eight of her ship's company perishing.

LOST:

Aldred, Leslie, AB
Anderson, Archibald F., Sto
Anderson, Cecil F., L.Sig
Annable, Grant C., OS
Banks, Merl A., AB
Benjamin, Stanley, AB
Bettess, Edward, AB
Campbell, William F., LCdr
Cournoyer, Roland, Sto
Forrest, George A.C., ERA
Garden, Rayburn V., ERA
Gauvin, Joseph M.R., OS
Gilbert, William M., Tel
Graves, Carleton S., AB
Griffin, Earle F., AB
Hall, James, AB
Lewis, William E., AB
McClellan, John F., AB
MacDonald, Donald M., LS
McDonald, Ronald J., AB
MacGregor, Duncan, Sto
MacLeod, Gordon I., Sig
McNeill, Donald, C.ERA
MacPhail, John A., Coder
MacPhail, Sidney J., Sto
Merryweather, Hugh, Coder
Morin, Joseph G.E.V., OS
Ninian, Thomas M., O.Tel
Paterson, Robert L., Sig
Rice, Stanley N., Sto
Robinson, Elwin, Tel
Smith, Arthur J., PO.Tel
Stevenson, James C.R., LS
Tanner, James A., AB
Vikstrom, Jack R., AB

SOURCES:

English, *The Hunts*, pp. 74-75, 102-103.

German, *The Sea is at Our Gates,* p. 108.

Johnston, *Corvettes Canada,* pp. 53-59.

Lenton, *German Submarines*, Vol.1, p. 29.

Macpherson & Burgess, *Ships of Canada's Naval Forces*.

Macpherson & Milner, *Corvettes of the RCN,* p. 70.

Rohwer, *Axis Submarine Successes 1939-1945.*

Schull, *Far Distant Ships*, p. 86.

CHAPTER 24

HMCS REGINA: A WELL CONDUCTED ATTACK SINKS AVORIO

Once in three years came the navy of Tarshish, bringing gold and silver, ivory[1], and apes and peacocks.

1 Kings Ch. 10, v. 22

Regina: Revised Flower class corvette
Builder: Marine Industries Ltd, Sorel, PQ
Comm: 22 Jan 42
Crew: 6 officers, 90 crew

Action: Sank Italian submarine ***Avorio***, off Algeria, Mediterranean, 8 Feb 43
Casualties: 3 officers, 16 crew

HMCS ***Regina*** in the spring of 1942, not long after her commissioning. Her much more spacious bridge is notable, as is the raised 4-inch gun forward. All the smoke is not explained; maybe part of an exercise.

As one of ten corvettes approved in March 1941 to meet the ever-increasing responsibilities of the Canadian Navy, ***Regina*** was built with great urgency. Laid down in March, 1941, she was one of the first built with both an extended forecastle and an improved bridge, lessons learned from hard experience with the earlier corvettes. Her mast, however, was still before the bridge, a nuisance corrected in later refits for most corvettes. In December 1941 she had to be towed to Halifax for completion to avoid being frozen in for the winter at Sorel. She commissioned there on 22 January 1942.

Defects plagued her during many months of her early service. She served briefly in the Halifax Force then in Western Local Escort Force, seeing several convoys safely outward and inward-bound and rescuing twenty-five survivors on one occasion. She also operated on the Halifax-Boston run for a period, identified with "lucky" convoys suffering little or no loss while others before and after suffered heavily. Four SC and HX convoys were part of her record where only one straggler was lost.

In late 1942 the Admiralty requested Canadian escorts to assist with Operation Torch convoys in support of the North African

1. Avorio means ivory in Italian.

invasion. ***Regina*** was one of seventeen corvettes assigned, fitted with additional Oerlikon guns required for anti-aircraft protection in the Mediterranean. In September a new commanding officer was appointed, LCdr Harry Freeland, RCNR, often known as "Harry The Horse" from his Atlantic convoy escort days and the adoption of Damon Runyan character names by the corvette COs. She started passage to England with Convoy SC-107 but had to return due to condenser problems, and sailed on 7 November with SC-108. This was perhaps fortunate, as SC-107 was one of the worst convoys, losing fifteen vessels to U-boat packs, while SC-108 was not seriously attacked.

Although the Torch landings had been made by the time ***Regina*** arrived, follow-on convoys were still required for supplies for the continuing battle. In December, 1942 ***Regina*** was part of the escort for KMS-5 to Gibraltar but due to damage in extremely rough weather wherein she lost her asdic dome, she had to return to Londonderry for repairs. On 25 January she was one of eight corvettes escorting KMS-8 to Gibraltar. Again the weather was severe: an RN trawler-minelayer, HMS ***Corncrake,*** foundered and was lost with all hands. Weather was as often the enemy as Germans or Italians.

This convoy entered the Mediterranean on 5 February. ***Regina*** was astern of HMCS ***Louisburg*** when that ship was sunk by an aerial torpedo on the 6th (See Chapter 23). There were several other air attacks and submarine alarms and excursions during the day. On the evening of 7 February ***Regina*** and HMS ***Rhyl***, a *Bangor* class minesweeper, were assigned to escort a ship of KMS-8 from Algiers onward to Bône, Algeria. There is some evidence that this "convoy" consisted of two ships, but there is only reference to the elderly little ex-coal carrier SS ***Brinkburn***. She was evidently carrying 1,500 tons of aviation fuel in cans in her holds. The crew had been overcome with petrol fumes from leaking and spilled cans and several men were replaced by an eight-man RN party from the trawler HMS ***Coriolanus*** for the short voyage to Bône from Algiers.

At 2310 ***Regina*** was 4,000 yards on the port bow of the convoy and ***Rhyl*** in the corresponding station to starboard. It was a quiet, dark night with stars out but no moon. ***Regina*** picked up a faint contact on her radar at a range of 6,200 yards, bearing 030°. Freeland altered toward and went to twelve knots. Radar contact was lost in five minutes as the submarine dived but at 2317 they obtained an asdic contact at about 1,000 yards. At full speed ahead the target was closed to 300 yards, moving left. At 100 yards contact was lost and a single ten-charge pattern was dropped, using the range recorder trace for "time to fire".

While nothing seemed to happen, at 2328 the spray and foam of the submarine surfacing was seen, then the wash of her wake and her hull were sighted, going away. A stern chase developed across the dark sea; the bridge Oerlikons immediately fired on the submarine and she returned fire with 12.5mm Breda machine guns. The Oerlikon tracer allowed the ***Regina's*** 4-inch gun to find the target in the dark. Eight rounds were fired and the submarine was struck at the base of her conning tower. This gunnery went on for some five minutes, then the fleeing submarine ceased firing and some of her crew started to jump into the sea. Those that remained on the casing were crying for surrender or help as ***Regina*** charged up. Freeland had planned to ram her but, when he saw the crew on the casing by a signal light shone on the boat, he stopped nearby. It was only then they realised their captive was an Italian submarine.

The ship carried out a precautionary sweep around the area to ensure there were no more submarines about. Then a boarding party under ***Regina's*** 1st lieutenant, Lt F.B. Marr, was put on board by boat. At first it was thought the submarine could be kept afloat and a tug was requested. At 0345 the tug HMS ***Jaunty*** arrived and a tow was attempted. By 0500 it was realised that the submarine was sinking and the boarding party had to jump into the sea as she sank at 0515.

Her own people and all the twenty-seven survivors of the Italian crew were rescued by ***Regina***, seven of the Italians wounded, two seriously, but most overjoyed to be saved and out of the war. They were taken into Bône by 1020 that day. The ship received numerous congratulatory messages and a few months later awards were made official: Harry Freeland received a DSO, SLt Roddick B. Thomas a DSC; CERA Allen Hurst and L/S Stan Heywood, the senior asdic rating, received DSMs; Mention in Despatches were awarded to the coxswain, CPO Jack W. Winn, ABs Joe Saulnier and Trevor Martin (who was the 4-inch gun captain), and to OS Vernon Cavanaugh.

Avorio was one of thirteen submarines of the 600-series ***Platino*** class, 710 tons,

The medium-sized Italian submarine *Avorio,* completed in March, 1942 and sunk just under a year later.

commissioned on 25 March 1942. One of her war patrols had involved her in attacks on ships of Operation Pedestal in August 1942 for the relief of Malta, where she had had no success. In February, 1943 she was operating out of a base at Cagliari, Sardinia on her sixth war patrol, although with no sinkings to her credit. Her new CO on this patrol was Tenente (Lieutenant) Leone Fiorentini.

Fiorentini had sailed from Cagliari on 6 February in company with the *sommergibili* ***Gorgo*** and ***Platino***, bound for Cape Bougaron, North Africa. He had sighted a convoy the next morning but depth charges from an MTB forced him to crash dive. Having remained submerged during daylight on the 8th, he had to surface that night to charge his batteries. ***Avorio*** was still on the surface when detected by ***Regina***, and in the dark of night, was dangerously close to the corvette before the Italians knew they were sighted. She crash-dived to 200 feet and stopped. The first depth charges were close and caused water to enter through distorted plates in the pressure hull, creating trimming problems. The next two explosions from the pattern caused further flooding in the control room and ballast tanks. When he surfaced, Fiorentini found his forward torpedo tubes were distorted and useless, and when he tried to escape on the surface he found the helm jammed and the boat could only move in a circle. It had been an excellent urgent attack by Freeland's team.

The gunfire from ***Regina*** had then been so effective that the captain, two other officers and sixteen ratings had been killed. The 4-inch shells had torn up plates and holed the conning tower. The corvette's only minor casualty was AB Henry Mortimer, who had a bullet scrape his rib cage.

Regina remained in the Mediterranean theatre for another month, during which she brought in the Portuguese vessel ***Nyassa*** which was trying to run the blockade from South America to Portugal and then transship her cargo to Germany. She then escorted an ancient side-wheeler tug bringing a damaged ship to Gibraltar.

The story of her remaining career and her loss are told in Chapter 48.

SOURCES:

Fraccaroli, *Italian Warships of WW II*, p. 143.

Macpherson & Milner, *Corvettes of the RCN*, pp. 127, 131.

Paquette & Bainbridge, *Honours & Awards.*

Pollina, Cocchia & Bertini, *I Sommergibili Italiani 1895-1968*, pp 178-182.

Schull, *Far Distant Ships*, pp. 157-158.

Smith, *Pedestal,* pp. 110-111.

CHAPTER 25

THE MINING OF HMCS WEYBURN

Weyburn: Flower class corvette
Builder: Port Arthur Shipbuilding, ON
Comm: 26 Nov 41
Crew: 6 officers, 71 crew

Fate: mined by *U 118*, off Strait of Gibraltar, 22 Feb 43
Casualties: 8 crew, 1 RN

It takes a heap of courage
Just to read the morning news

Wilma Coutts, *Saugeen Sonnets*

HMCS *Weyburn* in 1942, as built.

After work-ups, ***Weyburn*** transferred between the Halifax Escort Force in February, 1942, the Western Local Escort Force in April and the Gulf Escort Force in July. While off Newfoundland in early September ***Weyburn*** just missed sinking the notorious (in Canadian annals) KL Paul Hartwig who, in ***U 517***, was to be so successful in the St.Lawrence. When the two vessels suddenly encountered each other on the dark night of 2 September, in the usual dreadful asdic conditions caused by fresh ice-fed water coming down from the Arctic, only two depth charges were dropped, to no avail. ***U 517*** sank the small laker ***Donald Stewart*** and was seen twice by ***Weyburn's*** bridge personnel but escaped to press on into the Gulf.

Assigned to the North African operations for Torch, ***Weyburn*** departed Halifax on 16 September 1942 with Convoy SC-100, being taken in hand for modifications and additional Oerlikons in a brief refit at Liverpool, where she joined the RN EG-25 for a month. Assigned to another RN Group, EG-62, ***Weyburn***, under her only CO LCdr Tom M.W. Golby, RCNR, supported the North African landings together with seventeen other RCN corvettes, withdrawn from the Atlantic battle. It was felt by some RN personnel at the Admiralty that the RCN ships required additional training and closer supervision by more experienced RN group senior officers for that struggle. Naval Service HQ in Ottawa agreed that most Canadian Groups should be withdrawn for some sorely needed group operating experience. At the same time they agreed to make corvettes available, under British direction, for Torch as well. In the Mediterranean, ***Weyburn*** escorted convoys and helped beat off air attacks. She probably shot down one Heinkel and damaged two others.

That these corvettes were a useful addition is demonstrated in their senior officer's report at one stage: "The Canadian corvettes are excellent ships individually and have distinguished themselves against submarines during their services in the Med. But a collection of escort vessels hastily thrown together under an SO whom they have never met before is no substitute for an effective Group.... They are very keen, quick to learn, and, under RN leadership, will make a good team." Somewhat patronising, but praise nonetheless. This was also an accurate assessment of the problems the Canadians had suffered under in their hastily assembled Atlantic anti-submarine escort groups. It was exactly what Cdr "Chummy" Prentice had been saying for two years as training commander with the Newfoundland Escort Force, to little avail.

On the morning of 22 February 1943, ***Weyburn*** left Gibraltar where she had gone in for fuel as her group and its convoy passed westbound on the 21st, to rejoin the slow convoy MKS-8 bound from North African ports for the UK. In fact there were two convoys in the area, GUS-4 being bound for the US, the whole consisting of some 100 ships, with eight RN vessels and five RCN corvettes, so there was much manoeuvring about in the Straits.

There were known mine-fields off Cape Spartel, north and west of Tangier, Morocco, and the tanker ***Thorsholm*** in the US-bound convoy had exploded a mine at 0910 on the 22nd with minimal damage. ***Weyburn's*** convoy was well to port in the swept channel, forty miles west of Gibraltar. The day was clear, and with only a modest swell running. On moving up the port wing of the convoy to assume her assigned escort position at about 1017 ***Weyburn*** detonated a mine on her port side abreast her engine room, which at once flooded, killing one rating. She drifted to a stop but remained afloat, though the explosion had buckled her deck and split the funnel vertically. Confidential books were disposed of and an officer and a rating at once removed the primers from the depth charges on her quarterdeck to render them inoperative in case she did sink. The twisted wreckage of one rail prevented the removal of two primers, but the pistols were set to "Safe". It was hoped she might be towed back to Gibraltar.

Another escort of the group, the elderly W Class destroyer ***Wivern*** came carefully alongside ***Weyburn's*** quarter and started to take off some of those wounded by the mine's explosion, while the senior officer's sloop ***Black Swan*** provided anti-submarine protection as the convoy steamed on. ***Wivern*** lowered her sea boat to pick up survivors who had been catapulted or leapt overboard and were swimming in the water. In crossing from ***Weyburn*** to ***Wivern***, the 1st lieutenant, Lt W.A.B. "Hip" Garrard's leg was caught between the two ships and his ankle severely crushed.

Suddenly, twenty minutes later, an after bulkhead let go in ***Weyburn***, her bows reared up and the corvette sank quickly by the stern. Her whole complement, except the killed stoker, had either taken to the water or been transferred to ***Wivern***, especially the injured. But now, from not very deep below this scene of rescue, there were two violent explosions, presumably from the two depth charges whose primers had not been withdrawn. One suspects that in the rail's destruction from the mine explosion, their firing pistols had also been damaged, and that the "Safe" setting of the pistol had not operated. At the time it was thought that maybe another mine had exploded, or ***Weyburn's*** boilers, but these were later discounted. It was appreciated that mines were the cause of the original explosion, not a U-boat torpedo, even though a U-boat was reported by aircraft later that day further south down the African coast.

At any rate, these explosions killed five seamen in the water at once. Two more were to die in hospital later in Gibraltar, including an RN ordinary seaman who had been serving in ***Weyburn***. Many others were injured in the water by ruptures. ***Wivern***, still lying close to where ***Weyburn*** had gone down, was lifted bodily by the explosions to the extent her engines were distorted and her boilers heaved from their mountings so she could no longer move, and several men had bones broken by the concussion. This contributed to the atmosphere of chaos on board. In the water, Sto PO Sidney Day of ***Wivern***, who had leapt aboard ***Weyburn*** to help rescue the injured and then taken to the water when she sank, was then killed by the explosion. In all in the two ships there were eighty-four wounded. Rescue was not made easier by Spanish batteries who "fired an intermittent and ineffective bombardment at rescue operations".[1]

Black Swan picked up forty-one of ***Weyburn's*** survivors (one of whom died on board) and sixteen of ***Wivern's*** injured and took the latter in tow, being relieved by a tug as they approached Gibraltar. From ***Weyburn*** there were sixty-eight survivors in total, with eight fatalities, including two who died of their wounds in Gibraltar and the RN rating. One of those who died in the water was LCdr Tom Golby, ***Weyburn's*** CO. It took seventeen months to repair the damages to ***Wivern.*** HMCS ***Woodstock*** replaced ***Weyburn*** in the escort screen.

There were, even in this disaster, tales of uncommon valour. Lt Garrard insisting on his injured ship's company being treated before his ankle was taken care of and then, with only some "pusser's" rum as anaesthetic (all the bottles of regular anaesthetic had been broken in the explosions), said to the medical officer and his assistants "O.K., hack away, boys, I'm in favour of it!" when they explained the need for its amputation. The medical officer in ***Wivern***, SurgLt P.R.C. Evans, RNVR, had both ankles broken in the depth charge explosion, and was carried to their wardroom dressing station but at his orders propped up on the floor, supervising and examining all the wounded brought in before allowing treatment for himself. Coder Thomas Hird, RCNVR, of Calgary recalls: "I was in the water with AB William Shelley, swimming away from the sinking ***Weyburn.*** All of a sudden the sea seemed to explode and both of us were tossed high into the air by a gush of water. Shelley turned into me, sort of shielding me from the blast. He gave a loud groan, and at the same time I thought my legs had been blown off, and I felt a terrific pain around my stomach. I grabbed at Shelley just as we came down, but that was the last time I saw him."[2] Shelley died from his injuries; Hird survived. Also rescued was the ship's mascot, a cocker spaniel named "Posh".

Some days later, AB Dorn McGaw of Kincardine, Ontario, was buried at sea in the Straits, from a Polish trawler retained for the purpose, by a group of seamen from HMCS ***Algoma*** and ***Weyburn.***

Lt. Patrick S. Milsom was awarded the MBE "for gallant rescue work", as was Lt. Garrard. SLt Wilfred Bark was awarded a posthumous Mention in Despatches, being one who died in the water, and LSig. L. W. Murray also received an M.i.D.

The mines had evidently been laid in the channel undetected about three weeks before by ***U 118*** (KK Werner Czygan), a U-boat specifically designed to carry and lay up to sixty-six SMA type mines from vertical shafts built into the hull. Operating with X U-Flottille out of Lorient, France, she had laid mines that sank three merchantmen in the preceding MKS convoy, and the one that had damaged ***Thorsholm*** and at least one other ship. ***U 118*** was to be sunk later in June, 1943 off the Canary Islands by naval aircraft from USS ***Bogue***, with no survivors.

LOST:

Bark, Wilfred, SLt
Eisner, Eric E., Stwd
Golby, Thomas M.W., LCdr
Hall, Richard S., L.Sto
McGaw, Dorn M., AB
Morrison, Melvin C., Sto
Savoie, Maurice A., Sto
Shelley, William H., AB
Plus 1 RN rating

SOURCES:

German, The *Sea Is At Our Gates*, pp. 10, 118, 133-4.

Gröner, *German Warships, 1815-1945*, Vol. Two, pp. 76-77.

Herzog, *Deutsche U-boote 1906-1966,* p. 267.

Johnston, *Corvettes Canada,* pp. 193-4.

Macpherson & Burgess, *Ships of Canada's Naval Forces.*

Paquette & Bainbridge, *Honours & Awards.*

Schull, *Far Distant Ships*, pp. 116, 158-160.

1. ***Black Swan's*** report in DHist files, Ottawa.
2. DHist file narrative.

CHAPTER 26

THE SILK STOCKING RUN: HMCS SHEDIAC AND ST. CROIX WITH CONVOY KMS-10

Shediac: Flower class corvette
Builder: Davie Shipbuilding & Repairing, Lauzon, PQ
Comm: 8 Jul 41
Crew: 6 officers, 79 crew

St. Croix: (See Chapter 12 for details)

Action: Sank *U 87*, off Portugal, 4 Mar 43
Casualties: 49
No survivors

He chose history because we have no chance of understanding the present without understanding the past.

P.D. James, *Unsuitable for a Woman*

Shediac, still unmodified, but on the West Coast for her modernization on 21 May, 1944.

The Canadian Navy had contributed seventeen corvettes for the enormous effort in late 1942 and early 1943 to convoy hundreds of ships to the Mediterranean for Operation Torch, the landings in North Africa. There was a need to continue the flow of supplies to that area for the next phase, the invasion of Sicily and Italy. One of the convoys involved in that build up was the slow KMS-10 from the United Kingdom to Algiers. Assigned as convoy close escort was the Canadian C-1 Escort Group operating from Londonderry. This consisted of the elderly destroyer ***St. Croix*** (commanded by LCdr A.H. Dobson who had earned a DSC in July of 1942 for sinking ***U 90***–see Chapter 12) and the corvettes ***Battleford, Kenogami, Napanee*** and ***Shediac***, the last commanded by John Clayton, RCNR, who had commissioned that ship almost two years earlier.

Some of the history of ***St. Croix*** is chronicled in two other chapters of this book. For almost two years ***Shediac*** had toiled in the Atlantic with convoys where the balance sheet could be assessed only in the number of ships successfully brought to the United Kingdom or returned to North America in ballast for fresh cargoes. She had been with Convoy SC-67 in February 1942 when her sister-corvette ***Spikenard*** was lost. She was with Convoy ONS-92 in May, 1942 when five merchantmen were torpedoed in two hours, and she had been in the battle for Convoy ONS-154 in December of 1942 when fourteen ships were sunk. While she had attacked the marauding U-boats, none had been sunk. Now it was her turn.

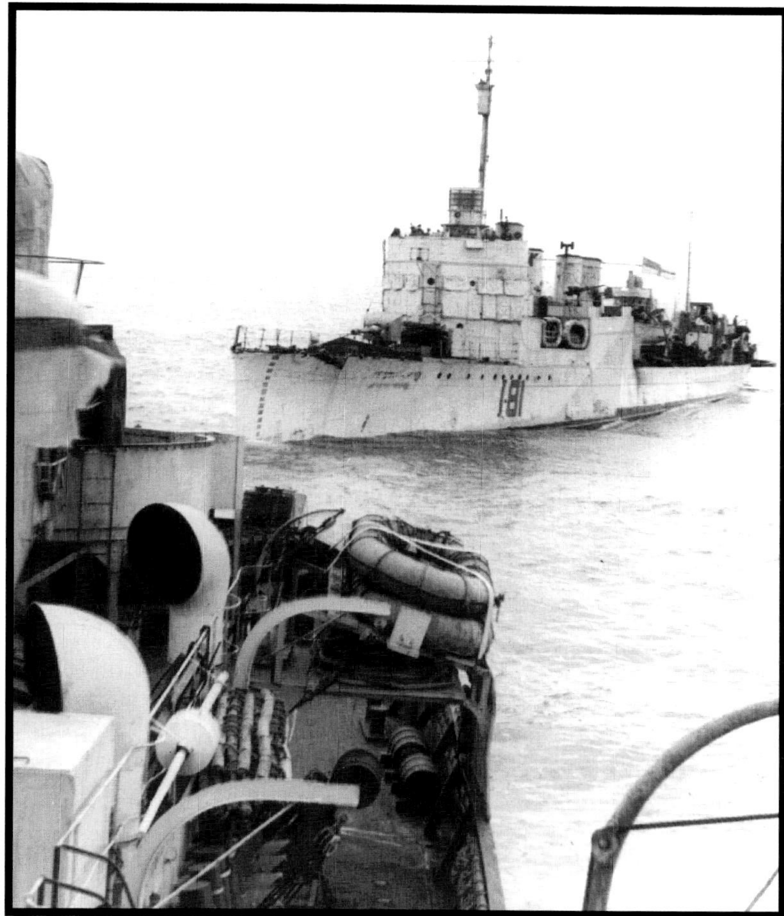

A nice view of *St. Croix* passing astern of HMCS *Arvida* in August, 1943.

The sources and official records are somewhat sparse concerning this event. Fortunately ***Shediac*** had aboard A.J. McWhinnie, the naval correspondent for the British newspaper the *Daily Herald.* He provided a contemporary account of a running battle between the escorts and merchantmen and German aircraft and submarines.

For some time the UK-Gibraltar convoys had experienced only minor attacks emanating from the German occupied French coast. Before C-1 sailed in March, 1943 they were told it was a "silk stocking run" and that they could look forward to arriving back in the UK with presents for the girls at home. This trip proved to be anything but a mere silk stocking run.

It started with two Focke-Wolfe *Condor* aircraft approaching the convoy, whose air escort was one quite slow *Catalina* flying boat. This aircraft's crew showed great gallantry in taking on one of the *Condors*. Those on board ***Shediac*** thought the *Catalina* was finished when it lost altitude but it had only done so to get rid of its load of depth charges to gain some speed. The F-Ws departed but the convoy's exact location was now known to the Germans.

The next day, 4 March, German aircraft arrived over the convoy again and three of them commenced bombing. They were met with a barrage of anti-aircraft fire from all the escorts and some of the merchantmen. In the middle of this air defence battle, now west of Oporto, Portugal, ***Shediac*** reported a submarine contact on her asdic. Postwar German records examined do not indicate whether this was one of three U-boats directed against the convoy as a result of earlier aircraft sighting reports, or whether it was an unlucky boat simply on transit through the area. At any rate, ***Shediac*** altered to attack this new threat, dropping ten depth charges initially. The convoy moved on.

St. Croix closed the area where ***Shediac*** was making a series of further depth charge attacks and, conned by ***Shediac,*** joined the battle, also dropping ten charges. There is no clear indication as to which ship contributed most to the ultimate kill. Their target disappeared after about two hours, even with a pass over the location with ***Shediac's*** echo sounder in case their target had settled on the bottom. In fact there was no substantial evidence at the time that a kill had been achieved. One of ***Shediac's*** plotting ratings, Coder Jim Gillick, later commented ruefully "We never saw anything!" But McWhinnie, who had been aboard many ships during numerous anti-submarine attacks commented: "I watched the underwater fight until the finish. Whatever decision the Admiralty may make about that particular U-boat, I am convinced we got a kill." It was some considerable time before it could be confirmed that ***U 87*** had gone missing and could only have been sunk in the ***Shediac-St. Croix*** attacks.

The chief ERA on board ***Shediac*** was William W. Maxwell who retired many years later as a commander. Maxwell confirms to this day that the ship's company shared McWhinnie's belief that they had finished the submarine.

The boat involved was ***U 87***, one of VI U-Flottille and a boat utilised for mine-laying, operating out of St. Nazaire, France. Launched in June, 1941, she made her first successful attack on 31 December that year when she sank the British tanker ***Cardita***. In 1942 she sank another four ships, all under KL Joachim Berger who commanded her when attacked by ***Shediac*** and ***St. Croix***. She disappeared without trace or survivors from these attacks.

Air and submarine attacks continued. ***Shediac*** ran so low in depth charges that she had to obtain some additional ones from other ships, transferring them in her sea boat despite their weighing over 300 pounds each. McWhinnie reports she did this three times. When an ammunition ship was damaged she was ordered to stand by her, having already picked up nine survivors from sunken ships.

Bill Maxwell recalls that one submarine contact was staying under the ammunition ship. ***Shediac*** was unable to drop charges too close for fear of a major explosion in the merchantman she was supposedly protecting. The submarine would slip from one side of the merchantman to the other, with ***Shediac*** fruitlessly pursuing her target from side to side. And most galling of all was that the ship they were protecting had a large supply of depth charges in her hold, but they could not be brought up for transfer to the corvette. As Sto PO Terry commented: "If this goes on much longer we'll just have to open the sea cocks and go down after him ourselves."

Shediac, although getting no further kill with this target, was detached from the convoy to be the sole protection of the damaged ammunition ship, SS ***Argonaut***. On the second night a tug and additional escorts arrived and the ship and cargo arrived safely in Gibraltar. Shediac returned to Canada after this action for a refit, spent some months in Western Local escort and was modernised with an extended forecastle at Vancouver in mid-1944. She spent the rest of the war on the west coast. Paid off in 1945, she was sold in 1951 and converted into the Dutch whale-catcher ***Jooske W. Vinke***. She lasted until 1965 when she was broken up in Spain.

Lt Clayton was awarded the DSC in 1946, "for outstanding services in anti-U-boat operations during the war", one of the decorations awarded not necessarily for a specific action but for a combination of many successes.

St. Croix had another six months of very active duty before being torpedoed in September, 1943 (See Chapter 29).

SOURCES:

German, *The Sea is at Our Gates*, p. 137.

Macpherson & Burgess, *Ships of Canada's Naval Forces.*

Macpherson & Milner, *Corvettes of the RCN,* p. 68.

McWhinnie, *Daily Herald*, 16 March, 1943.

Milner, *The North Atlantic Run*, pp. 205-210.

Paquette & Bainbridge, *Honours & Awards*, p. 109.

Rohwer, *Axis Submarine Successes 1939-1945.*

Schull, *Far Distant Ships*, pp. 102, 112, 140.

Showell, *U-Boat Command,* p. 107.

Tarrant, *The U-Boat Offensive, 1914-1945*, p. 143.

CHAPTER 27

A SKILFUL ATTACK BY HMCS PRESCOTT

Post varia studia quibus ab annis tenerrimis fideliter, nec infeliciter incubuit...[1]

John Donne's epitaph

Prescott: Flower class corvette
Builder: Kingston Shipbuilding Co, ON
Comm: 26 Jun 41
Crew: 6 officers, 71 crew

Action: sank *U 163*, Atlantic, 13 Mar 43
Casualties: 57
No survivors

HMCS *Prescott* in 1943-1944, with her forecastle extended and augmented A/A armament for Mediterranean service, but still with the annoying mast before the bridge and Canadian radar.

LCdr Wilfred "Red" McIsaac was one of those rather rare pre-war RCNVR officers, having joined at St. John, NB in the 1930s. He was to serve at sea for almost the entire war and HMCS ***Prescott*** was his first command. She commissioned at Montreal and served briefly at Halifax, then joined the Newfoundland Escort Force in August, 1941 escorting convoys to Iceland. She made two trips to Londonderry then was assigned to the Western Local Escort Force out of Halifax. Back to the 25th Escort Group at Londonderry, then, in February, 1943, ***Prescott*** joined the 27th Escort Group operating between Gibraltar and the UK and to North African ports in support of Operation Torch, the North African landings. It was in this latter role that she was belatedly credited with sinking ***U 163***.

While the seventeen RCN corvettes assigned to this task were vitally required, the RN also felt that many of the Canadian ships were lacking in training and group skills for the Atlantic anti-submarine war. This assignment would give them a chance to improve these skills.

U 163, a larger Type IXC 1,120-tonner under KK Kurt-Eduard Englemann, had had a successful patrol the previous November off British Guiana, where she sank three ships of 15,000 tons. This time she left Lorient at 1630 on 10 March, 1943, to rendezvous on the 20th with the homeward bound blockade runner ***Regensburg*** in mid-Atlantic, far to the southwest of Iceland. In the normal manner she was to have reported her safe passage out of the Bay of Biscay (this message known in German as a *Passiermeldung*) and, when this had not been received by 15 March, ***U 163*** was asked to give her position. When again nothing was heard, BdU presumed she was lost, initially

1. "After various studies, which he plied from his tenderest youth faithfully and not unsuccessfully..."

attributing this to air attack or mining although there was nothing in their records to support this assumption. She was one of many U-boats that, from a BdU perspective, just "disappeared" and after the war the Admiralty's Assessment Committee also attributed her loss to an unknown cause. But in some USN records it was maintained that ***U 163*** was sunk by their submarine USS ***Herring*** on 21 March. However this location of ***Herring's*** was far to the southeast of ***U 163's*** assigned track to meet in-bound ***Regensburg***. At 0040 local time ***Herring*** had fired a salvo of torpedoes at a target appearing to be a surfaced submarine at a range of a mile and a quarter. Two explosions were heard and hydrophone noises ceased. But to accept this assessment runs contrary to BdU information and ***U 163's*** orders. She would have reported meeting or not meeting ***Regensburg*** on the 20th, and to have been ***Herring's*** target would have been returning homeward contrary to orders to be in that location on the 21st. It is now presumed that ***Herring*** had mistakenly fired at Spanish fishing trawlers that were in her area at the time, and whose small wheelhouse could look like a conning tower at a distance.

This led Mr. R.M. Coppock, the RN researcher doing the 1980s studies into unproven U-Boat losses, to look elsewhere for the cause of ***U 163's*** unexplained disappearance. A meticulous search through escort reports and German radio traffic led to ***Prescott.***

On 13 March, 1943, ***Prescott*** was part of the screen for Convoy MKS-9 bound from North Africa to the UK, well out into the Atlantic around Spain to avoid attention from German aircraft. Five miles out on the convoy's starboard bow, at 2149 local time ***Prescott's*** radar watch obtained a contact at about 3,400 yards with her newly-fitted 271 radar,[2] coming from the east or the Bay of Biscay. Visibility was about five miles, a first quarter moon was up, the sea was slight in light winds.

McIsaac altered toward and increased speed and the echo closed rapidly. At just under three-quarters of a mile a U-boat could be seen just diving, and strong hydrophone effect was heard. A firm asdic contact was obtained at 1,200 yards and McIsaac set up a deliberate attack. Then, at only a short distance off ***Prescott's*** port bow another surfaced U-boat was reported, running fast on the surface toward the convoy. McIsaac at once altered course the few degrees needed to engage her, judging this to be the greater threat to the convoy.

However, McIsaac had forgotten to cancel his previously set up depth charge attack and, as he ran on, a five-charge pattern was fired but subsequently judged to be well off his original submerged target. He opened fire with his forward 4-inch gun on the second U-boat which was going away at high speed, two rounds of high explosive and one of starshell were fired, which clearly revealed the submarine on the surface, spray flying from her bows. When the range had closed to 700 yards the U-boat was seen to dive, and at 600 yards asdic contact obtained, held to 200 yards. As ***Prescott*** hustled across the U-boat's path a nine-charge depth charge pattern was fired, after which contact with her target could not be regained. Now joined by the corvette ***Napanee***, an organized search called Operation Observant was conducted around the target's last-known position.

This attack lasted thirty to forty-five minutes at the most. At 2319 ***Prescott*** obtained an asdic contact and, although classified as "doubtful", she ran over it, holding contact in to 400 yards, when it disappeared, indicating in those days before depth-measuring asdic that the target was about 400 feet deep. The echo was regained at 1,500 yards so ***Prescott*** attacked with another nine charges, some of which were right on target according to her plot. Thereafter, contact was lost for good. After sniffing about for a bit and finding nothing on or beneath the surface, ***Prescott*** and ***Napanee*** left to rejoin their convoy.

Coppock's examination of all relevant German and Allied naval and air attack documents reveals that only ***U 163*** could have been present that evening, her course to meet the blockade-runner passing close to the scene of ***Prescott's*** action on that date. It is now supposed that when she originally saw the attacking corvette, she dived, had a problem, or possibly Englemann had a change of mind when he appreciated that he was dealing with one corvette that he could probably out-run on the

---

2. These sets, fitted in UK refits, were greatly superior to the Canadian built SW1C sets originally supplied and even the later RXC sets. But the Canadian authorities would not accept the critical reports from the users at sea and it took some circumvention - and insistence by the RN when the corvettes were to be under their command - to allow for the 271 sets to be supplied . The SW1C set tended to shut down when guns were fired or depth charges went off.

surface, and re-surfaced. This led McIsaac to assume he was dealing with two U-boats, even though he neither saw nor was in contact with two at once. Since it was only two days later that ***U 163*** failed to respond to BdU's request for her *Passiermeldung*, it is reasonably certain that ***Prescott*** was responsible for her silence.

The corvette returned to Canada the next month for a refit at Liverpool, NS to extend her forecastle and for modernization, then joined EG-6 out of Londonderry, principally for West African convoys, until April of 1944 when the corvettes were replaced in the hunting escort groups by frigates. She was employed in invasion screening duties out of Greenock, Scotland, back to Liverpool for another brief refit, and over to the Nore Command in the UK until the end of the war. She was paid off at Sorel in July, 1945, and broken up at Hamilton in 1951.

A somewhat sad note is recorded in the future of Red McIsaac, who left ***Prescott*** in April, 1944, and was awarded an MBE for his wartime services, even without knowing of his success against ***U 163***. After the war he retired, and worked in sales, eventually out of London, Ontario. In 1955 he suffered a completely disabling stroke, which left him unable to speak, read or move about, although he understood what was read or told to him, for his wife went almost every day to his extended care home to read to him. When the story of his 1943 sinking of ***U 163*** was discovered in early 1987, his wife was able to pass this on to Red, to his very considerable delight. "He was sure," she said, "that he had sunk that submarine! He just was never credited with it." Red died in June, 1987.

SOURCES:

Johnston, *Corvettes Canada,* p. 195, 256.

Macpherson & Burgess, *Ships of Canada's Naval Forces,* p. 83.

Paquette & Bainbridge, *Honours & Awards*, p. 341.

CHAPTER 28

HMCS DRUMHELLER: SUCCESS AT LONG LAST

I'll yield him thee
Where thou mayst knock a nail into his head

Wm. Shakespeare, *The Tempest*

Drumheller: Flower class corvette
Builder: Collingwood Shipyards Ltd, ON
Comm: 13 Sep 41
Crew: 6 officers, 79 crew
HMS *Lagan* River class frigate
Builder: Smith's Dock Co, UK, 1942
Crew: 8 officers, 132 crew

Action: Sank *U 753*, mid-Atlantic, 13 May 43
Casualties: 47
No survivors

HMCS *Drumheller* in her 1942 short forecastle form, looking rather care-worn. It is now understood that this was a problem caused primarily by the steel not being prepared properly before painting during construction.

HMCS ***Drumheller*** is one of the most frequently mentioned corvettes in the annals of the RCN. After commissioning and a month with the Sydney Force, she was attached to the C-2 close Escort Group for two and a half years, There she participated in some of the most savage yet typical early convoy battles, operating out of Newfoundland and Londonderry with the likes of ***St Croix*** and HMS ***Polyanthus*** in the conflicts of 1942 and early 1943 against the BdU-directed wolf packs, and the first of the acoustic torpedo attacks. While she contributed to damaging or driving off several U-boats, it was not until May of 1943, at the very worst time of the Atlantic battle, that ***Drumheller***, commanded by Lt Les Denny, RCNR, got credit for her own U-boat kill.

Sailing in defence of eastbound Convoy HX-237 which had left New York on 1 May, this convoy and the Canadian C-2 Close Escort group were fortunate to have the small escort carrier HMS ***Biter*** in a support role. Within the month these carriers, more very long range shore-based aircraft, and the arrival of additional convoy escort warships were to temporarily drive the U-boats from the North Atlantic.

In the early morning hours of the 13th a straggling merchantman had been torpedoed by the circling U-boats. ***Drumheller*** was sent to rescue the fifteen survivors. This had just been accomplished when at first light the bridge watch noted a *Sunderland* aircraft on patrol several miles on the convoy's starboard side. Then ***Drumheller's*** lookouts reported the aircraft circling low over the water about six miles away. The OOW, the ship's 1st Lt, K.B. Culley, RCNVR, altered toward and called the captain just as the plane signalled ***Drumheller*** by lamp that she was over a submarine. The ship hastened toward the *Sunderland*, which was hotly engaged in a running gun battle with the aggressive U-boat, the lumbering *Sunderland* keeping its distance. Lt Denny ("a cool type" according to Culley) told him "Don't ring action stations. Have the pipe made 'Action stations bell will be in five minutes time.'"[1] That pipe brought all the crew to their stations just as quickly without the unnerving shock of being awakened by the clamour of the loud bell.

The U-boat's crew was so busy trying to shoot down the *Sunderland* that they didn't notice the approaching corvette. As Lt Culley reported, "the air was full of tracer... We opened fire at a relatively short range, about 400 yards, and, as soon as we started shooting, he dived." Taking on an aircraft with the U-boat's substantially augmented anti-aircraft guns was one thing but a warship's 4-inch gun was quite another. As a result of the ship's report to her senior officer of C-2 Group, the *Sunderland,* of the RCAF's 423 Squadron, had been joined by a *Swordfish* aircraft from ***Biter.*** These aircraft pounded the U-boat as she went under and dropped depth charges, circling as ***Drumheller*** arrived to prosecute the attack with heavier weapons and more depth charges.

Almost at once ***Drumheller*** picked up a strong asdic contact, altered course to the bearing and dropped a shallow pattern of ten depth charges. After this attack the asdic 1st operator reported he was still in contact, with the submarine moving slowly as the ship circled for another attack, even though her steering was somewhat damaged by the first explosions.

At this point the RN frigate HMS ***Lagan***, also from C-2, arrived on the scene to add her weight. ***Drumheller***, because she had the firm contact, conned ***Lagan*** over the target so she could quietly attack with her more effective ahead-throwing hedgehog weapon. ***Lagan*** fired one salvo, and the ships circled as the twenty-four bombs sank. There was the dull thud of an explosion, a hump in the water, and moments later a roiling of oil, air and debris broke surface. It had only required one direct hit. The ships collected some samples of the debris and oil, assessed the U-boat as sunk, the Sunderland and the *Swordfish* left, and ***Drumheller*** and ***Lagan*** rejoined their convoy.

Their target had been the Type VIIC ***U 753***, KK Alfred Manhardt von Mannstein. Operating as part of the III Flottille out of La Pallice in western France, Mannstein had commanded her for about a year and a half, with only modest success. He had sunk one 7,200 and one 6,600-tonner on his own, and given the *coup de grâce* to another 6,600 ton ship already hit by two acoustic torpedoes from another U-boat in February of 1943. The official RCAF history notes that ***U 753*** (although it refers to her as ***U 456***) had already been somewhat damaged by a *Liberator* of No. 86 Squadron when 423's *Sunderland*, commanded by F/L John Musgrave, RCAF, spotted her. There were no survivors from ***Drumheller's*** and ***Lagan's*** attack.

It was to be ***Lagan's*** first of two U-boats in two days, for she and HMS ***Broadway*** sank ***U 89*** the next day, the 14th. Sadly, within four months, ***Lagan's*** stern was to be blown off by one of the first acoustic torpedoes, although she survived to be towed home. Lt Culley, ***Drumheller's*** XO, had been ***Oakville's*** 1st lieutenant when she sank ***U 94*** in August, 1942. While Denny received no award for this neat attack, he did receive a DSC when in command of the larger Castle class corvette ***St Thomas*** when she and ***Sea Cliff*** sank ***U 877*** (see Chapter 57).

After a refit to extend her forecastle, ***Drumheller*** returned to serve in Operation Neptune in support of the invasion convoys, working out of Greenock, Portsmouth and the Thames. She returned to Canada in mid-May, 1945, was paid off on July 11th at Sydney, NS, but not broken up until 1949 in Hamilton, ON.

There has been considerable confusion over which U-boat was sunk by ***Drumheller*** and ***Lagan***, with some texts crediting them with the wrong U-boat. Several sources show ***U 753*** as lost due to "unknown causes". But in recent postwar research by the RN's historical section and examination of German radio logs and U-boat orders, it seems the ships' target was certainly ***U 753.*** With no named debris or prisoners to indicate a particular U-boat, it was often hard to tell with certainty which U-boat had been despatched, even if the interception staff at Bletchley Park knew some U-boats were sunk.

And it was an early example of excellent cooperation between aircraft of the RCAF and of the Fleet Air Arm, an RCN corvette and an RN frigate. It had not always been so. This cooperation was to herald a vast improvement in the forces' success rates over the U-boats in the next year.

SOURCES:

German, *The Sea Is At Our Gates,* p. 141.

Greenhous, Harris et al, *The Crucible Of War*, Vol.III (official RCAF history), p. 402.

Johnston, *Corvettes Canada*, p. 203.

Keatts, *Field Guide To Sunken U-Boats,* p. 65.

Macpherson & Burgess, *Ships of Canada's Naval Forces*, pp. 75, 131-132.

Macpherson & Milner, *Corvettes of the RCN,* pp. 61, 78, 99.

Milner, North *Atlantic Run*, pp. 125, 170, 240.

Paquette & Bainbridge, *Honours & Awards*, p. 141.

Rohwer, *Axis Submarine Successes*, pp. 97-99, 150, 166.

Schull, *Far Distant Ships*, pp. 172, 174-175.

There are four oil paintings by Tom Wood in the Canadian War Museum's collection showing scenes on board HMCS ***Drumheller*** about this time.

1. Correspondence with Lt Culley, 1995.

CHAPTER 29

THE LOSS OF HMCS ST. CROIX: A NEW WEAPON SINKS AN OLD BUT SUCCESSFUL SHIP

St. Croix:
(See Chapter 12)

Fate: Torpedoed by *U 305*, mid-Atlantic, 20 Sep 43

Casualties: 147, 1 RN; 1 survivor

II B. 105.) b) The attack should be carried out with indomitable resolution and steadfastness, until final success, resulting in annihilation of the enemy, has been achieved.

E.J. Coates, U-Boat Commander's Handbook

HMCS *St. Croix* in June, 1942, little modified from her USN days, with only the removal of one set of torpedo tubes and the addition of depth charges.

The story of the sinking of ***St. Croix*** involves a much larger battle that included three escort groups, two large convoys and one of the largest and best equipped groups of U-boats that the Germans had ever assembled. It was also the harbinger of a new BdU policy, to attack escorts as much as merchantmen. In September 1943 ***St. Croix*** was with Mid-Ocean Escort Group C-9, comprised of another of the ex-USN "four-stackers" ***St. Francis*** and the veteran corvettes ***Chambly, Morden*** and ***Sackville,*** plus the RN frigate HMS ***Itchen*** with A/Cdr C.E. Bridgman, DSO RNR, as SO.

The German wolf packs had found the Atlantic battle turning against them and by March 1943 were suffering unacceptable losses. They had rapidly been withdrawn from this theatre of operations until, in August, only four ships of less than 26,000 tons had fallen to U-boats in the whole North Atlantic. Their own losses had continued: in three months, June, July and August of 1943, seventy-nine U-boats had been destroyed.

But by the end of August a large number of submarines had been re-equipped and were ready to return to the convoy areas. Many were now fitted with the *wanze* radar detectors, a radar decoy called *Aphrodite* and additional anti-aircraft power to combat the Allies' escort carrier threat. They also carried an important new weapon, the T-5 or *Zaunkönig* torpedo which homed in on the sounds from the propellers of ships. The Allies were to call this torpedo by the acronym GNAT (for German Naval Acoustic Torpedo). As well, new BdU tactics called for the sinking of escort ships, then exploiting the resulting gaps in the screen.

St Croix, commanded by LCdr A.H. Dobson, DSC, RCNR, with C-9 was heading for the Biscay area when British intelligence became aware of German intentions to return in force to the main convoy routes. Two large west-bound convoys were assessed as their target. The faster one, ON-202 of forty-two ships, was overtaking a slower one, ONS-18 of twenty-seven merchantmen and a merchant aircraft carrier (MAC ship). These convoys were already under the protection of Escort Groups C-2 (Canadian) and B-2 (British) but additional escorts were felt required, so C-9 was ordered to assist.

The threat was very real. Grossadmiral Dönitz, the new commander of the German naval forces had gathered twenty-two U-boats from his Biscay bases and an additional six from Norway and Germany. Nine of these boats were equipped with the T-5 homing torpedoes. Designated *Gruppe Leuthen* this large pack was manoeuvring to place itself in the path of the converging convoys, of which they were well aware from their B.Dienst intelligence section reports.

The convoys were ordered by the Western Approaches operations section to join together in one very large group. The combined escort force amounted to fifteen warships, with Cdr Evans, RN in the destroyer HMS ***Keppel*** as senior officer.

On 19 September, before the main battle began, a *Liberator* of RCAF's 10 Squadron, operating out of Reykjavik, Iceland but on her way to Gander, Newfoundland, sank ***U 341*** some miles away from the convoys, confirming the wolf pack was indeed gathering.

The first blow was struck by KL Paul-Friederich Otto in ***U 270*** when he torpedoed the RN frigate ***Lagan*** in the early hours of 20 September. ***Lagan*** was eventually towed into port but ***U 238***, as foreseen, took advantage of the reduction in the escort screen and torpedoed the American merchant ships ***Theodore Dwight Weld*** and ***Frederick Douglas***. The former sank, the latter was later finished off by ***U 645***.

In the daylight hours of the 20th the weather cleared sufficiently for more RAF *Liberators* from Iceland to provide air cover. An aircraft of 120 Squadron sank ***U 338***. This latter boat had sunk five merchantmen in attacks in March on convoy SC-122. Also in the wolf pack now was ***U 305***, KL Rudolph Barr, who had also gone against SC-122, sinking two British ships.

Then at 2151 on the 20th Barr put two T-5 torpedoes into ***St. Croix***, hitting her near her propellers. The destroyer did not sink immediately and German records show that it was an hour later that Barr fired a third torpedo at her. The resulting explosion caused ***St. Croix*** to sink within three minutes. Her commanding officer and a number of her ship's company were lost in the sinking, but many of the crew were in the water looking for possible rescue.

Two RN ships from the escort force rushed to the area, now astern of the convoy, to see what had taken place and could be done. The frigate ***Itchen*** signalling to B-2:

"***ST. CROIX*** TORPEDOED AND BLOWN UP. FORECASTLE STILL AFLOAT. SURVIVORS IN RAFTS AND BOATS. TORPEDOES FIRED AT ME. DOING FULL SPEED IN VICINITY. WILL NOT ATTEMPT TO P.U. SURVIVORS UNTIL ***POLYANTHUS*** ARRIVES."

But the RN escort corvette ***Polyanthus,*** was herself torpedoed by ***U 952*** just after midnight, again in the stern by a GNAT. ***Itchen*** then had to become involved in attempting to locate the attacking U-boat. She was only later able to locate one survivor of ***Polyanthus*** in the dark, SLt Atkins, then looked for ***St. Croix*** survivors. She was joined by the Canadian corvette ***Sackville***. With ***Itchen's*** asdic now unserviceable, she was left as a rescue ship, but ***Sackville*** was told to rejoin the convoy screen. ***Itchen*** was eventually able to pick up eighty-one ***St. Croix*** survivors, five officers and seventy-six ratings, but only after they had been in the very cold water for thirteen hours. Most of those lost had perished in the sea after abandoning the ship. The next morning the RN corvette ***Narcissus*** and ***Itchen*** still searched and found some men from ***St. Croix*** on two floats and in a half-sunk whaler.

Throughout the 21st and 22nd six of the U-boat pack continued to fire GNATs at the convoy and escorts. Two U-boats, ***U 377*** and ***U 270,*** were damaged in counter attacks and had to withdraw. Two torpedoes exploded near ***Chambly*** and ***Morden*** but did no serious damage. None of the others made a kill, although many hits were reported by the submarines in subsequent reports. German torpedoes were usually set to explode at the end of their runs if they hit nothing, and this was quite often reported by the firing U-boat as a hit. The escort was able to retaliate when ***Keppel*** sank ***U 229.***

For the survivors of ***St. Croix*** and the single ***Polyanthus*** crewman the few hours of rescue

The RN corvette HMS *Polyanthus,* the second victim, sunk just after *St. Croix,* with a single survivor.

came to a bitter end at approximately 0200 on the 23rd as ***U 666***, again using a GNAT, sank ***Itchen*** in her turn. This time there were but three survivors, two from ***Itchen*** and Stoker W. Fisher from ***St. Croix***. They were rescued because the Polish merchantman ***Wisla***, Captain Kazimierz Lipski, Master, courageously stopped to pluck them from the ocean. One of those lost was Surg Lt W.L.M. King, RCNVR, the Prime Minister's nephew, who had been serving in ***St. Croix***. It was the second time ***Wisla*** had rescued Canadian naval survivors. She had picked up seamen when HMCS ***Otter*** burned and sank off Halifax in March, 1941. (See Chapter 6)

Two hours later ***U 238*** sank three merchantmen, and at 0800 ***U 952*** another. The acoustic torpedo had proved to be a very effective weapon in this initial surprise use. Three escorts were sunk and one damaged beyond repair. This contributed to allowing the pack to sink six merchantmen. The attacking force lost three U-boats, one of them to an aircraft far from the convoy itself. For BdU it was, after results had been analyzed, not as devastating a victory as hoped for; for the Allies, while it was about "honours even", the attacks on the escorts had been a nasty, although not entirely unexpected shock.

Many of the torpedoes that were fired had exploded prematurely or in the wake of the escort ships. The U-boats dived immediately after firing so that the torpedo would not home in on their own propellers. The boats heard explosions and as a result made grossly inflated claims of success.

British intelligence had anticipated an acoustic homing torpedo and were able to have a counter to it fitted to some ships within seventeen days. The RN's "Foxer" had some tactical problems and was somewhat complicated compared to the Canadian-produced simple CAT gear that was just as effective. These devices limited the ability of the Germans to exploit their new torpedoes to their full extent. These towed noise-makers were not an unalloyed boon, as they were necessarily noisy and masked the ship's asdic reception. Thus the ships were sometimes reluctant to activate them, and a few suffered torpedo hits as a result.

St. Croix had distinguished herself in the earlier days of the Atlantic campaign. Her two U-boat kills are described in Chapters 12 and 26. Of the elderly ex-American destroyers acquired by Canada, she was certainly the most successful.

The RN frigate *Itchen,* shown in 1943, the third ship of the trio of escorts lost to acoustic torpedoes in this action of September, 1943.

1944

The RCN pounds U-boats and
surface ships alike:
19 successful actions,
tempered by eight losses.

CHAPTER 32

HMCS CAMROSE AND HMS BAYNTUN GET U 757

This submarine menace is truly a terrible one for British commerce... for no means can be suggested at present of meeting it except by reprisals.

Admiral of the Fleet Lord Fisher , *Records*, 1919

Camrose: Flower class corvette
Builder: Marine Industries Ltd, Sorel, PQ
Comm: 30 Jun 41
Crew: 6 officers, 79 crew
HMS *Bayntun:* Captain class frigate
Builder: US Navy Yard, Boston Mass, 1942

Action: Sank *U 757*, mid-Atlantic, 8 Jan 44
Casualties: 49
No survivors

HMCS *Camrose* in November, 1943. A fine view of a modernized corvette with her extended forecastle.

This action is only briefly covered in occasional texts, yet it was a very creditable example of a cooperative effort between two COs who did not know each other or their operating methods. Each, by this stage in the Atlantic war, knew his job almost to perfection.

This was certainly true of Lt Louis Raymond Pavillard, RCNR, forever known in naval circles as "Pavillard the Mad Spaniard" (though now no one is quite sure why).

Camrose worked up at Halifax in the summer of 1941, then joined the Newfoundland Escort Force in EG-15, escorting convoys to Iceland, followed by a refit at Lunenburg late in the winter. In June, 1942, she made one escort round trip to Londonderry, then was assigned to Western Local Escort until October when she went to the UK for escort duties connected with the North African invasion. In April, 1943 she was taken in hand at Pictou, NS for modernization and forecastle extension. Assigned now to EG-6 she returned to Londonderry, for the most part on convoy work to Gibraltar and Freetown, West Africa.

She sailed from Londonderry on 5 January, 1944 with her group for operations in the Bay of Biscay. There they encountered fifty-two German survivors from a blockade-runner that had been sunk by RAF and RCAF aircraft of Coastal Command on 29 December. The corvettes ***Camrose, Snowberry*** and ***Edmundston*** took on these survivors to transport them to Britain and captivity, while the group's frigates continued with their support role. Returning to join EG-6, ***Camrose*** and the other corvettes were acting in support of outbound combined convoy OS-64/KMS-38, joined now by a British group, B-4, which included the Captains class frigate

Bayntun. These ships were very similar to the Canadian River class frigates, although a few feet smaller and three knots faster due to diesel electric propulsion versus the Canadians' steam triple expansion engines. Pavillard in ***Camrose*** was senior officer, standing in for the CO of HMCS ***Nene,*** the group's normal SO, as the latter had departed for the UK with fifty-two survivors of the RN frigate HMS ***Tweed,*** torpedoed on the 7th. B-4 had joined EG-6 under its orders, although Pavillard later commented that the RN group probably didn't realise that the normal senior officer was not present.

Well out in the Atlantic, at the end of the afternoon of 8 January, ***Bayntun*** gained a radar contact at four and a half miles, reported this, altered toward, and sighted a surfaced U-boat which then dived. ***Camrose*** had by this time reached the scene where the two ships attacked the contact with depth charges, while ***Edmundston*** and ***Snowberry*** carried out Operation Observant around the periphery in case their target should attempt to slip away from her tormentors. ***Waskesiu*** of EG-6 and the rest of B-4 Group were left to shepherd the convoy out of harm's way.

The attacks went on sporadically for two hours, five by ***Camrose***, three by ***Bayntun***, the last two (one each) on doubtful contacts. Lt Pavillard was helped by having on board the group anti-submarine officer to help assess the attacks. At this point ***Bayntun*** heard sounds as if the U-boat was trying to blow her ballast tanks. Soon a flood of oil was seen on the surface, plus some debris and wreckage including a German seaman's cap.

With sufficient escorts available for the convoy, ***Camrose*** and ***Snowberry*** searched around the area until 1000 the next day. Finding nothing further, they departed to join the others, satisfied that the U-boat had been sunk as they claimed, or at least damaged enough to be no further threat to the convoys.

Later, on March 30th, it was assessed by the Canadian Director of Warfare and Training/Tactics that:

"1. HMS ***Bayntun*** was almost too diffident and careful not to get in HMCS ***Camrose's*** way; but this is more of a virtue than a fault.

2. ***Bayntun's*** first attack caused no damage.

3. ***Camrose's*** first was fairly accurate. The U-boat was assessed as 'deep', but probably not as deep as the depth charge patterns were set.

4. ***Camrose's*** 4th attack was a good one."

It was later determined by the Assessment Committee that their U-boat was severely damaged, if not destroyed. In fact they had indeed destroyed the Type VIIC ***U 757***, KL Friedrich Deetz and his forty-four crew, operating out of St. Nazaire with VI Flottille. Under Deetz this submarine had sunk two ships in Convoy HX-228 in March 1943 and added a third victim in August 1943.

HMS *Bayntun,* built for the USN as a small *Evarts* class destroyer escort. Returned to the USN at the war's end.

Camrose had already come close to success a year earlier when, early on 7 February, 1943, bombers operating in support of the group had dropped flares exposing a U-boat on the surface. ***Camrose*** had on board 129 survivors from two merchant ships that had been sunk. On sighting the U-boat, Pavillard altered to ram but due to the submarine turning at the last moment, only managed to scrape along her side. AB Jack Hannam was in the magazine and remembers the crashing sound along his ship's hull. ***Camrose*** dropped a depth charge pattern and Hannam also remembers that some of the survivors assisted the depth charge party in hoisting the heavy charges by hand from the magazine. The submarine, likely an Italian, was assessed as "probably damaged." The action was not helped when the 4-inch gun was loaded with a day charge which created temporary night blindness on the bridge when it was fired.

Within a few days of the January 1944 attack, the corvettes, including ***Camrose***, were withdrawn from the support escort groups, being replaced by the larger and faster frigates. In February she joined EG-17 for invasion escort duties, followed by another Pictou refit, and in January to Plymouth again for duty with EG-41 until VE Day, when she was one of the first vessels into St. Helier in the Channel Islands for their relief. Returning to Canada, she was paid off in June of 1945, and broken up at Hamilton in 1947.

"The Mad Spaniard" was awarded a DSC for his efforts against ***U 757***, but not until mid-December, 1944, and the citation only referred to "attacking a U-boat".

SOURCES:

Johnston, *Corvettes Canada*, p. 233.

Macpherson & Burgess, *Ships of Canada's Naval Forces*, pp. 72, 191.

Rohwer, *Axis Submarine Successes*, pp. 156, 171.

Schull, *Far Distant Ships*, p. 217.

Tarrant, *The U-Boat Offensive*, p. 143.

CHAPTER 33

HMCS WASKESIU SINKS U 257: AND IS RARELY MENTIONED

Neat, not gaudy

Charles Lamb, 1806

Waskesiu: River class frigate
Builder: Yarrows Ltd, Esquimalt, BC
Comm: 16 Jun 43
Crew: 8 officers, 133 crew

Action: Sank *U 257*, mid-Atlantic, 24 Feb 44
Casualties: 30
19 survivors

Waskesiu in 1944, typical of the hard-worked frigates of the day. Note the unusual provision of mine-sweeping davits aft in connection with potential requirements for the Normany landings.

The name ***Waskesiu,*** was adopted in lieu of the actual name for the city of Prince Albert, Saskatchewan as there was already an RN ship of that name. HMCS ***Waskesiu*** was the first Canadian-built frigate commissioned. This "new breed" of anti-submarine escort ship represented a major advance over the doughty corvettes in speed (by three to four knots); asdic capability, with the most modern set coupled to the type 147 depth predictor set; and two and a half times the number of depth charges. While the corvettes and the hard-worn destroyers had held the bridge during the early and desperate convoy battles, these frigates and the squid-equipped Castle class corvettes effectively ended the hopes of Dönitz for at least a stalemate with the new classes of U-boats and their increased effectiveness and weapons. These frigates could remain away from their convoy charges while hunting U-boats and yet catch up again, unlike the corvettes that on occasion were left far behind for days, or had to give up even promising hunts in order to regain their vital station with a convoy. As well, the numbers of the new frigates in late 1943 and 1944 allowed for the formation of roving support groups ancillary to the close escorts, with speed, weaponry and flexibility to hunt their quarries to exhaustion. The new generations of U-boats would have posed a serious problem even for these ships, but they were too few, too late.

Waskesiu came around from the west coast to Halifax in July, 1943, completed work-ups at Bermuda and sailed for Londonderry with EG-5 in October. She was largely employed in UK waters with out- and in-bound convoys and in escort duties to Gibraltar and Sierra Leone. While she had hunted a suspected U-boat in December 1943, she had no successes to her credit.

Convoy SC-153 of thirty-two merchant ships had sailed from Sydney in early February, 1944, supported by C-5 escort group (led by the second HMCS ***Ottawa***) and the British escort group EG-3. ***Waskesiu's*** EG-6 (the group was renumbered in November, 1943) had sailed from Londonderry on 7 February after a day of intensive exercises and practices, and conducted a variety of A/S hunts and support duties into the Bay of Biscay. In very rough weather the group's corvettes had returned to Londonderry for fuel, while ***Waskesiu*** and HMS ***Nene*** (Cdr J.D. Birch, RNR as senior officer) joined SC-153 in support as they moved toward the UK just east of mid-ocean. This convoy had the startlingly large escort protection of five destroyers, four frigates, eleven Captains class frigates, four corvettes, two A/S trawlers and one rescue tug. It was literally surrounded by escorts.

On 24 February, at a few minutes after 0200 on a very dark morning in poor visibility and moderate seas, ***Waskesiu's*** asdic 1st operator, PO M.J.T. Fortune, reported a possible submarine contact. Her ASCO confirmed the target and a series of attacks were made. Her CO, LCdr James P. Fraser, RCNR (ex-RCMP Marine Division) had been in command for only nineteen days. Following current doctrine, he elected to try a slow speed deliberate hedgehog attack first. This was about half an hour after initial contact. Asdic contact was lost at 400 yards, indicating a deep submarine, and there was no explosion from the hedgehog attack. (Unlike depth charges, one of the twenty-four bomb salvo needed to strike the target to detonate). A flare was dropped when "over by plot" to mark a datum for the next attack. Fraser then opened out to 1,000 yards, increased speed to fifteen knots, altered back and, without an asdic contact, dropped one depth charge to keep the U-boat unsettled and on the defensive. He reduced to ten knots, regained contact on the U-boat now heading south and at 0226 increased to fifteen knots for a full pattern attack, losing contact at 350 yards. With a bold attack-course throw-off, Fraser later estimated he had dropped the pattern well ahead of his target but shaken it severely. He then hunted around the area at various speeds, regained a contact at 1,500 yards and made another full ten charge attack on a target assessed as moderately deep–around 300 feet. Contact was then lost again for half an hour. Using the flare still burning on the surface, Fraser carried out a box search Operation Observant. At 0327 contact was regained at 1,600 yards and Fraser set up another attack, at first for 400 feet, then at 350 feet as they closed. Cdr Bush in ***Nene,*** hastening to join the hunt, ordered Fraser to delay his next attack until ***Nene*** joined and could gain contact as well. Those in the slowly circling ***Waskesiu*** could now see a faint oil slick even in the dark and noted a strong smell of oil when they searched about four miles north of their last attack. All this was progressing at such a controlled and leisurely pace that the engineer officer, not feeling he was required in the engine room, played solitaire in the wardroom.

At 0410 a firm contact was regained with ***Waskesiu*** idling along at only five knots on a target moving slowly ENE and apparently very deep, for contact was lost at 750 yards, regained at 800 yards. (For deep submarines, the distance in yards at which a target was lost as it passed under the asdic beam was roughly equivalent to its depth in feet). ***Nene*** ordered Fraser to hold contact but suggested they wait until dawn. Then, when she also gained contact, her staff officer A/S (a "Long Course" A/S specialist) classified their contact as "non-sub" and Bush ordered ***Waskesiu*** to abandon the unproductive hunt and rejoin their convoy.

But Fraser still trusted his asdic team's judgement, backed by his navigator, Lt Williams who was keeping the plot. Fraser asked Cdr Bush's permission to make one more attack. Bush agreed. The plot suggested the U-boat's course as 092°, the ship increased to ten knots and set a depth charge pattern for J, very deep. This was quickly changed to G and speed increased when contact was held until 350 yards, indicating the submarine had come up several hundred feet, and the ten charge pattern dropped accurately.

As the ship opened out from the explosions, at 1,400 yards a submarine blowing tanks could suddenly be heard plus submarine motor hydrophone effect The CO was confident enough of success that he secured the hedgehog mounting and cautioned the gun armament to

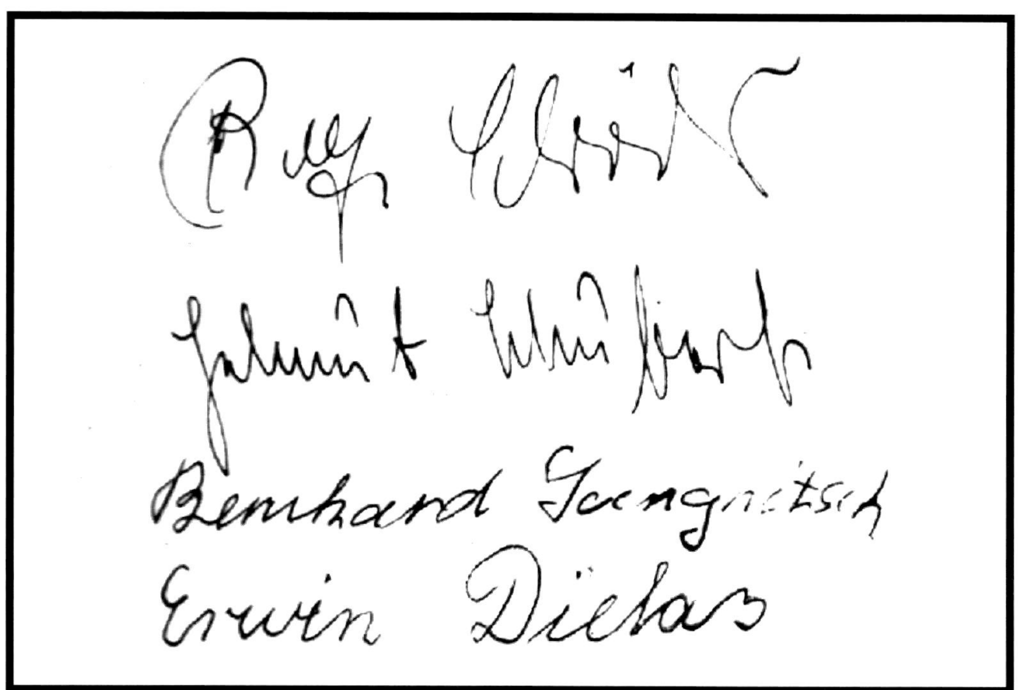

Autographs of four *U 257* survivors collected by AB Gordon Arnold, RCNVR of HMCS *Waskesiu* on 24 February, 1944.

be prepared for surface action.[1] Then, at 0550, a surface radar contact was gained, 285°, 1,800 yards, fifteen degrees on ***Waskesiu's*** port bow. This was illuminated by starshell and there was the U-boat on the surface, leading to the coded TBS message to ***Nene:*** "HEARSE PARKED".

Waskesiu at once closed this target and opened fire with both of her 4-inch guns and her Oerlikons and, as they closed, even the two Bren guns from the bridge locker which got off 170 rounds. As well another rating fired a burst from a machine gun from beside the hedgehog mounting on the forecastle. ***Waskesiu***, in a flurry of belligerence, fired nineteen starshell rounds and thirteen high-explosive direct-action fused shells (HE-DA); the Oerlikons 406 rounds. Fraser claims the first HE rounds from his 4-inch guns hit "dead centre on the conning tower" and that AB Thomas Stephenson on No. 1 Oerlikon "never wasted a cartridge." The ship's gunnery officer was Lt G. Peter Nares, RCNVR, who had been ***Ville de Québec's*** gunnery officer when she had bagged ***U 224*** in the Mediterranean in January, 1943. The submarine crossed ***Waskesiu's*** bows about 100 yards away, and passed slowly down her port side, now also illuminated by searchlight with the frigate unable to alter around fast enough to ram her as was Fraser's initial intention.

On receipt of ***Waskesiu's*** startling message, ***Nene*** of course turned back, just in time to get off a few rounds. Her CO admitted in his reports that they were "just spectators in that one." The U-boat sank vertically, stern first, about fifteen minutes after surfacing, leaving survivors struggling in the bitterly cold Atlantic in heavy swells and sea. The ships lowered their whalers to rescue whom they could, with cries in the still dark night from the submariners "Hallo - Hallo - Kamerad" who were also blowing shrill lifejacket whistles. It was difficult to locate them in the dark and broken seas and ***Waskesiu*** took aboard only four over the ship's stern. Her whaler had broken two oars when it was lowered into the surging sea and the crew considered themselves fortunate to be rescued themselves. ***Nene*** was able to rescue only another 15, even utilising the ship's searchlights. As a bit of a needle, when the two ships later rejoined Convoy SC-153 whose escorts had been able to follow the progress of the battle by radio, one irreverent escort asked ***Nene*** if she had "any 'non-sub' prisoners aboard."

1. Notes and diary kept by AB George Devonshire, a rating on the hedgehog mounting.

In typical Canadian fashion, the prisoners in ***Waskesiu*** were treated more as distressed mariners after their rescue than dangerous *Kriegsmarine* warriors. The next morning AB J.G. Arnold obtained their autographs when he took them some hot chocolate. One crew member asked the captain if the survivors could come down to their mess deck to listen to the radio, and each went ashore later in England in new clean survivors' clothing provided from a stock in ***Waskesiu.***

The rescue operation was all over by 0852, seven hours and fifteen minutes after first contact. There was only one officer rescued, LtzS. Waldmar Nickel, the 2nd watch officer, newly joined and "a real Nazi type". In addition to five chiefs and POs and twelve other crew of the U-boat, they rescued one seaman who had been a survivor of the U-boat tanker supply ship ***Charlotte Schliemann*** and of ***U 178.***

U 257 of II U-Flottille from Lorient, France (and ex-III Flottille of La Pallice), had commissioned in January, 1942, and sailed on this, her fifth patrol, from St. Nazaire at 1500 on 2 January, 1944, under KL Heinz Rahe. She had no successes recorded for her previous patrols in the Atlantic and in the Gulf of Guinea, nor on this one, although she had seen convoys she could not catch. In fact neither Rahe himself nor ***U 257*** appear to have ever fired a torpedo at a target. On her first patrol she had been damaged in a *Sunderland* attack and hunted by a destroyer which did not damage her further.

U 257 was to have rendezvoused with a blockade-runner to pass that ship charts but the ship had been sunk by the time the U-boat arrived at the rendezvous. By 23 February she was homeward bound. At 2300 her Naxos radar detector warned of the presence of ***Waskesiu*** and Rahe dived. ***Waskesiu's*** first single depth charge was fairly close but didn't damage the boat. He went deeper, received some damage in subsequent attacks, decided to surface, heard H.E. and went deep again. In the last attack the pattern was very close, damaging the main motors and causing uncontrolled leaks in the outboard vents in the control room and the diesel engine room. Rahe ordered the boat surfaced. It was the feeling of the survivors that he deliberately went down with his U-boat, as he threw his lifejacket and one-man dinghy to men in the water and re-entered the boat.

The rest of the trip for the convoy was uneventful. ***Waskesiu*** and ***Nene*** detached on the morning of the 28th to land their prisoners at Londonderry. The crew were told to keep quiet about the sinking and not exhibit any cockiness, as some RN ships had sunk more U-boats than the whole RCN!

LCdr Fraser was awarded a DSC as was the 1st lieutenant, Lt J.H. Lincoln, RCNVR. AB Stephenson was awarded a DSM as was AB J.H. Rickard and AB B.M. Stoner. Mentions in Despatches went to four others of the crew.

Waskesiu continued her escorting duties for the remainder of the war, including one Murmansk convoy. In June, 1945 she arrived in Esquimalt for tropicalization for the Pacific war, which ended before anything was done. Towed to Vancouver for disposal, she was sold locally then passed to the India Supply Mission, her conversion overseen by German & Milne of Montreal. She became the Hooghly River pilot vessel ***Hooghly*** in 1949. Her bell was presented to Prince Albert in October, 1946.

SOURCES:

Note: This is another case of almost no mention of the above action except a line or two. The cover painting by Bo Hermanson is of this action between ***Waskesiu, Nene*** and ***U 257***, taken accurately from crew descriptions and LCdr Fraser's reports.

Lawrence, *Tales of the North Atlantic*, p. 161.

Macpherson, *Frigates of the RCN,* pp. 53-54.

Macpherson & Burgess, *Ships of Canada's Naval Forces*, pp. 54, 202, 230.

Milner, *The U-Boat Hunters*, pp. 114-115.

CHAPTER 34

THE HUNT TO EXHAUSTION OF U 744. C-2 SUPPORT GROUP SHOWS VETERAN'S SKILLS

The fundamental object in all military combinations is to gain local superiority by concentration.

Captain A.T. Mahan, USN *Naval Strategy*, 1911

Chaudiere: River class destroyer
Builder: Vickers-Armstrong Ltd, Barrow UK
1st Comm: as HMS *Hero*, 1935
2nd Comm: 20 Mar 43
Gatineau: River class destroyer
Builder: Swan Hunter & Wigham Richardson, UK
1st Comm: as HMS *Express*, 1934
2nd Comm: 3 Mar 43
Crew: 10 officers, 171 crew
St. Catharines: River class frigate
Builder: Yarrows Ltd, Esquimalt, BC
Comm: 31 Jul 43
Crew: 8 officers, 133 crew
Fennel: Flower class corvette
Builder: Marine Industries Ltd, Sorel PQ
Comm: 15 May 41
Crew: 6 officers, 79 crew
Chilliwack: Flower class corvette
Builder: Burrard Dry Dock Co, Vancouver
Comm: 8 Apr 41
Crew: 6 officers, 79 crew
HMS *Icarus*: RN destroyer
Comm: 1937
HMS *Kenilworth Castle*: RN Castle class corvette
Comm: 1944

Action: Sank *U 744*, Atlantic, 6 Mar 44
Casualties: 12; 39 survivors

The destruction of ***U 744*** was an event that, with hindsight, can be seen as one of the continuing signals that the tide was finally turning to favour the hunted over the hunter in the Battle of the Atlantic.

The participants were now veterans. The number of warships available allowed the close escorts to continue to protect their convoys while the so-called "support groups" settled to the task of remaining in contact with a located

HMCS *Gatineau* in 1943.

The frigate *St. Catharines.*

submarine until it could no longer remain submerged or was sunk. The mixed RCN and RN groups were working together comfortably. Tactics had been developed so that each commanding officer could fit into the team without excessive direction by the senior officer.

One of those commanding officers was A/LCdr C. Patrick Nixon, RCN, commanding ***Chaudière.*** That destroyer had seen service as HMS ***Hero,*** with ***U 50*** and ***U 568*** to her credit before acquisition by the RCN. In late 1942, with more trained officers and seamen now available, the Canadian War Cabinet had requested additional destroyers for escort duties from the Admiralty. With Canada assigning her four new Tribal class destroyers to fleet operations in UK waters, the British were receptive to the Canadian request.

Six older fleet destroyers were modified for escort duties and by the fall of 1943 had all been commissioned into the RCN. Two had been assigned to the C-2 (Canadian) Support Group, ***Chaudière*** and ***Gatineau,*** the latter commanded by LCdr H.V.W. Groos, RCN. Cdr P.W. Burnett, RN, was the senior officer, riding in the RCN frigate ***St. Catharines*** (LCdr A.F. Pickard). Normally the other members of the group were the Canadian corvettes ***Fennel*** and ***Sackville***, and the British destroyer HMS ***Icarus.***

In March, 1944 the group was in the fourth and last week of supporting convoys north of the Azores. The greatest excitement up to that point had been when the group had passed an American aircraft carrier and her four protective destroyers. USS ***Cory*** mistook ***Chaudière*** for a surfaced submarine and in misplaced zeal fired over 100 rounds of 5-inch ammunition before discovering that her target was an Allied ship. (See Chapter 60 for another instance of more tragic mistaken identity, involving HMCS ***Trentonian***).

HMCS *Chilliwack* in fine form with her extended forecastle, at the end of the war. She helped sink two U-boats.

On the morning of 5 March, C-2 was augmenting the close escort of Convoy HX-280 in a screen five miles ahead of it, eastbound to the UK. The weather was clear and, for the North Atlantic, calm with the first warmth of spring in the air. However the Type VIIC U-boat ***U 744*** was approaching from the east, submerged for fear of air attack.

U 744 was commanded by OL Heinz Blischke. She had commissioned in 1943 and had had limited success to date. On 3 January 1944, she had finished off the already-damaged

Built for the RN, HMCS *Fennel* was taken over by the RCN. In this view looking singularly well turned-out for a 1945 period.

Empire Housman, and on 2 March had sunk the Royal Navy's ***LST 362.***

The first contact was at 1000 yards by ***Gatineau***, about to depart for Londonderry, who made one depth charge attack. ***U 744*** evaded by turning sharply and going deep. Next ***St. Catharines*** dropped a pattern of depth charges. ***Chilliwack***, temporarily replacing ***Sackville*** in the group, tried a hedgehog attack but the U-boat was too deep for the accuracy required. Continuing to hold the shifting contact, over the next five hours a series of creeping attacks were conducted by ***Chilliwack, Gatineau*** and ***Icarus***, as well as three squid attacks at about 1500 by ***Kenilworth Castle*** which had joined from the close escort B-1 Group with her valuable depth predictor 147B asdic. These attacks produced no visible results. The creeping attacks were done at slow speeds, aimed primarily at deep-running U-boats (***U 744*** was now at about 600 feet), with the attacking ship moving quietly without asdic, being controlled by another ship holding the asdic contact from a distance. ***Gatineau*** detached at 1600 to return to port with defects requiring repair.

The submariner was proving to be a competent and courageous opponent, taking advantage of the disturbed sea conditions after every attack. At one point contact was lost but soon regained. At 1640 two more attacks were made by ***Fennel*** and ***St. Catharines***. In late afternoon, ***Chaudière*** and ***Icarus*** were ordered to return to the HX convoy which was facing other U-boats, but fortunately both were able to return for the finale before dawn the next morning. As night approached there was concern that the submarine would surface and escape in the dark. In the belief that the U-boat might have fired an acoustic torpedo, occasional single charges were dropped to make her CO think he had made a hit and surface to check.

A slender contact was maintained throughout the night in worsening weather and rising seas, with the corvettes patrolling around the perimeter of the "box" in which ***St. Catharines*** held contact. Attacks commenced again at 0751. Over the next three hours ***Fennel***, then ***Icarus, Chaudière, St. Catharines*** and again ***Chaudière*** and ***Icarus*** moved in and dropped charges. For one period of half an hour contact was lost once more but, with an organized search pattern, was regained. Then it was decided, in view of the lack of success in getting depth charges close enough to the elusive U-boat, to sit on top of him until his battery was exhausted and he had no choice but to surface. It was suspected by the attackers that conditions in the U-boat must by now be almost intolerable. The boat would be running short of oxygen and the chlorine fumes, darkness, dampness and damage as well as remaining battery power would not permit her to remain submerged much longer. In fact, her engine base plate and cylinder block were cracked, the hull had sprung small leaks, and the air purifier was damaged.

At 1520 on the 6th, almost thirty hours after the first contact, their patience was rewarded. The conning tower of ***U 744*** was first seen by the corvette ***Chilliwack***, who had also joined the hunt from C-1 Group. That ship, warned by the sound of blowing ballast heard by her asdic team, immediately opened fire with her Oerlikons, 4-inch and 2-pounder pom-pom. In some excellent shooting, she hit the U-boat's conning tower with her first 4-inch round and smothered the boat with Oerlikon fire. ***Fennel*** soon joined in and the submarine was taking

Chilliwack's whaler alonside *U 744*, with its Flottille swordfish emblem, and showing the extensive shell damage.

frequent hits. Her captain was struck while standing in the conning tower. The crew made no attempt to man their guns but started jumping into the sea. Gunfire was halted. ***Chilliwack*** had intended to ram but with no return fire her CO, LCdr C.R. Coughlin, RCNVR, decided it was worth trying to board the U-boat.

Both ***Chilliwack*** and ***St. Catharines*** sent their whaler crews to try to secure code books and signal equipment from the wallowing submarine, just barely awash. The seamen got aboard and went down into the boat's control room, while Signalman John Starr hoisted a triumphant White Ensign. With their salvaged gear, when they tried to re-board their boats the sea had by now become quite rough and both whalers were capsized by the U-boat's out-thrust saddle tanks. Much valuable booty was lost.

Chaudière also lowered both her whaler and her motor cutter, and ***Fennel*** her whaler. ***Chaudière's*** whaler crew under Lt C.I. Rathgeb, RCNVR, boarded the submarine, no mean feat with the seas running, while SLt D.S. Boyle, RCN in the motor cutter rescued the crews of the capsized whalers. Rathgeb found the boat flooded, pitch black and apparently sinking. ***Chaudière*** took aboard twenty-two survivors of the U-boat, of whom thirty-nine were saved in all, plus all the RCN boats' crews also in the frigid water. Some valuable papers were also rescued. Had the weather remained calm, an attempt to tow the submarine to port might have been made but, in view of her condition, the decision was made to sink her, and ***Icarus*** did so with a torpedo.

This was an epic hunt. It took more than thirty-two hours from first contact to the end. Two hundred and ninety-one depth charges were dropped; the ships made over 1,500 signals during the action. Canadian sources have since called it the longest hunt to exhaustion, but John Tremaine, in *The U-Boat Wars* identifies the destruction of ***U 358*** by EG-1 four days earlier, on 1 March in the same general area, as the longest, at thirty-eight hours.

While the senior officer, Cdr Burnett was somewhat critical of his various ships' asdic teams' inability to assess the U-boat's movements when at 500 to 600-foot depths, he considered "the team" worked excellently to control the whole action and hold the boat. C-in-C WA, Admiral Sir Max Horton, later noted "The hunt and destruction of ***U 744*** is a classic example of anti-U-boat warfare in which the operations of the opponents were conducted by experts of their profession." The use of the plural is significant, as Sir Max, an ex-submariner himself, was not given to accepting less than perfection.

Patrick Nixon, who retired as a captain in the 1960s, still speaks with pride of his ship's company. They had been assembled "from three ships which had serious personnel troubles in UK waters", and he says "they were to say the least a mixed lot." But he concludes,

Aboard *Chaudière* after the battle: the U-boat's first watch officer, Lt Tom Pullen, the U-boat's engineer officer and *Chaudière's* medical officer.

"In over thirty years of naval service it was never my good fortune to have as shipmates a more cheerful, enterprising and loyal group of men."

Medals were awarded: among others Signalman Starr and ERA Longbottom received well-deserved DSMs. Coughlin got a DSC for ***Chilliwack's*** part; Nixon and Boyle collected Mentions in Despatches. The senior officer ordered "Splice the Mainbrace" and the group returned to Londonderry with the prisoners whose "façade of superiority" was shattered by the carefree attitude of the Canadians and the abundance of fresh bananas and pineapples (recently acquired during a fuel stop-over in the Azores.)

SOURCES:

German, *The Sea is at Our Gates,* pp. 151-153.

Lenton, *Navies of World War II.*

Milner, *The U-Boat Killers*, pp. 116-119.

C.P. Nixon, unpublished notes.

Paquette & Bainbridge, *Honours and Awards.*

Rohwer, *Axis Submarine Successes 1939-1945.*

Schull, *Far Distant Ships,* pp. 217-223.

Tremaine, *The U-Boat Wars 1916-1945,* p. 754.

Tucker, *Naval Service of Canada*, Vol.II, pp. 80-81.

CHAPTER 35

ESCORT GROUPS C-1 AND EG-9 COMBINE TO SINK U 845

By the way that he came, by the same he shall return

2 Kings, Ch.9, v.33

St. Laurent: (See Chapter 20)

Swansea: River class frigate

Builder: Yarrows Ltd, Esquimalt, BC

Comm: 4 Oct 43

Crew: 8 officers, 133 crew

Owen Sound: Increased Endurance Flower class corvette

Builder: Collingwood Shipyards, ON

Comm: 17 Nov 43

Crew: 6 officers, 79 crew

HMS *Forester*: RN destroyer

Launched: 1934

Action: Sank *U 845*, mid-Atlantic, 10 Mar 44

Casualties: 3 officers, 10 crew; 42 survivors

HMCS *St. Laurent* in mid-war camouflage colour. Often called *"Sally Rand"* by her crew and friends.

In March of 1944, while the U-boats' attacks were being contained, there were still enough of them in the open Atlantic areas to be a very real danger for the ever larger and more vital convoys still crossing to the UK in preparation for the invasion of Europe. C-1 Escort Group now consisted of HMCS ***Assiniboine*** as senior officer (Cdr John Byron, DSC and Bar, RNR) with the RN destroyer HMS ***Forester, St. Laurent*** (LCdr George Stephen), the corvettes ***Fredericton, Giffard, Halifax*** and ***Regina***, and the new frigate ***Valleyfield. St. Laurent*** had carried a major share of Canada's escort war since the first days in 1939, including involvement in one of the worst convoy battles, for ON-154 in the winter of 1942. In this battle of March, 1944, she gained a victor's laurels.

C-1 had sailed on 1 March from St. John's to undertake the mid-ocean portion of escorting the forty-ship Convoy SC-154. The group was at first shorthanded as ***Assiniboine*** had been delayed with generator problems and then trapped in St. John's by ice blocking the harbour entrance. As well, ***Halifax*** and ***Valleyfield*** were delayed with problems. By 4 March, after a storm scattered some of the convoy, all the escort group's ships had joined. Then more problems intruded, again not enemy-caused. On the 5th most of the group had fuelled from a convoy oiler, but the weather began to blow up and Cdr Byron cancelled further fuelling until the weather moderated. The convoy course could hardly be adjusted to suit the oiling convenience of the escorts. However ***Regina*** became entangled in the fuelling steadying line which fouled her propellor, jamming it stopped, and it could not be freed. There was no option but to tow the incapacitated ship to the Azores. This was started skilfully by ***St. Laurent's*** George Stephen, the two ships protected by ***Valleyfield.*** When the tow parted late that night, C-in-C WA ordered the convoy's rescue vessel

The Flower class corvette in its final form: HMCS *Owen Sound* on commissioning. An Increased Endurance corvette, she has no engineroom ventilators by her funnel, her mast behind a larger bridge and a squared-off stern.

(the motor vessel ***Dundee***) to take over the tow and, with ***Valleyfield*** still in attendance, they reached Horta. ***St. Laurent*** re-joined the convoy.

At 0410 on the 8th, HMCS ***Halifax*** reported a fire aboard the 7,700-ton Swedish motor vessel ***San Francisco***, which soon spread to her flax cargo and became uncontrollable. To prevent it reaching the bridge, the ship hove to. With no U-boats threatening just then, Cdr Byron ordered ***Halifax*** and, shortly after, ***St. Laurent*** to stand by the burning vessel and try to help; Stephen had a well-deserved reputation for dealing with just such situations as this. Two loads of heavy salvage and fire-fighting equipment were transferred from ***St. Laurent*** to the freighter by whaler in heavy seas under her 1st Lieutenant, Lt T.C. Mackay, RCN. Then the whaler was swamped trying to take over a third load and, although the men were all rescued by the ship's second whaler and Carley floats, all the gear was lost. More men and gear were

Arguably the most famous photo of the war, taken by Lt Gib Milne, RCNVR, of the frigate HMCS *Swansea* during her work-ups off Halifax in January, 1944.

transferred until there were three officers and twenty-six naval ratings aboard the merchantman. With all the equipment and help, this was enough to control and then beat back the fires.

At 1300 ***Halifax*** was ordered to rejoin the convoy escort, as Western Approaches staff suspected they were heading into a U-boat concentration. The newly formed 9th Escort Group was nearby, providing additional escorts for the fast convoy HX-280 which was ahead of SC-154. On instructions from C-in-C WA, that group was ordered to close SC-154 to augment its diminished escort protection. EG-9 consisted of the frigates ***Matane*** (Cdr A.F.C. Layard, DSO, RN as senior officer) and ***Swansea*** (LCdr Clarence King, DSO, DSC, RCNR) and the corvettes ***Owen Sound, Frontenac, North Bay*** and ***Baddeck. Owen Sound*** (A/LCdr J.M. Watson, RCNR) was sent to replace ***Halifax*** and defend the two ships following far astern of the convoy.

By 1600 ***San Francisco*** and her escort were under way again at eight knots, starting to overhaul the now-distant convoy. At 1845 ***St. Laurent*** recovered twelve men by whaler, the rest remaining to help quell the still smouldering fire in the hold. All through the night the three plodded along, not gaining much on the convoy. On the morning of the 10th ***St. Laurent's*** remaining fire party left the still smouldering cargo to the ***San Francisco's*** crew and were re-embarked. She would shortly need them aboard.

Then, at 1324, there was a report from ***St. Laurent's*** HF/DF operator of a U-boat radio transmission nearby and almost dead ahead, between her and the convoy. This was also picked up on board ***Assiniboine*** of C-1 and ***Swansea*** of EG-9. ***Forester*** was sent to search the bearing reported for twenty miles and, half an hour later, ***Assiniboine*** went out also on another HF/DF contact, both finding nothing and returning to the convoy.

St. Laurent, now about thirty miles on the convoy's port quarter, altered course slightly at 1500 to pass through the area of her first HF/DF signal, with ***Owen Sound*** and ***San Francisco*** following more slowly. At 1647, over three hours since the first report, ***St. Laurent's*** 2nd OOW and a signalman saw an object almost eight miles away and not far from the plotted HF/DF fix. It developed later that the CO of ***U 845,*** KL Werner Weber, concentrating on the convoy ahead, had surfaced to re-charge his 60% depleted batteries in preparation for a night attack on 10 March and had not noticed ***St. Laurent*** with her charges astern of him.

When the object in the distance disappeared suddenly a few minutes later, ***St. Laurent*** cracked on full speed and altered directly toward, reporting what she had observed. After several minutes, watchers saw a swirl in the water only 300 yards on her starboard bow just as the asdic team picked up a firm contact. Despite slowing down to A/S attacking speed, she was too close to set up a satisfactory attack, passed over the U-boat and opened to 1,000 yards. As she did so, Stephen directed ***Owen Sound,*** who had abandoned her charge and hastened after the destroyer, onto the target as the corvette had not yet gained contact. ***Owen Sound*** dropped a ten-charge pattern at 1657, with ***St. Laurent*** coming back in for another ten-charge attack at 1705. Asdic conditions were ideal, the submarine easily held even in the disturbance of the attacks. ***St. Laurent*** again came in for a hedgehog attack, without results. The depth charges had thrown off ***Owen Sound's*** asdic electrical breakers so ***St. Laurent*** directed her in another attack. By 1730 they had determined that their target was very deep, maybe as much as 700 feet. ***St. Laurent*** ordered ***Owen Sound*** to carry out an Operation

The destroyer HMS *Forester,* in January, 1943.

Observant square search around the area to prevent their quarry sneaking off, and tried to line up astern of the U-boat to carry out a creeping attack. By 1815 ***Forester*** had joined to relieve ***Owen Sound*** who was sent back to protect the forsaken ***San Francisco.***

St. Laurent ran through a patch of diesel oil, later found to have been released by the wily U-boat CO as a decoy. Even with ***Forester*** assisting, due to the U-boat's twisting and turning through ninety degrees on a generally northerly course and still very deep, they could not set up the creeping attack. The ships' COs were growing concerned that, with the coming of dark about 2030, a creeping attack would be more difficult to control or require lights for directing the ships. Also the submarine would have an increasingly favourable chance of escaping on the surface. So ***Forester,*** as senior officer on the scene, stopped asdic transmissions and had ***St. Laurent*** direct her over the U-boat from 1,500 yards, although Stephen still wanted to delay until the U-boat steadied on a course, as they usually did. But at 1922 ***Forester*** delivered her twenty-two charge attack, followed by ***St. Laurent's***, fired by eye just ahead of ***Forester's***.

Bubbles were seen rising to the surface and an underwater explosion was heard from ***St. Laurent's*** engine room five minutes after the last of her depth charges. Nothing was found on the surface, however. Contact was briefly lost and then regained twenty minutes later, at 2,200 yards by ***St. Laurent***, just as ***Forester*** reported her asdic was now unserviceable. They resolved to await moonlight to enable another creeping attack, meanwhile carrying out an Operation Observant holding pattern with ***St. Laurent*** still in firm contact. While a bright moon cleared the low clouds at 2130, ***Swansea*** was on the way to join them and the two resolved to hold off until her arrival. When she joined at 2205 she was assigned to the opposite side of the box from ***Forester***, still with unreliable asdic. When the U-boat finally settled on a course of 215° at two and a half knots, ***St. Laurent*** set up her creeping attack from astern in improving moonlight.

A 50th reunion of some of the survivors of *U 845* at Dolmen, Westfallen in June, 1994: (left to right) G.Klauke, E. Hennig, G. Wilske, G. Hochhuth, H. Bühnert, H. Frubrich, A. Helfers, W. Hennig, H. Kling, F. Heger, E. Torunski, R. Vaas and J. Müller.

Their plans were abruptly suspended at 2234 when the U-boat suddenly surfaced in a flurry of foam, moving at increasing speed to the southwest. Later prisoners reported that Weber had decided that he stood a better chance of escape on the surface if the moon was at least partly clouded, thinking his speed was superior to that of the corvettes he believed were hunting him. It says something for the level of his asdic team's training that they were not able to distinguish between the single triple expansion engine of the corvette, the two engines of the frigate and the turbines of ***St. Laurent*** and ***Forester.***

She surfaced 1,400 yards ahead of ***St. Laurent*** and on ***Forester's*** starboard bow. All ships opened fire with their 4.7 and 4-inch guns and the Oerlikons that would bear on the twisting, fleeing U-boat, ***Swansea*** at least making the traditional but electrifying signal "AM ENGAGING S/M AHEAD OF ME BY GUNFIRE".

Fortunately Weber was more intent on escape than challenging his pursuers, for ***Swansea*** and ***Owen Sound*** did not stream their CAT gear at all and ***St. Laurent*** only after seventeen minutes, which was noted critically later by WA staff. The former two COs had not yet attended the Tactical School at Liverpool, but Stephen did not have this excuse. A GNAT might have sunk one of the U-boat's tormentors. In the running gunfight that developed, the bright moonlight and ***St. Laurent's*** type 271P radar were of great help and she scored several hits on the U-boat, as evidently the others did as well. The U-boat replied vigorously, but soon her forward 88mm gun was hit and her return Oerlikon fire suppressed. ***Forester*** was left behind at first until she could develop full speed as she had no foxer anti-GNAT gear fitted, but caught up for the finale. ***St. Laurent*** closed, intending to ram, as did ***Swansea*** (King had rammed ***U 94*** in the Caribbean when CO of ***Oakville*** two years before. See Chapter 15), but they were discouraged by ***Forester*** as the U-boat was obviously badly damaged already although still moving quickly. ***St. Laurent*** swept past, firing all available guns including pistols at the damaged U-boat, and dropped a shallow-set depth charge pattern just ahead of the submarine. She opened out to 1,000 yards and, by the time she had turned, the U-boat lay stopped and sinking and survivors were leaping into the frigid ocean. ***St. Laurent*** alone had expended 119 rounds of 4.7-inch and 1,440 Oerlikon rounds. The U-boat sank at 2338.

The captain, the 1st watch officer and the bridge watch of ***U 845*** had all been killed in the gun duel. Whalers were dropped from the three ships to rescue survivors. ***Forester*** picked up two officers and fifteen men, ***St. Laurent*** five men and ***Swansea*** one officer and twenty-two men. Several were wounded, but all survived to go into POW camps in England and later in the USA. As often happened, the Canadian sailors treated their prisoners more as distressed seamen and many busily collected autographs from them.[1]

U 845 had been on the coast of Newfoundland where she had torpedoed a freighter but not sunk her. It was her only wartime success. She had gone aground off St. John's, damaging a propellor, and had one rating killed by machine gun fire from an attacking RCAF aircraft. Although built in 1942, she had left Lorient on 1 January 1944 on her first war patrol. She was on her way home when BdU directed her to join in an attack on SC-154. Weber, at age thirty-five, was considered old by U-boat standards of 1944.

The attacking warships were fortunate that none of them had been hit either by the U-boat or by each other's cross-fire. (The only casualty reported was LCdr George Stephen's cap brim which he tore off in a moment of excitement during the chase!)

The victors returned to their escort duties with the convoy. ***Owen Sound*** and ***San Francisco*** also rejoined at last. While some attacks were made by the escorts on possible submarines, nothing further developed and the convoy reached the UK safely. The ships of C-1 group arrived at Londonderry on 13 March, with those of EG-9 on the 14th, to land their prisoners and refuel. All four Allied ships survived the war, ***Swansea*** remaining in naval service until 1966.

SOURCES:

Bishop, *Courage At Sea,* pp. 94-95 (Caution: several details in this story are incorrect)

Johnston, *Corvettes Canada*, pp. 236-237.

Lenton, *German Submarines*, Vol.1, p. 95, & Vol.2, p. 28.

Macpherson & Burgess, *Ships of Canada's Naval Forces.*

McKee, *HMCS Swansea, The Life And Times of a Frigate,* Chapter 4.

Schull, *Far Distant Ships,* pp. 224-227.

Milner, *The U-boat Hunters,* pp. 109, 119-121.

1. In 1995 and again in 1996 co-author Fraser McKee stayed several days with Herr Herman Frubrich in Hamm, Germany. Frubrich had been ***U 845's*** helmsman during the battle. Others have also developed correspondence with their ex-prisoners since the war.

CHAPTER 36

HMCS PRINCE RUPERT, THE USN AND U 575

Prince Rupert:
River class frigate
Builder: Yarrows Ltd, Esquimalt, BC
Comm: 30 Aug 43
Crew: 8 officers, 133 crew

Action: Sank *U 575*, Atlantic, 13 Mar 44
Casualties: 19
13 Survivors

[Dönitz] argument was that, by remaining where they were, these U-Boats were tying down vast enemy forces at sea and, in particular, in the air.

Jochen Brennecke, *The Hunter and the Hunted*

A view of *Prince Rupert* in 1944, emphasising the mass of depth charges carried by these anti-submarine frigates.

The destruction of ***U 575*** was an example of the level of interservice co-operation that had come into effect by the spring of 1944. It involved not only the RCN frigate HMCS ***Prince Rupert*** but the USN's destroyer ***Hobson,*** destroyer-escort ***Haverfield***, their escort carrier ***Bogue*** and its air group, and RAF Squadrons 172 and 206. Times had certainly changed since the days when Allied ships and aircraft could not even communicate easily with each other, let alone understand each other's anti-submarine tactics.

After commissioning, travelling around from the west coast and work-ups, ***Prince Rupert*** joined EG C-3 as the senior officer's ship in January, 1944, commanded by LCdr R.W. Draney, RCNR. She at once began escorting ocean convoys with her group, a job which was to last throughout 1944 with no more than a day or two's respite.

On 13 March 1944, the USN's anti-submarine hunter-killer Task Group 21.11 led by the escort carrier USS ***Bogue,*** and including ***Hobson, Haverfield,*** and the destroyer-escorts ***Jansen, Swenning*** and ***Willis***, had been dispatched to an area in the open Atlantic well north of the Azores to investigate a reported U-boat rendezvous. One suspects that this was as a result of the code-breakers at Bletchley Park reading German Enigma-cyphered messages directing their U-boats to the location, although Captain J.B. Dunn in ***Bogue*** would certainly not know this. Extreme care had to be exercised when sending escorts to such locations to avoid the Germans guessing "their mail was being read".

For several days the task group had bad weather and, although the destroyers picked up occasional echoes, nothing developed. Then at 0650 ***Bogue*** got an HF/DF bearing on a submarine, and sent ***Hobson*** and an aircraft to investigate. Nothing was found but the US destroyer history comments "there were indications of U-boats in the area." This was probably from hearing local U-boats' radio transmissions, even if they could not be deciphered.

Then late in the morning one of ***Bogue's*** searching *Avenger* aircraft spotted an oil slick. This, slight evidence as it was, indicated a possibility. The pilot, LCdr John Adams of VC-95 squadron dropped a sono-buoy at 1115, but at first had no indication of a submarine. At 1235 another *Avenger* joined in the hunt and dropped another sono-buoy. This time, to the operator listening in the aircraft, the buoy transmitted faint engine sounds of a submarine operating in the vicinity, the advantage being that the U-boat would not know she was detected. From this time on the aircraft were in continuous sono-buoy contact. Adams radioed a call for surface warship support, and ***Haverfield*** was despatched. As the US history phrases it, "The hunt was under way."

At 1251 USS ***Haverfield*** arrived on the scene. She searched about, pinging and listening for almost two hours. Persistence finally paid off and at 1509 she made contact in excellent sonar conditions (the USN's name for asdic) at 1,700 yards. Passing over at 1517 ***Haverfield*** fired a hedgehog salvo, followed by two more, with no audible or visible results. At 1547 she then tried a thirteen charge depth charge pattern, explosions this time at least bringing some oil to the surface.

In the meantime, just before this last attack, by chance ***Prince Rupert*** passed nearby heading westward, escorting Convoy ON-227 with her C-3 Group. Captain Dunn, controlling events from ***Bogue,*** asked if a ship from that group would join in the hunt that seemed to be developing, allowing him to retain his other escorts for carrier protection. LCdr Draney was delighted at the opportunity to help and set off in ***Prince Rupert*** at once, although her asdic had broken down by the time she reached ***Bogue's*** position.

While there seems to be a difference of opinion between those that were present for the attack and the official reports as to whether her asdic worked or not, ***Prince Rupert***, probably controlled by the American destroyer, delivered at least one depth charge attack and then hedgehog attacks. Marc Milner notes that heretofore the ability of the USN and the RCN to control each others' attacks hasd usually failed due to communications problems and presumably to lack of familiarity with tactical terms used in the two navies. By this stage of the war the RCN and RN were usually able to carry out coordinated attacks with few problems. In this case the coordination with the USN worked remarkably smoothly as well.

Prince Rupert then stood off while ***Haverfield*** depth charged the twisting and turning target in further attacks. Both ships continued their bombardment, ***Haverfield*** at 1638 and 1651, again with hedgehog, and ***Prince Rupert*** with depth charge patterns at 1701 and 1729. ***Haverfield*** continued with another thirteen charge pattern. Lt Donald Pattie joined in with his *Avenger*, dropping more sono-buoys to help in the maintenance of the contact. ***Prince Rupert*** directed ***Haverfield***

USS *Hobson,* one of the large *Bristol* class of 1940 destroyers, she was launched in 1941, and in 1944, after the action here, was converted to a destroyer minesweeper.

The *Edsall* class destroyer escort USS *Haverfield*, launched in late 1943, she was one of a class of 85 similar ships, indicating the remarkable capacity achieved by the US shipbuilding industry.

in making a very deep attack, and then made "an excellent attack" herself, as she reported.

Now USS ***Hobson*** arrived on the scene and entered the fray. After ***Haverfield's*** next two deep-set barrages, ***Hobson*** also dropped two successive patterns, the last at 1933, directed by ***Haverfield***. This was four hours and fifteen minutes of continuous attack; it was enough for OL Wolfgang Boehmer in ***U 575***. He surged to the surface at 1935, with cries from a ***Prince Rupert*** lookout "She's coming up!"

Prince Rupert, Hobson and ***Haverfield*** at once opened fire with their main armament and Oerlikons, riddling the conning tower and hull. Even one of the circling *Avengers* dropped two bombs, circled, and fired rockets into the port side of the battered U-boat. The U-boat tried briefly to return fire but this was soon suppressed. Boehmer was able to send off a partial message as to his fate to BdU. In less than ten minutes flames and smoke were issuing from the conning tower and forward hatch; the German crew was appearing and leaping into the sea. The boat settled lower until her casing was just awash. Her bow suddenly rose and she sank stern-first.

Of the U-boat's crew of fifty-six, ***Haverfield*** picked up seven survivors, ***Hobson*** sixteen, including the CO Boehmer, and one corpse. ***Prince Rupert*** took aboard fourteen whom she took on to St. John's. Eighteen of the crew died in the boat or by gunfire.

It was a satisfying riposte, for ***U 575***, operating out of St. Nazaire in France as part of the VII Flottille, had sunk the RN corvette ***Asphodel*** a couple of hundred miles to the east on 9 March. This had led to aircraft attacks on the U-boat, for shortly after midnight ***U 575*** was strafed by a British Azores-based *Wellington* which the U-boat repelled before submerging. At 0830 she re-surfaced only to be attacked by a *Fortress* which dropped bombs and strafed the boat again. Neither attack caused apparent damage, but may have lead to the oil slick seen by Adams in his *Avenger* just before noon. During most of the later hedgehog and depth charge attacks ***U 575*** was at 450 feet, and the last three caused most of the damage, forcing Boehmer to surface his boat.

Robert Draney received a DSC for his work that day. ***Prince Rupert*** continued with C-3, had a three-month refit at Liverpool, NS during the winter of 1944, joining EG-27 just before the end of the war. She went to the West Coast, and paid off in January of 1946. In 1947 her hull was expended as part of a breakwater at Royston, BC, just south of Courtenay on the northeast shore of Vancouver Island. By chance, the vessel was towed to the site by a tug commanded by Captain Bob Draney, DSC who had resumed that profession after the war.

USS ***Hobson*** was retained after the war, but was sunk in a collision with the carrier USS ***Wasp*** in 1952.

SOURCES:

Macpherson & Burgess, *Ships of Canada's Naval Forces,* p. 51

Milner, *The U-Boat Hunters,* p. 121-122.

Roscoe, *Destroyer Operations In WW 2,* pp. 300-1.

Y'Blood, *Hunter-Killer,* p.151.

CHAPTER 37

HMCS SWANSEA AND HMS PELICAN SHARE IN THE END OF U 448

Thus they realized from the outset that a greater advantage than mere numbers was on their side, and that they could count on eventual success, however brave and skilled in their own ways of war their enemies might be.

John Richard Hale, *The Great Armada*

Swansea:
(see Chapter 35 for details)
HMS *Pelican*:
Bird class sloop
Builder: John I. Thornycroft & Co, Southampton
Comm: 2 Mar 39

Action: Sank *U 448*, Atlantic, 14 Apr 44
Casualties: 9
42 survivors

HMCS *Swansea* during work-ups off Halifax in January 1944, one of a series of photos taken by Lt Gib Milne, RCNVR. In this case, she is preparing to take *Matane* in tow as part of an exercise.

HMCS ***Swansea*** assisted in the destruction of ***U 845*** on her way overseas. The destruction of ***U 448*** was ***Swansea's*** CO, LCdr C.A. King's fourth U-boat credit in two wars. ***Swansea*** was one of the earliest commissioned frigates, joining EG-9 in February, 1944 and sailing for Londonderry on 1 March.

While each ship was assigned to an escort group, it was not unusual by 1944 for them to work individually or as a group with other ships of the Royal or US Navies for particular requirements. Such was the case when EG-9 joined the RN group EG-7 to form part of the protective screen for the escort carrier HMS

Biter operating in the open Atlantic area west of Spain.

One ship in the RN group was HMS ***Pelican,*** a Bird class anti-submarine sloop, originally destined to have been a survey sloop, then for service with the China squadron, but actually completed as an A/S escort. They were nearly ideal in this role throughout the war, carrying heavy armament, a large stock of depth charges and hedgehog, and having the speed (over nineteen knots) to hunt U-boats away from the convoys and yet catch up. The most successful and famous of the U-boat hunters, Captain F.J. Walker, CB, DSO and three Bars, RN made all his kills when commanding near-sister sloops, HMS ***Stork*** and ***Starling.*** At the time of this action ***Pelican*** was temporarily commanded by Lt Jack Bathurst, RN. He was later to comment to the author that "contrary to popular belief I did not push the captain, Cdr John Dalison, off the bridge ladder whereby he broke his ankle, even though this did leave me in command!" It was unusual for a lieutenant to command these valuable A/S vessels.

On 9 April 1944, EG-9 sailed from Londonderry with orders to join EG-7 on the 12th for protection of Convoy OS-73 and U-boat hunting as support groups on call as needed. The British group comprised two sloops and three or four frigates. On the 14th the two groups were operating with HMS ***Biter***, an escort carrier converted in the US from a merchant ship hull and carrying six aircraft. The CO of ***Biter*** was senior officer of the force. The smaller ships formed an extended screen around the carrier as they moved northwards into an area where they were told they could expect good hunting. The Canadian group formed an outer screen in order to provide HF/DF fixes. In the morning ***Swansea*** and EG-9 fuelled from ***Biter*** to ensure they were topped up in case of need. EG-7 fuelled next in a moderate swell and sea which caused some problems in keeping station astern of ***Biter***. The ships were zig-zagging occasionally, all asdics closed up and operating. ***Swansea*** was about two miles on the starboard bow of the carrier. While no U-boats had been reported in their immediate vicinity, it was known that due to pressures by numerous anti-submarine forces in waters around the UK, Grossadmiral Dönitz had moved his forces outwards and south into the Atlantic.

At 1118 ***Swansea's*** 1st operator reported a contact on their starboard bow at a range of about 2,200 yards, "possible submarine". The officer of the watch altered toward at once, rang "Action stations", increased speed, streamed CAT and called the CO to the bridge. He informed both Cdr Layard with EG-9 and ***Biter*** that he had a contact. ***Pelican*** was at once ordered to join ***Swansea*** in her hunt and she hastily broke off fuelling. ***Biter*** altered away out of danger with the remaining ships of EG-7 and EG-9 for her protection.

In excellent asdic conditions, ***Swansea*** had meantime made an urgent depth charge attack to discourage the U-boat from setting up her own attack on the carrier. There were no visible results from this attack. Later questioning of prisoners revealed that it did no damage but did cause the CO to abandon his stalking of the carrier. Another attack was set up at seven knots, this time by hedgehog, but the target was lost at 500 yards, indicating the U-boat had gone deep. Target movement signified it had turned away, so LCdr King went full speed ahead and dropped a ten-charge depth charge pattern. This was close but not right over his target. The frigate was having some problems retaining contact as the U-boat released a continuous series of SBTs (submarine bubble targets) and altered course and depth to throw off her pursuer. On ***Pelican*** joining, she and ***Swansea*** carried out an Operation Observant to relocate their target for certain. When ***Pelican*** obtained a firm contact, she carried out one attack without result.

Since Bathurst agreed that the U-boat had gone very deep (he was an A/S specialist and had been the group A/S Officer), he then recommended to LCdr King that they carry out a creeping attack with ***Pelican*** directing ***Swansea*** over the target. King promptly agreed. ***Swansea*** switched her asdic to listening only and ***Pelican*** directed her along the U-boat's course at almost 2,000 yards distance. As Bathurst says, "The beauty of this type of attack was that the firing ship did not operate her asdic when closing the target so the U-boat, only hearing the long-range pinging of the conning ship, was not aware that she was about to be attacked and therefore took no evasive action." The directed ship also operated as quietly as possible, and usually tripped her CAT gear so it didn't rattle. When ***Swansea*** was over the target the first time, however, the U-boat altered sharply away so the attack was cancelled and re-organised, with the sloop again directing the frigate over the submarine. All this took more than half an hour, giving King time to work out a leisurely sun sight for his position. ***Pelican*** gave the order to fire and ***Swansea*** dropped a line of twenty-six depth charges across the U-boat, running at about 600 feet. Then ***Pelican*** passed over dropping a ten-charge pattern.

That was all it took and, within minutes, at 1528 the submarine surfaced. Both of the circling ships at once opened fire on her with their 4-inch guns and Oerlikons. In all, ***Swansea*** fired thirty-two rounds from her two 4-inch mounts.

The ships ceased fire when it was obvious that the boat was sinking, as she never fully surfaced and her crew appeared out of the hatches and leapt into the ocean. The U-boat's engineer opened the vents and the submarine sank at 1535. Both warships dropped their whalers so that they need not stop to pull aboard the Germans in case there was another U-boat about. ***Pelican*** picked up the CO, OL Helmut Dauter, three other officers and twenty-one of the crew, while ***Swansea*** rescued one officer and sixteen men. One of the officers picked up by ***Pelican*** was a prospective U-boat CO under training. Their average age was twenty-three and some were reported by ***Swansea's*** medical officer as really being unfit for service at sea by Canadian standards.

Launched in August, 1942, ***U 448*** was based on St. Nazaire, France, as part of VII U-Flottille, and was on her fourth war patrol without any ships sunk or even damaged to her credit. She had left St. Nazaire on 14 February to seek targets off Iceland but found none. While the first attacks had not damaged the boat, Dauter had taken her very deep, about 700 feet, to avoid the next expected attacks. The creeping attack had put out almost all lights, caused flooding in the engine room and, by the seventh explosion, the charges were detonating almost alongside, blowing a six-inch hole in the hull. The crew later did not even remember counting the rest of the charges. The damage made the CO realise the situation was hopeless. On surfacing he ordered the crew overboard at once. Nine were killed and several wounded by the ships' gunfire. The crew was scattered over quite an expanse, so it took some time for the two whalers to round them all up and haul them aboard. In ***Swansea's*** whaler, commanded by her 1st lieutenant, Ian MacDonald, one of the U-boat officers pulled out a pistol which was seen by LS Albert Hurtubise who grabbed his arm, hit the man and threw the gun overboard. Whether the German was planning to throw it away or use it was never determined. Hurtubise received a Mention in Despatches. Once the prisoners were aboard, the wounded treated and all provided with new dry clothing from a Red Cross supply, the sailors of ***Swansea*** seemed more interested in collecting autographs than oppressing their captives.

The U-boat survivors in ***Swansea*** were transferred to ***Pelican*** after two days, to be landed at Greenock. Most were later transferred to prison camps in the central US, not returning to Germany until the fall of 1947.

As well as having assisted with the destruction of ***U 845***, after this action ***Swansea*** sank ***U 311*** a week later with HMCS ***Matane*** (although this was not known until the mid-1980s), all under LCdr King. Then under Cdr Layard she got a fourth U-boat in September, 1944, in those cases in conjunction with other ships of EG-9. She was retained after the war as an ocean escort and training ship until 1967. ***Pelican*** as well was a very successful ship, with two U-boats to her credit already by the time she sank ***U 448***, and another in June, 1944. She too was retained after the war and served in various stations around the world, being paid off in 1957. Bathurst moved to Canada after the war, serving in the RCN and then becoming a master mariner. Cdr King retired as a Captain, RCNR and returned to apple farming in southeast British Columbia.

SOURCES:

Hague, *Sloops*, pp. 67-71.

Macpherson, *Frigates of the RCN*, pp. 48-50.

McKee, *HMCS Swansea*, pp. 82-92.

Milner, *The U-Boat Hunters,* pp. 130-131.

Schull, *Far Distant Ships,* p. 227.

CHAPTER 38

HMCS MATANE SWANSEA AND U 311: A CHANGE IN THE RECORDS

Matane:
River class frigate
Builder: Canadian Vickers Ltd, Montreal
Comm: 22 Oct 43
Crew: 8 officers, 133 crew
Swansea:
(see Chapter 35 for details)
Action: Sank *U 311*, mid-Atlantic, 22 Apr 44
Casualties: 51
No survivors

21. On the bridge, a "Captain's Bearing Instrument" indicates the transducer bearing to the Captain and shows him the course to steer offered by the bearing recorder... The latter information is conveyed to the helmsman, and to a "Weapon Control Unit"

BR 1671, Handbook Of Asdic Set Type 164.

In examining German records post-war there was no doubt that U-boat **U 311** had disappeared in mid-April, 1944. This was confirmed shortly afterwards by the Admiralty through secret intelligence sources.

At first her destruction was attributed to a very good attack by *Sunderland* aircraft A of 423 Squadron, RCAF, FL F.G. Fellows, operating out of Castle Archdale on Lough Earne, Northern Ireland. She had attacked a surfaced U-boat from astern at 1347 local time on 24 April when west of Ireland, straddling her with six depth charges, one of which detonated prematurely, somewhat damaging the aircraft itself. The aircraft's gunners also smothered her with 1,600 rounds of .303 machine gun fire (the *Sunderland* wasn't known as "the flying porcupine" for nothing), and the U-boat disappeared. A "probably damaged" was recorded at the time and a kill credited when ***U 311***'s disappearance was deduced later. It was not the first for 423 Squadron.

However, in the mid-1980s the British Ministry of Defence historical section began reviewing all U-boat kills, especially where there was no absolutely conclusive evidence of which U-boat had been sunk, and how. In checking German radio logs at BdU, U-boat logs for reported attacks from which boats survived, and Allied records of attacks , it was discovered that ***U 672*** had been attacked by a *Sunderland* on the 24th at the time and in exactly the method described. She had been extensively damaged but had reached her base to report. But then ***U 311*** had indeed disappeared about that time, although she should have been northwest of the area of the *Sunderland* attack. As well, she had not reported in since 2 April, when she had reported failing to meet ***U 358*** for a transfer of diesel fuel as ordered, a rather longer silence than

HMCS *Matane* in June 1944.

A *Sunderland*, well-weathered, of 422 Squadron, RCAF.

expected. (In fact ***U 358*** had already been sunk by EG-1).

If Fellows' attack had been on ***U 672***, what had happened to ***U 311***? A close and extensive investigation by the historian eliminated several possibilities of attacks on her, including another attack by a *Liberator* of the RAF's 120 Squadron on the hapless ***U 672*** earlier on the 24th. He then could only conclude that a good attack on April 22nd by the EG-9 ships ***Matane*** and ***Swansea*** on an unidentified submarine must be the cause of the sinking of ***U 311***. Thus the records have been amended, over forty years after the events.

In the early morning of 22 April, Canadian EG-9 under Cdr A.F.C. Layard, DSO, RN, acting as an extra convoy support group, received a message ordering his group to cooperate with a Leigh-light *Wellington* of the RAF's Coastal Command that had obtained a good radar contact of a possible U-boat in a neighbouring area. By 1700 ***Matane*** (Cdr Layard) and ***Swansea*** (A/Cdr C.A. King, DSO, DSC, RCNR) were in the middle of the possible area of the reported contact and commenced sniffing about in an organised search with their asdics. At 2000 ***Matane*** got a firm asdic contact, ordered the frigate ***Stormont*** and the corvette ***Owen Sound*** of his group to join in a hunt, and started a deliberate hedgehog attack at a slow seven knots. The submarine's range began to close rapidly and its bearing moved rapidly right. Almost at once a swirl and a periscope were seen at 200 yards on ***Matane's*** starboard bow.

Due to the vulnerability of the rest of the group still approaching the area and to discourage the U-boat's plans, Cdr Layard says "I then got thoroughly rattled [his officers say Cdr Layard *never* got rattled!] and in case he should fire a torpedo I reckoned I must go for him. Went full ahead and dropped a [five-charge] pattern by eye which was probably too early. However we picked him up astern and the other ships were now on the scene." ***Swansea*** then reduced speed and carried out a full pattern deliberate attack. Asdic conditions shortly became awful and contact was lost, although an Operation Observant square search was carried out. The ships remained in the area all night, illustrating the happy circumstances by the spring of 1944 whereby there were enough escorts to spare them for such extensive efforts. No further contact was gained, the group returned to her convoy support on the 25th... and ***U 311*** disappeared, with her entire complement. A Type VIIC, she had been launched in Jan. 1943, and had left Brest on 9 March 1944, commanded by KL Joachim Zander. He had torpedoed and sunk the 10,300-ton American merchantman ***Seakay*** on 19 March in mid-Atlantic, so was evidently returning home when encountered by the *Wellington* and then EG-9.

Cdr Layard's group was eventually to be credited with six U-boat kills by the end of the war, for which he received a well-merited DSC. And this was Clarence King's fifth U-boat kill. When serving in a sailing "Q" Ship in World War I he had received a DSC for a spirited action against a U-boat presumed sunk; a DSO when CO of the corvette ***Oakville*** (see Chapter 15) for sinking ***U 94***, and ***Swansea*** had already sunk two U-boats earlier in March and April (see Chapters 35 and 37) about which there was no doubt, as many prisoners were picked up from those two. ***U 311*** counts as an unexpected "extra", although Captain King had died in February, 1964, never knowing that he had gained yet another U-boat credit. Commander Layard is still alive, in his late 90s, to appreciate his added success.

SOURCES:

McKee, *HMCS Swansea*,pp. 94-96.

Milner, *The U-Boat Hunters*, p. 131.

Unpublished notes from MoD (Navy), UK.

CHAPTER 39

HMCS HAIDA, HURON & ATHABASKAN HELP SINK THE GERMAN DESTROYER T 29

There must be a beginning of any great matter, but the continuing unto the end until it be thoroughly finished yields the true glory.

Sir Francis Drake, 1587

Athabaskan, Haida, Huron:
Tribal class destroyers
Builder (all):
Vickers-Armstrong Ltd, UK
Comm:
Athabaskan, 3 Feb 43;
Haida, 30 Aug 43;
Huron, 19 Jul 43

Action: Sank German destroyer *T 29*, N of Brittany, 26 Apr 44
Casualties: 137

Two Tribal destroyers and a supporting cruiser of the 10th DF: (from the left) *Huron, Haida* and *Black Prince* (above *Haida's* B gun) in the Channel in 1944.

Four Canadian Tribal class destroyers were assigned to the 10th Destroyer Flotilla, the "Fighting Tenth" in January - February, 1944, commanded by Cdr St.John Tyrwhitt, RN, and after March by Cdr Basil Jones, DSO, DSC, RN. For their commanding officers and indeed for the RCN, this was the achievement of the ideal of the Navy. The 10th DF was to conduct fighting patrols, called Tunnel Operations, in the Channel and Bay of Biscay against any German convoys or destroyer patrols. They were to make the area theirs and deny it to the enemy, an ideal proposition for large and well-armed destroyers. Convoy escort was all very well, but destroyer battles were closer to the great fleet actions of the legends which inspired most regular naval officers.

At this time the flotilla consisted of HMS ***Tartar*** (as senior officer, although Jones occasionally had to travel in another ship if ***Tartar*** was out of service), HMS ***Ashanti***, HMCS ***Haida*** (Cdr Harry DeWolf) and ***Huron*** (LCdr Herbert Rayner, DSC) as the 19th Division, and HMS ***Eskimo,*** HMCS ***Athabaskan*** (LCdr John Stubbs, DSO), and the Polish destroyers ***Blyskawica*** and ***Piorun*** as the 20th Division.

When the Canadian Tribals had commissioned they had each spent some time on Home Fleet destroyer flotilla duties, including difficult convoys to north Russia in late 1943. The Canadian ships included HMCS ***Iroquois***, which supported convoys to Gibraltar and Freetown. She then went to Canada for a refit in early 1944, while ***Athabaskan, Haida*** and ***Huron*** were assigned to the 10th DF.

Iroquois was to join later in the summer. Between February and April several Tunnel Operations had been undertaken, largely unsuccessful, in part due to lack of group training, mis-matched ships and the slow development of an aggressive policy.

Jones' policy was based on bringing the enemy to action with gunfire rather than torpedoes. Against fast, weaving, small targets, frequently at night, and with the Tribals' single four-tube torpedo mounting, this seems to have been a reasonable policy, although sometimes criticised by Admiralty staff. On 25 April four destroyers and a supporting cruiser as the force senior officer were to comprise Force 26 and sweep along the French coast in the expectation of catching three *T 22* class Elbing-built German destroyers. They had been sheltering in St. Malo harbour, revealed by aerial reconnaissance on the 23rd.

The force was to sweep from west to east along the Brittany coast. On this occasion Force 26 consisted of the cruiser ***Black Prince*** with ***Ashanti*** and ***Huron*** as a sub-division ahead to port and ***Haida*** and ***Athabaskan*** as the sub-division to starboard. After some ineffectual radar-controlled German shore battery fire, of which ***Black Prince*** was forewarned by her "headache" operator (a German-speaking radio operator who listened in on German radio instructions to coastal batteries as well as German inter-ship voice traffic), the force turned eastward. At 0207 on the 26th, ***Black Prince*** reported an initial radar contact ahead at 21,000 yards - over ten miles - then confirmed as up to four ships at 18,000 yards range, moving at twenty-four knots. It developed that these were the three Elbing fleet destroyers, each equipped with six torpedo tubes and four 4.5-inch guns. They were on their way from St. Malo to Brest, commanded by KK Franz Kohlauf. At this point they also detected the Allied force, reversed course and fled.

Force 26 went to thirty knots with the range closing slowly. At 0220 ***Black Prince*** illuminated the targets by starshell at 13,000 yards and, as Jones phrases it, "released the destroyers": ENGAGE, BEARING 090. Being nearer, ***Haida*** and ***Athabaskan*** opened fire at 10,900 yards on the Germans' starboard quarter, followed by ***Black Prince***, and ***Ashanti*** and ***Huron*** to port of the German ships. The German ships also fired illuminating starshell and, in their usual fashion and as anticipated, altered enough to fire torpedoes. ***Black Prince*** stepped aside to avoid them and the gun action continued with the four destroyers firing steadily, although the German ships tended to open the range as they were somewhat faster at thirty-four knots. By 0231 hits were being obtained by our destroyers and, before the enemy could out-distance their attackers, ***T 29*** was severely damaged aft and in the engine room. Again at 0254 the "headache" operator warned the force that "the enemy is firing torpedoes." They passed harmlessly. By 0332 ***T 29*** slowed and coasted to a stop while another, later identified as ***T 27***, retreated inshore and was lost among the radar echoes of the rocks and small islets after receiving considerable damage. The third German ship, ***T 24,*** fled east and escaped but with damage and casualties as well.

The Canadian and British destroyers returned to ensure the destruction of ***T 29***, which the four Tribals circled at about 700 yards range. As many as sixteen torpedoes were fired at her without effect, at least without visible hits. The German was still defiant and fired back at her tormentors, hitting all the Allied destroyers with 20 mm fire. The confusion as to identity is illustrated by a signal at 0336 by ***Ashanti*** to ***Huron:*** SWITCH ON FIGHTING LIGHTS FOR 15 SECONDS, so she could be identified in the smoke and darkness. At 0355 ***Haida*** sent the same message to ***Athabaskan***. The German gunfire at ***Huron*** caused considerable minor wiring damage, killed LS Henry Gosnell, RCN, of the pom-pom crew when its feed tray was hit, wounded the director layer and several others, and punched a small hole in her gunnery control officer's steel helmet - Lt Alan Watson, RCNVR. In 1995, he commented with some enjoyment that both ***Huron's*** CO, LCdr Rayner, and the XO, Lt Patrick Budge, RCN were torpedo specialists but of all the torpedoes fired by German, British and Canadian destroyers that night not one hit a target. As ***Ashanti*** signalled to ***Haida*** rather plaintively: ALL TORPEDOES FIRED. THEY MUST HAVE GONE UNDERNEATH. ***Haida*** also suffered several 20 mm hits, causing damage and some casualties. Her report notes damage also caused by blast of her own guns when trained close aboard on an aft bearing.

At 0420 the battered and blazing ***T 29*** rolled onto her side and sank from the cumulative effects of gunfire alone, with 137 killed, including the squadron commander and her CO Seventy-three men were later rescued by German patrol craft. The 10th DF set course for Plymouth, arriving at 0821 on the 26th. Just as the action against ***T 29*** ended ***Huron*** and

Ashanti were in a glancing collision which added some damage to that done by German gun fire, seriously damaging ***Ashanti's*** bow.

As the force approached Plymouth, the senior officer in ***Black Prince*** signalled: FORCE 26 WILL WEAR BATTLE ENSIGNS ON ENTERING HARBOUR. There was no rest on arrival as all ships had expended a considerable quantity of gun ammunition and all their torpedoes, so they had immediately to re-ammunition and then re-fuel in preparation for another night's Operation Tunnel.

While the fighting formation proved effective, and C-in-C Plymouth approved the night's action, the Admiralty staff were considerably more critical. They noted that the attention of four large Tribals concentrated on sinking ***T 29*** was an error and permitted at least one other damaged ship to escape when she should have been pursued. They were also critical of the torpedo firing drills in the destroyers that failed to hit the stopped German with sixteen torpedoes. Little was developed from these criticisms however, and Canadian officers do not appear to have been even aware of them at the time.

Two nights later ***Haida*** and ***Athabaskan*** (taking the damaged ***Huron's*** place) were in the same area to cover coastal forces on a mine-laying foray off Île de Batz. (The story of the sinking of ***Athabaskan*** by a German torpedo and the destruction of the German Elbing ***T 27*** by ***Haida*** is told in Chapter 40 and not repeated here.)

Haida and ***Huron*** and the other destroyers of 10 DF achieved another success on 8/9 June, described in Chapter 42.

SOURCES:

Brice, *The Tribals*, pp. 61-62; 130-131; 141.

German, *The Sea Is At Our Gates,* pp. 159-161.

Gröner, *German Warships, 1815-1945*, Vol. One, p. 195.

Jones, *And So To Battle,* pp. 74-79.

Keene, *The Ship That Voted No,* pp. 65-66.

MacBeth, *Ready, Aye, Ready,* p. 145.

Roberts, *Canada and the War At Sea*, p. 72.

Schull, *Far Distant Ships,* pp. 251-253.

Sclater, *Haida,* pp. 65-81.

Smith, *Hold The Narrow Sea,* pp. 210-211.

Venier, *Ready, The Brave,* pp. 258-272.

Whitby, *Canadian Defence Quarterly,* Dec. 1989, pp. 54-59.

Whitley, *Destroyer!,* p. 205.

CHAPTER 40

TRAGEDY IN THE CHANNEL: THE LOSS OF HMCS ATHABASKAN

Athabaskan:
(see Chapter 39 for details)

Crew: 16 officers, 245 crew

Action: Sank German destroyer *T 27*, English Channel, 29 Mar 44

Casualties: 11

Fate: Torpedoed by German destroyer *T 24*, English Channel, 29 Mar 44

Casualties: 128 killed, 86 captured

With arrested step he cries
Weeping, "What place, Achates, or what clime
But with the story of our grief o'erflows?"

Virgil, *Aeneid*

HMCS *Athabaskan* in 1944.

The story of the Tribal destroyer HMCS ***Athabaskan*** has been very completely told in *Unlucky Lady* by Len Burrow and Emile Beaudoin. Together with ***Haida*** and ***Huron*** their three histories are comprehensively documented.

These modern destroyers met two requirements: the need by the RCN for modern destroyers in its desire to be other than just a "small ship" Navy; and the trade off with the Admiralty whereby Canada built corvettes, *Algerine* minesweepers and other smaller vessels for which its shipyards were suited in exchange for the destroyers built in warship-experienced UK yards. These negotiations were difficult and protracted, as British yards were already fully occupied with RN orders. Australia made the same decision, electing to build the Tribals in their own yards, of which only three were completed. Canada, probably wisely, decided to have the first four built in Britain, followed by four more built in Halifax which, however, were not completed until after the war.

On 29 March 1943, after work-ups, ***Atha B***, as she was often known, commanded by Capt

G.R. Miles, OBE, RCN, joined the Home Fleet in the Shetlands, and made patrols in the Faeroes-Iceland passage. After repairs of weather damage, this was followed by Operation Gearbox III, the relief of Spitzbergen, more repairs, and then she was on A/S patrols in the Bay of Biscay. On 27 August she was hit by a German glider bomb off the Spanish coast, but reached Devonport, where she once again was repaired. Now commanded by LCdr John Stubbs, DSO RCN, she returned to Scapa and escorted a convoy to North Russia and back. In February, 1944 she left for Plymouth to join the RN's newly formed 10th Destroyer Flotilla under Commander Basil Jones, RN for service once again in the Biscay and Channel area. The flotilla was supported by the cruisers HMS ***Bellona*** and ***Black Prince***, and made up of four Canadian Tribals, ***Athabaskan, Haida, Huron*** and ***Iroquois***; two Polish destroyers, ***Piorun*** (RN N class) and ***Blyskawica*** (Polish Grom class); and the RN destroyers ***Tartar*** (usually as SO), ***Ashanti, Eskimo, Javelin*** and ***Nubian***. At any one time not all were on operations, either due to battle damage or because only certain ships were selected for a night's operation.

Captain Jones remarks in his book *And So To Battle* that "the Canadian COs were highly efficient and full of aggressive spirit... and that although it was fashionable for a new leader to throw his weight about a bit to indicate to all that he was in charge... I appreciated that a gratuitous attitude like that would not go down too well with the Canadians, who could be somewhat touchy if provoked unnecessarily." When ***Haida's*** CO, Cdr Harry DeWolf was promoted Captain by the RCN, the RN perforce had to promote Cdr Jones, the "senior officer", to acting captain to his delight and their annoyance.

After flotilla training and escorting exercises in March, during April several operations involving ***Atha B*** were undertaken, the one on 25 April resulting in the destruction of a German destroyer (see Chapter 39). But it also left two of the 10th DF destroyers damaged, and one was in short refit, the SO's HMS ***Tartar.***

Thus two nights later only two ships of the 10th DF were able to be out again, ***Haida*** and ***Athabaskan***, this time to screen and provide distant defence cover for coastal force motor boats laying a disruptive minefield east of the Île de Batz near the tip of the Brittany peninsula. This force consisted of eight MLs and two MTBs. It was known that two small German Elbing-built ***T 22*** class destroyers, ***T 24*** and ***T 27*** of their 4th Flottille, were in the French port of Morlaix for repairs after the running fight two days before, and that they might try that night to reach their base at Brest to the west and south.

After their mine-laying protection responsibilities ended about 0300, the Canadian destroyers swept in line ahead, ***Haida*** leading, southwest down the coast. They were warned by Plymouth radio at 0313 that an enemy force, tracked at eighty miles distance by Plymouth radar, was near them and would pass close to Île de Batz, hugging the coast. In exceptional radar conditions the two German ships were detected by the destroyers at fourteen miles. The Canadian ships altered to head them off, but keeping their opponent forty-five degrees on their port bows so all guns would bear when the enemy was sighted. At 0400 ***Haida*** and ***Atha B*** were both in contact, the latter firing starshell to the southeast on ***Haida's*** order ten minutes later. This exposed two destroyers and possibly a third small ship at a range of some 7,300 yards. Despite being completely surprised by the sudden starshell illumination, the Germans at once turned away as they usually did, and fired torpedoes, twelve in all. Some confusion still reigned aboard the German destroyers as ***T 24*** fired three of her torpedoes on the side away from the RCN ships. The Canadians, concentrating on a gun action and preventing the faster German ships from escaping, did not fire torpedoes, which would have entailed at least a partial turn aside from their closing course.

Although the Canadian ships turned thirty degrees toward to present a narrow target, "combing the torpedo spread", but at the same time allowing the after 4-inch guns to continue firing illuminating starshell, at 0415 one of the torpedoes hit ***Atha B*** in the gearing room, just before her after superstructure, as she steadied on her new course. A great column of flame and white water rose from her port side aft. The ship coasted to a stop with considerable damage and no steering, turning slowly to port and settling aft. Post-war checking indicates the torpedo was fired by ***T 24.*** Stubbs reported to ***Haida***: I'M HIT AND LOSING POWER.

Large fires broke out aft and amidships, although the crew worked valiantly to move heavy pumps and get them connected and working. On the forecastle, a team prepared for towing by ***Haida***. LCdr Stubbs ordered the boats turned out but not lowered yet, and torpedo tubes trained inboard. Just after the forward seventy-ton pump had been hauled aft and was being connected to fight the worst oil fuel blaze, the ship's after 4.7-inch magazine blew up with a tremendous roar and flames that were seen thirty miles away. Blazing and unignited fuel oil was thrown in the air across the whole forward part of the ship. Many of the surviving crew were blown over the side or fell overboard. One of these was the ship's CB officer, criticized by the subsequent Board of Inquiry for not having assured the destruction of his CBs. There have also been official questions as to why Captain DeWolf did not fire torpedoes at the German destroyers. But since the Germans themselves fired twelve for a single hit, and two nights before the Allies had fired dozens with no hits, DeWolf's feeling was that against small, fast and weaving destroyers it was a waste of money and effort. Thus they were often used as a tactical threat to cause an adversary to alter course, and a hit was a bonus.

Haida, in the meantime, altered across the bows of the slowing ***Athabaskan*** and paused only long enough to lay a smoke screen to protect her. Captain DeWolf later recalled that he was not sure whether she had been torpedoed or possibly mined. (The latter preyed on the minds of those operating in inshore waters quite frequently and, DeWolf feels now, in a 1995 interview, he was possibly too conscious of the mine threat at the time.)

As Schull says, "The grim priorities of sea warfare had to be maintained." Thus DeWolf took up the chase of the two German ships that were departing toward the coast at maximum speed, obtaining hits on both of them. They split up, so ***Haida*** concentrated on ***T 27***, gaining more hits and causing explosions on board. That ship elected to run herself ashore at Meneham, where ***Haida*** pounded her again to ensure she stayed there, then returned to the scene of ***Atha B's*** damage, the other German destroyer having disappeared up the coast. ***T 27***, deemed by the British to be salvageable, was later torpedoed on 6 May by an MTB that went close inshore among the rocks for a clear shot. Eleven of her crew had been killed. The other destroyer, ***T 24,*** who had turned back east, was herself driven ashore by rocket-firing RAF aircraft four months later, in August, 1944.

The blast on board ***Atha B*** was seen in ***Haida*** of course, but the ship only lasted for another couple of minutes, rolling to port and quickly sinking by the stern. There was only time for the survivors of the two explosions to shove a few Carley floats over the side and jump after them. ***Athabaskan*** sank at 0442.

A survivor credited the saving of many lives to the fact that all had been issued the new style life vest that not only protected them but had lights attached, a lanyard to clip them to rafts, and straps on the shoulders to haul weakened swimmers from the water.

As she approached, ***Haida*** fired a starshell to see what had happened to ***Atha B*** and her crew, not yet knowing that the ship had already sunk. When she reached the scene of ***Atha B's*** destruction, all that was to be seen were many small scattered lights on the life vests and a mass of oil and wreckage. She dropped scramble nets over her sides as she coasted to a stop amidst the larger group of men, dropped floats and lowered all her boats, including her port motor cutter. DeWolf called out to his crew amidships he would stay for fifteen minutes. He was within fifteen miles of the German-held coast, air attacks would occur with first light, and current doctrine was to be clear of the coast by first light (dawn was at 0711, British double summer time). He radioed for air cover but was told that none was available, a point that caused considerable ill feelings in later years.

Also ***Haida*** was drifting quite swiftly to starboard in the coastal currents and DeWolf was much concerned with drifting into a nearby minefield and thus losing two ships. While guns' crews were to remain at their guns, all who could be spared of her men went to the scramble nets to help the dazed and often injured survivors up both sides. Thirty-eight were hauled aboard. Those in the dark waters forward and aft of the scramble nets were thrown heaving lines, towed to the nets and helped up the ship's side.

At fifteen minutes, ***Haida's*** navigator told DeWolf time was up. He passed the word to the rescuers on the iron deck "I'll give you five minutes more. And I'll call out the minutes." There was already a cry from the water, reportedly by LCdr Stubbs, ***Athabaskan's*** CO who well appreciated the dangers of staying: "Get the hell out of it ***Haida!*** We'll be all right." Then even when asked by his 1st lieutenant if he was ready to move DeWolf waited for another few moments. Then at 0515, he bitterly gave the order "Slow ahead". Some men clinging to the lower edge of the nets were swept away as speed increased. This included two of ***Haida's*** own seamen, P.O. H.P. Murray and Tel. S.A. Turner, the latter being towed through the water at gradually increasing speeds because he had clipped a line from his belt to the scramble net and it took some minutes before he could cut himself free.

DeWolf had ordered his boats lowered for the survivors, but intended them to be unmanned, to let the ***Atha B*** crew man them. However, either deliberately or unintentionally, the motor cutter was manned by ***Haida's*** Leading Seaman William A. McClure, AB Jack Hannam and Sto W.A. Cummings. Despite the motor failing at one point, they picked up six ***Atha Bs*** from the water, including the badly injured torpedo gunner's mate, and then by pure chance the two ***Haida*** seamen that had been washed off her scramble net. Then German minesweepers were seen coming out from the coast so the cutter set off for England, 120 miles away! One minesweeper chased after them briefly, then turned back when she judged they were motoring into a minefield.

Eighty-six men in the water were taken prisoner by the German ships, one of them ***T 24*** who had returned when ***Haida*** had turned after ***T 27***. She picked up forty-seven of ***Atha B's*** survivors, and then was somewhat damaged when she set off a ground mine on her return to harbour. All Canadians survived their year of hardship in North Germany POW camps. Some bodies were picked up by the rescuing German ships, others drifted ashore all along the coast. These are all buried in nine cemeteries, about half of the men identified, including LCdr Stubbs. Forty-nine bodies were not identifiable, even through research after the war. And another thirty-seven lie beneath the sea, "missing, presumed dead". Two of those lost were special branch Lieutenants, along that night as part of a photographic unit.

Meanwhile the motor cutter sputtered toward home with fuel for a theoretical thirty hours. The balky motor, typical of its kind, stopped twice more, eventually only making three knots. A little after 1600 two aircraft flew over very low, greeted by enthusiastic waves and a red flare from a Very pistol, until the black *Luftwaffe* crosses were seen and the planes identified as ME 109s. The tired and hungry crew were more circumspect about 1830 when again two planes approached, but these were RAF *Spitfires* which flew a patrol around them. These two were relieved by two more and a *Lancaster* and, at last, during the evening, an RAF rescue launch arrived to take them aboard and to hospital. Their arrival at Penzance on Cornwall's tip brought the total of survivors that reached England to a modest forty-four. The motor cutter itself was towed into Falmouth by a Fairmile ML. LS McClure and Sto Cummings received Mentions in Despatches for their valiant rescue, a very modest reward for a valiant effort. Hannam was not mentioned.

There has been speculation that the torpedo that hit ***Athabaskan*** was fired by German E-boats or even in error by one of the MTBs returning from the mine-laying operation. Or that the second explosion on board was from a second torpedo. This is not considered possible, as there were no E-boats in the area and the MTBs were all much too far away, even though at 0448 they were ordered to proceed to rescue survivors. They could not even have been at the site by first light, so they were ordered home by C-in-C Plymouth. Neither reported even firing a torpedo that night. DeWolf knew they had been ordered to the scene and he hoped that they could rescue more survivors and yet not be in as much danger as ***Haida*** due to their small size and speed, and the prospect of air cover. But he did not know until returning to Plymouth that they had been called off later and that there was to be no air cover. This too caused some post-action ill feeling and sour comments by Canadians.

While the actions and control exercised by Harry DeWolf were supported by his C-in-C Plymouth, again the Admiralty staff tactical section were critical, without much justification or understanding of the situation at the scene.

SOURCES:

Brice, *The Tribals*, pp. 66-70.

Burrow & Beaudoin, *Unlucky Lady*.

German, *The Sea Is At Our Gates*, pp. 162-163.

Jones, *And So To Battle*, pp. 79-80.

Keene, *The Ship That Voted No*, pp. 66-67.

Lenton, *German Surface Vessels 1*, p. 120.

Macpherson & Burgess, *Ships of Canada's Naval Forces*, pp. 42, 209.

Paquette & Bainbridge, *Honours & Awards*, p. 332.

Reader's Digest, *The Canadians At War*, Vol.2, pp. 399-407.

Schull, *Far Distant Ships*, pp. 253-258.

Sclater, *Haida*, pp. 86-120.

Tucker, *Naval Service of Canada*, Vol.II, p. 329.

Whitby, *Canadian Defence Quarterly*, Dec. 1989, pp. 59-61.

Whitley, *Destroyer! German Destroyers In WW II*, pp. 205-206.

LOST:

Adams, John C., AB
Agnew, John, AB
Allison, Albert E., AB
Amiro, Irvin V., Tel
Annett, Robert I.L., SLt(E)
Armstrong, George A., AB
Ashton, Percy G., AB
Barrett, Arthur E., AB
Bell, Donald A., Sto
Berkley, Alfred G., OS
Bertrand, Laurent J.L., CPO
Bianco, Anthony D., AB
Bieber, Edgar E., Sto.PO
Blinch, Harry C., AB
Brandson, Thomas L., Lt(S)
Brighten, Victor H., ERA
Burrow, William O., LS
Chamberland, Paul H.A., AB
Cookman, Edgar A., LS
Cooney, Stewart R., Stwd
Corbiere, Vincent G., AB
Corkum, Gordon F., AB
Cottrell, Sydney A., AB
Croft, Mayle H., AB
Cross, Alfred T., O.Tel
DeArmond, Gordon L., LS
Dillen, Stewart C., Stwd
Dion, A. Jean G., L.Sto
Edhouse, Donald W., Sto
Fleming, Harold L., AB
Forron, Jack E.A., Sto
Fralick, Earl I., AB
Frith, William A., LS
Fuller, Eugene M., AB
Gaetano, Valentino J., AB
Gibbons, Marshall L., AB
Goldsmith, T.H., C.Yeo.Sig
Gordon, Lloyd M., AB
Goulet, Robert J., Sto
Grainger, Roy J., LSA
Guest, Carlton G., AB
Hayes, Christopher, OS
Heatherington, John T., Sto
Henry, Robert J., AB
Houison, George D., L.Wrtr
Hurley, Michael P., Sto
Irvine, Leonard C., AB
Izard, Theodore D., Lt(E)
Jarvis, Edmund A., LS
Johnson, Elswood S., AB
Johnson, Richard R., L.Sto
Johnston, Lawrence R., AB
Kelly, Lionel D., Stwd
Kobes, John R., LS
Lamoureux, André, LS
Lawrence, Ralph M., Lt
Lea, Eric E., Sto
Ledoux, Louis, AB
Lewandowski, Stan. S., Sto
Lind, Mekkel G., Sto.PO
Love, Walter M., ERA
Lucas, Donald O., Sto
MacAvoy, Gerald W., PO.Cook
MacDonald, Ashley K., AB
MacKenzie, Alexander, AB
Maguire, John W., L.Sto
Mahoney, John D., Lt(SB)
Manson, John L., Cook
Matthews, George H., AB
McBride, John L., AB
McCarroll, Thomas G., Sto
McCrindle, William D., AB
McGregor, William, L.Sto
McLean, Daniel H., AB
McNeill, John J., Sto
Meadwell, Richard G., AB
Mengoni, Eric J., AB
Metcalfe, Donald I., Elec.Art
Millar, Victor, AB
Mills, Ernest G., C.ERA
Mumford, Leonard K., ERA
Nash, Robert A., SLt
Nicholas, Joseph R., L.Sto
Ouellette, Joseph E.V., AB
Peart, Hubert J., AB
Phillips, John D., AB
Pike, Brenton J., AB
Pothier, Charles L., AB
Rennie, John E., PO
Riendeau, Joseph A.L., AB
Roberts, John C., ERA
Roberts, Raymond L., AB
Robertshaw, Eric, AB
Robertson, Ian A., AB
Robertson, William, Sto
Roger, Leo A., Sto
Rolls, Raymond B., AB
Ryan, Norman V., AB
St. Laurent, Joseph L.M., AB
Sampson, Francis L., AB
Sanderson, Earl H., AB
Senecal, Jean G.L., AB
Sherlock, Albert V., Stwd
Sigston, George D., Gnr
Singleton, John C., AB
Skyvington, Francis G., SBA
Sommerfeld, Samuel W., AB
Soucisse, Paul E., Coder
Stevenson, Elmer H., Sto
Stewart, John L., AB
Stewart, William G., Sig
Stockman, Ernest O., Lt(E)
Stubbs, John H., LCdr
Sutherland, John W., AB
Sweet, Charles C., CPO
Thompson, Harry, Sto
Tupper, Allister R., Ord.Art
Vair, James A., L.Stwd
Veinotte, Joseph V.W., Sy.PO
Waitson, Maurice, AB
Wallace, Peter W., AB
Ward, Leslie, Lt(SB)
Watson, Reginald J., Tel
Williams, Kenneth W., ERA
Wood, John A., AB
Yeadon, Robert L., AB

Plus 2 RN ratings.

CHAPTER 41

HMCS VALLEYFIELD: THE ONLY FRIGATE SUNK

Halfway between truth and endless error the mold of the species is permanent. That is earth's burden.

Barbara Tuchman, *The First Salute*

Valleyfield:
River class frigate
Builder: Morton Shipbuilding Ltd, Quebec City
Comm: 7 Dec 43
Crew: 15 officers, 148 crew, (6 RN)
Fate: Torpedoed by *U 548*, off Cape Race, NF, 6 May 44
Casualties: 12 officers, 111 crew, 2 passengers

There are few photos of HMCS *Valleyfield* as she only survived five months. Here she is seen in the St. Lawrence just after commissioning, with visitors from her name-sake city of Valleyfield, Quebec on board for a few hours.

Of the sixty frigates built for the RCN and the ten acquired from the RN, ***Valleyfield*** was the only one sunk. When she was commissioned in December 1943, she barely made it through the ice in the St. Lawrence to Halifax, in company with three other RCN and RN ships before freeze-up. On arrival she had to be dry docked to check for damage due to the ice.

Valleyfield became operational in February 1944 and was assigned to C-1 Escort Group. Within three months she was sunk with a heavy loss of life.

After a convoy escort task to the UK the group left Loch Foyle on 29 March to pick up the forty-eight ship convoy ONS-32 bound for North American ports. After a difficult passage due to heavy weather, the group was relieved by W-2 of the Western Local Escort Force out of Halifax and the C-1 ships carried on to St. John's. There the group's senior officer, Cdr John Byron, DSC, RD, RNR (known by those who worked in the group as "The Brain") transferred from the destroyer ***Assiniboine*** to ***Valleyfield*** as the former was assigned to other duties. The group then consisted of the one frigate and four corvettes, ***Fredericton, Halifax, Frontenac*** and ***Giffard.*** The group sailed in four days to Londonderry, where the corvette ***Edmundston*** was added to their number, and sailed again on the afternoon of 27 April to escort Convoy ONM-243 westward. It crossed the Atlantic without incident except that ***Fredericton*** was detached on 3 May to escort a straggling merchantman to Newfoundland. At 1736 on 6 May C-1 Group turned over convoy responsibilities to a Western Local group and once again headed at a modest thirteen knots almost due north for St. John's.

The ships were in line abreast about 2,000 yards apart, in order from port to starboard ***Halifax, Frontenac, Valleyfield, Giffard*** and ***Edmundston.*** The weather was clear and bright and, by nightfall, with an almost full moon dead astern. Visibility was good, with objects out to 4,000 yards and more clearly visible through binoculars. There were small growlers or "bergy bits" of ice about, which the ships passed through all afternoon and evening. The sea temperature was 32°. Due to this ice, which was largely submerged, hard to see and almost undetectable on radar, yet dangerous to hit, Byron ordered zig-zagging cease at 2030. In ***Valleyfield***, the RXC radar was inoperative (not for the first time) and so the OOW had switched to the older (and already obsolete) SW1C set. ***Frontenac's*** radar was also not functioning due to problems.

At the subsequent Board of Inquiry the base radar officer was asked, regarding the RXC sets: "Has it always worked well?" To which he responded "It has never worked well to my knowledge." The Board also noted that at 2000 a signal had been received by the group that a submarine was believed operating within 150 miles southeast or east of the Avalon peninsula; a rather vague threat for the group coming up from the south. Also the Board noted that CAT gear was not streamed by the ships. But due to its annoying rattling noise masking the asdic, thus reducing the effectiveness of the sweeps, and because the ships were not in contact with any threatening U-boats, survivors felt it quite normal not to have streamed CAT.

The group had to some extent advanced into clearer water by 2230 but the zig-zag was not resumed, mainly because both Cdr Byron and the ship's CO, LCdr D.T. English, RCNR, were asleep, exhausted from long watches during the convoy operation and while avoiding the ice.

Lt Ian Tate, ***Valleyfield's*** ASCO and one of only two officers to survive, was on her bridge that evening as OOW. The asdic loud-speaker was turned on on the bridge, Tate noting its customary "ping..... rattle.. ping..... rattle.. ping....." as the set transmitted and then the operator trained it five degrees for the next transmission, then a long rattle as the set was trained to the opposite beam to start again. At about 2335 he was startled by a cessation in that rhythm, replaced by a tentative series of rattles as the operator (ABSD Russ) investigated a suspicious sound broad on the ship's port beam. Tate then comments "I heard this ticking sound over the loud-speaker, jumped to the voicepipe and immediately ordered the operator 'Investigate 250 to 290'. He started to investigate this arc, and about five seconds later the torpedo struck." What they had heard was the sound of the electric motor of an acoustic torpedo.

Valleyfield was hit on the port side in the boiler room. Although "Action stations" was ordered rung, power failed almost immediately and no more than a brief alarm was sounded. The ship split in two halves at once; the bow rose, rolled to starboard and sank vertically within two minutes of the explosion. The after part also sank quickly, damaged section first, and there was but one survivor from this part of the ship. Within four minutes there was nothing left but a mass of debris, floats, survivors and oil on the surface. The explosion was so violent that there was uncertainty among the survivors on which side the torpedo had hit. ***Halifax*** and ***Frontenac***, to port of ***Valleyfield***, were now ahead of the ship's position and outside visibility range, although the CO of ***Frontenac*** reported later he had heard the thump of what he took to be a single depth charge. His OOW even saw a plume of shadowy smoke in ***Valleyfield's*** direction and also presumed it to be a depth charge. There was some unintelligible signal flashing and, when the corvette's signalman-of-the-watch was called, he could not make out anything. With the loss of the group's senior officer, unknown to the other ships, there was some confusion, and later Board criticism, as to what should be done about these vague sounds and sights.

The ship was hit at 2340 ship's time on the 7th (0040 Newfoundland time). At 2345 ***Giffard*** signalled by RT (voice radio) to ***Valleyfield*** "Is there anything wrong?" She tried this query several times, with no response. Then at 2400 she asked ***Edmundston*** "Are you in radar contact with ***Valleyfield?"*** When that ship replied simply "Negative", ***Giffard's*** CO took it on himself to close the frigate's last known track and, within minutes, found only the litter of a ship's destruction.

U 548, KL Eberhard Zimmermann, had been in commission eighteen months as part of II U-Flottille and had an experienced crew although this was Zimmermann's first war patrol as a CO. She had departed six weeks before, from Narvik in Norway, on 23 March on her current patrol. After a shot on 4 May at what Zimmermann recorded as an RN or RCN escort (which missed and which was, in fact, a damaged merchantman), he had been attacked by aircraft and dived, not too sure of his position due to fog and the need to detour around icebergs. Having heard his signals to BdU, the operating authority in Newfoundland knew a U-boat was in the area and sent ***Agassiz*** and ***Timmins*** to hunt her. These two had passed C-1 Group at 2100.

The U-boat had been trimmed down on the surface since 2040, with Zimmermann in the conning tower. Paradoxically her *wanze* radar-detector was also not operational. Not expecting anything in particular, at 2300 Zimmermann sighted the faint shadow of ***Valleyfield*** fine on his port bow, closing rapidly. He crash dived and, to gain time, turned to parallel ***Valleyfield's*** course which he estimated correctly within one degree and her speed within one knot. He was not aware of the other ships in company until his hydrophone operator advised him of engine noises to port and starboard of the

The Canadian ships opened fire on ***Z 32*** at 0254, hit the German as she turned south at thirty-one knots and then eastward, entering a known minefield area. ***Haida*** and ***Huron*** skirted the minefield to the north, DeWolf presuming the German would continue toward Cherbourg if possible. At 0422 ***Haida's*** radar picked up the German ship at long range, and the two set off in pursuit. Then a destroyer of the 20th Division encountered the Canadians and, mistaking them for a possible enemy, illuminated them by starshell, which gave the chase away. So all opened fire on ***Z 32*** which again altered to the south toward the coast, firing ineffectually at her pursuers. Now assisted at long range by the 20th Division and ***Tartar***, and despite cover of a smoke screen, the German ship was driven ashore in flames close to the Île de Batz light. The next day photo reconnaissance revealed her well ashore and still on fire. Attacks by RCAF Beaufighters, to finish her off for certain with rockets, were driven off by local AA batteries and an attempt to torpedo the hulk from seaward by an MTB (as had been done in the case of ***T 27,*** driven ashore by ***Haida*** when ***Athabaskan*** was sunk, Chapter 40) were not successful. But the ship was a total loss in any event.

At 0530 the flotilla turned for Plymouth and home. A brief attack by JU 88s was driven off by the flotilla's AA fire. ***Tartar*** was again able to lead at twenty-nine knots. Word of the flotilla's success had spread at their base, and they received a hero's welcome from cheering crowds on their entry into Plymouth harbour. ***Tartar*** was the only ship damaged to any extent, ***Haida*** having only a splinter hole in her engine room. The close control between Plymouth Command, who were in constant W/T connection with the ships, and between the ships themselves to ensure they did not fire on each other and that damaged ships were protected is indicated by the eighty-two W/T messages and 147 voice tactical messages recorded by Sig (TO) George Mannix in ***Haida*** alone, between 0102 and 0518 that night, one a minute.

The Admiralty signalled: "The Board of Admiralty convey their congratulations to Officers and Ships' Companies on the spirited action which has caused a potential menace to the main operation to be removed." In fact the senior officer of the German 3rd Naval Defence Division was later to conclude that, partly due to the Luftwaffe's refusal of any air defence, "this action has demonstrated that no further possibility existed of moving larger units along the coast of Brittany." This was a most valuable outcome to the Allies. DeWolf and Rayner were awarded DSCs.

Of the Germans who escaped, ***T 24***, not much damaged in her running battle with ***Haida*** and ***Huron***, was sunk on 24 August 1944 in Le Verdon roads in an RAF raid. ***Z 24***, considerably damaged and not fully repaired, was also sunk in Le Verdon roads by RAF fighter-bombers the next day. The German ships had not been able to escape to Germany or to influence the Normandy battle because of the sea control exercised by the destroyers of 10 DF. Of survivors of ***ZH 1***, twenty-seven reached the French shore, and 140 were picked up as prisoners by HMS ***Fame*** and ***Inconstant***, sent to the area of the battle for that very purpose.

Some verses from a poem " The Fighting Tenth", by the WRNS of the Long Room Signal Station, Plymouth, tell the story well:

There are specks on the horizon
As familiar as can be,
D.10 with his flotilla
Proceeding in from sea.

The pendants now come visible
Four-three, Five-one, Two-four,
Tartar, Ashanti, Huron,
Astern there loom five more.

Blyskawica, Haida, Javelin,
Piorun, Eskimo,
Buntings on the signal bridge,
Stokers down below.

Battle ensigns at all mastheads,
An impressive sight to see,
The ***Tartar*** with the Tenth DF
Come in Triumphantly.

Passing through the gate at last
They move more cautiously,
The same old signal flying
"Act independently".

We hope we'll always see you thus
With ensigns flying free,
For the Fighting Tenth's a lovely sight
When coming in from sea.

SOURCES:

Brice, *The Tribals,* pp. 239-240.

German, *The Sea Is At Our Gates,* p. 163.

Gröner, *German Warships 1815-1945*, Vol.One, pp. 195, 203-204, 212.

Jones, *And So To Battle,* pp. 81-89.

Paquette & Bainbridge, *Honours & Awards*, pp. 143, 453.

Schull, *Far Distant Ships,* pp. 286-295.

Sclater, *Haida*, pp. 141-160.

Smith, *Hold The Narrow Seas,* pp. 237-241.

Venier, *Ready, The Brave,* pp. 303-313.

Whitley, *Destroyer!,* pp. 205-211.

CHAPTER 43

SINKING GERMAN COASTAL FORCES: A SERIES OF STORIES

The real war will never get in the books

Walt Whitman

Actions against merchantmen and minor war vessels are much harder to describe accurately and verify than those against larger surface units and U-boats. Records that accurately identify destroyed ships tend to be sparse on both sides. The following are probably not the only cases of success against smaller enemy warships, but are typical and verifiable. Small vessels that appeared to be sunk, at night or in smoke, sometimes were salvagable or struggled into nearby harbours, to be repaired. Probably others, recorded in German records as "Sunk about" or "Loss unknown" should be credited to Canadian forces but records of these minor battles were often not as carefully preserved as those for larger warships.

* * * * * * * * * * * * *

HMCS *Sioux*: V class destroyer

Action: Sank German E-boat *S 136*, off Barfleur, 11 Jun 44

Sioux: German records indicate that their *schnellboot* (E-boat in Allied terms) ***S 136*** was sunk on 11 June, 1944 off Barfleur by an Allied force consisting of HMCS ***Sioux*** (LCdr E.E.G. Boak, RCN), the RN Captains class frigate HMS ***Duff*** and the Polish Hunt class destroyer ***Krakowiak***. No Canadian reference to this action has been found but it was presumably in defence of the invasion routes to Normandy.

SOURCES:

Whitley, *German Coastal Forces,* p. 180.

* * * * * * * * * * * * *

MTB 748: D class Fairmile

Action: Put minesweeper *M 133* out of action, St. Malo, 14 Jun 44

MTB 748: Operating out of Brixham, just before transfer to Ostend and rather far from home, on 5 August the 65th Flotilla encountered a southbound German convoy off St. Malo. The convoy was not aware of danger and was attacked from its port bow, from the dark landward side. In the ensuing action the four Canadian boats, ***748*** (LCdr J.R.H. Kirkpatrick, SO), ***735, 736*** and ***743*** sank two merchant ships by torpedo and set on fire the minesweeper ***M 133*** by gunfire. Although ***M 133*** reached St. Malo, she was sunk in the harbour in an air attack on 6 August 1944, evidently later the same day.

SOURCES:

Law, *White Plumes Astern,* p. 135.

Schull, *Far Distant Ships,* p. 337.

* * * * * * * * * * * * *

HMCS *Iroquois, Haida*: Tribal class destroyers

Action: Sank minesweepers *M 263* and *M 486*, two auxiliaries and merchant ships, Biscay coast, 6 Aug 44

Iroquois & Haida: This action was part of the 10th Destroyer Flotilla's sweeps along the French coast to prevent enemy ships interfering with the ongoing invasion traffic or of escaping back to Germany as French ports fell to the Allies. Titled Force 26, the cruiser HMS ***Bellona*** (as senior officer) and the RN Tribal destroyers ***Tartar*** (D.10, Cdr Basil Jones, DSC, RN) and ***Ashanti*** and the Canadian HMCS ***Haida*** (Cdr Harry DeWolf) and ***Iroquois*** (Cdr J.C. Hibbard, DSC) sailed from Plymouth on 4 August 1944. By the evening of the 5th they were closing the French Biscay coast south of St. Nazaire, the destroyers in loose line abreast, with the cruiser two miles astern to provide for illumination when required and to be out of the way of any torpedoes fired by an enemy. At 2355 when thirty-five miles south of Belle Île and heading southward, ***Tartar's*** radar picked up an echo astern at great range. This was plotted, identified as several ships heading south at twelve knots and zig-zagging.

The destroyers and cruiser altered about and set course to put the destroyers between the German convoy and the coast, crossing the enemy's course fifteen miles ahead. Speed was increased to twenty-five knots.

At 0035 ***Bellona*** fired starshell from seaward of the target and ordered "Engage." The ships could now be seen as seven or eight vessels and fire was opened at 9,000 yards, just under five miles. ***Tartar*** took the lead ship and the other three were to spread their fire among the remainder as the destroyers all altered to port toward the enemy in staggered line. At 0102 ***Haida*** accurately identified the enemy ships as a minesweeper and two trawler/coasters. Fire was opened by all the destroyers. ***Tartar*** to ***Iroquois:*** FINISH OFF LEFT HAND SHIP. And to the senior officer: WE ARE FINISHING OFF 3 SHIPS. The ships fired steadily; it was not long before two escorts had been torpedoed and blown up and all the rest were damaged. ***Bellona*** signalled the destroyers: INTEND TO FORM SINGLE LINE AHEAD, STEER PAST BURNING TARGETS AND DESTROY. CO. 270, SPEED 15. In Cdr Jones' words, "the remainder of the convoy were then circled and destroyed." During the height of the action a premature explosion had occurred when loading a shell in one of Y mounting's guns on ***Haida's*** quarterdeck. This killed two gunners, LS Gordon Rowe and AB Roy Betts, and wounded eight and put the mounting out of action, but the ship was not otherwise seriously damaged and the fight continued. Rowe's was a sadly ironic case, for he had missed his ship ***Haida*** when she had sailed from Plymouth but was able to catch HMCS ***Saskatchewan*** who transferred him to ***Haida*** the night before the action.

While it was not possible to tell who had sunk which ship, the German records show that a large cable layer, ***Hoher Weg***, was sunk as well as another merchantman, the 775-ton minesweepers ***M 263*** and ***M 486***, and the smaller armed escorts ***SG 3*** and ***V 414.***

As the ships turned for home another action ensued with another southbound convoy. This time, in difficult conditions of smoke screen and unfavourable moonlight, and with an enemy minefield parallel to the course and to seaward, the force set another minesweeper, ***M 304*** and the flak ship ***Richthofen*** afire and damaged others, although they all survived the night. The 10 DF destroyers and ***Bellona*** reached Plymouth with only ***Haida's*** killed and injured as the cost.

Jimmy Hibbard, who died much lamented in early 1996, was well respected as a CO and a person. He insisted on ensuring those who should be aware knew he was in charge. It is naval custom that the senior officer, when of equal rank, is the one who has the earliest promotion date. When driving ***Iroquois*** in mid-1943 and ***Assiniboine*** joined his group, commanded by Cdr Ken Adams, also with a puckish sense of humour, Hibbard sent the signal: J.C. HIBBARD, DSC; ONE STROKE ONE STROKE 43. In response he received from ***Assiniboine:*** KENNY ADAMS WEIGHS A TON; ONE STROKE ONE STROKE 41!

SOURCES:

Jones, *And So To Battle,* pp. 95-98.

Schull, *Far Distant Ships,* pp 349-351.

Sclater, *Haida,* pp. 192-199.

* * * * * * * * * * * * *

HMCS *Qu'Appelle, Restigouche, Saskatchewan, Skeena:*
River class destroyers
Action: Sank two or three armed U-boat escorts, off Brest, 6 Jul 44

In an action sometimes referred to as "The Battle of Pierres Noires", ***Qu'Appelle*** (Cdr A.M. McKillop, RN as senior officer), ***Restigouche*** (LCdr D.W. Groos, RCN), ***Saskatchewan*** (LCdr A.H. Easton, DSC, RCNR) and ***Skeena*** (LCdr P.F.X. Russell, RCN) were part of EG-12, sent in Operation Dredger to destroy escorts that had been protecting U-boats entering and leaving Brest. In the same operation EG-14 Group was to follow them and attack the U-boats when the heavily armed escorts were disposed of. The Canadian destroyers were steaming east and then north along the rugged and island-strewn Brittany coast when at 0113 on 6 July radar reported three or four contacts, outbound from Brest Roads at nine knots. At least ***Iroquois*** and ***Skeena*** had Action Information Organization (AIO) systems, based on radar and other input, making the picture clear of what was occurring, both as to enemy movements and own forces.[1] Speed was increased to 30 knots until the enemy were closer, course altered to the west to parallel them, then speed reduced to sixteen knots so the bow waves would be less visible. The escorts were sighted at 3,000 yards at 0137, with two U-boats in their midst. They were illuminated by starshell and fire opened by the destroyers, which the escorts returned with a vengeance. The two U-boats turned at once and fled back toward Brest. In two passes the destroyers eventually appeared to sink at least two of the escorts and set a third afire, but the return fire injured several aboard the Canadian ships, including Cdr McKillop and killing a seaman gunner in ***Saskatchewan***. While EG-12's responsibilities had been carried out to the letter, EG-14 could not catch the U-boats. In a search of German coastal force records it has not been possible to identify with any certainty the escorts destroyed. They were likely ex-fishing trawlers, at least one armed with a 3-inch or 4-inch gun, 37mm and 20mm Oerlikons. Also the heavily damaged ships may have been towed back into the Brest area by ships sent to their aid when the Canadians withdrew after the twenty-five minute action.

Another Operation Dredger on 12 August also resulted in apparent destruction of one or two large escort trawlers in the same area, off the isle of Ushant. This time ***Saskatchewan*** was not present, but the River class HMCS ***Assiniboine*** and the small RN Hunt class destroyer HMS ***Albrighton*** were part of the force. Again, the German ships, one at least driven ashore and one set afire, have not been identified.

1. From Peter Chance, ***Skeena's*** navigator.

SOURCES:

Milner, *The U-boat Hunters*, pp.160-162 and 167.

Schull, *Far Distant Ships*, pp. 341-342.

* * * * * * * * * * * * * *

HMCS *Iroquois*: Tribal class destroyer
Action: Sank minesweeper *M 385*, Biscay, 14 Aug 44

Iroquois: As part of Operation Kinetic to cause maximum disruption to German forces moving along the French coasts, on the night of 14 August 1944, the RN cruiser HMS ***Mauritius*** and two 10 DF destroyers, HMS ***Ursa*** and HMCS ***Iroquois*** (Cdr J.C. Hibbard, DSC, RCN) were proceeding south off La Rochelle. They encountered an armed merchant ship and then an Elbing class destroyer. These the force engaged and damaged and then withdrew as the enemy made smoke and retreated under the cover of heavy coastal guns.

The force continued southward, then turned back for home parallel to the coast. At 0540 ***Iroquois's*** radar detected ships to the north at about 11,000 yards. At 0615 three minesweepers were sighted inshore of the destroyers, who engaged them by gunfire at 3,200 yards. The destroyers claimed two driven ashore and one sunk in an explosion. An examination of German records indicates that the two minesweepers driven ashore must have been salvaged or were smaller auxiliaries, but ***Iroquois*** and ***Ursa*** had indeed sunk the large M261 class minesweeper ***M 385***.

On 23 August the same ships were back again on the Biscay coast, where ***Iroquois, Ursa*** and ***Mauritius*** detected vessels inshore at 0117. They stood out into the bay to entice the German ships to venture farther and then at 0209 the destroyers and ***Mauritius*** opened fire at 4,000 yards at four vessels. The two destroyers took on the escorts, sinking one and driving another ashore. From the two gun battles, at least one Allied report claims victories over not only ***M 385*** but also the armed auxiliaries (ex-fishing vessels) ***V 702*** (the 444-ton ***Memel), V 717*** (***Alfred III*** of 1,000 tons), ***V 720, V 729*** (the 282-ton ***Marie Simone***) and ***V 730*** (***Michel François*** of 535 tons). Prisoners were taken from stranded vessels by local Free French partisans, and although it is not possible to allocate sunken ships to particular destroyers, the success of the night sweeps deserves recording as a "credit".

SOURCES:

Brice, *The Tribals*, pp. 151-152.

Schull, *Far Distant Ships,* pp. 351-352.

* * * * * * * * * * * * * *

HMCS *Algonquin*: V class destroyer
Action: Sank minesweepers *M 416* and *M 427*, off Norway, 12-13 Aug 44

Algonquin: After a series of carrier and shore-based air strikes against the German battleship ***Tirpitz*** in northern Norway, in which ***Algonquin*** and ***Sioux*** acted as support (the former helping rescue the Canadian-manned carrier HMS ***Nabob*** when she was torpedoed) a welcome, purely naval surface operation was planned against German vessels passing along the coast of Norway.

Operation Counterblast was mounted in November, 1944 to destroy German shipping operating off the southern Norwegian coast.

CHAPTER 45

HMCS HURON AND HMS ESKIMO IN A GUN BATTLE THAT SINKS...SOMEONE

HMCS *Huron*: (see Chapter 39 for details)

HMS *Eskimo*: (see Chapter 44 for details)

Crew: 190 total

Action: Sank trawler *Vp 213 (Claus Bolten)* & *M 4611 (Etienne Rimbert)*, off Channel Islands, 28 Jun 44

When first under fire an' you're wishful to duck,
Don't look nor take 'eed at the man that is struck,
Be thankful you're livin' and trust to your luck
And march to your front like a soldier

Rudyard Kipling, "The Young British Soldier"

While this story is well covered in general reports, it has proven difficult to determine what actually happened on the German side of events. While ***Huron*** and ***Eskimo's*** reports both refer to sinking a German minesweeper, German reference texts report no minesweepers lost on this date. But the UK Ministry of Defence (Foreign Documents Section) finally solved the puzzle.

Huron (LCdr H.S. Rayner, DSC, RCN as senior officer) and ***Eskimo*** (LCdr E.N. Sinclair, RN), were units of the 10th Destroyer Flotilla. On the night of 27 June the pair were designated Force 27, to sweep through the area south of the Channel Islands to St. Malo. They were to look for German surface ships that had been in Cherbourg, which had just fallen, to prevent them escaping south along the Brittany coast. They sailed from Plymouth at 1900 on the 27th aiming to be off Roches Douvres by 2330.

The sea was slight, the wind SW just over five knots, with visibility about five miles, and when the action opened there was no moon. The two ships were in line ahead, ***Huron*** leading, heading east at twenty-three knots and weaving on either side of the base course. At 0053 on the 28th, when about twenty miles NW of St. Malo, ***Eskimo*** reported a radar contact at five miles fine on their starboard bow. Within two minutes ***Huron*** picked up the echo on her 271 radar. By 0057 the enemy's course was estimated as 040° at seven knots. The two destroyers increased to twenty-five knots and altered course together to lead the enemy. At 0059 both ships opened fire with starshell on the enemy's bearing.

This revealed three ships that appeared to be minesweepers or trawlers, a larger one and two smaller, moving from right to left. ***Huron*** at once opened fire on the largest ship with A and B guns at a range of some 6,000 yards or three nautical miles, scoring hits almost with her first rounds and setting her target afire. While she could still see her target, the other two were promptly obscured in smoke. Speed was increased to thirty knots and course altered toward to close the range. Then ***Eskimo*** reported that she thought she was being fired at by shore batteries, so the ships altered to starboard to draw off the shore and to investigate yet another echo at three and a half miles - which turned out to be a large whistle buoy.

At 0112 the two destroyers altered again to the east "to re-engage the enemy" as LCdr Rayner put it in his subsequent report. ***Huron's*** initial target was now burning furiously and its ready use ammunition began to explode. The other two were still obscured by smoke but held on radar. To starboard of ***Huron, Eskimo*** had circled the smoke and encountered one of the other vessels at which she opened fire at once and which returned fire in a spirited manner with an 88mm (3.5-inch) deck gun, a 37mm and several Oerlikons. Rayner's description gives a good impression of events:

> Altered course 180° to port and reduced speed to twenty knots to keep [in] touch with but avoid the melee a short distance on my starboard beam. It was not possible to distinguish which was ***Eskimo*** and which was the enemy, as streams of tracer were being

fired by both ships. Rounded a buoy during the turn which normally shows a fixed red light, but it was not lit on this occasion.

Over the next ten minutes Rayner fired starshell on various bearings to try to illuminate both ***Eskimo's*** battle and the third ship that had been present. At 0137 ***Huron*** opened fire with main armament on a target hidden by smoke but with a radar range of 5,600 yards. Almost at once her target exploded with a very large flash and the radar echo disappeared.

At 0158 ***Huron*** queried ***Eskimo***: ARE YOU JOINING ME? ***Eskimo*** replied: I AM TRYING TO SINK THIS CHAP.

By now ***Eskimo*** had reported she had been hit by an 88mm shell in No. 1 boiler room and a 37mm round had cut the main steam line in No. 3 boiler room, with other hits elsewhere. She lost all steam power and electrics, including radar and the steering motor. She continued firing her 4.7-inch guns in hand control at her trawler, which then moved off to the eastward and escaped further attention. Rayner ordered ***Eskimo*** to withdraw to the west at 0207.

Both Rayner and Sinclair felt the trawler had been badly mauled, and for another ten minutes opened fire sporadically on what seemed to be a blazing trawler partly obscured by drifting smoke. There is much confusion as to their targets during this period as well, and it is likely their later targets were the first and second ships ***Huron*** had attacked earlier, although there may have been a fourth trawler present for a short while as well. At 0214 Rayner sighted German survivors on a raft and was tempted to pick them up for evidence and interrogation but was involved in sorting out ***Eskimo*** and her victim and did not encounter the raft again. Later evidence shows the third ship escaped relatively unscathed into St. Helier, Jersey.

Eskimo was able to raise steam for six knots and Rayner ordered her to withdraw as he felt he could take care of their remaining German ship himself. However by this time, 0221, no other enemy ship could be found, so ***Huron*** returned to her first victim and finished her off with close range fire at 0250.

Huron then took off after ***Eskimo*** who, by this time, had restored power for twenty knots, and the two arrived back at Plymouth at 0830 without further incident. ***Huron*** had fired 496 4.7-inch rounds and 166 4" starshells, as well as almost 1,100 pom pom and Oerlikon rounds.

Although the two did not know it for many years, their targets were the auxiliary minesweeper ***M 4611**** (the ex-French 197-ton fishing vessel ***Etienne Rimbert*** of Dieppe), and the armed trawler ***Vp 213*** (*Vorpostenboot.* ***Claus Bolten***, a 282-ton ex-fishing trawler of Cuxhaven) both of which were sunk. The vessel which escaped was also an ex-fishing trawler, ***Vp 203*** (***Carl Röver***, 390 tons, of Wesermünde), the largest of the three.

It was a typical destroyer night action of the period, with some radar assistance but much uncertainty in the dark and smoke, with tracer and explosions everywhere, and at considerable speed requiring instant decisions to avoid firing on or running into friends. Herb Rayner in his report's section entitled "Lessons Learnt" comments that he thought at first the vessels were destroyers and being intent on not letting them escape, operated at higher speeds than was necessary. Also he had got in too close before he appreciated the situation, exposing his ships to the small ships' close range weapons while being unable to make full use of his own infinitely superior gunnery control and main armament. A very honest and judicious assessment by an officer who was to rise to be a vice admiral and the Navy's last Chief of the Naval Staff before unification cancelled the position.

Huron had already helped dispose of two German destroyers and a large minesweeper earlier in June with 10 DF. ***Eskimo's*** damage was to cause further problems, on the night of 1 July, when she and four 10 DF destroyers were off Ushant. It says something for the keenness of her CO and ship's company not to miss a single operation that she was out that night at all. With her radar still inoperative and in hand steering from aft, she collided in thick weather with HMS ***Javelin,*** badly damaging her bows. She was towed back into Plymouth by ***Huron*** and out of service for repairs until 31 October.

Huron continued to serve until the war ended and went to the Far East for the Korean War. She lasted in peacetime service until 1965. ***Eskimo*** was broken up in 1949.

SOURCES:

Brice, *The Tribals,* pp. 122-123.

German, *The Sea Is At Our Gates,* p. 164.

Jones, *And So To Battle,* p.91.

Lloyd's Register, 1941-1942.

Schull, *Far Distant Ships,* pp. 339-340.

Venier, *Ready, The Brave* pp. 241-242, 320-321.

Warship 1996, p.172.

****M4611*** was sunk in April 1943, salvaged and renumbered as ***M4260*** when sunk as described in this action.

CHAPTER 46

TOO OFTEN FORGOTTEN: MTBs 460 & 463

From Corvette returning to base,
to MTB setting out on night patrol:
GOOD NIGHT. GOOD LUCK
Reply from MTB:
THANKS. ACTUALLY WE RELY ON SKILL

Captain Jack Broome, *Make Another Signal*

MTBs 460 & 463:
G type motor torpedo boats
Builder: British Power Boat Co, Hythe, UK
Comm in Flotilla: Mar 44
Char: 71.5 X 20.5 feet, speed 41 knots max.
Crew: 2-3 officers, 14-17 crew
Fate: mined, English Channel off Normandy, *MTB 460* 2 Jul 44; *MTB 463* 8 Jul 44
Casualties: *460*, 2 officers, 9 men; *463*, none

Lt Dave Killam's *MTB 460*, followed by another boat of the 29th Flotilla, travelling at speed.

Canadians served from very early in the war in British MTBs and MGBs (the gunboat variant). They gained much valuable experience and no little praise for their quickly-learned skills and daring, in both night actions in the Channel and forays in the Mediterranean, particularly among the Greek Islands.

In 1942 the Admiralty suggested that the RCN form at least one flotilla of MTBs of their own. Because Canada had no such boats (although plans developed in late 1939 had suggested thirty-two of them for the RCN), the offer was turned down at the time. Quite a few Canadians went to serve with the RN in lieu of Canada providing actual boats. Then, in mid-1943, the RN offered to supply the boats, if the RCN would man them, due to manpower shortages in the UK. This time the offer was quickly accepted, and two flotillas were formed. The 29th, under A/LCdr C.A. Law, of eight boats, were to be "Short" MTBs built by the British Power Boat Company, of the well-known hard chine design. The 65th Flotilla, formed at the same time and commanded by A/LCdr J.R.H. Kirkpatrick, were to be Fairmile Type D or "Dog Boats", somewhat slower, but much longer and carrying more armament. In fact, both classes were several knots slower than their German counterparts, the diesel-driven *schnellboote* or E-boats, which caused much frustration when the latter decided to break off actions and depart.

The 29th's boats worked-up at Holyhead in North Wales and had the torpedo tubes removed and replaced with depth charges, to the annoyance of the COs. (They were re-installed later). The 300-pound depth charges were intended for dropping close alongside their ship targets, set to shallowest depth and, it later developed, against German frogmen and miniature submarines in the Normandy anchorages. In early May 1944 the flotilla proceeded to their operational base at Ramsgate at the north end of the Strait of Dover and under Dover command.

Invasion was obviously in the air, and on 22 May the 29th's boats undertook their first operational patrols off the coast of France with an RN flotilla. When Operation Neptune, the naval portion of the invasion, took place on 5 and 6 June, the flotilla became involved in protecting the outer fringes of the landing beaches. They were at first protecting the minesweepers, then the anchorages against infiltrating E-boats trying to lay mines or shoot up the huge crowd of vessels.

On 1 July, MTBs ***459, 460*** and ***465*** were on their way to Normandy once again after brief refits to repair damages, often caused by masses of floating debris from either sunken ships, bombed shore installations or other battle wreckage. LCdr Law's ***459*** hit some unseen underwater timber, bent her props and had to retire to Portsmouth. Lt Dave Killam in ***460*** and Lt Charley "Chuff-Chuff" Chaffey in ***465*** continued, and that night patrolled the landing area looking for any enemy intrusions near Cap d'Antifer.

There were none, but on the way back to their mother ship (an RN frigate) early in the morning, travelling at moderate speed and in line ahead, ***460*** evidently hit a floating mine and disintegrated in a crash, a sheet of flame and an immense column of water and pieces of the boat. This before the horrified eyes of Chaffey and his crew in ***465***, 150 yards astern. Chaffey's boat was showered with the falling wreckage and water.

Chaffey sheared clear at once, then slowed and swept around to carry out a careful search of the area where the disaster had occurred. He succeeded in picking up six dazed survivors and two bodies from the water, those of ABs George Ashmore and George Grant. The upper deck gunners had survived due to their life vests and flack jackets, although knocked senseless by the explosion. After a long search another MTB flotilla relieved them and continued searching, just in case. Nothing more was ever found. The CO, Lt Killam and nine of his men had been killed in all, their bodies never found.

The two men whose bodies were recovered were buried a few days later in Haslar Cemetery on the outskirts of Gosport, across from Portsmouth. The mines could have been laid as recently as the night before by E-Boats or dropped from aircraft, a threat which continued throughout the Normandy campaign.

Then on 7 July, a new danger was reported, the German "Human Torpedo" or "Neger" of the German *Kleinkampferbände*, (small battle units). These small one-man double torpedo self-propelled units had sunk several ships in the Normandy anchorage. The MTBs were assigned, particularly at night, to search for the small glass domes that protruded above the surface as the attackers approached and to finish them off with light depth charges, of which each boat carried six. It was dull but vital work, as the anchored Allies' ships were very vulnerable at night to these diminutive pests.

That night the patrol off Sword Beach was carried out by Lt Glen Creba in ***463*** and Lt Barney Marshall in ***466***. They were both under strain due to the presence of small German mines that they and other patrolling ships constantly set off, many pressure-activated. At 0500 on the 8th, ***463*** and ***466*** were still searching for the human torpedoes along the eastern side of Sword, travelling at a modest fifteen knots. Suddenly Creba's ***463*** set off a submerged mine just at her stern, a gigantic column of water rising high above the boat and descending on her with an immense crash. Although she emerged from this geyser, she started to settle quickly by the stern as ***466*** came hastily alongside. Although no-one was killed, there were five wounded, mostly sprained legs and arms and bad bruises. ***466*** took aboard all the crew of ***463*** except Creba and his 1st lieutenant, Dick Paddon, who hoped to save the boat by lightening her, jettisoning any moveable objects. She was taken in tow and two RN MTBs arrived to help. But it was in vain, as her plywood hull had been opened up too much to survive.

Lt Tony Law's *MTB 459*, badly damaged, but being towed home, 15 July, 1944. From a drawing done by Law at the time.

The two officers scrambled aboard ***466*** and the last they saw of ***463*** was the triangle of her bow as it slipped below the surface in a welter of bubbles at 0700, two hours after the explosion.

Glen Creba and the others were put on board a Polish destroyer in the assault area, where they were given warm dry clothes and their bruises attended to. They returned to Portsmouth and, after a week's leave, got a newer - and faster - boat, ***MTB 485.***

LOST:

Note: This listing has been checked against various sources, who do not all agree as to some names. It would appear accurate.

Ashmore, George, AB	Killam, David, Lt
Button, E.A., Sto(M)	Lawson, L., Sto(M)
George, D., PO.MM	Lee, J., LS
Grant, George, AB	Thompson, Peter, Tel
Hartley, J., Sto(M)	
Hunt, Howard, Lt	Plus 1 RN listing.

AB J. Allingham is sometimes shown as missing, but PO André Rousseau, the flotilla historian and Coxswain of ***460*** advises that he was a survivor.

SOURCES:

Borthwick, *History of the 29th Canadian MTB Flotilla,* pp. 25, 27, 37.

German, *The Sea Is At Our Gates*, p. 167.

Law, *White Plumes Astern*, pp. 102, 106-108.

Nolan & Street, *Champagne Navy,* pp. 156-158.

Schull, *Far Distant Ships,* pp. 332-334.

Tucker, *Naval Service Of Canada*, Vol.II, pp. 28-29, 48, 85-86.

CHAPTER 47

HMCS OTTAWA & KOOTENAY AND THE SINKING OF U 678: INNOVATIVE TACTICS

Place in the forefront of the record the plain fact that they were men who had grasped the new conditions of naval war, prepared in advance the necessary forces for the coming conflict.

John Richard Hale, *The Great Armada*

Ottawa (2nd): River class destroyer
Builder: Vickers-Armstrong Ltd, UK, as HMS *Griffin*, 1935
Comm in RCN: 20 Mar 43
Kootenay: River class destroyer
Builder: John I. Thornycroft & Co, Southampton, as HMS *Decoy*, 1931
Comm in RCN: 12 Apr 43
HMS *Statice*: Increased Endurance corvette
Builder: Collingwood Shipyards, ON, for USN
Comm in RN: Summer 1943
Action: Sank *U 678*, English Channel, 7 Jun 44
Casualties: 52
No survivors

The second HMCS *Ottawa* on August 20,1944, the day the group sank *U 984*. She has sacrificed A gun for a hedgehog mounting and Y gun for more depth charge armament.

In July 1944 the powerful Canadian support group EG-11 consisted of five destroyers: the second ***Ottawa*** (Cdr J.D. Prentice, DSO as senior officer); ***Kootenay*** (A/LCdr W.H. Willson); ***Gatineau*** (LCdr H.V.W. Groos); ***Chaudière*** (A/LCdr C.P. Nixon, all RCN officers) and ***St. Laurent*** (LCdr A.G. Boulton, RCNVR). Commander Prentice's name appears more than once in these chapters, and as senior officer he occasionally travelled in other ships of the group during operations. On this occasion his own ship and ***Kootenay*** were in company when they responded to a call for assistance.

The group was operating along the English south coast when the RN corvette ***Statice*** reported late on 5 June she was in contact with a submarine by asdic and could use help. ***Ottawa*** and ***Kootenay*** were ordered to her assistance, arriving at 0715 the next morning, when Prentice took over as senior officer for the hunt.

The Channel was one of the most difficult areas in which to conduct anti-submarine operations. The depths were not great, often 200 to 300 feet, with an irregular bottom which posed many problems for even the most experienced operators. There was often heavy surface traffic about, particularly in the post-D-Day build-up of Allied armies in Normandy; there were strong tidal currents

A nice portrait of *Kootenay* taken in February, 1944 with her hedgehog "split" on either side of A gun.

which not only degraded echo quality but also carried depth charges and hedgehog bombs away from their intended targets. Perhaps the most serious difficulty for the attacker was the proliferation of wrecks on the bottom. Centuries of sunken ships had created numerous anomalies. The destroyers had all been provided with "wreck charts" showing the approximate location of all the identified casualties. But the German submariners were also aware of most of these, and a simple tactic was to lay their U-boats on the bottom close alongside a wreck, creating doubt and confusing echoes for searching ships. Many a depth charge and hedgehog attack only battered an old wreck. It was not always possible to fix a ship's position with exactitude, and it was better to be sure than to let a possible U-boat escape. Two days before, ***Ottawa*** and HMS ***Forester*** had spent all day pounding a target later identified as one of these wrecks.

As well, a U-boat could use a tidal stream to lie still just above the bottom and let it carry her silently out of the area without using even electric motors. In addition to their asdics; the warships were all fitted with echo sounders to determine depth and bottom contours, normally for navigational use. The sounder produced a paper "trace" and a ship proceeding slowly could develop an outline of the shapes along the bottom, including the distinctive one of a submarine. In Channel waters, it was one of Prentice's preferred methods of target classification.

Ottawa and ***Kootenay*** on joining ***Statice*** commenced a square search of the area around the contact, with no immediate results. ***Statice*** became dubious about her earlier contact, decided it was probably "non-sub" and as she was not under Cdr Prentice's command, departed for Portsmouth. However Prentice was not so easily dissuaded, and ordered the Canadian destroyers to continue the search.[1] An echo sounder pass by ***Ottawa*** seemed to clearly reveal the outline of a bottomed U-boat. ***Ottawa*** gained a firm submarine contact at 0938, while ***Kootenay*** maintained an excellent plot of the action, location and movement of the ships. The submarine appeared to be on or near the bottom, in about 225 feet.

Attacks were made with both depth charges and hedgehog until approximately noon but results were inconclusive. There was a two knot tide running 080°, across the attack direction. Some light oil was seen glistening on the surface after a hedgehog attack by ***Ottawa*** at 1059 produced an extra explosion, and more debris of German origin came to the surface after one of ***Kootenay's*** depth charge attacks. Although never proven, it was widely suspected a U-boat might deliberately discharge such evidence in the hope of misleading the attackers, encouraging them to depart, sure of a kill. Cdr Prentice didn't accept the good evidence in hand as the final proof of destruction. The submarine at one stage seemed to be moving across the tide flow, and once was even thought to have been detected at only sixty feet, but by 1130 she did not appear to be moving.

1. From information provided by Lt (later Rear Admiral) R.W. Timbrell, CMM,DSC, CD, and Capt(N) W.H. Wilson, OMM,CD, then a seaman gunner in ***Ottawa.***

LCdr Willson, many years after the war, said that Commander Prentice encouraged the ships in his group to develop new tactics in the anti-submarine war. Now, with depth charges in short supply from days of wreck-pounding, there was an opportunity to try another tactic. The destroyers were quite sure they had the submarine carefully localized by depth sounder trace and SLt Peter Berry's careful plot in ***Kootenay***. It was the group anti-submarine officer who thought that in this case it would be possible to lower a depth charge on a wire fitted with a grapnel-hook and detonate it electrically when it was firmly hooked to the U-boat's hull.

Lt R.W. Timbrell was one of the very few RCN officers who had taken the long anti-submarine specialist course in the UK. As a sub-lieutenant he had already won a DSC taking soldiers of the British Army off the Dunkirk beaches in 1940, and was a survivor of HMCS ***Margaree*** when she was sunk in a collision later the same year. Now he set up the depth charge and grapnel system, which worked to the extent that additional evidence of destruction appeared on the surface and was recovered by ***Ottawa's*** whaler under command of her 1st lieutenant, Lt E.P. Earnshaw. LCdr Willson recalls that he preferred to drop a series of depth charges at slow speeds for accuracy. These were set to maximum depth and were allowed to "cook off" after lying at the submarine's shallower depth (the pistol operated on a combination of time and water seepage through small holes in a diaphragm). It was effective, but "a damned dangerous procedure", as sometimes they went off too soon after dropping, with the ship moving away at slow speed.

Because the evidence didn't guarantee the certain destruction of the U-boat, more attacks were carried out throughout the afternoon, depth charge, towed charge and hedgehog, none producing the clear evidence desired, although Schull reports they did get a tin of German butter, censor stamps, and a worn blue serge coat with three German buttons attached.

Ottawa now left to pursue another possible nearby contact, leaving ***Kootenay*** and ***Statice*** (who seems in some reports to have returned on ***Ottawa's*** more favourable messages) to hold the contact throughout the night. In the morning those two attacked one last time and produced a few more bits of debris including a locker door of German origin, a code book and some papers. At this time the hunt was judged a success and ***Ottawa*** returned to Portsmouth with the evidence. The code book was hurried ashore for study by the Intelligence Branch, and the papers were shown to the ship's company, and then cut up, each man receiving a small piece as a memento of a success.

It was enough to convince the Assessment Board, so ***Ottawa, Kootenay*** and ***Statice*** were credited with destroying ***U 678.*** While Prentice was commended for his thoroughness and for "absolutely correct tactical handling of his group", Commodore (D) Western Approaches, Cmdre "Shrimp" Simpson and Admiral Sir Max Horton, his chief, (both ex-submariners themselves) felt he had gone on rather too long in trying to "open up" the evidently defeated U-boat.

U 678 was another of the large class of Type VIIC overseas boats. Commissioned in October 1943 she was part of VII U-Flottille operating out of St. Nazaire, France. There is no indication in German records available after the war that the boat ever made a single attack on Allied shipping, at least under her CO at this time, OL Hyronimus. The imagination and ingenuity of EG-11 had indeed succeeded in destroying the boat before she had any opportunity for establishing a record.

Prentice received a DSC to add to the DSO from his ***Chambly*** and ***Moose Jaw*** action (see Chapter 7); Lt P.G. Hadrill, RCNVR ASCO of ***Ottawa*** at this time also received a DSC. DSMs were awarded to CPO G.W. Candy, ERA2 P. Emberley and CERA P.P. Salsiccioli. Willson was Mentioned in Despatches, as was SLt Berry, Lt Timbrell and four others from the two ships. All these awards were for "courage and skill in anti-U-boat operations", not specifically mentioning ***U 678,*** for at that date the number was not known. These same two RCN ships were in successful actions again the following month (see Chapter 49), and both Willson and Berry had successful RCN careers post-war.

SOURCES:

German, *The Sea Is At Our Gates,* p. 174.

Lenton & Colledge, *Warships of WW II*, Part Three, p. 63.

Milner, *The U-Boat Hunters,* pp. 156-159.

Paquette & Bainbridge, *Honours & Awards,* pp. 43, 445, 581.

Schull, *Far Distant Ships,* pp. 344-345.

Tarrant, *The U-Boat Offensive,* p. 143.

CHAPTER 48

A CASUALTY OF THE INVASION: HMCS REGINA

Regina:
(see Chapter 24 for details)
Fate: Torpedoed by *U 667*, off Cornwall, 8 Aug 44
Casualties: 1 officer, 29 crew

Look how the pale Queen of the night
Doth cause the ocean to attend upon her,
And he, as long as she is in his sight,
With his full tide is ready to her honour.

Charles Best, "Of the Moon", 1602

For the first eight months of her service life, ***Regina*** was with the Halifax and Western Local Escort Forces. In September with seventeen other Canadian corvettes she joined in Operation Torch, escorting convoys to North Africa in support of the forces fighting there. Her success in destroying the Italian submarine ***Avorio*** is described in Chapter 24.

In March 1943 she returned to Canada, where many of her ship's company were replaced during a refit. Her new commanding officer, Lt Jack Radford, RCNR, joined her in September. In February, 1944 she was assigned to C-1 Escort Group. By March the build-up for the planned invasion of Europe necessitated additional escorts in UK waters so ***Regina*** returned to England and Western Approaches Command to escort local convoys in the Channel area.

Most convoys were formed up in two main collecting areas. The Thames estuary served the eastern side of the British Isles, and the Bristol Channel ports the west. From there they moved into the assembly areas, thence to the invasion beaches or small ports as they were captured and cleared. The Canadian corvettes were extremely busy from early May throughout the summer, always on call, making frequent trips to the Normandy area.

For the bridge personnel it was a type of duty unlike the Atlantic or Mediterranean convoys that had been their principal experiences to date. This time they often had large convoys that could travel only when passages through the minefields had been swept and marked. Precise navigation was vital. In addition to the mines there were constant and variable threats of U-boats, E-boats and air attack, including glider bombs.

Regina was the sole escort for the west coast convoy EBC-66 of ten ships in two columns. Proceeding southwesterly along the north coast of Cornwall on a clear, calm night of 8 August, 1944, ***Regina*** was carrying out a broad zig-zag sweep from ahead of the starboard column to ahead of the port. At about 2130, when some eight miles from Trevose Head, Lt Radford was on his bridge when an explosion was heard. He saw steam coming from the 7,200-ton US Liberty ship ***Ezra Weston***, third ship in the starboard column, so closed her to investigate.

The master of the ***Ezra Weston*** signalled that he had hit a mine forward. Radford later estimated that the merchantman was slightly outside the swept channel, so mining was a consideration. This was to some extent a critical misapprehension that had an effect on ***Regina's*** later fate. Radford could see that the ship's back was broken so advised the master to try to beach his ship on the shore near Padstow, the nearest port, about seven miles off. HM ***LCT 644*** (a Landing Craft, Tank) was in the convoy as the last ship in the port column. SLt L.G. Read, RNVR, the captain of the LCT, turned toward the stricken ship and arrived near her about the same time as ***Regina.*** Read was told to go alongside the merchant ship's starboard side. The master had by now decided to get his crew off the evidently sinking vessel and they went aboard the LCT with their personal gear in suitcases. This took almost an hour, while the possibility of saving some of her deck cargo of vehicles was discussed with the master and chief engineer. This was not practical as by then there was no steam to operate winches, so the

LCT drew clear. The master and three officers stayed on board the merchantman.

Regina remained idling in the vicinity of the ***Ezra Weston*** throughout this whole period. The merchant ship was moving slowly ahead for about half an hour but then stopped. ***Regina*** used her engines only to stay within hailing distance.

Read in the LCT decided to try to tow the ***Ezra Weston*** stern-first to shallower water and had actually started to take the strain on the manila tow line when ***Regina*** was hit by a torpedo at 2248, when she was just 200 to 300 feet from the LCT. At the time, no-one knew whether it was "another" mine or a torpedo. The resulting explosion sank the corvette in seconds. Most of the ship's company not on watch below had been on the upper deck watching the towing operation and the men were thrown, jumped or were simply washed overboard into the water. AB T.D.H. Malone had set the depth charges to "safe" before the ship was struck and this action undoubtedly saved many lives. But he himself was not one of the survivors. Malone received no official recognition for doing his duty but he is remembered with gratitude by those who were rescued. In other rapid sinkings many Canadian sailors were lost while they were in the water, through the explosion of depth charges of foundering ships.

Thirty of the crew were killed on board or drowned in the immediate aftermath as the ship reared up and sank stern first. Some of those died later from their injuries. Most of those killed on board were engine and boiler room personnel. The sixty-six survivors from ***Regina*** and the four officers who had remained aboard the ***Ezra Weston*** until she broke in two and also sank were rescued by the LCT, assisted by HM Trawler ***Jacques Morgand*** which was in the vicinity, but there were serious injuries. The survivors had been in the water for only about thirty minutes but were covered in bunker fuel oil.

The rescue operation was carried out with skill and gallantry by SLt Read and his small crew, considering they had no asdic or anti-submarine weapons. ***Regina's*** medical officer, Surgeon Lieutenant Grant A. Gould, RCNVR, was rescued but was in shock and choking on fuel oil. Some medical supplies had been brought from the ***Ezra Weston*** with her survivors and, after first recovering with a morphine shot, Surg. Lt Gould spent the night attending to the wounded, assisted by his own LSBA Bill Oneschuk, also among the survivors. His work included a leg amputation of ERA Lionel Racker who had joined the ship just that morning. Gould's surgery was the small quarterdeck of the LCT lit by flashlights, his scalpel a sterilized carving knife and the anaesthetic a few ounces of brandy. Gould and Oneschuk were awarded Mentions in Despatches for their heroic work under very difficult circumstances, and Racker survived his ordeal. It is interesting to note that in a post-war (1945) article Dr. Gould concluded that the injuries "were of the type typically found in torpedoed vessel survivors. There was an absence of compression fractures associated with mined vessels."

The customary Board of Inquiry was held immediately after the sinking of ***Regina*** and its report rendered on 12 August. The Board focused much attention on trying to determine the still unidentified cause of the sinkings and positions of the three participants relative to each other. The ***Regina*** survivors questioned could not even be entirely sure that the explosion was on the port side though most thought so. The Board did not conclude whether ***Regina*** was sunk by a mine or a torpedo. Certainly she had no indication of a submarine on her asdic but she had also searched unsuccessfully for mines with the asdic short transmission unit.

When the master of the ***Ezra Weston*** told Radford that his ship was mined, it certainly contributed to the loss of ***Regina.*** His assumption was probably based only on negative evidence: no sighting of either a U-boat or a torpedo track. Had Radford considered the presence of a U-boat it is doubtful that he would have stopped his ship near the sinking merchantman, or even reduced his speed. His unprotected convoy had continued and he was not formally criticized for leaving them. But by remaining stopped, he was considered by the Naval Board, many months later, to have made a grave error. The RN director of anti-submarine warfare division also noted ***Regina's*** CO had erred in presuming the danger was from mines and that he had left his convoy unescorted.

LCT 644 took the wounded and oil-soaked survivors to Padstow harbour where they were taken off by an RAF crash boat, the ***Sir William Hillary*** (the ex-Dover RNLI[1] lifeboat), the Padstow RNLI lifeboat ***Princess Mary*** and

1. Royal National Lifeboat Institute, who maintain sophisticated rescue lifeboats all around the British and Irish coasts.

other small boats. The Padstow RNLI staff were puzzled and somewhat annoyed that they had not been called out for the rescue itself. Surg Lt Gould later mentioned that due to the low tide, some of the wounded had to be carried the last 100 yards to shore through mud and shallow water. Two had died on board the LCT from severe head wounds.

Regina's and ***Ezra Weston's*** antagonist was ***U 667***, commanded by KL Karl-Heinz Lange, although this was not discovered until German records could be searched post-war. She had not had a very distinguished career since her launching in 1942: by the spring of 1944 she had not recorded a single successful attack. In May, 1944, under KL Heinrich Schroeteler, ***U 667*** had been one of the early boats fitted with *schnorkel,* allowing air to be drawn into the submarine while remaining submerged, permitting boats to run on their diesels, saving battery power. He had sunk ***Regina*** with a GNAT.

Lange scored again six days later, sinking the American ***LST 921*** and ***LCI(L) 99*** out of convoy EBC-72, but he did not return to his home port, as ***U 667*** struck a mine off La Pallice, France eleven days later and was lost with all hands.

A touching aftermath to the loss of ***Regina*** is in the 1985 story of Mr. and Mrs. Ivor Jenkins of Bideford, Cornwall. When they came across the badly neglected graves of ***Regina*** casualties AB T.D.H. Malone, Sto 1 A.E. Dawson and Sto PO W.J. Cramp in the churchyard of Poundstock St. Neots, they took it upon themselves to restore and care for the graves. They have since added two other ***Reginas*** to their charge, SA J.G.M. Rathbone and AB J.M. Saulnier, buried in St. Merryn Naval Cemetery near Padstow.

A new and very powerful Canadian Patrol Frigate has been named HMCS ***Regina***, perpetuating the memory of the lost corvette. Several of the latter's survivors attended the commissioning of the new vessel in the spring of 1995, fifty-one years after their rescue.

LOST:

Arkell, Joseph W., AB
Asselton, J. Derek, L.Tel
Beaton, Neil K., AB
Blain, Ronald G., AB
Burrows, Ernest D., Sto
Cramp, William J., Sto.PO
Dawson, Alfred E., Sto
Denoncourt, Charles O., L.Sto
East, Richard G., AB
Ferron, Kenneth M., Sto
Harrison, Robert M., AB
Helis, Joseph F., ERA
Loney, Donald C., Sto
Lovell, Alec S.M., Sto
Lusty, Frank O., AB
Malone, Thomas de la H., AB
McCarron, Francis J., AB
Moore, Harold B., LS
Pound, Francis J., AB
Rathbone, John G.M., SA
Robertson, Douglas P., Sto.PO
Rodseth, John N., AB
Rutter, James A., Coder
Saulnier, Joseph M., AB
Simpson, Frederick W., AB
Smith, Adam J., AB
Sutherland, Robert, Tel
Swalm, Charles H., Lt
Taylor, Albert D., Tel
Thompson, John, Cook

SOURCES:

Bishop, *Courage At Sea,* pp. 139-141.

Gould, *The Journal of the Canadian Medical Services,* November, 1945.

Johnston, *Corvettes Canada,* pp. 261-262.

Lenton, *German Submarines,* Vol.1, p. 126.

Lenton & Colledge, *Warships of WW II.*

Macpherson & Milner, *Corvettes of the RCN,* p. 131.

Paquette & Bainbridge, *Honours & Awards,* pp. 210, 416, 479.

Richards, *Operation Sick Bay*, p. 107.

Rohwer, *Axis Submarine Successes.*

Schull, *Far Distant Ships,* pp. 328-329.

Van der Vat, *The Atlantic Campaign,* p. 373.

CHAPTER 49

ESCORT GROUP 11 SCORES TWO KILLS

Their souls may make a peaceful and a sweet retire from off these fields.

Shakespeare, Henry V

Ottawa (2nd), Kootenay:
(see Chapter 47 for details)
Chaudiére: River class destroyer
Builder: Vickers-Armstrong Ltd, UK, as HMS *Hero*
Comm in RCN: 15 Nov 43
Crews: 10 officers, 171 men each

Action: Sank *U 621*, Bay of Biscay, 18 Aug 44
Sank *U 984*, Brest, 20 Aug 44
Casualties: 101
No survivors

Chaudière in the Bay of Biscay on 20 August, 1944, the day she, *Kootenay* and *Ottawa* (seen in the right background) sank their second U-boat in two days.

The invasion of Normandy necessitated many changes in the operations of Canadian naval forces. Not the least of these was the need to screen the cross-channel traffic and to prevent its disruption by German submarines and E-boats.

The 11th Escort Group was newly organized, was all Canadian and consisted of five River class destroyers: ***Ottawa*** as senior officer, (Cdr J. Douglas "Chummy" Prentice); ***Chaudière*** (LCdr C. Patrick Nixon); ***Kootenay***, (LCdr W.H. "Bill" Wilson); ***St. Laurent***, (LCdr A.G. "Gus" Boulton RCNVR); and ***Gatineau***, (LCdr H.V.W. Groos). ***Restigouche***, (LCdr David W. Groos), was to transfer from EG-12 later in the month of August. Their base for Channel operations was Plymouth where they arrived in June, 1944.

Before the events described in this chapter, the group had fought two actions against German E-boats in a dense fog, been bombarded by shore batteries, attacked by a torpedo-carrying Junkers 88, bombed by two Dornier 217s with radio-controlled glider bombs, attacked submarine targets, and expended much ammunition on half-sunken derelicts to get them out of the way of shipping. Two of the group, ***Ottawa*** and ***Kootenay***, had sunk ***U 678*** in July (see Chapter 47).

In August, 1944, ***Ottawa, Chaudière, Kootenay*** and ***Restigouche*** (loaned in from EG-12 in anticipation) were in the Bay of Biscay, off La Rochelle, halfway down France's Biscay coast when despite poor asdic conditions ***Kootenay*** at 0953 reported "another in a seemingly endless series of contacts" (Milner). The COs began to put their hard-won experience of five years of war into action.

At 1012 ***Ottawa*** carried out a hedgehog attack which appeared to produce one hit about 160 feet above the sea bed. When the target settled to the bottom and an echo sounder trace indicated a submarine which did not move again, Prentice considered he had at least disabled the U-boat. But without confirmation of a kill, the four Canadian destroyers made repeated attacks with depth charges. While no debris surfaced, the group was sure that there was a submarine on the bottom despite confusing asdic echoes, and that she was damaged but not yet certainly destroyed. ***Kootenay*** tried laying a single charge set for 500 feet right over the target by echo sounder at slow speed but it exploded prematurely, damaging the destroyer. Then Willson in ***Kootenay*** again tried with his Mark X depth charge, a ton of explosive fired from a torpedo tube. To the consternation of all it failed to explode, which rather worried David Groos in ***Restigouche,*** ordered by Prentice to make the next depth charge attack. He brashly suggested to ***Ottawa*** by TBS: "Suggest SO make the next attack!"

Ottawa then fired a Mark X which did detonate, but without producing the required results. All her ship's company that could be spared off watch were on deck to see this abnormal explosive trial. Finally ***Ottawa*** and ***Kootenay*** had to detach at 1800, ***Restigouche*** left for Plymouth with defects and ***Chaudière*** was left in sole contact.

Their opponent was also a veteran of the Atlantic war. ***U 621*** was one of the numerous Type VIIC submarines that made up the majority of the German ocean-going force. She had commissioned in 1942 and was now under her third skipper. On 23 October 1942, under KL Horst Schünemann she had torpedoed the British ship ***Empire Turnstone***. Her second CO, OL Max Kruschka from December 1942 to March 1943, had sunk three ships, one Greek and two British. Now in August, 1944 her CO was OL Hermann Stuckmann, who had the RN infantry landing ship ***Prince Leopold*** and the large passenger liner ***Ascanius*** to his credit in two days among the invasion traffic at the end of July. So ***U 621*** had to her account over 32,000 tons of shipping in two years of operations.

Although she maintained the contact overnight only with difficulty and even started for home, ***Chaudière*** was ordered back and, during the following morning and early afternoon, made a further series of meticulous depth charge attacks on her own. Her final attacks at 1607 and 1609 were rewarded with a loud underwater explosion. Soon she was able to retrieve from the debris in the water a German letter dated seven days before and a chocolate bar wrapper from Berlin. When the authorities evaluated all the evidence, the track and attack charts, the group was given official credit for a submarine which was subsequently confirmed as ***U 621***.

Two days later, the same three ships of EG-11, ***Ottawa, Chaudière*** and ***Kootenay***, were again in company but on their way back to Plymouth. They had operated at high speeds and were now short of fuel. When passing along the Finisterre coast, at 1935 the asdic operator in ***Ottawa*** reported a good contact at 500 yards. The experienced group soon classified it as a submarine. "Chummy" Prentice's group anti-submarine officer was Lt Bob Timbrell, a long course A/S officer. Hedgehog and depth charge attacks were made over several hours, with their limited fuel constantly on the minds of the commanding officers. ***Chaudière*** had both a depth-predictor 147B set and a depth-estimating asdic Q attachment and was able to obtain accurate depth estimates, using the last of her hedgehog projectiles to drop bombs close to the target.

In poor visibility, however, no wreckage was found and the ships were eventually forced to break off at 2300 and head for Plymouth, ***Kootenay*** having developed a feed pump problem. In fact when ***Chaudière*** got to within 100 yards of the tanker her fuel supply was exhausted and without power she drifted alongside the resupply ship. The Canadians were in no doubt that they had destroyed a U-boat but the strict requirements for confirmation prevented any credit to them at that time. The U-boat Assessment Committee decided it must have been a wreck that they were pounding. But the sailors in ***Chaudière*** were already positive that it was a kill and even painted two swastikas on their funnel. It was not until after hostilities, when the German BdU records became available, that a confirmed kill was credited once again to the three destroyers of EG-11.

Their victim was ***U 984***, another Type VIIC. This one had commissioned only months before and was operating under her first captain, OL Heinz Sieder. On 7 June he had fired three GNATS (homing torpedoes) at the Canadian destroyers of EG-12. One had exploded in the CAT gear towed by HMCS ***Saskatchewan*** although Sieder claimed a possible sinking. The others missed. Sieder, however, had been singularly successful among the invasion traffic. On 25 June he had torpedoed the RN Captains class frigate HMS ***Goodson.*** She was towed to harbour by HMS ***Bligh*** but never repaired. Four days later Sieder torpedoed four American 7,000-ton freighters in the invasion build-up fleet. Of these, ***H.G. Blasdell, A.A. Treutlan*** and ***J.A. Farrell*** were either beached or towed in but not repaired, while ***E.M. House*** was eventually repaired. Sieder escaped a massive hunt by running on schnorkel. His action was an indication of the potential damage the U-boats could have inflicted had Hitler concentrated more of his available fleet on the Channel area.

Commander Prentice finished the war with four submarines to his credit, while Nixon and Willson had shared in three each. The young Canadians in these ships had learned how to fight the U-boat war. All five of EG-11's destroyers survived the war but were promptly paid off in 1945 and 1946.

SOURCES:

Lenton, *Navies of World War II.*

Macpherson, *The River Class Destroyers of the RCN,* pp. 63-73, 87-91.

Macpherson & Burgess, *Ships of Canada's Naval Forces.*

Milner, *The U-boat Hunters,* pp. 167-170.

Rohwer, *Axis Submarine Successes,* pp. 178, 181-182.

Van der Vat, *The Atlantic Campaign,* p. 374.

CHAPTER 50

HMCS ALBERNI SINKS IN THIRTY SECONDS

Alberni:
Flower class corvette
Builder: Yarrows Ltd, Esquimalt, BC
Comm: 4 Feb 41
Crew: 7 officers, 83 crew
Fate: Torpedoed by *U 480*, English Channel, 21 Aug 44
Casualties: 4 officers, 55 crew

Hath made...an invisible eel to swim the haven at Dunkirk,
and sink all the shipping there.
But how is't done?
I'll show you sir. It is automata, runs under water... and sinks it straight.

Ben Jonson, *Staple of News*

Alberni in 1944. Although time had been taken during a refit to move her mast behind the bridge and equip her with a new radar and AA armament aft, there was not the opportunity to extend her forecastle before she was sunk in mid-1944.

Named after a town on Vancouver Island (and thus after Captain Don Pedro Alberni who commanded the Spanish soldiers sent to occupy Nootka in 1790), HMCS ***Alberni*** was one of the earlier RCN corvettes to see service, with a minimum of time allowed for work-ups upon arrival at Halifax in April, 1941.

She escorted convoys to Iceland, participating in the desperate fight around Convoy SC-42 in September, when fifteen merchantmen were sunk and ***U 501*** was destroyed by ***Chambly*** and ***Moose Jaw*** (see Chapter 7). ***Alberni*** was then based on Londonderry, and made a name for herself during 1942 by rescuing over 145 torpedoed merchant seamen on two occasions. She was assigned to escorting convoys in support of the North African landings between Britain, Gibraltar and North African ports. She was present with the Mediterranean convoys when ***Ville de Québec*** and ***Regina*** obtained their submarine kills but, as with ***U 501,*** did not have the chance for direct participation and credit. Reports did give ***Alberni*** a "probably damaged" verdict after an attack in 1941. Returning to Canada in March 1943, she served in the Western Local and in the Gulf Escort Force in the St. Lawrence. Time was taken for a modest and partial refit. In April 1944 she was one of seventeen RCN corvettes sent to the UK in support of Operation Neptune, the landings at Normandy. In June and July she escorted a miscellaneous collection of landing craft and ships, barges, tugs and floating piers for Mulberry and merchant ships between Southampton Water and the beaches.

On 26 July she shot down a German Junkers 88 that had attacked her at almost sea level. ***Alberni*** opened fire with her starboard Oerlikons and her after pom-pom as the plane tore toward her. The *Junkers* climbed and banked to clear ***Alberni*** and her port Oerlikons scored direct hits at close range. The enemy burst into flames and exploded in the sea 100 yards off ***Alberni's*** port bow with no survivors. On 28 July she narrowly missed an aircraft-laid mine, then a depth charge laid over an asdic contact set off another mine 200 yards off ***Alberni's*** starboard beam without significant damage. It was an exciting time.

After brief maintenance at Southampton, ***Alberni*** was ordered to relieve HMCS ***Drumheller*** on patrol for U-boats to the eastward of the swept channel leading to the Normandy beaches. At 1145 on 21 August she was steaming south at fourteen knots in fair weather with a NNE wind of five knots but State Four seas for the rendezvous, sweeping by asdic eighty-degrees on either bow, radar operating. "Hands to dinner" had just been piped. Four minutes later, with no asdic warning whatsoever, she was hit by a torpedo on her port side just aft of the engine room. In less than ten *seconds* she was awash from the funnel aft, listing to port and sinking fast. In another twenty seconds she was gone, sinking stern first. Most of the off-watch hands were trapped in their mess decks, and only one stoker escaped from the engine and boiler rooms.

Her CO, A/LCdr Ian H. Bell, RCNVR, a twenty-six-year-old former lawyer, leaped out of his cabin at the explosion, planning to dash to the bridge. He was washed over the side as the ship foundered rapidly by the stern, with no time for orders or damage control. There was not even time to release Carley floats, and men, many without time to put on life belts as the ship foundered, had to cling to odd pieces of debris. Fortunately the depth charges did not explode, although there was a muffled boiler explosion which did not seem to cause much harm. One seaman credited the new-style RCN life jackets, with protective crotch sections buckled to the upper jacket, with preventing groin injuries. One rating in boots and trousers, struggling in the sea, cast off his boots and then pushed down his trousers to be able to swim more easily. He suddenly recalled that his dentures were in the trouser pockets, so pulled them back up again. As an intelligence officer commented later after questioning the survivors, "He seemed to have all his teeth when I spoke to him."

A/Lt Frank Williams, a former football player and strong swimmer, was credited with saving several lives including those of Donald Wood, the ship's writer, and Ian Bell who was dazed by the suddenness of his ship's destruction. Williams was later, in January, 1945, awarded the Royal Humane Society's bronze medal for saving life at sea for his efforts on this day.

For forty-five minutes the dazed survivors struggled to keep from drowning or giving up in heavy seas. Providentially HM motor torpedo boats ***469*** and ***470***, returning from duties off Normandy and having seen an explosion and the startling disappearance of the corvette on their horizon, altered course to investigate. They came across the survivors and rescued three officers and twenty-eight men of the ship's company of ninety. They were taken to Portsmouth, where two moderately injured were admitted to hospital.

TO: CAPT COASTAL FORCES
FROM: HMCS ALBERNI

ON BEHALF OF THE SURVIVING OFFICERS & RATINGS IT IS REQUESTED THAT OUR GRATITUDE & THANKS MAY BE TRANSMITTED TO THE OFFICERS & SHIPS COMPANIES OF MTBS 470 & 469 FOR THEIR SPLENDID SEAMANSHIP & RESCUE WORK IN CONNECTION WITH THE RECENT LOSS OF HMCS ALBERNI.

TOO: 29/1605B

The U-boat that had destroyed ***Alberni*** with an acoustic torpedo was not identified at the time. In fact it was suspected that ***Alberni*** might have been mined, as seven anti-submarine craft hunted through the area the next day and found nothing. Post-war review of German records indicate she was the first victim, of several ships in the area, of ***U 480*** (OL Hans-Joachim Förster) of the IX U-Flottille, operating out of Brest, France. Less than twenty-eight hours later Förster sank the RN *Algerine* minesweeper ***Loyalty*** in almost exactly the same location, with nineteen killed. She and her flotilla had been sweeping the area for suspected mines, partly as a result of ***Alberni's*** still unverified sinking. ***Loyalty*** had fouled her sweep with another *Algerine's*, dropped back to recover her gear in hazy weather and was catching up when Förster hit her in the stern with a GNAT. Fortunately that day the minesweeper took twenty minutes to sink, although her CO was lost. The lack of detection of the U-boat may have been, at least in part, due to its all-over *Alberich* rubber coating, designed to absorb asdic sound waves.

Over the next two days ***U 480*** sank two more merchantmen in the area. After sinking another, also in the Channel the following February, Förster and ***U 480*** were in their turn sunk by the RN frigates ***Duckworth*** and ***Rowley*** on 24 February 1945. There were no survivors.

In the mid-1980s there were diver's reports that the remains of ***Alberni*** had been located just off the Isle of Wight. But these are discounted by others who note the location is far too close to the island near where she was sunk, and the description of the vessel located does not appear to be that of a corvette.

LOST:

Allan, John M., AB
Angell, Bruce, AB
Barss, Walter C., ERA
Bosworth, Robt. C., Coder
Bouchard, J.J., ERA
Brock, George M., OS
Buchanan, G.W., AB
Campbell, Donald W., Sto
Carder, Wilfred W., OS
Clinton, Elmer J., L.Sto
Cosgrove, C.T., AB
Cox, Henry J.M., Sto PO
Culpepper, J.A., Sto PO
Currie, Wm. P., Sto PO
Dittloff, William, Sto
Drew, Robert F., Tel
Erickson, Ingvi S., Tel
Evans, Albert K., L.SA
Fulton, Hugh C., Lt
Gallagher, G.J., LS
Garvey, Donald N., Sto
Graham, Alvin J., Sig
Grais, Donald B., ERA
Grant, Malcolm S., Lt
Griffiths, Ed. S., Sto
Hamilton, John P., Lt
Hammond, John A., Sto
Hatcher, Arthur M., LS
Henderson, Hugh M., Surg Lt
Horley, Wallace C., Sto
Irving, James C., L.Coder
Jenks, Keith W., O.Tel
Jones, Donald O., AB
Karns, Robert J., Sto
Kirkpatrick, S.M., Tel
Koster, John B., ERA
Kowbell, Morris, AB
Laing, Wallace W., OS
Lang, Robert A., ERA
Lee, Donald, F., PO
Lighthall, A.E., CPO
McDermott, Joseph G., Sto PO
McGrath, James D., LS
McInnes, Wm. S., AB
Merk, George A., Stwd
Moffat, Cyril B., AB
Page, Ivan E., OS
Paquet, J.A.R., L.Stwd
Pilon, Joseph G., Sto
Plott, John, L.Sto
Rogers, Nicholl, Cook
Smith, Thomas A., L.Cook
Stephen, Donald, L.Tel
Stuart, George A., AB
Turner, Alan T., AB
Walker, James, AB
Whyte, John W., AB
Wilkinson, H.E., L.Sto
Wright, Thomas, Sto.

SOURCES:

Bishop, *Courage At Sea,* pp. 141-143.

Johnston, *Corvettes Canada,* pp. 250, 261, 263, 269.

Macpherson & Burgess, *Ships of Canada's Naval Forces,* pp. 68, 190, 231.

Macpherson & Milner, *Corvettes of the RCN,* pp. 55, 90.

Milner, *The U-Boat Hunters,* p. 174.

Paquette & Bainbridge, *Honours & Awards,* p. 578.

Schull, *Far Distant Ships,* p. 330.

Williams, *They Led the Way,* pp. 145-146.

CHAPTER 51

A LONG HUNT: HMCS SAINT JOHN & SWANSEA

Saint John: River class frigate
Builder: Canadian Vickers Ltd, Montreal
Comm: 13 Dec 43
Crew: 8 officers, 133 crew
Swansea: (see Chapter 35 for details)
Action: Sank *U 247*, off Cornwall, 1 Sep 44
Casualties: 52
No survivors

Sir, for the love of God and our country, let us have with some speed some great shot sent us of all bigness, for this service will continue long.

Howard of Effingham to Lord Walsingham, 1588

A typical frigate picture, of *Saint John* in May, 1944. Her hedgehog is on the forecastle and she has reasonable radar and HF/DF. A good anti-submarine fighting ship of her day.

The ships of EG-9 were notably successful in sinking U-boats. ***Saint John*** was credited with two, ***Swansea*** with four, ***Matane***, ***Nene*** and ***Owen Sound*** with one apiece, all of them shared with other RCN or RN forces. By the late summer of 1944, the group was working well together, each CO knowing his job and the capabilities of the others. In addition, there were enough ships in the group to spend long hours hunting elusive U-boats from an initial contact, without depriving convoys of vital protection. The senior officer was the much respected Cdr A. Frank C. Layard, DSO, RN. His service dated from World War I, and he had earned his DSO in the 1943 landings at Algiers when commanding HMS ***Broke,*** the only destroyer of four to land her troops that day. In EG-9 he commanded successively ***Matane, Swansea, Saint John*** and finally ***Loch Alvie***, in each case also as senior officer.

In August 1944 the group was based on the much-bombed city of Plymouth in Devon. At 0900 on the 31st EG-9 sailed to patrol an area fifteen miles south of the Scilly Isles off Cornwall's southwest tip, a busy traffic lane for ships and material coming down the Irish Sea and heading for the Normandy beaches and ports. Thus it was known to be a favourite waiting ground for U-boats. When the group was at sea, the C-in-C Plymouth sent a message directing them to search in the shipping lane on Cornwall's north coast, where an aircraft radar contact at 0330 that morning indicated something suspicious off Trevose Head, half way along the coast between Land's End and the entrance to the Bristol Channel.

At 1815, just as the group was about to sweep around the Scilly Isles and head northeast, ***Saint John*** (A/LCdr William R. Stacey, RCNR; and ***Saint John*** was always to be spelt in full, to avoid confusion with St. John's Newfoundland, St. John Antigua, St. Jean, PQ.) obtained what her asdic operator considered a promising although short-lived contact five miles off Wolf Rock. LCdr Stacey suggested to Cdr Layard that it was worth a more careful investigation. Layard agreed, and sent ***Monnow, Meon*** and ***Stormont*** on to scout out the earlier aircraft report, while retaining ***Swansea, Saint John*** and ***Port Colborne*** to sniff out ***Saint John's*** contact, which had now disappeared.

Having established a square area search that expanded with time, some three hours later, at 2115, ***Swansea*** obtained a possible submarine contact under difficult asdic conditions, as did ***Port Colborne***. There was quite a tide race and a rough rocky bottom in relatively shallow water. ***Swansea*** dropped only one depth charge as a trial, as the asdic team considered it could have been just a shoal of fish. However ***Saint John***, following astern of ***Swansea***, reported a meagre oil slick glistening slightly on the surface. She made a hedgehog attack which brought more oil to the surface. Careful asdic searching produced no firm or lasting contacts for any of the ships, although ***Saint John*** fired another hedgehog pattern at 2300. By this time it was too dark to observe any results, and they had no contact.

It is illustrative both of the availability of anti-submarine ships, and of Commander Layard's perseverance that when the contacts so far indicated a submarine *was* in the area, that he was determined to stay at the site. At midnight he organised his three ships on a parallel sweep to the west past Land's End, south around Wolf Rock and then east again, along likely paths for a U-boat trying to slide away from her tormentors into deeper waters. At 0155 on the 1st he was justified when ***Saint John*** obtained a firm contact just south of Wolf Rock.

This time, instead of attacking at once, she passed slowly over the target and was rewarded with a possible Type 147 (depth predictor) asdic contact and a good echo sounder trace indicating a likely U-boat on the bottom at 250 feet. It was not moving nor could the listening ships detect any hydrophone effect of motors or machinery running.

Saint John then carried out an attack with five depth charges, three heavy and two light, which brought up more oil and seemed to cause a minor additional explosion deep underwater. She tried again at 0330, although ***Swansea*** could obtain no contact when passing over the area. Meanwhile ***Port Colborne*** patrolled the perimeter of the field to prevent any outside interference and watch for signs of their target trying to escape. It was a veritable cat-and-mouse enterprise with deadly stakes, played by patient experts.

The C-in-C had been advised of their progress and directed them to remain with the hunt until told otherwise. ***Saint John*** made another hedgehog attack without results and ***Swansea*** was only able to obtain the most dubious of indications of a U-boat below. But if they were to ensure she wasn't just lying doggo, waiting to move away and fight another day, and if they were to obtain enough evidence to convince the Assessment Committee that they had indeed destroyed a submarine, more concrete proof was needed.

At 0410 no contact could be obtained, even by echo sounder. So at daylight Cdr Layard decided to reinvestigate the area of their first contact from the day before, to the northeast. There they found again faint traces of oil and some dead fish, but no sign of a bottomed U-boat. With ***Port Colborne*** still sweeping around the outside, ***Saint John*** and ***Swansea*** returned to circle at slow speed the larger oil slick of their second attack of the evening before. At 1310, after careful positioning, ***Saint John*** made another pass over the contact area, this time getting a good clear trace on her echo sounder. She ran out and turned to attack again, using only her echo sounder, but conned by ***Swansea*** as her asdic had now broken down. ***Saint John*** fired five depth charges as she passed over the target at 1404, nineteen and a half hours after the first contact the day before. This time, in Cdr Layard's words, "Results were startling!"

LCdr Bill Stacey, RCNR, with a small cupboard door panel recovered from *U 247* as proof of her destruction.

The resulting explosion brought up not only more oil but a great deal of definitive evidence: letters, photographs, a certificate certifying ***U 247's*** ten millionth engine revolution, an engine maintenance log book with the same boat number, German seamen's clothing, a diagram of a radio set, a light list for the Bay of Biscay (which usefully also indicated the German swept channels in the area), a rubber raft, a leather coat, several portions of panelling and other items. With considerable difficulty in a rising sea these were collected by whalers lowered by the two ships.

The weather now became rougher but, just to make sure, ***Saint John*** and ***Swansea*** rained down another twenty-three depth charges at the head of the slick. The destroyer HMCS ***Assiniboine*** joined, sent by C-in-C Plymouth from EG-11 to reinforce the hunt if need be. ***Swansea*** and ***Port Colborne*** left to join the rest of EG-9 on their search for the possible target off Trevose Head, which revealed nothing. The watch over ***U 247*** was given up thirty-seven hours after the initial contact, and ***Saint John*** and ***Swansea*** were credited with the kill.

This caused some ill feeling in the ship's company of HMCS ***Port Colborne***, some of whom recall that their asdic team also picked up the contact with ***U 247*** in the initial stages, but it was taken over by ***Saint John*** and ***Swansea.*** While the official records only credit these latter two, ***Port Colborne*** and her CO, LCdr Colin J. Angus, RCNR would seem to have merited at least an "honourable mention." It seems that Cdr Angus was also very dubious about the contact and backed off on his own accord, with Cdr Layard's agreement.

U 247 was not a fortunate boat. Although launched in September, 1943, the Type VIIC U-boat had but one success under OL Gerhard Matschulat. On 5 July 1944, she had sunk the twenty-eight-year-old steam fishing trawler ***Noreen Mary*** off northwest Scotland by gunfire.

TO: HMCS ST JOHN/HMCS SWANSEA
FROM: ADMIRALTY
(R) C-IN-C CNA, C-IN-C WA, C-IN-C PLYMOUTH

TOP SECRET

WE CONGRATULATE HM CANADIAN SHIPS SAINT JOHN AND SWANSEA ON DESTRUCTION OF U 247 ON 1ST SEPTEMBER. THE TENACITY OF SAINT JOHN IN HOLDING A DIFFICULT CONTACT WAS MOST COMMENDABLE

TOO: 20 1022A 44

The RN's Assessment Group commented that the sinking of this U-boat demonstrated "the skill and efficiency of the commanding officer and A/S team of HMCS ***Saint John*** and the expert and firm control of operations maintained and exercised throughout the varying phases of the hunt by the operating authority, Commander in Chief, Plymouth." While true enough, and LCdr W.R. Stacey of ***Saint John*** and his expert team did the work, Cdr Frank Layard's persistence in keeping his ships searching for their elusive target, based on experience and his knowledge of the reliability of his COs, warranted the inclusion of his name in this praise as well.

LCdr Bill Stacey is an interesting study on the background of several of the RCNR officers: he went to sea at age sixteen, served in a five-masted schooner and in ships of the Dollar Line, Union Oil and the Canadian Government's merchant marine. From 1930 to 1939 he was master of Boeing Aircraft's 125-foot steam yacht ***Taconite.*** During the war he served in examination vessels, the *Bangor* ***Malpeque***, and when ***Saint John*** had problems with her work-ups Stacey was sent to straighten her out, which he did. His new crew thought highly of him, and with two U-boat kills to the ship's credit by the war's end, he was obviously good at his naval job too.

In April 1945 awards were accorded to various members of ***Saint John's*** company, for both this persistent attack and for a later one (when the ship was commanded by Cdr Layard) that sank ***U 309*** the following February (see Chapter 59). Stacey and Lt J.R. Bradley received DSCs; the HSD A/LS L.P.A. Haagenson and LS W.E. Royds received DSMs, and Mentions in Despatches went to Lt Henry Blanchard, the Coxswain CPO R.W. Warburton, and Chief ERA H.V. Liabo (a Norwegian) and AB T.A. McMullin. Cdr Layard also was awarded a DSC at the end of the war.

SOURCES:

McKee, ***Swansea***, pp. 114-118.

Milner, *The U-Boat Hunters*, pp. 171-172.

Rohwer, *Axis Submarine Successes,* p. 183.

Schull, *Far Distant Ships,* pp. 346-347.

CHAPTER 52

HMCS DUNVER AND HESPELER SINK U 484 USING ALL THREE A/S WEAPONS

They are bold and daring to excess, though the latter are no longer all that they once were.

Emperor Leo VI, 905 AD

Dunver: River class frigate
Builder: Morton Engineering & Dry Dock, Quebec City
Comm: 11 Sep 43
Crew: 8 officers, 133 crew
Hespeler: Castle class corvette
Builder: Henry Robb Ltd, Leith, Scotland as HMS *Guildford Castle*
Comm in RCN: 28 Feb 44
Crew: 8 officers, 112 crew
Action: Sank *U 484*, N Irish Sea, 9 Sep 44
Casualties: 52
No survivors

The frigate HMCS *Dunver* in 1944. A lovely photo of a working frigate at sea, showing clearly her extensive depth charge armament in two rails at the stern, in "haystacks" beside the throwers, and additional stowage under the 4-inch gun on each side. Note the "Barber pole" stripe on her funnel.

HMCS ***Dunver*** was the first RCN frigate launched, on 10 November 1942, and received the unusually low pennant number of ***K 03,*** transferred from HMS ***Heliotrope*** which had been given to the US Navy. It was thought at first that the large building programs might require re-use of numbers, although this did not prove necessary and was stopped shortly after ***Dunver.*** On completion and after work-ups she was assigned to C-5 Escort Group in December 1943, known as "The Barber Pole Brigade" from the diagonally red and white striped identifying band on the ships' funnels. She began convoy escort duties at once. She was active in this role with the group for almost a year without respite.

HMCS ***Hespeler*** was laid down for the RN at Leith but taken over by the RCN before completion, the first of the twelve RCN Castles acquired in exchange for the *Algerine* minesweepers built in Canada for the RN. These Castle class corvettes were a wartime development arising from the experience gained with the earlier Flower class corvettes and the frigates in anti-submarine warfare. With the latest asdics, including 145Q and 147

HMCS *Hespeler*, fifty feet shorter than *Dunver* but designed around improved asdics and with an ahead-throwing squid mortar, between the forward 4-inch gun and the bridge.

depth-predictor sets, they carried only one depth charge rail, two throwers and fifteen depth charges. Their primary A/S weapon was the ahead-throwing three-barrel squid mortar. Additionally they had four modern radar sets and a Loran navigating set.

Hespeler joined the Mid-Ocean Escort Force in April, 1944 in C-5 Group, escorting HXF and ONF convoys, operating out of St. John's and Londonderry.

On 9 September ***Dunver*** with Cdr George Stephen, RCNR as senior officer of C-5 and LCdr W. Davenport, RCNR as her CO, and ***Hespeler,*** LCdr N.S.C. Dickinson, RCNVR had detached from Convoy HXF-305 and the rest of C-5 group to take a section to Loch Ewe in western Scotland. That morning at 0400 two merchant ships, one of them the 15,700-ton ***Empire Heritage***, had been torpedoed by ***U 482***. During the day a *Sunderland* aircraft of RCAF 423 Squadron operating out of Lough Earne reported a surfaced submarine nearby. Thus there was clear evidence of at least one U-boat operating in the vicinity.

At 2018, just after dark, ***Dunver*** reported a radar contact at 4,000 yards, altered toward and increased to full speed, firing starshell. Some of those aboard thought they saw a surfaced submarine revealed in the starshell's glare. Cdr Stephen ordered ***Hespeler*** to assist ***Dunver*** due to her superior A/S equipment. The radar target disappeared at 2027. Another target appeared one minute later and was assessed by the operator as being a decoy balloon released by the still-submerged U-boat. At 2052 ***Hespeler*** picked up an asdic contact at 1,400 yards but did not attack as it was not clear if it was the submarine or a bottom echo. LCdr Dickinson recalls he never saw any sign of a U-boat on the surface from ***Hespeler***. The two ships searched around the area for two hours until, at 2329, ***Dunver*** again picked up a good asdic contact at 1,100 yards. She attacked with a ten-charge depth charge pattern, followed at 2350 by a hedgehog attack. No results were seen, although one hedgehog bomb seemed to explode above the bottom which was only thirty to fifty fathoms (180 to 300 feet).

The ships continued circling in an organized search pattern. At 0319 on 10 September ***Dunver*** sighted a thin oil slick near the scene of their hunt, but obtained no definite asdic echoes worth attacking further. Nothing more was detected until, at 0445, a very faint and questionable asdic echo was obtained in ***Hespeler***. She made two squid attacks, followed by ***Dunver*** with a depth charge and one final hedgehog attack.

LCdr Dickinson recalls in 1994 that the two ships searched the area until first light when Cdr Stephen in ***Dunver*** ordered Neville Dickinson by signal lamp to close him for a consultation by loud hailer. Despite reservations at this procedure with a probable U-boat nearby, Dickinson brought his ship over to ***Dunver*** where an assessment of the situation took place by loud-hailer, the two ships idling along at minimal speed.

At this point ***Hespeler's*** starboard bridge lookout shouted a report of a torpedo approaching fine on the starboard bow. It was too late to take evasive action so the bridge personnel "held their breath and prayed." The torpedo passed down their starboard side and as it cleared the stern an increase in engine revolutions was rung on and ***Hespeler*** proceeded up the track from which the torpedo had approached. The asdic team gained a firm contact and a squid attack was carried out. The explosion of the three squid projectiles was followed in short order by another explosion and two huge upheavals of water about 100 yards apart.

One of ***Dunver's*** crew, Robert F. Gall, recalls that all they ever saw was a wooden platform or grating which was not picked up, and both ships reported a considerable quantity of oil on the surface which later proved to be diesel fuel. But there was no other debris that would positively indicate a sunken U-boat. At the time Commodore (D) Western Approaches noted "Lack of concrete evidence prevents any estimation of the amount of damage this U-boat might have obtained."

The two ships stayed in the area carrying out an expanded "box search" until late afternoon, at which time, having detected nothing further, they broke off and proceeded to Londonderry.

Although it was noted that ***U 484*** had disappeared around that date, it was not until post-war examination of German records that it could be ascertained that these two ships certainly could have disposed of her. There were no survivors. In 1997 Mr. Robert Coppock of the British Admiralty Historical Section found evidence that ***U484*** may have been sunk by the RN corvette ***Portchester Castle*** and frigate ***Helmsdale***. Launched in late 1943 and on operations in January 1944 ***U 484*** was a III U-Flottille boat out of La Pallice and commanded by KK W.A. Schaefer when lost. No attacks or sinkings are credited to her.

Both RCN ships survived the war, and Neville Dickinson was eventually awarded a Mention in Despatches, in October 1945, for his part in the U-boat's destruction. ***Dunver*** was expended as part of a breakwater at Royston, BC. ***Hespeler*** had a life extension as a merchant ship. Paid off in November 1945, she became the Union Steamship Line's ***Chilcotin***, then under other owners, ***Capri***. Around 1960 she was again sold to Greek owners who registered her as the Liberian ***Stella Maris*** for passenger cruising, with accommodation for 140 and a crew of 69, and moved her base to the Mediterranean.

SOURCES:

Coppock research notes, MoD (Navy), to author, Dec. 1997

Herzog, *Deutsche U-Boote 1906-1966,* p. 275.

Macpherson, *Frigates of the RCN,* p. 22.

Macpherson & Burgess, *Ships of Canada's Naval Forces*, pp. 46 & 106.

Macpherson & Milner, *Corvettes of the RCN,* p. 154.

Milner, *The U-Boat Hunters,* pp. 189-190.

CHAPTER 53

AN ALERT RADAR WATCH: HMCS ANNAN & LOCH ACHANALT SINK U 1006

Unmentioned at home in the press;
Heed it not: no man seeth the piston,
But it driveth the ship none the less.

R.A.Hopwood, "Laws of the Navy"

Annan: River class frigate
Builder: Hall, Russell & Co, Aberdeen, Scotland
Comm in RCN: 13 Jun 44
Crew: 8 officers, 133 crew
Loch Achanalt: Loch class frigate
Builder: Henry Robb Ltd, Leith, Scotland
Comm in RCN: 31 Jul 44
Crew: 8 officers, 133 crew
Action: Sank *U 1006*, S of Faeroes Islands, 16 Oct 44
Casualties: 6 crew
46 survivors

HMCS *Annan*, showing distinctive whaler davit fittings in RN Rivers frigates, in particular the outboard brackets. In September 1944, just before sinking *U 1006*.

While official records show that ***U 1006*** was sunk by EG-6, those who participated, especially in HMCS ***Loch Achanalt***, differ quite markedly in their memories and records of what actions the two ships took and in which order when compared with the official and semi-official descriptions available. Some deck logs have been lost, and Admiralty assessment reports conflict with facts from the ship's logs that survive and reports of A/S actions.

Annan was acquired as one of seven River class frigates from the RN, as were three very slightly larger Loch class ships, including ***Loch Achanalt***. These transfers were a result of an agreement reached in Quebec in 1943 whereby the RCN would take over and man ten British-built ships of these classes. ***Annan*** joined EG-6 in August and ***Loch Achanalt*** in September, 1944, working out of Londonderry as a support and hunting group. ***Annan*** was commanded by LCdr C.P. Balfry, RCNR who was to be her only CO while with the RCN, and ***Loch Achanalt*** by A/LCdr R.W. Hart, RCNVR.

On 16 October the group, commanded by the well-known ex-CBC broadcaster A/Cdr W.E.S.(Ted) Briggs, DSC, RCNR in ***New Waterford***, was patrolling west of the Shetlands, hunting for U-boats departing Norwegian bases. They had left Skaalefjord, Faeroes, on 14 October and were steaming at eleven knots in line abreast at 4,000 yard intervals, a bit more than usual due to excellent asdic conditions. The weather was clear with calm seas and only a slight swell. The ships had detected several HF/DF transmissions during the afternoon and at 1858 ***Annan*** had dropped a pattern of depth charges on what seemed at first to be a good submarine contact, but which turned "woolly" after her attack. No further contact was obtained despite a long search by ***Annan*** and ***Loch Achanalt***, assigned to prosecute the possible U-boat. With nightfall they headed back to rejoin the group, classifying ***Annan's*** target as non-sub.

Just as they reached the group, at 1906, ***Annan's*** surface warning radar operator, AB Fred Davies, reported a small contact astern at about three miles, as did ***Loch Achanalt's*** operator. These reports were transmitted to the senior officer who ordered them to investigate their contact. Both ships swung about, sounding action stations, ***Annan*** near-missing her senior officer in ***New Waterford*** as she reversed course in the dark. The two closed in on a steadily improving echo, soon assessed as a surfaced submarine moving away at maximum speed and zigzagging sharply. ***Annan***, working up to her maximum speed, headed directly for her target, closed to within 2,700 yards and fired 2-inch illuminating rockets from rails affixed to her 4-inch gun shield at 1912, revealing a submarine almost beam on. LCdr Richard Hart in ***Loch Achanalt***, to the distress of his gunnery officer Lt J.A.P. Clark, followed normal tactical procedure established to avoid possible GNAT counter-attacks. This involved advancing in a series of course alterations devised to "step aside" from torpedo attacks while the ship streamed her Foxer gear, thus somewhat delaying her arrival on the scene.

U 1006 was an ocean-going Type VIIC, 769-ton boat, built by Blohm & Voss in Hamburg, launched in April of 1943. She had an operating range of some 6,500 miles and was fitted with their *schnorkel* breathing mast. The U-boat had recorded no successes since her commissioning.

She was, in fact, accompanied by ***U 1003*** and other submarines of *Gruppe Rita*. They had sailed on 9 October from Bergen, Norway, and were heading for an Atlantic patrol west of Ireland. (Years later, at a dinner in Toronto, the CO of ***U 1003*** claimed to have seen ***Annan*** and ***Loch Achanalt*** firing on ***U 1006***, and even fired at the frigates as they were rescuing survivors. No ship in the group reported hearing torpedoes running, and German records do not show any *reported* attack by ***U 1003*** that night, although there are notes left by ***Annan's*** quarterdeck party that a torpedo's track was seen to pass down her port side.) ***U 1003*** was to be sunk next spring by HMCS ***New Glasgow*** (see Chapter 63).

HMCS *Loch Achanalt* in RCN hands in August, 1944, fitted with the much heavier mast than the River Class.

A Type VIIC U-Boat of *U 1006's* class. In this case *U 96* entering a French Biscay harbour.

U 1006 had been the U-boat detected in the afternoon's abortive depth charge attack and suffered damage in the hydroplanes and torpedo firing mechanism. She had been forced to surface, hoping to slip away unnoticed in the dark. When ***Annan*** and then ***Loch Achanalt*** opened fire with their 4-inch guns, ***U 1006*** responded sharply with her short range weapons, and not unsuccessfully. Fortunately the U-boat's 37mm gun had also been damaged in the late afternoon attack. Eight of ***Annan's*** crew were wounded by the U-boat's gunfire over the next few minutes and ***Loch Achanalt*** also had several rounds fired at her as she joined ***Annan***. The rounds fortunately passed through her rigging, to the discomfiture of seaman Bob Watkins in the crow's nest above. In true Hollywood fashion, a bridge signalman in ***Annan*** at one stage grabbed his head and cried out "They got me!" He was taken to the sick bay, a head laceration dressed and he returned to work.

By the time ***Annan*** had closed to eight hundred yards her radar and asdic were knocked out by damaged wiring, she had no signal projectors, and several men had been wounded. She closed further, firing continuously with her 4-inch and midships Oerlikons, hitting the U-boat frequently, and maintaining continuous illumination with the 2-inch rockets. Eighteen minutes after opening fire ***Annan*** ran close alongside her target and fired two shallow-set depth charges from the starboard throwers, one of which even landed on the enemy's deck and rolled off, exploding just below the U-boat as ***Annan*** sped out of harm's way. She had fired fifty-four 4-inch rounds.

Although LCdr Hart in ***Loch Achanalt*** had planned to ram the U-boat, he sheered away as ***Annan*** passed close to the U-boat to drop the charges. Even so, her guns had been firing continuously as well. In fact one Oerlikon gunner had to be pushed off his weapon by the gunnery officer to cause him to cease firing at the now-foundering U-boat.

The U-boat began to settle, her hatches opened and men were seen to be jumping into the sea. In two minutes, ***U 1006*** sank on an even keel at 1932 as other frigates of the group arrived, ***New Waterford*** and ***Outremont*** firing illuminating starshell over the scene and ***Outremont*** even getting away several 4-inch rounds that passed close over ***Loch Achanalt.*** These two then dropped their whalers at 2038 to join those of the attacking ships and help in the rescue of the forty-six survivors, including three officers. ***Outremont*** recovered twenty-four including the U-boat's CO, OL Horst Voigt. The enemy were by no means yet accepting utter defeat, for one officer was described by Lt Joe Clark of ***Loch Achanalt*** as "...a snooty bugger. We tried to treat him properly but he was just a horse's ass." ***Loch Achanalt*** picked up twenty and ***Annan*** two. Surg Lt Dick Galpin, RCNVR, in ***New Waterford,*** operated for many hours on the

German survivors transferred from other ships with leg and abdominal wounds. One was the CO, who gave him his monocle as a souvenir, which Dick still wears. An ***Annan*** officer, on having some shell fragments removed from his arms and legs, handed them to a ***U 1006*** survivor commenting "You can have these back!" Two PMOs in the group, Surgeon Lieutenants R.M. MacDonald of ***Loch Achanalt*** and J.L. Fitzgerald of ***Annan***, undertook a serious three-hour operation on Lt David Howitt, ***Annan's*** gunnery officer, wounded in the abdomen, as a result of which a kidney was removed. An RN W/T operator was blinded in one eye by a 20mm fragment. All the wounded, both Canadians and those that were picked up, survived. The prisoner survivors were landed in Greenock the next day.

LCdr Balfry of ***Annan*** received a DSC in March, 1945, "For services in destroying enemy submarines", implying he had been involved with other cases before, although these are not identified. Lt Howitt also received a DSC with the same citation. No awards have been identified for ***Loch Achanalt's*** part; certainly her CO received none and his ship is often omitted from credits for ***U 1006's*** destruction. ***Annan*** survived the war, was returned to the RN, and in November 1945 was transferred to the Danish Navy, renamed ***Niels Ebbesen,*** being scrapped in 1963 at Odense, Denmark. ***Loch Achanalt*** was sold by Britain to the New Zealand Navy as HMNZS ***Pukaki***, being broken up in Hong Kong in 1966.

SOURCES:

Clark, *HMCS Loch Achanalt*, pp. 32-46.

German, *The Sea Is At Our Gates,* pp.177-8.

Herzog, *Deutsche U-Boote,* p. 284.

Lawrence, *Tales of the North Atlantic*, pp. 244-246.

Lenton, *German Submarines*, Vols.1 & 2, pp. 51 & 50.

Macpherson, *Frigates of the RCN,* pp. 91-92.

Rohwer, *Axis Submarine Successes,* p. 186.

Schull, *Far Distant Ships,* pp. 381-2.

CHAPTER 54

HMCS SKEENA AGROUND IN A GALE

The disadvantages of the stockless anchor are that it has less holding power, weight for weight, than an Admiralty pattern anchor.

Manual Of Seamanship, 1937

Skeena:
(ee Chapter 13 for details)
Fate: Stranded & lost, Videy Island, Reykjavik, Iceland, 25 Oct 44
Casualties: 15

Skeena aground at Videy Island, Iceland.

The story of the acquisition and early career of ***Skeena*** is told in Chapter 13. This is the story of her tragic end.

By the fall of 1944 ***Skeena*** had been in the forefront of the battles of the Atlantic convoys for five difficult years. She had served in the 25th, 15th and 11th Canadian Escort Groups, then for two years in the 3rd. After a refit in Canada in the spring of 1944, and some repairs in Plymouth in September, the ship had worked with the 11th and 12th Escort Groups out of Londonderry. Her eighth wartime commanding officer was A/LCdr P.F.X. Russell, RCN.

In October, 1944 the ship was on patrol south of Iceland with two other ships of EG-11. The senior officer was Cdr James D. Prentice, RCN in command of HMCS ***Qu'Appelle*** with ***St. Laurent*** the third ship. A fourth ship of the Group, HMCS ***Chaudière***, was already at anchor in a shallow bay behind Videy Island on Iceland's rough west coast.

The weather on 24 October was of gale proportions, and the admiral commanding Iceland Command signalled EG-11 giving Prentice the decision to return to the Reykjavik area if conditions were unfit for operations. Cdr Prentice signalled the group that his intentions were to return to harbour for the night.

The navigating officer of ***Skeena*** was Lt Peter G. Chance. When the order was received to anchor independently off Videy Island he discussed the situation with his captain. He knew from earlier experience that the sea bottom in the Reykjavik area was volcanic ash and provided very poor holding ground. The ship had anchored there before. He was also concerned because ***Skeena*** was fitted with a single centre-line capstan, meaning only one anchor could be worked at a time.

Lt Chance selected an anchorage in the centre of a basin with at least 800 yards to shore in all directions. His response to the order to anchor had been to ask his commanding officer to relieve him of his duties as navigating officer because in his considered opinion this was not a safe undertaking in the weather extant and with ***Skeena's*** equipment. The navigator felt it was better to remain at sea and clear of the land, even in very rough weather, than accept an unsatisfactory and possibly dangerous anchorage. But he accepted the responsibility of bringing the ship to the best location he could select. Another possible factor was "Chummy" Prentice's hard-won reputation as an expert, for one didn't argue matters of practical seamanship with him lightly.

It was close to midnight when the ship came to single anchor with six shackles on the starboard cable. According to Lt Chance this much cable was paid out to allow for its extra weight on the bottom to help in the poor holding conditions. In his report of grounding, LCdr Russell stated that he remained on the bridge for ten minutes after the ship had got her cable. He gave orders for a full anchor watch to be set and to maintain steam at immediate notice in two boilers. The starboard cable was left around the capstan to facilitate working the cable should the anchor drag. All were exhausted from days at sea in violent weather, with little sleep, tried to the extreme.

Before going to bed in his cabin, the CO also satisfied himself that the four anchor bearings were fully understood by the experienced and reliable officers who were to stand the anchor watch. Lt Chance also remained for another ten minutes to check that the anchor bearings were not changing. When he considered that the ship was riding steadily, with only a slight yaw, he turned the watch over to the 1st lieutenant, William M. Kidd.

Lt Kidd also provided a full narrative for the report of grounding. After assuming the watch he confirmed that the full anchor watch was closed up, and then began checking anchor bearings, the ship's head being to seaward, into the high winds and sea. He did so every five minutes when the visibility cleared somewhat for about an hour. Throughout this period heavy hail and snow flurries were experienced and LCdr Patrick Nixon in ***Chaudière***, anchored nearby with both anchors down and considerable cable out on both, reported winds of nearly 100 miles an hour. Due to ground clutter, their radar was of no use in position fixing.

Just after one of the obscuring hail flurries, Lt Kidd noticed that one of the arcs between the shore bearings was closing rapidly, indicating the ship was dragging astern, toward the island. He at once ordered half ahead on both engines, for twelve knots, closed up the cable party and called the captain and the navigator. He then went to fifteen knots, followed quickly by "Full speed ahead". At that point the ship struck ground, stern first, then she lurched to port and swung around onto the rocks ninety yards off Videy Island, listing to starboard.

Both the commanding officer and the navigator rushed to the bridge, both awakened only by the ship's jarring as she grounded. The engines were stopped, then the captain ordered "Half ahead," followed by "Full ahead". ***Skeena*** remained hard aground, so he dropped the port anchor to try to prevent the ship from broaching to incoming heavy seas.

At this point many things were happening and a clear picture of events is not possible due to the varying perspectives of the participants. The captain recalls sending signals to the admiral commanding Iceland and Commander Auxiliary Vessels. He also asked a nearby trawler for assistance to hold his bows off the rocks. He subsequently instructed the trawler not to come closer because she would herself be endangered. The ship's company was ordered to the upper deck, watertight doors and hatches ordered closed, depth charges had their primers removed for safety, and preparations made for being taken in tow forward. Carley floats were ordered dropped over the lee side with lines at each end, so that if they had to go to the beach they could be hauled back to the ship.

Lt Chance wrote in 1990 that the cautionary order "Stand by to abandon ship" given by the captain was misunderstood as "Abandon ship!" by some. At the Board of Inquiry which was held in Iceland three days later, LCdr Russell was asked why he gave the order to abandon ship so soon. His answer indicated that order was in fact given as Lt Kidd confirmed, but that it was cancelled very soon after when he appreciated that abandoning the ship would be more hazardous than staying on board. In the event, twenty-one men responded to their understanding of that order, misunderstood in the gale of wind and roar of the seas breaking, and leapt over the side. Although most of them climbed onto one or other of the three Carley floats, only six men were to survive the cold and the wave-lashed volcanic rocky shore as three of the floats, their tail ropes to ***Skeena*** parted or cut, were swept onto outlying rocks or off along the shoreline. One seaman who had earlier been washed or leaped into the surging surf reached shore, and in ***Skeena's*** searchlight could be seen on the high rocky cliff over the ship. Shortly, to avoid a possible explosion, the boilers were shut down, and all power was then lost. AB Ken Kelpin described how he eventually reached shore, frozen, wet, oil-soaked, and climbed the rocks to reach a farmhouse where he passed out. The men still on board, seeing those in the floats being swept away, remained aboard, and all of them survived. At 0300 two RN landing craft approached ***Skeena*** and the shoreline from seaward, but due to the storm could not get close enough to be useful. Guided by an Icelandic

Another view of *Skeena* aground on Videy Island at the end of October, 1944.

pilot, Einar Sigurdsson, they made their way to the leeward side of Videy Island and their men crossed it on foot to the cliff facing the stranded ship by 0740. A Coston gun line fired from ***Skeena*** reached this party. They tied it to one of the ship's salvageable Carley floats and hauled all the remaining crew ashore. The rescue party, including Einar and the largely RN Patrol Service RNVR seamen, were labouring neck-deep in the freezing surf. Many of the survivors were taken by the RN ratings to the crofter's hut first seen, although at least one died from exposure on the way.

The following day parties from the other RCN destroyers boarded the ship to examine the damage. With rocks showing through the lower spaces, her salvage was deemed impractical especially this late in the war. They removed whatever valuable stores and equipment that could be saved as the weather moderated. The hulk was later sold to some Icelanders who eventually moved her and dismantled the ship for scrap value. Even so, ***Skeena*** defied this fate when the barge transporting the scrap to England sank while under tow.

It is not the purpose of this chapter to attempt to review or pass judgement on any of the actions of the participants in the loss of ***Skeena***. The results of the Board of Inquiry contained some elements of criticism or second guessing. They were issued from the office of the staff officer (Navigation), area combined headquarters on 31 October 1944. They contained a number of positive assessments of actions taken and recognized the presence of confusion given the constant and heavy pounding of the seas. The Report noted that the indirect cause of the deaths was the cutting of the "tails" fitted to the Carley floats, allowing them to be swept along the coast onto the rocks, and concluded that "No death can be attributed to the negligence of anyone."

Two ships that were also at anchor had observed ***Skeena*** apparently dragging, and ***St. Laurent*** tried to signal her. There is no evidence ***Skeena*** received the signal. No conclusions were drawn concerning the lapse of time between ***Skeena*** commencing to drag, the realization of that by the officer of the watch, or the time or duration of squalls which obscured the lights of the anchor bearings.

In due course there was a court martial and the captain and first lieutenant faced charges of "hazarding" and "stranding" the ship. In both cases the charges were considered proven, and penalties assessed.

It was not until 16 May, 1945 that the loss of ***Skeena*** was announced in a press release from NSHQ. Even it has some confusion in the orders given regarding abandoning ship. It would have been normal routine to give a warning order, the Royal Navy stipulating that "Hands to Emergency Stations" should precede "Abandon Ship" for the express purpose of avoiding confusion.

The fifteen dead from the ship were buried in Fossaburg cemetery at Reykjavik with full naval honours. Each man rests with a white cross bearing his name and number at his head. The cemetery slopes down to a quiet bay and in the near distance are snowclad mountains.

LOST:

Apostolos, Archie, Stwd
Blais, Joseph F.A., LS
Cook, Desmond B.W., Cook
Davidson, Gordon, AB
Ellis, Melvin N., AB
Gabourel, Lloyd A., AB
Hancock, Ralph G., L.Sig
Janos, Joseph F., AB
Johnston, Joseph N., AB
Pressner, Edward J., Stwd
Seath, Richie O., Coder
Silk, James E., LS
Stewart, Kenneth W., AB
Unger, Abraham, AB
Watson, Leonard, AB

SOURCES:

Chance, P.G., *Last Days Of Skeena* in the Bulletin of the Chief and Petty Officers Association, Nov. 1990.

Hadley, *U-Boats Against Canada*, pp. 241-242.

Macpherson, *The River Class Destroyers*, pp.22-25.

Macpherson & Burgess, *Ships of Canada's Naval Forces*, pp. 228-229.

Royal Navy Manual of Seamanship, Vol.II, 1967.

Schull, *Far Distant Ships*, pp. 382-384.

Unger, *Skeena Aground.*

of Halifax, transferred to the Gulf Escort Force, and in September 1942 rescued survivors of HMCS ***Charlottetown*** (see Chapter 18). She then worked out of Sydney until January 1944. After nine months as a training ship at HMCS ***Cornwallis***, the base on Annapolis Basin, NS, she returned to escort work out of Halifax.

In July 1944 when A/LCdr A. Craig Campbell, RCNVR, took command, he was the seventh officer to do so, and the third Campbell. A pre-war member of the Vancouver Division, RCNVR, he was one of a considerable group of Canadian 'VRs sent to fill some of the shortages in the Royal Navy in the early days of the war. After two years, on returning to Canada he commanded the Fairmile ***Q 090*** and the 76th ML Flotilla, then was appointed to ***Clayoquot***.

On 22 December 1944, ***Clayoquot*** was in Halifax harbour and many of the ship's company were on short Christmas leave. Campbell himself was at his home in Chester, a few miles from Halifax.

The situation leading up to the events of 24 December began three days earlier with an attack by ***U 806*** on convoy HHX-327. The U-boat was commanded by KL Klaus Hornbostel, who had been a gunnery officer in ***Admiral Scheer*** during her attack on HX-84 when she sank HMS ***Jervis Bay***. While not a volunteer for U-boats, due to heavy losses he was appointed to that command. ***U 806*** had been launched at Bremen early in the war, and was part of the XXXIII U-Flottille based in Flensburg, but when she sailed in October for the Halifax area it was her first war patrol. Hornbostel arrived off the coast in mid-December and spent some time becoming acquainted with navigational marks and ship traffic patterns. He had one close call when a minesweeper's wire swept across his deck and caught his net guard, snapping the steel cable. The minesweeper was unaware of what had happened to break her sweep; it happened periodically for quite innocent reasons.

On the evening of the 21st, Hornbostel had his first partial success when he hit the British-flagged Liberty ship ***Samtucky***, one of four ships in Convoy HHX-327. He fired four torpedoes and achieved two hits, believing he had finished off ***Samtucky,*** but she was beached and later repaired. Although in no doubt that the attack would cause a heightened response, on the 22nd he was again off Chebucto Head where he made another unsuccessful attack. By the morning of the 24th he was idling in the vicinity of the Sambro Light Vessel, awaiting targets.

The damage to ***Samtucky*** was assessed in Halifax as being probably caused by a mine, thus it was imperative to get minesweepers to the area through which so much of the convoy traffic was routed. One "minesweeper" selected was ***Clayoquot***. Although she had been operating as an escort, with much of her sweeping gear removed, she had retained the heavy minesweeping winch on her quarterdeck.

On the 22nd LCdr Campbell was called on the phone by Captain(D) and ordered to return immediately. A similar recall of his ship's company was only partially successful: Campbell found he was twenty-two men short and his request for assistance was met by drafting replacements from the manning depot. At the French Cable Wharf on the Dartmouth side of the harbour the necessary paravanes and oropesa floats for minesweeping were lifted on board.

In company with the frigate ***Kirkland Lake*** (Cdr N.V. Clark, RCNR as SO) and the *Bangor* ***Transcona*** (A/LCdr A.E. Gough, RCNR), ***Clayoquot*** sailed on the morning of the 23rd. The sweepers had been ordered to carry out an anti-submarine sweep through the area in which the liner ***Pasteur***, a twelve-ship merchantman convoy bound for Boston, XB-139, and the CNR troopship ***Lady Rodney*** were scheduled to pass. Convoy HJF-36 (***Lady Rodney***) was heading for St. John's with escorts ***Fennel*** and ***Burlington.***

Hadley, in his book *U-boats Against Canada*, aptly describes the situation: "The swiftly changing combat picture becomes obscure at this point." By mid-morning ***U 806*** was about two miles from the Sambro Light Vessel when the three ships of the hastily formed escort group approached in line abreast on their way to take screening stations around XB-139. The COs were aware there was possibly a U-boat about, and were zig-zagging. Although U-boats were known to be in the area (in fact there were three around), CAT gear was not streamed because the ships were not in actual contact with any of these boats and because of the annoying masking of their asdics by these noise-makers. Minesweeping was postponed until the two convoys had been escorted out of the area.

When the U-boat sighted the ships of convoy XB-139 which Hornbostel intended as his target, she was 400 yards on its port side. The senior officer in ***Kirkland Lake*** had just ordered the warships to break their formation and take up screening positions as Hornbostel observed them astern of him through his small attack periscope. On receipt of the flag signal ***Clayoquot***, in the middle position, altered away, which, perchance, took her directly toward the track of the submarine from astern of her. Hornbostel assumed that he had been spotted and that an attack was being made by ***Clayoquot***. He temporarily abandoned his attack on the convoy ships and fired a GNAT homing torpedo in his defence at the on-coming ***Clayoquot*** and dived to 155 feet. The torpedo struck sixty-nine seconds later, at 1140. The ship was only three miles from the light vessel.

Craig Campbell, in his cabin, had just been informed by the OOW that the signal for assuming the assigned escort positions had been executed. He ordered speed of fourteen knots and went to the bridge. Moments later he was talking to the OOW as the ship was hit in the stern and immediately listed to starboard. The torpedo explosion was not particularly violent. But almost immediately there was a further thunderous explosion aft as some of the depth charges countermined. This explosion blew thirty-eight feet of the stern section into a vertical position. Parts of the minesweeping winch flew over the mast and landed on the forecastle; parts of depth charges landed on the bridge itself. Campbell ordered "Action stations", but when he ordered "Damage control parties" to be piped the seaman could not find his bosun's call amid the destruction on the bridge. Parts of another depth charge crashed through the galley skylight onto the cook's stove. Dense clouds of steam and smoke obscured Campbell's view aft, and there was a tremendous roaring noise from escaping steam.

Three men on watch aft and two officers in an after cabin were killed outright in the explosion. The toll would have been much higher but for the timing, as all off-watch personnel were forward drawing their rum tot before the noon meal. Two other officers, Lt Paul Finlay and SLt William Munro, were trapped in an after port side cabin. As the ship quickly settled lower in the water they yelled out a scuttle for help or an axe to chop themselves free. LS Atherton went below into the obviously foundering ship in search but by then the axes were under water, and the two had to be left to their fate.

One twenty-seven-foot whaler was cut adrift from the starboard side as it reached the water and many of the ship's company were saved by that means. When Campbell ordered "Abandon ship" as she rolled more to starboard, the ship's company went to their stations in an orderly fashion then leapt into the frigid 38° December seas. It took only about ten minutes for the ship to turn turtle and sink, stern first. There had been no opportunity to withdraw the primers from some of the emergency pattern depth charges on ***Clayoquot's*** stern, so when she sank they detonated. The newly developed life jackets with a crotch piece for protection meant fewer serious injuries, although men in the water suffered. Campbell himself lay on his back in the water as a result of recalling the advice of a ***Charlottetown*** survivor whom they had rescued in like circumstances. Even then he described the sensation as "being lifted to the deck head and then dropped onto a concrete slab."

Transcona, Kirkland Lake and ***Fennel***, the last with the ***Lady Rodney*** convoy following the others out of Halifax, had all seen ***Clayoquot's*** torpedoing. ***Transcona*** streamed her CAT and altered toward ***Clayoquot's*** position to rescue survivors. But just then a freighter signalled she had sighted a submarine on the surface. ***Transcona*** passed near the survivors, dropping four Carley floats for them but continued on the more urgent task of hunting this threat. Within ten minutes of ***Clayoquot's*** torpedoing, another GNAT fired by Hornbostel was exploded by ***Transcona's*** CAT. ***Kirkland Lake*** also was searching for the elusive U-boat, reporting possible contacts, but without attack results. ***Fennel***, ordering ***Lady Rodney*** and ***Burlington*** back into Halifax and considering the desperately cold water, moved to rescue survivors. With ships about for rescue, some men in the water and on rafts even managed to sing and joke. One shouted out a news broadcast: "Flash! Canadian minesweeper destroys German torpedo!"

For a change there was little diesel oil on the survivors which made the rescue somewhat easier and faster. All seventy-six in the water were picked up in about forty minutes and taken into Halifax. LCdr K.L. Johnson, RCNVR, ***Fennel's*** CO was awarded a Mention in Despatches for his "leadership, initiative and good judgement." Others involved also received M.i.D.s including Lt H.C. Campbell of ***Fennel*** and two ***Clayoquot*** seamen who had helped those in the water, Coder W. Petrie and AB B.E. Williams for their example and leadership. Some Carley floats were later found along the shoreline by "coast watchers" and compensation paid. But there was no indication that these were available to or required by the survivors.

After firing at ***Transcona*** Hornbostel dived to 185 feet and turned to pass under the ships of the XB-139 convoy, which had continued outbound. At 1310 he settled on the bottom in shallow waters at 210 feet, virtually in the track of the many ships hastily sent out from Halifax to join the massive hunt. Cdr Clark in ***Kirkland Lake*** initially took charge, later replaced by an RN staff officer brought out by Fairmile. In the end the four ships of the two escort groups (***Fennel*** returned after dropping her survivors in the dockyard) were joined by another frigate, four corvettes, two minesweepers, seven Fairmiles and three trawlers. Although they hunted until 26 December, and made some attacks on suspected targets, nothing was seen. An aircraft sighted a periscope at 1310 Christmas day and depth charged it, without visible results. As there were two U-boats suspected to be in the area, and in fact there were three, it might have been one other than ***U 806.***

Hornbostel remained on the bottom until almost midnight. His crew lay quietly while he spent the time recording his assessment of the tactics and equipment of the Canadian Navy. They heard numerous asdic contacts against the hull and noises he described as "circular saws", which were either ship's echo sounders searching for the bottomed submarine or distant CAT gear. All depth charges dropped in the hunt were far from where they lay. He finally moved away after eleven hours on the bottom.

He then raised the boat until it was thirty to sixty feet clear of the bottom and for ten hours moved slowly south. During that time he recorded a ship over him six times, but the hunt presumed he would retreat north and east, into deeper and safer submarine waters, and would not remain so close to shore. Admittedly shallow water detection is difficult, due to bottom conditions, and possibly the inexperience of the asdic teams. It was not until 2000 on the 25th, after twenty-four hours of undetected movement that Hornbostel finally used his *schnorkel* to drive out the stale air that must have been at extreme levels for the crew, and recharge his batteries.

The Board of Inquiry held on 26 December made only two recommendations and attributed no blame. It recommended that greater use should be made of CAT gear in swept channels, and that the other ships present should report their searches subsequent to the torpedoing for purposes of analyzing submarine tactical procedures.

Craig Campbell had two more commands before the war's end, the corvette ***North Bay*** and the frigate ***Ste. Therese.*** He transferred to the RCN in 1945 and served until 1967.[1]

U 806 survived the war, surrendered to the Allies at Wilhelmshaven in May, 1945 and was eventually scrapped.

LOST:

Bate, John R., OS
Brozovich, Walter, OS
Colbeck, Arthur W., SLt
Finlay, Paul W., Lt
Hilyard, Edmond, AB
Munro, William J., SLt
Neil, John D., Lt(E)
Smith, Lloyd W., AB

SOURCES:

German, *The Sea Is At Our Gates,* pp 178-180.
Hadley, *U-Boats Against Canada,* pp 252-258.
Lawrence, *Tales Of The North Atlantic,* pp. 188-190.
Lenton, *German Submarines*, Vol.2, p.25.
Macpherson, *Minesweepers of the RCN,* pp 19 & 24.
Macpherson & Burgess, *Ships of Canada's Naval Forces*, pp 113 & 234.
Milne, *Shawinigan And The War,* pp. 113-114.
Milner, *The U-Boat Hunters,* p. 224.
Paquette & Bainbridge, *Honours & Awards,* p. 279.
Rohwer, *Axis Submarine Successes,* p. 188.
Schull, *Far Distant Ships*, pp 157-158.
Tarrant, *The U-Boat Offensive*, p. 144.
Tucker, *Naval Service of Canada*, Vol II, pp 21-228.
Watt, *In All Respects Ready*, pp 189-191.

1. Klaus Hornbostel and Craig Campbell have since become friends. Hornbostel returned to the German Navy, the Bundesmarine, and retired as a captain in 1974. Campbell has corresponded for some time and visited him twice and also met the 1st watch officer of ***U 806***, OL Gert Kappen. During a 1994 visit to Hornbostel Campbell accidentally cut his hand and spilt some blood on a lovely white carpet. He jokingly explained to Hornbostel that that was his way of repaying him for the loss of his ship. They signed each other's copies of Hadley's book, Hornbostel writing "At the beginning you were searching for an adversary; at the end you found a friend for life."

CHAPTER 57

HMCS ST. THOMAS AND SEA CLIFF: A SECOND SQUID SUCCESS

St. Thomas: Castle class corvette
Builder: Smith's Dock Co, UK, as *Sandgate Castle*
Comm in RCN: 4 May 44
Crew: 8 officers, 112 crew
Sea Cliff: River class frigate
Builder: Davie Shipbuilding Co, Lauzon, PQ
Comm: 26 Sep 44
Crew: 8 officers, 133 crew
Action: Sank *U 877*, mid-Atlantic, 27 Dec 44
Casualties: none
55 survivors

They sacrificed unto devils...to new Gods that came newly up, whom your fathers feared not.

Deuteronomy, Ch.32, v.17

HMCS ***St. Thomas*** was one of twelve Castle class corvettes acquired by the RCN from Britain in exchange for minesweepers built for them in Great Lakes yards. As Marc Milner puts it, these Castles were "a radically new kind of corvette... the pursuit of the basic corvette design to its ultimate form." fifty feet more length in the hull made them good, and much more stable, anti-submarine platforms. The single three-barrel second generation ahead-throwing weapon, the squid A/S mortar, when connected directly to the new Type 144Q/147B A/S range and depth asdic sets proved a formidable weapon, producing up to a 50% kill rate. So reliable was this slaving of set to the mortar bombs that these ships only carried one depth charge rail, two throwers and fifteen depth charges as a back-up.

Sea Cliff was the standard A/S frigate with masses of depth charges (they were supplied with up to 200) and the original ATW hedgehog, both weapons controlled more or less manually by the asdic team and the CO on the bridge.

St. Thomas was taken over by the RCN on commissioning on the Tees in May of 1944, and after work-ups at Commodore G.O. Stephenson's formidable base at Tobermory in western Scotland, joined the close escort C-3 Group. She at once began escorting outbound ocean convoys. ***Sea Cliff,*** after her work-ups in Bermuda, also joined C-3 but much later, in December, 1944. Their group

A lovely, and all-too-typical North Atlantic photo of a frigate at sea. HMCS *Sea Cliff*, named for Leamington, Ontario as there was already an HMS *Leamington*. The twin 4-inch was not usual in Canadian frigates until late in the war.

senior officer was Cdr Clarence A. King, DSO, DSC & BAR, RCNR, of HMCS ***Oakville*** and ***Swansea*** fame (See Ch. 15, 35, 37 and 38.)

On the morning of Wednesday 27 December, in miserable, cold, windy and rainy weather, the group, having sailed from St. John's, was escorting eastbound Convoy HX-237 in mid-Atlantic, well north of the Azores. At 0600 local time the RCN corvette ***Edmundston*** of EG C-8 with the same convoy picked up a possible submarine echo on asdic but classed it as "non-sub." However, Cdr King, rich in available escorts and with no other U-boats threatening as far as he knew, thought it worth further investigation so he ordered ***St. Thomas*** and ***Sea Cliff*** to join ***Edmundston*** and check. After a bit of searching and also gaining contact, ***St. Thomas's*** asdic team classified the echo as a submarine. Ironically, the asdic 1st operator in ***St. Thomas*** had only recently transferred from ***Edmundston***.

St. Thomas's CO, LCdr L.P. Denny RCNR, set up a careful squid attack, joined by ***Sea Cliff*** under LCdr J.E. Harrington, RCNVR, who stood off and held asdic contact. At first there were problems with the contact due to fish noises, and the asdic showed the target depth as 520 feet.

LCdr Denny later described his attack: "I only fired two rounds. The first fired manually to keep ***U 877*** down (at 100 feet), and the second (at 400 feet) fired by the anti-submarine system as I slowly advanced over the U-boat. It was as easy as duck soup!"

After this attack, the two ships shifted away a bit, circling at modest speed, watching the sea and listening, although they lost contact. Suddenly the U-boat surfaced about two and a half miles away. Both ships opened fire at the stopped U-boat but didn't seem to hit the small target at that range; by this time ***St. Thomas's*** radar was inoperative. They altered quickly toward the submarine but could see survivors leaping from the casing into the sea. Within a few minutes, the U-boat, scuttled by her engineers, slid beneath the swells, leaving fifty-five survivors swimming in the bitterly cold and choppy seas in their yellow life jackets or in small rubber life rafts. The ships cautiously approached and picked them up; one officer and twenty men by ***Sea Cliff***, four officers, including the CO and thirty men by ***St. Thomas.*** For a change this was the whole crew of the U-boat. By far the majority of boats were sunk with no or few survivors. The two ships then rejoined their convoy and headed east at the end of a darkening December afternoon.

U 877, a Type IXC/42 U-boat commanded by KL Eberhard Findeisen had left Kiel on her only wartime patrol at midnight on 11 November 1944, planning to be out for 120 days attacking North Atlantic convoys. She anchored in the Kattegat due to very heavy weather, undertook some schnorkeling exercises and deep diving tests and arrived at Kristiansand on Norway's south tip on the 26th. She sailed that day, in a convoy of minesweepers, a *sperrbrecher* and three U-boats, only to be attacked, without damage, by two Beaufighters of RAF Coastal Command. Submerged by day, at only two and a half to three knots due to just this sort of harassment, and snorting by night at six knots to re-charge batteries, Findeisen found he could not surface for more than half an hour due to radar-detected aircraft contacts. Once in the open Atlantic, he was able to surface for up to three days, each time sending weather reports which, despite the possibility of radio-detection, were considered vital for the German land offensive then under way, particularly around Bastogne, Belgium. For three days even these were impossible to transmit due to aerial damage sustained when diving. ***U 877*** was then told to operate at the CO's discretion, so Findeisen decided to try conditions off the Canadian-American coast and was detected purely by chance by ***Edmundston and St. Thomas*** as he headed west.

In the attack, the first squid bomb had detonated as LCdr Denny estimated, fairly far astern, although doing some damage. The second flooded the U-boat's stern, damaging her propellers, and the boat sank to a reported 1,115 feet at an angle estimated at forty degrees while the crew tried to regain control.

This was probably when ***Sea Cliff*** and ***St.***

HMCS *St. Thomas*, showing her excellent late-war spacious bridge, RN radar and her single Squid mounting (under canvas) above and behind her 4-inch gun with its illuminating rocket rails.

Thomas lost contact. ***U 877's*** pumps were now no longer working, so Findeisen ordered the tanks blown and full speed ahead. The boat rose to 524 feet and he tried to hold her there but, stern-heavy, she started to slide back again. At three-quarter speed, he ordered all tanks blown and the boat surfaced at once. On surfacing and opening the upper conning tower hatch, there was so much positive pressure in the boat that the CO and the coxswain/navigator were both blown out of the hatch and injured. They were hospitalized later in the UK.

When the two victors rejoined the convoy, ***Edmundston*** signalled her congratulations to ***St. Thomas.*** LCdr Denny, unable to resist the opportunity, replied: THANKS. CREDIT LARGELY DUE TO YOUR LATE HSD.

Peter Chance, a lieutenant in ***Sea Cliff***, describes the plight of the submariners:

> They were a sorry lot: in a state of shock, cold and very frightened as to what we might do next. A humanitarian attitude was something they didn't expect from their captors. After rescue from the sea, huddled on the upper deck, each was provided with a blanket and then escorted to the warmth of a mess deck. They seemed very young - younger than we, anyhow.
>
> There were requests for combs to disentangle long blond hair made more unpleasant with traces of diesel oil. *'Unser schiff war ein salat'* was a phrase I heard referring to the terrible destruction wrought by the squid bombs. They were not wanting to talk much. We knew that each submarine carried a Gestapo member, which could have accounted for the reluctance of the crew to talk to us. Our innovative captain [LCdr Eric Harrington] resolved this by quietly telling his ship's company of his plan and not to be alarmed. During the latter part of the First Watch, steaming at 10 knots, Action Stations was sounded. The hatch to the prisoners' mess deck was slammed down and dogged. Very soon a depth charge pattern, set to 25 feet, was fired. The shock throughout the ship was formidable but not damaging beyond a few light bulbs. For the prisoners it was another dreadful reminder–but with a happy ending. The Gestapo member was identified somehow and isolated. Smiles and chatter replaced glum silence. There were requests for paper and pencils to write home.
>
> We had the boat's executive officer [1st watch officer], and after trying my high school Deutsch and our BR *German/English Naval Equivalents*, neither of much use, a 22-year-old Austrian acting lieutenant suggested we speak English, his second language. He had not served for long; crews were increasingly difficult to find, let alone train. Morale was still quite remarkable in light of the low survival rate beyond one cruise.
>
> On December 31st we berthed in Gourock on the Firth of Clyde. ***U 877's*** ship's company was formed up in two ranks, facing our ships. They were first mustered and inspected by their own officers and then, prior to being marched off to the prison camp train, they gave us three cheers' as a thank you gesture for their rescue and our compassion in victory.

The same experiences occurred in ***St. Thomas***, where the rescued U-boat officers played chess and bridge with their captors.[1] LCdr Denny received a DSC for this success, well-merited, as he had already sunk a U-boat when commanding the corvette ***Drumheller*** in early 1943 (see Chapter 28), and had been a watch-keeper in ***Oakville*** when Clarence King sank ***U 94.***

Continuing with uneventful convoy escorting, in April of 1945 ***St. Thomas*** left Londonderry for the last time to refit at Halifax. With the war ended, she transferred to the west coast and was paid off on 22 November, 1945. Sold to commercial interests, she served as the coastal passenger vessel ***Comosun*** and later as ***Chilcotin*** (when the name was given up by the ex-Castle class corvette ***Hespeler***) and ***Yukon Star.*** She was broken up in Tacoma in 1974.

Sea Cliff also continued convoying, leaving Londonderry for the last time on 12 May, 1945. Planned for Pacific war operations, work was halted on her, and she was paid off on 28 November at Halifax. In 1946 ***Sea Cliff*** was sold to the Chilean Navy and renamed ***Covadonga***, being broken up in 1968.

SOURCES:

Johnston, *Corvettes Canada,* pp. 252-253.

Macpherson, *Ships Of Canada's Naval Forces,* pp. 62. 108, 229, 235.

Macpherson & Milner, *Corvettes Of The RCN,* pp. 74-77, 158.

Unpublished narrative by Peter Chance.

1. In May of 1960, Mrs. Stan Déry (her husband, Stan Déry, had been ***St. Thomas's*** 1st lieutenant) flew to Europe, spending part of her time in Germany as a guest of Dr. and Mrs. Peter Heisig, ***U 877***'s ex-1st watch officer. When she left his home, Dr. Heisig gave her his naval sword to pass on to Stan. A fitting end for seamen appreciating each other's position in the naval war.

1945

*Ending on a sad note,
with more late
losses than successes*

CHAPTER 58

THE DESTRUCTION OF THE 29th MTB FLOTILLA

29th MTB Flotilla: Motor torpedo boats (see Chapter 46)
Fate: Destroyed by fire, 5 RCN boats, Ostende Harbour, Belgium, 14 Feb 45
Casualties: 1 officer, 25 crew

They shall go out from one fire, and another fire shall devour them; and ye shall know that I am the Lord.

Ezekiel, Ch. 16, v. 7

The remains of RCN and RN Motor Torpedo Boats (MTBs) in the harbour at Ostende, Belgium.

After their D-Day duties off the Normandy beaches, the loss of two boats and severe damage to some others, the 29th MTB Flotilla at last got away from the boring but dangerous anti-*Kleinkampferbände* slow speed sweeps through the anchorages off the eastern beaches. They went back to the more interesting although just as exhausting night sweeps after E-boats along the French and Belgian coasts. These German boats spent many nights trying to lay mines in the swept channels along the British coasts and out into the North Sea and setting up attacks on Normandy supply shipping and convoys entering the French and Belgian ports as they were captured by the Allies.

The MTBs usually had a frigate with good radar accompanying them, to vector the boats onto the Germans. They were also sent after small coastal convoys of German R and flak boats, heavily armed minesweepers and local transports trying to move supplies to their beleaguered forces in ports up and down the coast.

In most cases, when attacked by the boats of the 29th Flotilla, after exchanging hot gunfire, the enemy retreated. The E-boats made off under a smoke screen with their superior speed (five to eight knots faster), and their convoys escaped into the nearest defended port.

On at least one occasion, on 1 September, the boats evidently hit and probably sank a flak trawler and torpedoed some unidentified ship in the smoke as she tried to reach Cap Griz Nez.

Officers and crew changed somewhat frequently, as lieutenants were given their own boats, boats were withdrawn for much needed maintenance and even engine changes, and new boats - ***485, 486, 491*** - replaced damaged or destroyed vessels. By October, the MTBs moved to Felixstowe and were either on defensive patrols across the North Sea defending shipping to Antwerp and preventing mining, or on more offensive patrol sweeps along the Dutch and German coasts. Winter was cold, wet and rough; patrols continued. On 15 January the 29th Flotilla was moved to Ostende in Belgium, to be nearer the action along the coast, against German E-boats coming down from the Hook of Holland area. Patrols became more boring, with less and less German action at sea. Ostende was sadly battered and short of everything.

On 14 February, LCdr Tony Law, the Squadron's senior officer in his MTB ***486,*** fitted with a new and excellent radar but which had temporarily broken down, left for Felixstowe for a day to have it repaired, there being as yet no such facilities in battered Ostende. This annoyed him, but may have saved his crew's lives.

The rest of the flotilla, and several groups of RN MTBs and MGBs, were in an inner *crique* well up inside Ostende Harbour. Maintenance was being carried out in preparation for possible night sweeps up the coast and many of the crew were below sleeping in preparation for the usual sleepless night. The boats were berthed in several trots of three or four. At 1630 on 14 February some 100-octane gasoline had been vented into the restricted calm water of the harbour from one of the boats when pumping out a fuel tank contaminated with water.

An accidental spark, possibly even a cigarette, ignited the gasoline floating on the surface and in moments the whole basin was aflame with a roar. The wooden boats, themselves impregnated to some extent with oil and the floating gas, caught fire almost at once. The on-deck torpedoes and depth charges exploded with thunderous crashes, heard as far away as England, as boat after boat was swept up in the conflagration.

The devouring flames and explosions went on for about two hours. Three boats of the 29th were saved by the crew of one who fought down the initial flames, got their boat started and towed two others to safety into the outer harbour. Those saved were MTBs ***464, 485*** and ***491***. By evening, twelve boats had been burned out, and sixty sailors, twenty-six RCN and thirty-five RN, had been killed. The flotilla medical officer, SurgLt W.L. Leslie, RCNVR, and LSBA W.R. Fraser, RCNVR were returning with medical supplies from a local hospital to the harbour when they saw the explosion. They and the flotilla chaplain worked on injured men and were assisted by soldiers, sailors, marines and nurses from an evacuation train nearby. MTBs ***459, 461, 462, 465, 466*** were lost. A Board of Inquiry was held, but its findings are not readily accessible.

The 29th Flotilla had effectively been wiped out, and on 8 March 1945, it ceased to exist on the books. Only LCdr Kirk Kirkpatrick's 65th Flotilla of "Dog Boats" was left to carry Canadian colours to the end of the war for the MTB/MGB Squadrons.

SurgLt Leslie and LSBA Fraser were both mentioned in despatches "for good services in the fire at Ostende."

LOST:

Note: This list is compiled from several sources, and although most records show the casualties from the Ostende fire to have been one officer and twenty-five men, the list gives only one officer and twenty-three men.

Bahleda, Tel
Broadley, H., AB
Byrne, J., AB
Brush, J.C.
Bond, ____
Cathcart, N., AB
Cross, A., OS
Crang, W.R.N.
Hayle, W.F., Lt
Hunter, E.R.
Kenny, J.
Long, G.P.
Long, W.W., Sto(M)
MacRae, J.R.
Motley, D., AB
Natdo, M.J.
Newbigging, W.J.
Park, E.W.
Pa (?),___
Routh, J.
Rowe, A.J.
Watt, J., L.Sto(M)
Wellington, W.E., PO(MM)
Wright, J.A., AB

SOURCES:

German, *The Sea Is At Our Gates,* p. 167.
Law, *White Plumes Astern,* pp. 161-163.
Lawrence, *Victory At Sea,* p 285.
Nolan & Street, *Champagne Navy,* pp. 225-234.
Richards, *Operation Sick Bay,* pp. 115-116.
Schull, *Far Distant Ships,* pp. 390-392.

CHAPTER 59

HMCS SAINT JOHN SINKS U 309, HER SECOND SUCCESS

Saint John: River class frigate
Builder: Canadian Vickers Ltd, Montreal
Comm: 13 Dec 43
Crew: 8 officers, 133 crew
Action: Sank *U 309,* Moray Firth, Scotland, 16 Feb 45
Casualties: 47
No survivors

O cunning enemy, that, to catch a saint,
With saints doth bait thy hook!

Wm. Shakespeare, *Measure For Measure*

The September 1944 success of EG-9 (see chapter 51) in which ***U247*** was sunk and for which A/LCdr William R.Stacey in ***Saint John*** was awarded a DSC indicated a well trained crew. In May 1944 she joined the 9th Escort Group in Western Approaches Command, based on Londonderry. By the summer of 1944 the group consisted of seven frigates, with Cdr A. Frank C. Layard, DSO, RN, as senior officer. The frigates in the group were rarely all operational at the same time. Repairs, damage, modifications, leave and other operational demands meant that not all ships were available, and the senior officer could choose which ships best served his purposes for certain operations. On 12 November, Layard selected HMCS ***Saint John*** to be senior officer's ship when Stacey returned to Canada for a course, leave, and eventually to command the repaired ***Matane.*** But the ship's company of ***Saint John*** were Stacey-trained.

An unusual 1943 photo of *Saint John*, a bit care-worn, but resting quietly for a change.

From mid-November to mid-February the ship was almost continually at sea, much of the time in northern waters. In November she and other frigates of EG-9, ***Monnow, Nene, Port Colborne, Stormont*** and ***Loch Alvie,*** escorted Convoy JW-62 to the Kola Inlet in North Russia and in December brought Convoy RA-62 back to Loch Ewe; in January she was on operations off Cornwall and in early February returned to the area of the Orkneys, north of Scotland.

Saint John was in company with EG-9 ships ***Nene, Loch Alvie*** and ***Monnow*** in the Pentland Firth between Scotland and the Orkneys when Layard was ordered to support Convoy WN-74 (Loch Ewe to Methil on the Firth of Forth) on 16 February. The convoy was inside the Moray Firth at 1315 on the 16th when ***Saint John's*** asdic team of William Royds and Cable Freeman reported a stationary submarine contact on the bottom.

Leaving the other frigates to protect the convoy, Layard began a most persistent series of depth charge and hedgehog attacks. His first pattern of ten charges brought up some diesel oil and paper. This convinced him he was onto a U-boat and not a wreck. He followed his first attacks at 1500 with another five-charge pattern, producing more oil. He held the contact until 1600 when he fired a hedgehog salvo; at 1714 another five depth charges; at 1735 ten more; at 1800 another hedgehog pattern, and at 1900 ten more depth charges.

The contact was maintained throughout the night without further attacks, as it would have been difficult to see or assess results. At 0800 on the 17th ***Saint John*** began again with ten more depth charges, hedgehog at 0815 and another five charges at 0830. This steady battering by hedgehog and depth charges went on through the morning, producing more papers, maps, cork and other debris not identifiable as to a particular U-boat. ***Loch Alvie*** and ***Monnow*** joined again to hold the contact and drop charges in passes over the target lying on the bottom. Between 1005 and 1500 Layard carried out seven more attacks, expending thirty-one depth charges and one further hedgehog pattern. At this they abandoned their victim, certain that whoever the U-boat was, she was destroyed.

Despite all this battering and the odds and ends of debris recovered, when the hard-nosed official assessment was later made, only a "probable" was allowed. But those on board assessed their quarry as a "dead duck" and AB Joe McLaren painted a second submarine silhouette on the forward 4-inch gun shield. Joe McLaren was a member of the seaboat's crew sent to collect debris sufficient to prove that they had made a kill. He recalls attempting to rip an eagle and swastika emblem off a jacket he had pulled inboard while still attempting to row. Layard was in no doubt and his subsequent recommendations confirmed the DSM for A/PO William Royds who manned the asdic as 1st operator for the majority of the attacks, although his DSM award had originated due to ***Saint John's*** earlier destruction of ***U 247.*** J.R. Bradley was awarded a bar to his DSC for this action, and DSMs went to A/Leading Seamen N.V. Hoffner and L.A. Stannard and to ERA 2 T.W. Whittemore. Lt Charles McIntosh, AB J.W. Hughes, SPO E.P. Seymour and A/LSto G.M. Styles received Mentions in Despatches. Similarly, Commander Layard was awarded a DSC for his succession of U-boat kills while senior officer of EG-9, but only after the war's end.

The tremendous number of depth charge and hedgehog attacks carried out at minimal speeds had caused some flooding in ***Saint John***. She proceeded to Scapa Flow where divers confirmed hull damage. Temporary repairs were made in Cardiff in south Wales and the ship returned to Canada for more permanent repair at Saint John, New Brunswick, the city for which she had been named. These repairs were still unfinished when the war ended, so she was placed in reserve in November, 1945 and broken up in 1947.

When she left Scapa Flow, Layard transferred to yet another of his diminishing number of frigates in EG-9, ***Loch Alvie.*** The group was now reduced to four, ***Monnow, Nene, Loch Alvie*** and, in April, ***St. Pierre***, for the rest of the European war, all the others being under repair in Canada or the UK

Post war assessments of German records confirmed that ***Saint John*** had indeed destroyed ***U 309*** and she was given full credit. The U-boat was commanded by OL Herbert Loeder, who perished with all forty-six of his crew. Commissioned in 1943 and later operating as part of IX U-Flottille out of Brest and later Norway under OL H-Gert Mahrholz, she had made one unsuccessful attack on Convoy ONS-20 in mid-October and, in July, 1944, damaged the merchantman ***Samneva***, the boat's only success.

SOURCES:

Herzog, *Deutsche U-Boote*, p. 271.

Macpherson, *Frigates of the RCN,* p. 44.

Macpherson & Burgess, *Ships of Canada's Naval Forces,*

Milner, *The U-Boat Hunters,* pp. 235-236.

Paquette & Bainbridge, *Honours & Awards,* pp. 52, 339, 471, 510.

Rohwer, *Axis Submarine Successes,* pp. 173, 182-183.

1. At the time of writing this, in September 1996, Cdr Layard is still able to correspond with the writers, in retirement outside Portsmouth in his mid-90s.

CHAPTER 60

THE LOSS OF HMCS TRENTONIAN

Preparations will be made to abandon her in an orderly manner and with the least possible loss of life.

Seamanship Manual, 1951

Trentonian: Increased Endurance Flower class corvette
Builder: Kingston Shipbuilding Co, ON
Comm: 1 Dec 43
Crew: 6 officers, 95 crew
Fate: Torpedoed by *U 1004*, S of Falmouth, England, 22 Feb 45
Casualties: 1 officer, 5 crew

HMCS *Trentonian*, as built, on work-ups at Bermuda in February 1944; already showing signs of paint problems due to poor steel preparation.

Built as an Increased Endurance extended forecastle corvette in the 1942-43 program and launched at Kingston ***Trentonian*** fitted out at Quebec City, went to Halifax in January 1944 for her armament and to Bermuda for work-ups. She was employed in local escort work out of Halifax until April, assisting an RN submarine broken down off Newfoundland. Arriving in Londonderry 1 May, she was allocated to RN escort groups. For the D-Day landings she escorted the huge cement "Mulberry" caissons and block-ships to be used for the artificial harbours, arriving off the beaches the morning of 7 June.

While escorting the cable ship ***Monarch***, laying operational telephone cables across the Channel, she was heavily fired on by a USN destroyer who for some inexplicable reason mistook them for enemy ships. While ***Trentonian*** was most fortunately only slightly damaged by a shell which passed through her engine room but failed to explode, ***Monarch*** was very badly damaged and beached, her captain was wounded and died in ***Trentonian*** later that day. Both ships' companies were naturally furious with the inept Americans, but the story was hushed up for diplomatic reasons, and no explanations were provided to the two ships.

Operating as an escort with groups out of Milford Haven in southwest Wales, ***Trentonian*** sailed on 21 February 1945 to escort Convoy BTC-76 bound for the Thames and Antwerp, Belgium. It consisted of fourteen ships in two columns, proceeding along the English south coast at seven knots. ***Trentonian*** was zigzagging about 3,000 yards ahead, with the RN Fairmile motor launch ***ML 600*** astern. While the night had been foggy, the 22nd was clear, with six to ten miles visibility. Her CO, Lt Colin

S. Glassco, RCNVR, had joined her only a few weeks before, replacing the popular LCdr W.E. Harrison, RCNR, who had been her CO since commissioning and who had been appointed to a frigate's command.

At 1320 the second freighter in the port column, the small British 1,300-ton ***Alexander Kennedy,*** was torpedoed with, at first, no U-boat detected. ***Trentonian*** altered to port to run back down the port side of the convoy, presuming that was the direction from which the attack came. However, as she was coming about, streaming her CAT gear and increasing speed, her asdic operator reported an echo from almost ahead of the convoy. At the same time, ***Trentonian's*** CO signalled the convoy commodore asking on which side the ***Kennedy*** had been hit. When told ON HER *STARBOARD* SIDE, he appreciated that the submarine echo detected before could well have been the perpetrator. In pursuit of a U-boat now presumed to be ahead of the convoy, he elected to pass through the convoy's two columns between the first and second ships of each column.

U 1004, under Oberleutnant Rudolf Hinz, a new CO, had been built by Blohm & Voss, Hamburg, and commissioned at almost the same time as ***Trentonian,*** in December, 1943. On completion of training and in operations she had had no successes until encountering this lightly guarded convoy. She had fired at the lead ship of the columns, hitting the ***Kennedy*** instead. Now, still undetected, she had another target for a quick shot, ***Trentonian***, although it is likely the CO would actually have preferred another of the larger and more valuable merchantmen.

As ***Trentonian*** came clear of the starboard side of the convoy, another explosion was heard astern, although no ship was hit. Hinz reported firing three torpedoes and this must have been one of the first two, detonating at the end of its run. At 1330 the third hit ***Trentonian*** aft on the starboard side, slewing the ship's bows around to starboard. First Lieutenant Burnley Kinsman and the engineer officer made a quick check below and, due to the obviously uncontrollable flooding of the engine room, considered it was impossible to save the ship. Illustrating good ship's discipline instilled in the crew and experience gained in five years of sea warfare, without further orders the depth charges were set to "safe" and their primers withdrawn so that they would not explode when the ship sank. The CO, who had earlier been somewhat shocked at the number of seamen, even Maritimes fishermen, who could not swim, had ruled that all the crew were to wear their life jackets when at sea, which they did.

Fortunately ***Trentonian*** settled on a relatively even keel, so there was time and the opportunity to send a distress message indicating she had been torpedoed, and to launch the ship's twenty-seven foot whaler and her Carley floats before the order to abandon ship was given ten minutes later. The navigator had time to destroy the ship's charts, which had secret details of minefields and swept channels indicated on them. The CO and 1st lieutenant were the last to leap overboard, having ensured there was no-one else left alive on board. In fourteen minutes ***Trentonian*** had sunk, stern first.

One officer and five men lost their lives, all in the initial explosion or due to injuries therefrom. Eleven others were wounded, several quite badly, two requiring considerable hospitalization in Cornwall. The RN ML and another from a convoy just astern safely rescued the ***Trentonian*** survivors. (Several of the survivors complained that they had just completed repainting Trentonian before they sailed!) Evidently the U-boat, satisfied with two hits, both of which sank their victim, did not tempt fate further and slipped away.

HMCS ***Calgary*** and, later, ships of the RCN's 6 and 26 Escort Groups hunted the area that afternoon and all night, but ***U 1004*** had got away undetected. She accomplished nothing further in the way of attacks, surrendered at the war's end the following May and was scuttled by the RN at sea.

Trentonian was the tenth and last RCN corvette sunk during the war, although two more ships, *Bangor* class escorts, were yet to be lost before the end.

LOST:

Beck, Moyle K., LS
Catherine, Robert T. AB
Founier, John A., LS
Harvey, Colin B. LS
McCormack, John, Sto
Stephen, Gordon K., Lt

SOURCES:

Bishop, *Courage at Sea*, pp. 163-165.

Gregory, *Memories of HMCS Trentonian.*

Johnston, *Corvettes Canada,* pp. 265-266.

Lamb, *Corvette Navy,* pp. 137-8.

Macpherson & Burgess, *Ships of Canada's Naval Forces,* pp. 99, 214, 233.

Rohwer, *Axis Submarine Successes,* p. 191.

Schull, *Far Distant Ships,* p. 390.

Winser, *The D-Day Ships.*

CHAPTER 61

THE FRIGATES OF EG-25 COMBINE TO SINK U 1302

The fox knows many things - the hedgehog one big one

Archilogus, 7th C B.C.

Strathadam: all River class frigates
Builder: Yarrows Ltd, Esquimalt, BC
Comm: 29 Sep 44
Crew: each ship, 7-10 officers, 170 crew
La Hulloise: Builder: Canadian Vickers Ltd, Montreal
Comm: 20 May 44
Thetford Mines: Builder: Morton Engineering & Dry Dock Co, Quebec City
Comm: 24 May 44
Action: Sank *U 1302*, off St. David's Head, S Wales, 7 Mar 45
Casualties: 48
No survivors

Strathadam shortly after commissioning, on the west coast.

In the fall of 1944 the Canadian 25th Escort Group was formed with four frigates fresh from the builders and work-up programs. Their operating base was to be Londonderry, Northern Ireland. The group was led by A/Cdr V. "Starchy" Browne, RCNVR, CO of ***Orkney*** (a frigate named after Yorkton, Saskatchewan, whose name could not be used because of possible confusion with USS ***Yorktown)*** and included ***Strathadam*** (LCdr H.L.Quinn, RCNVR), ***La Hulloise*** (LCdr John Brock, RCNVR) and ***Thetford Mines*** (LCdr J.A.R. Allan, RCNVR). At this late point in the war, the Germans were concentrating submarines in the busy convoy arrival and departure area between Ireland and the west coast of England and Scotland. EG-25 was to assist the close escorts of convoys as merchantmen broke away to head to various ports, and to prosecute suspected submarine contacts. On the night of 13 February, 1945 the frigates were covering ships moving into the Mersey River leading up to Liverpool. The weather was foul, with rain and poor visibility when ***Orkney*** struck the new

One of the truly great photos of a wartime frigate, in typical Atlantic weather. *La Hulloise* entering Liverpool, England, in 1945, looking somewhat care-worn but efficient, in a strong wind and difficult chop. Fitted with twin 4-inch guns.

ship ***Blairnevis,*** loaded with bauxite, which had to be run aground to prevent her sinking in the swept channel. ***Orkney*** herself was damaged and was sent to Scotland for repairs.

In early March the group was down to three ships with Howard Quinn in ***Strathadam*** as acting senior officer. One year earlier, in April, 1943, Quinn, in command of the corvette ***Eyebright***, had towed the corvette ***Mayflower*** commanded by Browne for 600 miles in bad weather and had been awarded a Mention in Despatches. He had asked for command of ***Strathadam*** to serve under his friend Browne.

On 6 March, 1945 EG-25 had been directed to patrol the southern entrance of St. George's Channel between Ireland and south Wales. Brock, in ***La Hulloise,*** obtained a contact on what could have been a submarine and had pounded away at it with hedgehog and depth charges. That he was attacking one of the numerous sunken wrecks became evident when debris came to the surface in the form of large round cheeses!

The group was then ordered to a patrol area northwest of Ireland. The ships were proceeding northward in St. George's Channel intending to pass up the Irish Sea, searching as they went in line abreast, ***La Hulloise*** to port, ***Strathadam*** in the middle and ***Thetford Mines*** to starboard. The sea was very calm and the ships were holding speed to ten knots to reduce cavitation from their screws and thus minimize the chance of being struck by homing torpedoes.

At about 2123 ***La Hulloise*** picked up a small blip on her radar which was at first thought to be a buoy. This in itself was remarkable, as it was an early instance of initial U-boat *schnorkel* detection by radar, and nearly miraculous with ***La Hulloise's*** Canadian-designed RXC set, much maligned elsewhere as not being up to service usage. It had been modified, even mostly rebuilt, by her assigned radar maintainer, Lloyd Dawson, and worked excellently. Then an asdic contact was obtained on the same bearing, which was closed. The other ships picked up the target on their radars as well, at 1,400 yards. Brock stopped engines and ***La Hulloise*** drifted slowly toward the target, the CO concerned in case it was simply a small fishing vessel or coaster. When his radar reported it as still "a good big echo", at 300 yards he illuminated the target with his twenty-inch searchlight and recognised at once the *schnorkel* and periscope of a U-boat fine on his port bow. The light glaring at him through his periscope alerted the U-boat's CO who dived at once. But Brock had expended all his hedgehog ammunition in his earlier "attack" so he moved to port to position the target between himself and Quinn in ***Strathadam*** and transmitted a Flash report.

HMCS *Thetford Mines* in the St.Lawrence shortly after commissioning. By this stage in construction all new frigates had twin 4-inch guns forward.

By 2157 all three frigates were in asdic contact and Quinn made one run at 2212, firing hedgehog, while ***Thetford Mines*** and ***La Hulloise*** held the target. This attack produced an underwater flash and an enormous explosion, and Quinn states the hedgehog projectiles had reached only a shallow depth when they struck the U-boat. One end of the submarine was then seen briefly rising out of the water astern of the group but Quinn cannot remember whether it was bow or stern. Some wreckage came to the surface and was collected as evidence, including a blackboard from the engine room showing the remaining fuel state and the U-boat's number. ***Strathadam*** made two more hedgehog attacks to be certain, without additional surface proof of a kill.

One more attack was made by ***La Hulloise*** with depth charges using the ship's echo sounder to show the target on the somewhat flat bottom of the Irish Sea. The group decided to wait until morning to see if they could recover more evidence of their kill. The Royal Navy group EG-18 approached and signalled to Quinn to proceed with his earlier orders to move north. Quinn, incensed at this suggested take-over, told the RN senior officer that if he wanted to take over the contact he would have to come in shooting. The British group moved on. The Canadian ships remained circling and, at first light, lowered sea boats to recover more floating wreckage. No survivors reached the surface as far as the group could tell. At noon it left the area to return to Londonderry on 9 March.

Those in Western Approaches Headquarters, assessing the attack later, were full of praise for the group's preparedness and professionalism. Commodore(D) commented: "***La Hulloise's*** decision to direct instead of attacking with depth charges or attempting to ram is considered eminently sound and indicative of the good teamwork displayed generally by the group and particularly in this action." Even the Admiralty's Anti-U-boat Division assessed it as "most satisfactory". Quinn himself was most complimentary in his post-action report of the actions of the other two COs during the attack.

Referring to Brock in ***La Hulloise*** he commented, "His steady accurate reports were a masterpiece of direction, and in fact his and ***Thetford Mines'*** grand performance bore positive evidence of... a well developed appreciation of team work."

Although still a Type VIIC boat, ***U 1302*** was one of the more recently commissioned submarines, commanded by KL Wolfgang Herwatz, one of two brothers commanding U-boats. In the week preceding her loss she had sunk one Norwegian, one Panamanian and two British ships, two of them from Convoy SC-167 on 2 March.

Just three weeks later ***Strathadam*** was again in contact with a submarine when there was a premature explosion of one of her hedgehog bombs. The ship had six dead and seven wounded in her fore upper mess deck immediately below the mounting, along with fires, a cut anchor cable and other damage. There were thirteen projectiles remaining on the hedgehog spiggots, all leaking torpex, their safety pins removed and some with their impellers partly wound off, arming the bombs. Quinn and LCdr Bill Wilkinson gently screwed the impellers back in and replaced the safety pins. Wilkinson was awarded a Mention in Despatches.

Howard Quinn transferred to the RCN after the war and at one point served in a NATO appointment in Norfolk, Virginia. When he met the German naval attaché he asked about the identity of the commander of ***U 1302***. The German captain was able to tell him that the parents of KL Herwatz had been informed that their son had been captured by the Russians. Quinn wrote to them so that they would not hold vain hopes of his eventual release. Herwatz' brother had survived the war and wrote to Quinn with the family's thanks.

Quinn received a DSC for the action and retired as a commodore. John (Panner) Brock also got a DSC to add to his M.i.D. earned for earlier Atlantic service. John Allan had won a DSC as a sub lieutenant in ***Chambly;*** for his part in this action he was given a Mention in Despatches.

All three frigates had new careers after the war ended. ***Strathadam*** was acquired by the Israeli navy in 1950 and served until 1959 under the name ***Misgav***. ***La Hulloise*** was recommissioned for service with the RCN from 1949 until 1953, converted to a *Prestonian* class frigate and continued in training roles until 1965. ***Thetford Mines*** was sold to a Honduran buyer for service as a fruit carrier.

SOURCES:

Lenton, *German Submarines, WW II,* Vol II, p. 192.

Macpherson, *Frigates of the RCN*, pp. 30, 51, 87.

Macpherson & Burgess, *Ships of Canada's Naval Forces*.

Milner, *The U-Boat Hunters,* pp. 126, 238-241.

Paquette & Bainbridge, *Honours & Awards,* pp. 6, 70, 450.

Rohwer, *Axis Submarine Successes,* pp. 191-192.

Schull, *Far Distant Ships,* pp. 392-393.

CHAPTER 62

HMCS GUYSBOROUGH: OUR LAST OVERSEAS LOSS

Exigui numero, sed bello vivida virtus[1]

Virgil, *Aeneid*

Guysborough: *Bangor* class minesweeper
Builder: North Vancouver Ship Repairs Ltd, BC
Comm: 22 Apr 42
Crew: 8 officers, 83 crew
Fate: Torpedoed by *U 878*, off Ushant, France, 17 Mar 45
Casualties: 4 officers, 47 crew

A nice photo of *Guysborough* in March, 1944. The ex-RN ships all had low yet very prominent hull numbers.

HMCS ***Guysborough*** was one of six *Bangor* minesweepers ordered for the RN from the North Van shipyard in 1940 as part of the exchange whereby the British built destroyers for the RCN and Canadian shipyards built smaller, less complicated corvettes and minesweepers. They were technically "on loan to the RCN" and the surviving five were returned to the RN at the war's conclusion.

Manned from her commissioning by Canadians, she served as an ocean escort on the West coast, and then in Western Local Escort until refitted in the US in late 1943. In February, 1944 she sailed with three other *Bangors* for minesweeping duties in support of the D-Day landings. On that momentous day she served with the RN's 14th M/S Flotilla with three other RCN ships, ***Georgian, Kenora*** and ***Vegreville***, sweeping mines from the approaches to the American beaches.

Completing her sweeping duties to clear the areas and local harbours, in particular around Brest, she returned to Canada in December, 1944 for a refit at Lunenburg. In March 1945 she headed back toward the UK for further minesweeping duties, pausing at Horta in the Azores for fuel. Apart from her normal crew, she had given passage to a Fleet Air Arm pilot, Lieutenant E.M. (Ted) Davis, RCNVR "...additional for return on loan to R.N." His brother, LCdr Jim "Foghorn" Davis was commanding the frigate ***Royalmount*** on mid-ocean escort duties. Although not required to do so, Ted stood watches crossing the Atlantic.

By 17 March, after her brief fuelling stop she was heading steadily northeast at thirteen knots for Plymouth. ***Guysborough*** was all alone, about 200 miles off the Spanish coast, in a moderate but rising sea and swell, light winds and, by 1815, in early evening sunlight. Possibly due to the war in Europe obviously drawing to a close as the Allies entered Germany from east and west, it seemed almost a peacetime patrol. Although she had CAT gear streamed, it was some 250 yards astern, a distance failing to give adequate protection and

1. "Small in number, but their valour tried in war, and glowing."

criticised at the subsequent Board of Inquiry. To conserve fuel she was not zig-zagging as there had been no U-boat warnings taken in. The *Bangors* were not designed for long ocean passages, and as in the case of the loss of ***Esquimalt*** the next month (See Chapter 64), an additional telegraphist was required if all intelligence broadcasts were to be read, and she did not carry that extra man.

With no warning or alarm whatsoever, at 1850 an acoustic torpedo from ***U 878*** struck her dead astern, curling up the minesweeping deck, littering the after part of the ship with debris, and damaging her two boats. ***Guysborough*** settled somewhat by the stern and took on a slight port list. So far no lives had been lost. The CO went forward, because he thought at first that was where the torpedo had struck, to find debris from the quarterdeck on the forecastle.

Initially it appeared that although some flooding continued, the ship might be saved. Damage control parties shored up bulkheads forward of the damaged stern and pumps were started to keep up with the flooding. The ship lay stopped. The crew were mustered, told to put on warm clothing and ordered to the upper deck. Guns were manned, gear needed for the damage control parties moved aft and, apart from feverish efforts below, all was quiet for forty-five minutes. The whaler was lowered and five Carley floats supposedly secured alongside, although two floats drifted away and had to be hauled back by the whaler.

The lack of immediate vital damage allowed a message to be sent:

TO: WHITEHALL W/T
FROM: GUYSBOROUGH

> EMERGENCY. HAVE BEEN STRUCK BY TORPEDO PORT SIDE. MY POSITION COURSE AND SPEED AT COMMENCEMENT OF CURRENT WATCH WERE 046°40'N, 009°30'W ....
>
> 1835Z

Then, again with no warning or even asdic contact, another torpedo hit the little ship amidships at 1935 and she was obviously doomed. There was evidently no time left to add the course and speed, for just then the order to abandon ship was given. In this second explosion and its aftermath only two lives were lost, First Lieutenant Oscar H. Rumpel and Petty Officer Dicks, the former when he went below to ensure all men were out safely. He did not return.

This time her two sea boats were destroyed, and several men injured. On orders from her CO, Lt B.T.R. Russell, RCNR, the last Carley float was released overboard. In the best of Service traditions, Lt Russell was the last to leave the ship.

To quote Joseph Schull in *The Far Distant Ships*: "All men had got away from the ship, and in spite of a moderately heavy swell the situation did not seem too threatening.... [But] four of the Carley floats with about twelve men on each were carried well away from the ship before other men swimming in the water could reach them. Onto the fifth, which remained alongside, forty-two men [and two officers], some of them injured, had to be crowded." Such a float was designed for about twenty survivors, twelve sitting inside with their legs in the water and eight clinging to life-lines around the outside.

Guysborough slowly settled as she flooded, and sank stern first thirty-five minutes later, given three cheers by the survivors still in the area. The four errant floats were soon swept out of sight of the fifth with the rising seas and strengthening wind. These unwieldy floats were designed to simply save lives, and were really not capable of being paddled far in winds or a heaving sea. Alongside the single float remaining in the area, some of those in the water and holding to the life-lines as darkness fell, numbed and in shock, and with no room on the little float for them, simply relaxed their grip and floated away, almost unseen. Some of the injured on the float itself died from their wounds. The sea rose, and this float capsized twice, whereby thirty-six of the occupants or those around the outside died. They were either trapped underneath or tossed away from their hand grips, or in some cases were unable to release the spring hook of their life-vest strap due to numbed fingers.

Lt Ted Davis was on one of the floats that drifted away, commenting "Ours seemed crowded enough with twelve or fourteen aboard and I don't recall anyone hanging onto the life-line on the outside... Four of the five floats were then lashed loosely together but the fifth, the one that was so overcrowded, drifted away and was unable to get back to the others." On his group of floats, someone attempted to muster spirits by having the wet and shocked crews sing the naval hymn "Eternal Father, strong to save," but his efforts were not appreciated and were greeted mainly with catcalls. It was the popular song hits of the day that drew enthusiastic vocal support throughout the long hours of darkness.

Ted Davis recalled: "The frigid water took its toll. The cold, the darkness, the apparent futility of it all was an ever increasing drain on our resources, both physical and mental. It was to become a test of will and endurance. Stay awake. Don't fall asleep. I kept telling myself to concentrate on what was going on around me and not let my thoughts wander. But the cold had a numbing effect, and I would suddenly awake with a start. You're not just trying to stay awake, you're trying to stay alive."

Some just slipped into a final sleep and died, their bodies committed to the sea after their coats had been removed for the living. At daylight an aircraft was sighted, but turned away apparently without seeing the floats. A ship appeared in late morning, lifting the hopes of the survivors, but altered away, as the crew on the floats found later, to first search for the attacking U-boat in case it had remained in the vicinity. Nothing was found. Fifteen men died in this cluster of floats, from injuries or exposure (now called hypothermia).

It was 1400 the afternoon of 18 March, nineteen hours after the ship went down before the Captains class frigates HMS ***Inglis*** and ***Loring*** picked up the survivors, rescuing those from the two widely separated groups of floats. Thirty-seven men and four officers were saved altogether, forty by ***Inglis*** who had a medical officer, while ***Loring*** carried out an Observant search of the area, in case the U-boat had lingered, and took aboard one man. From the ship's company of ninety-two, four officers and forty-seven men were lost.

The ships then conducted a further search of the area for fifteen miles around, ***Loring*** encountering only a Portuguese or Spanish trawler with a suspicious amount of electronic and HF/DF antennas. The frigate's CO was very annoyed and suspicious that she had been involved in the attack on ***Guysborough*** and told her to clear the area at once, firing her Oerlikons close to the trawler. ***Inglis*** then took her survivors to Plymouth, her sick berth attendant doing minor surgery to close wounds in some cases. Ted Davis's injuries were sufficiently severe to prevent him resuming flying duties for six months.

The Board of Inquiry was held on 29 March aboard the cruiser HMS ***Cleopatra*** with her CO as President. The findings tended to be somewhat critical, as described above, of the end-of-the-war atmosphere. In August, 1945, two officers and four men were awarded Mentions in Despatches "for service in ***Guysborough***", three of them posthumously, although no mention is made if this was for unusual valour in her sinking.

U 878 under KL Johannes Rodig was part of the XXXIII U-Flottille operating out of Flensburg on the German-Danish border, northwest of Kiel. She was not long to enjoy her victory over ***Guysborough***, her only success in one year of operations. Less than a month later, on 10 April, 1945, she was sunk south of Ireland in the outer Bay of Biscay by HMS ***Vanquisher*** and ***Tintagel Castle.*** Of her crew of fifty-one, there were no survivors.

LOST:

Note: There is some difference in the records as to the numbers lost. The following are the names in the DND file on ***Guysborough***, and are reflected in the numbers at the top of the chapter.

Andrews, Joseph C., L.Sto
Ballantyne, Roswell A., Sto
Barnett, Charles A., AB
Bell-Irving, Charles A., Lt(E)
Berryman, Jack G., L.Sto
Bishop, Robert J., Sig
Bodeux, Joseph M., Sig
Bouchard, Joseph E.P.E., AB
Bourbonnais, J.J.G., Sto.PO
Bury, James E., Sto
Chalmers, Robert J., Tel
Clarke, James P., OS
Cox, John D., ERA
Crosson, Abraham B., L., Coder
Densmore, Wilfred H., Cook
Dicks, George R., PO
Downey, Dale G., Sto
Eddy, Donald C., SBA
Gair, Alexander H., L.Sig
Garvey, William, Sig
Geddes, Frederick E., Sto.PO
Gibson, Alvon R., OS
Gohier, Joseph V.M., AB
Gray, Gordon T., L.Sto
Hamilton, William A., ERA
Holland, Thomas V., Lt
Hunter, William A., AB
Konsmo, Ole B., Cook
Lapp, John R., Sto.PO
McCluskey, Henry, AB
McCutcheon, Wm. A., L.Wrtr
McGuigan, John D., L.Stwd
Mallette, Joseph A.M., Stwd
Matthews, Paul J., Sto
Mitchell, George T., Sto
Mountain, William T., AB
Mutcheson, John E., OS
Neufeld, Arthur, Sto
Paul, Kenneth B., L.Sto
Payne, Harry A., LS
Renaud, Maurice J., Sto.PO
Robertson, Robert G., Tel
Rumpel, Oscar H., Lt
Schmidt, Alfred H., Sto
Shinewald, Sydney J., Tel
Slade, Richard S., Lt
Smardon, Walter E., L.Tel
Sorrell, William W., AB
Stevenson, Robert G., Sto
Williams, Roland G., LSA

Plus 1 RN rating.

SOURCES:

It is a melancholy indication of the tendency of both the naval staff and historians to become inured to five and a half years of naval losses during the war that there is so little recorded of ***Guysborough's*** loss. No more than a line or two appears in any other publications reviewed.

Gröner, *German Warships, 1815-1945,* p. 74.

Macpherson, *Minesweepers of the RCN*, p. 42.

Macpherson & Burgess, *Ships of Canada's Naval Forces*, p. 119.

Rohwer, *Axis Submarine Successes 1939-1945*, p. 192.

Schull, *Far Distant Ships*, pp. 393-394.

Williams, *They Led The Way*, pp. 5, 8, 34.

CHAPTER 63

SUNK "BY OTHER MEANS": HMCS NEW GLASGOW AND U 1003

New Glasgow: frigate
Builder: Yarrows Ltd, Esquimalt, BC
Comm: 23 Dec 43
Crew: 8 officers, 133 crew
Action: Sank *U 1003,* off Lough Foyle & Londonderry, 20 Mar 45
Casualties: 18
31 survivors

Les méchants sont toujours surprise de trouver de l'habileté dans les bons.

Luc de Vauvenargues, *Reflexions,* 1740

New Glasgow, in 1944 just after commisioning. These frigates still had single 4-inch guns.

The sinking of ***U 1003*** was unique in that in postwar records its loss is shown in a column headed "By other means", rather than by depth charges, bombing, mines, accident and so on. But ***New Glasgow*** still gets the credit in the tables.

She came around to the east coast after commissioning at Esquimalt, undertook work-ups in Bermuda, and joined the close convoy escort group C-1 for the next five months, until September, 1944 when she joined EG-26 support group at Londonderry.

By this time the hunting or support groups, assigned to add strength to convoy defence if called upon when wolf packs threatened, or to go on roving anti-U-boat hunts, were being comprised of frigates as they became available. These ships were faster and more heavily armed than the corvettes they replaced, whose lack of speed (at fifteen or sixteen knots) over their opponent submarines and even over fast convoys had always been a major handicap. The corvettes were being withdrawn from these groups and assigned to the convoy close escort groups.

New Glasgow remained with EG-26 until the war's end, based part of the time in early 1945 on England's south coast, then on Londonderry.

Late on the evening of 20 March, 1945, after fuelling from the tanker at Moville, she left the Foyle estuary with three others of her group, all RCN frigates, ***Sussexvale, Beacon Hill*** and ***Ribble***. They were to go to Loch Alsh for group training. ***New Glasgow*** was on the port wing of the group, each ship carrying out an independent zig-zag, all sweeping forward at fifteen knots in line abreast at visibility distance. It was a very dark night but with a moon, and relatively calm seas. Nothing untoward was really expected so close inshore and those on the upper deck were still securing for sea.

The CO, LCdr Ross M. Hanbury, a well experienced RCNVR officer, came to the bridge in carpet slippers for a last check of the watch before trying to get a good night's sleep, anticipating the next busy days.

At 2317 the port bridge lookout heard a motor noise, and reported "Low-flying aircraft approaching from port", highly unusual in that area and at night. Suddenly, not twenty-five yards off ***New Glasgow's*** port bow, a U-boat's *schnorkel* and periscope were seen by the lookout and the CO, heading right for them, sticking three feet out of the water, emitting yellowish exhaust smoke. It was the thrumming of the diesel engine exhaust through this *schnorkel* that the lookout had heard. "Action Stations" was rung instantly, but a collision could hardly be avoided.

The *schnorkel* and conning tower hit ***New Glasgow*** just below the bridge wing with a grinding crash. ***New Glasgow*** reared up and lurched over to starboard, throwing many off their feet, followed by a crashing and banging down the port side of the ship as the U-boat scraped aft and clear. The poor navigator, Lt Jack MacBeth, at his chart table in the wheelhouse below, dashed for the bridge, yelling "Holy Christ, we've run aground!!" Despite considerable damage, ***New Glasgow*** altered sharply around to port, fired starshell in an attempt to illuminate the U-boat if she surfaced and carried out a couple of depth charge and hedgehog attacks without really gaining a verified contact with the submarine. By this time, her damage had been assessed, consisting of a bent propellor that reduced her to one engine, some holes and splits in her hull along the port side and damaged asdic. Even with shoring of flooding compartments, LCdr Hanbury felt it was wiser to return to Londonderry since the rest of the group could carry on the hunt for their presumably damaged enemy. He reported his assessment of ***New Glasgow's*** damages to the new group senior officer, Cdr R.M. Aubrey, DSC, RN, (replacing Cdr E.T. Simmons, DSO, DSC, RCNVR who was ill) and asked permission to return to Londonderry. Aubrey concurred, knowing the other three frigates could cope.

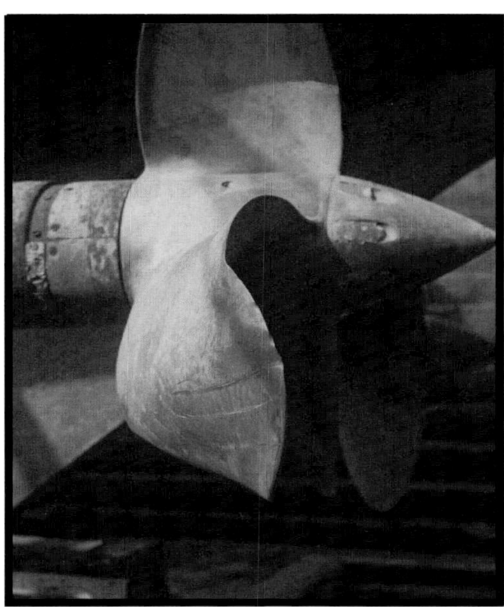

New Glasgow's bent propeller, seen later in dry dock, as a result of *U 1003* hitting it ... or vice versa.

While ***New Glasgow*** had to retire, the other frigates in her group searched around for the U-boat, dropped occasional depth charges on dubious contacts that produced no results, then continued with their planned course for Scotland, finding nothing of the U-boat that had been involved.

Ross Hanbury tells of reporting to Cmdre G.W.G. Simpson, Commodore(D) Londonderry, on arrival with his damaged ship: "Sir, I have just completed a *happy accident*, and I don't think you will want to court martial me for it!"

In a few days, after temporary repairs, ***New Glasgow*** then moved around to Rosyth naval dockyard in eastern Scotland for much more extensive repairs that would make her again operational, which took until 5 June.

Also back in Londonderry, LCdr Howard Quinn, a long-time pre-war RCNVR, was acting senior officer of EG-25 in ***Strathadam,*** with ***La Hulloise*** and ***Thetford Mines***, a companion group to ***New Glasgow's*** EG-26. He continues the tale: "We are refuelling alongside the tanker in Moville, after one of our routine stints pulverising old shipwrecks lying on the bottom of the Irish Sea.[1] Commodore 'Shrimp' Simpson, a born sceptic,[2] has reason to believe the U-boat is still alive, mayhap not alive and well but capable of escape. He orders every escort in the country to search. EG-25 is assigned the western outer limit off Tory Island. About 48 hours later, a cold, dreary March morning, we sight the crew of ***U 1003*** huddled in a damn great yellow inflatable boat, 34 of them, give or take."

U 1003, a 1944-built Type VIIC boat of the XI U-Flottille operating out of Bergen, Norway, had been on her second war patrol, under OL W. Struebing. The collision with ***New Glasgow*** had wrenched off the *schnorkel,* filling the conning tower with sea water and breaking her periscopes. After creeping off to seaward slightly, the boat settled on the sea bottom at 180

1. These were a perpetual problem all around the UK coast for A/S ships trying to locate bottomed U-boats, who knew this perfectly well.

2. And an ex-submariner himself.

feet, while her pumps tried to cope with the flooding. She could now only operate fully surfaced, a very poor choice in the busy waters off Londonderry, or very temporarily on her electric motors; and when her batteries gave out she would be unable even to surface.

During daylight on 21 March, in a daring escape attempt, Struebing quietly eased his boat, sightless without her periscopes, westward and to seaward at sixty feet and after dark surfaced, hoping to air out the boat and charge his batteries. Forcing open the damaged conning tower hatch, he found not only the *schnorkel* and periscopes destroyed but the radar receivers torn away, one 20mm gun dismounted and the bridge wrecked. His U-boat was detected by escorts' radar almost at once and forced to dive again. After trying to cope with the flooding, now as well through the conning tower hatch which would not re-seal properly, and again exhausting his batteries, about midnight on 22 March, Struebing realised it was futile. He brought his boat to the surface, hoping he could reach the Irish Free State and beach her. Almost at once escort radar was detected on his portable search receiver, so he resolved to scuttle ***U 1003*** without further ado. His crew abandoned the dying boat and she promptly sank, leaving the men to struggle in the bitterly cold water, where several perished. This was the unhappy, cold, dirty and miserable bunch Howard Quinn's EG-25 found sixteen miles off Inishtrahull, Ireland, and took prisoner. Two of them died on board and were buried at sea on the way in.

This destruction, unintentional as it may have been, was the RCN's last in the war - in fact the last for over fifty years, if one excludes the intentional sinking of the surrendered ***U 190*** off Halifax in 1947.

Howard tells the concluding part of the tale as well: "Later the scene shifts to the seagoing officers' club in 'Derry, home of post mortem tribunals. So, with minds honed to razor sharpness by infusions of grape and juniper, the 20/20 Hindsight Committee buttonholes ***New Glasgow's*** CO, Ross Hanbury, and needles him: 'What you should have done,' they said, 'was to say in your Report of Proceedings, on sighting the *schnorkel,* I turned to ram. Not too late old boy, get it back, say you forgot something and insert that simple phrase, then you'll collect a DSC for destroying ***U 1003.'*** 'Tis said that the CO was quite stirred by the Committee's brilliant assessment and kindly advice. He supposedly set off to recover his Report of Proceedings. But alas, the telling document had already ascended to the seventh astral plane and was now in the gnarled hands (gnarled from peeling strips off COs) of C-in-C Western Approaches, Admiral Sir Max Horton." Ross Hanbury later said he in fact thought better of this questionable plan, given Admiral Horton's reputation, and did not try to retrieve his report.

Even so, the various reports on the action caused considerable confusion and much mirth when they reached the Assessment Committee. In fact ***New Glasgow's*** EG-26 had already tried to claim a "kill" when ***U 1209*** grounded on Wolf Rock off Cornwall during a hunt on 18 December 1944, contending it was their attacks that had led the hapless boat "to reckless manoeuvres" that caused the grounding. Here they were again, claiming a U-boat rammed, when the detailed reports obviously described something quite different. After many memos back and forth, the committee allowed ***New Glasgow*** the credit for sinking ***U 1003*** "By other means", but no DSC for Hanbury.

In another odd coincidence, several ***New Glasgow*** ratings tell of a clandestine visit to Eire a night or so before this action, and getting into a conversation in a pub with some foreign-language-speaking sailors who turned out to be off a U-boat, in an Irish harbour for brief repairs (as allowed under international law). In typical friendly Canadian style, the two groups exchanged drinks and halting conversation and parted. They might have been off ***U 1003***... no one ever checked.

After her repairs at Rosyth, ***New Glasgow*** returned to Canada, being paid off into reserve in November. Rebuilt in a long refit to a Prestonian frigate design, she recommissioned on 30 January, 1954 and served in a multitude of training duties until paying off finally on 30 January, 1967. She was broken up in Japan later that year.

SOURCES:

Edge, *First, The Navy,* p. 13-14.

Hoyt, *Death of the U-Boats,* p. 202.

Keatts, *Sunken U-Boats* p. 72.

Lawrence, *Tales of the North Atlantic*, pp. 215-6.

MacBeth, *Ready, Aye, Ready*, pp. 98-9.

Macpherson & Burgess, *Ships of Canada's Naval Forces,* p. 50.

Milner, *The U-Boat Hunters,* pp. 214-244.

NOAC, *Starshell*, October, 1986, p. 17.

Schull, *Far Distant Ships*, pp. 394-5.

CHAPTER 64

HMCS ESQUIMALT: A LATE AND LAST LOSS

All service ranks the same with God -
With God, whose puppets, best and worst,
Are we: there is no last or first.

Robert Browning, "Pippa Passes"

Esquimalt: Diesel *Bangor* class minesweeper
Builder: Marine Industries Ltd, Sorel, PQ
Comm: 26 Oct 42
Crew: 7 officers, 64 crew
Fate: Torpedoed by *U 190*, Halifax approaches, 16 Apr 45
Casualties: 5 officers, 39 crew

Esquimalt in November, 1944, just five months before her loss.

HMCS ***Esquimalt*** was one of a small class of ten diesel-engined *Bangor* class minesweepers. But there were delays in the delivery of the Sulzer diesel engines from Dominion Engineering Company in Montreal and the builders did not complete the ships as early as planned. ***Esquimalt*** was laid down in December, 1940 but not commissioned until 22 months later. Diesel engines took 28,000 man-hours to build; the steam triple-expansion engines only 10,000 man-hours. The big advantage of the diesels was the ability to get under way quickly, if required. ***Esquimalt*** was not fully equipped for minesweeping.

Esquimalt's early career was marred by mechanical problems. It was not until June 1943 that she was assigned to the Newfoundland local force for escort duties. In September 1944 she returned to Halifax as part of the Local Defence Force for escort and if need be, for minesweeping operations. After another lengthy refit Lt R.C. Macmillan, DSC & Bar, RCNVR, took command in early February, 1945, the ship's sixth commanding officer. He was due for promotion to lieutenant commander and had been awarded a DSC and then a Bar to it in quick succession in the Mediterranean. The latter Bar was "for bravery and endurance" in August, 1941 when serving in the Royal Navy minesweeper HMS ***Skudd III***, a converted Norwegian whaler (similar to the RCN's ex-Norwegian *Suderöys*). He was at Tobruk when his vessel was sunk by enemy aircraft when sweeping there. It was this dangerous sweeping that had earned him the initial DSC only a few months before in the 1941 New Years' Honours List.

By early 1945 the Atlantic war had turned decisively against the U-boats. But this did not deter Hitler from directing his remaining strength to try to destroy the Allied re-supply at its sources in the ships leaving North American ports. ***U 190*** was one of the larger type IXC fast-diving boats of the XXXIII U-Flottille, directed to operate in Canadian waters. The U-boat had been launched in 1942, but had limited success. Under another CO she had sunk a straggler, SS ***Empire Lakeland***, from Convoy SC-121 in March, 1943. ***Esquimalt*** was to be her only other success, just two weeks before the war's end.

OL Edwin Reith sailed from Norway on his boat's sixth war patrol at about the same time as MacMillan took command of ***Esquimalt***. By mid-April, after familiarising himself with traffic in the area, ***U 190*** had taken up a position in the vicinity of the East Halifax Light Vessel where earlier U-boat successes had been attained. (See Chapter 56, loss of ***Clayoquot***)

Esquimalt sailed from Halifax late in the evening of 15 April, postponing the completion of installation of her minesweeping gear. Her orders were to conduct an anti-submarine sweep in one of the areas near the approaches to the harbour. The ship was to be alone during the middle and morning watches but was to join another *Bangor* class escort, HMCS ***Sarnia***, at 0800 and sweep outwards from the light vessel for ten miles in anticipation of the passage of an HJF convoy to St. John's. It was a slightly misty day with good visibility, improving as the morning wore on. The sea state was moderate although with an occasional uncomfortable swell. Despite the fact that the Board of Inquiry that considered ***Clayoquot's*** loss three-and-a-half months before had recommended increased use of CAT gear in the swept channels, ***Esquimalt*** did not stream hers because of its asdic interference. Her obsolete SW2C radar set had apparently been switched off because of the ten miles visibility and the relatively calm seas. In accordance with her orders she was conducting an asdic sweep in her patrol area but was doing so without zig-zagging.

Reith in ***U 190*** thought he had been detected. ***Esquimalt's*** asdic beams were heard on the submarine's hull but the ship was not aware that a contact had been made. There is much similarity here with the action of ***U 806*** and ***Clayoquot*** since Reith, believing a depth charge attack was imminent, fired a GNAT from his stern tube as he altered away from the escort as a defensive measure. The range was very close and ***Esquimalt*** was steering directly for the submarine, although the torpedo would be programmed to "seek" the noise of the ship's engines or propellers.

It was still before dawn when the torpedo struck ***Esquimalt*** on the starboard side at the engineroom, about 0630. It was here that the relatively few deaths from the explosion occurred. MacMillan rushed to the bridge but his ship was already sinking, rolling to starboard. In the four minutes it took the ship to sink, due to loss of electric power and no doubt broken batteries it was impossible to send off any radio messages or distress signals. Had ***Sarnia*** been aware of the situation many lives might have been saved.

Sarnia moved toward the rendezvous position, failed to see ***Esquimalt*** as planned and then, paradoxically, became involved in a hunt herself for a possible U-boat when an asdic contact was made. Although she sent a signal to Halifax reporting the non-appearance of her sister-ship, her "Immediate" report of her submarine attack arrived first and distracted those ashore. She depth charged a contact without results, was delayed returning to the rendezvous and it was only then, when she again failed to find the other *Bangor*, that her CO, Lt R.P.J. Douty, RCNVR, appreciated that ***Esquimalt*** was really overdue. Just after 1000 both those in Halifax and on board ***Sarnia*** became conscious that the ship was indeed missing.

For the ship's company of ***Esquimalt*** each hour in the water meant more deaths. Before it could be released, the starboard whaler was underwater at its davits, and had been damaged by the fallen mast due to its proximity to the explosion. While four Carley floats were released through the exertions of some men, the automatic release mechanisms of two others did not work even when the ship sank. Some of the crew suggested this was due to debris thrown up from the quarterdeck by the explosion just below and aft of them. The Board implied it might possibly be due to inadequate, or lack of, regular maintenance or to painting over the release gear during previous years, a suggestion of lack of professionalism found most annoying to surviving ship's company. A photo of men on a float being picked up later by ***Sarnia*** shows several in only the undershirts they were wearing as they dropped out of their hammocks to begin the day. The water in mid-April off Halifax was still too cold for long survival. It was more than six hours before ***Sarnia***, hurrying back along the track from the buoy where she had been supposed to meet ***Esquimalt***, at last found the survivors. Only then did Halifax know for certain of the disaster.

MacMillan had been the last to leave his ship and he tried to keep the floats together and keep up the spirits of those crowded on them or clinging to them. Only MacMillan and SLt Mike Kazakoff survived of the seven officers. None of those on watch on the bridge survived to report anything seen before the torpedoing. As the hours passed, aircraft flew over but mistook the yellow Carley floats for fishermen at work. About 0900 two minesweepers passed within sight of the survivors in the water but did not see them, despite their waving shirts and other garments, possibly due to the sweepers' concentration on a change of course just then, with paravanes and sweep wires to be adjusted. Men succumbed to the cold, injuries, exhaustion and despair. Of the total crew of seventy-one, ***Sarnia***, when she eventually found the small cluster of floats, was able to save only twenty-seven, twenty-four from the floats. Three, including Mike Kazakoff, managed to paddle their Carley float almost to the East Halifax Light Vessel whose small dinghy brought them aboard, but five had died from exposure on the way. ***Sarnia*** also brought in twelve bodies.

By 1005 two Fairmile MLs, ***Q 091*** and ***Q 099***, were in the area and depth charged a contact. This turned out to be the sunken ***Esquimalt***. The MLs brought in four more bodies they recovered.

After firing the torpedo ***U 190*** simply moved somewhat inshore, dived to seventy-five feet and waited. After ***Sarnia*** reported ***Esquimalt*** missing and then finding the survivors, ships of EG-28 and four others were sent out to hunt for the U-boat but concentrated their searches in deeper water, along the 200-foot line to seaward, where they anticipated an escaping U-boat might lie. No contacts were reported and later in the day Reith moved his boat cautiously south parallel to the shore and escaped. He remained in the general Halifax area until the end of April and then set course for Norway, via Newfoundland waters.

However another U-boat, ***U 879***, was sunk on 19 April by a hedgehog attack south of Sable Island by two USN destroyers who were helping the Canadians in the futile search for ***U 190.***

The later Board of Inquiry's findings were inconclusive and very controversial, certainly to the surviving crew, as well as to the senior naval officers. There were a number of points considered: the non-streaming of CAT gear; the fact that the radar had possibly been turned off, although this was never ascertained for certain; that the ship was not zig-zagging; the failure to recognize an asdic contact (the 128A asdic was an elderly and by now obsolete set); the failure of the life saving equipment to release automatically as designed; and the fact that those in the ship had not read the daily intelligence situation reports on estimates of likely U-boats operating in the local areas. Also the state of some of the crew in not wearing adequate clothing while on operations. What Hadley calls a surprising "apparent lack of battle readiness". Many of these conditions were not covered by specific instructions, but the Board did not direct any criticism toward those responsible for issuing orders covering these various areas. Quite adequate clothing was worn by many, who therefore objected to the Board's findings. The fact that ships who did not carry extra telegraphists were not able to receive the U-boat situation reports contributed to the crew's criticism of the Board's recommendations. Some postwar bibliographies have accepted the Board's criticisms as fact without a more critical examination of crew evidence.

The Board, presided over by LCdr D.W. Piers, RCN, of HMCS ***Algonquin,*** was subsequently criticised by Ottawa staff for not producing more useful findings but by this time the staff had the hindsight from questioning personnel of the surrendered ***U 190***. There were indeed some areas where Halifax Patrol Orders regarding zig-zagging and streaming CAT had not been followed. But then Ottawa also criticised the staff of the light vessel for not reporting anything though the sinking had occurred within at least their distant vision, and the aircraft crews for not being able to distinguish between fishermen and Carley floats. The light vessel captain commented that they were always hearing distant bangs from training exercises and thought nothing of the one early on the 16th.

When the war ended for the Germans in May, Reith and ***U 190*** were still at sea. In accordance with instructions from BdU he surfaced and surrendered to HMCS ***Thorlock*** and ***Victoriaville*** off Newfoundland. Initially escorted into Bay Bulls the U-boat then was taken on the surface to Halifax by a small crew of RN submariners flown hurriedly to St. John's from an RN submarine under refit in New England (they retained most of the U-boat's engine room personnel to run their diesels). She was the object of great interest and much visiting to those who had spent much of the war trying to sink her and her sisters. ***U 190*** was taken into the RCN for tests. By the fall of 1947 the Navy decided she was no longer of practical use except as a target. An exercise was planned for Trafalgar Day, 21 October, which would involve a synchronised attack by surface vessels firing guns and torpedoes and naval fighter aircraft with rockets, culminating in a final run by an *Algerine* escort firing hedgehog as the submarine sank.

The exercise did not come off quite as planned. The two destroyers, ***Nootka*** and ***Haida***, had to abort the first run as the *Algerine*, ***New Liskeard***, fouled the range. The second run at thirty knots was "delayed", some present saying because the senior gunnery observer inadvertently leaned on the "Check Fire" bell-push on ***Nootka's*** bridge. By the time the destroyers finally started to shoot, the aircraft were on target with their rockets and ***U 190*** was already settling. Surface and air components of the RCN have never agreed who sank her.

At a naval conference in Halifax in 1994 a member of ***Esquimalt's*** crew met the engineer officer from ***U 190***, both treating the 1945 tragedy as an acceptable but sad outcome of war. Local news reporters were unable to stir up any residual animosity, after forty-nine years.

LOST:

Bellazzi, Joseph O.F., Skpr
Berge, Olaf E., Sto
Bland, John B., Sto
Carlsen, Harvey M., Sto
Clancy, Gregory J., Tel
Conn, James R., L.Stwd
Devins, James E., Sto
Downie, Bryan R., L.Tel
Ducharme, Joseph R.D., AB
Dunlop, Ronald E., MM
Eadie, Clifford J., AB
Edwards, Charles, AB
Fanning, Huntley A., Elec.Art
Fitzpatrick, William, AB
Gallagher, Anthony, Sto
Granahan, Edward J., L.Sig
Hedstrom, Arnold D., L.SBA
Hughes, David A., LSA
Jacques, Carlton J., ERA
Johnston, Howard E., MM
Knowles, John C., PO
Knight, Herbert R., LS
Kynman, Albert, CPO
Le Drew, Frederick, L.Sto
Leroux, Leo J., AB
McConnell, Lawrence M., LS
McIntyre, Thomas J., L.Cook
Monaghan, John M., AB
Parker, Jack R., Lt
Partington, Richard, LS
Peddie, Roy N., Stwd
Pool, Ralph B., Shpwt
Porter, John C., C.MM
Roberts, James E., Wt.Engr.
Shave, Chesley N., C.ERA
Smart, John M.G., Lt
Smith, Kenneth H., AB
Stafford, John H., L.Coder
Stanley, James C., AB
Trudel, Joseph M.R., Sto
Ware, William J., Tel
White, Donald W., AB
Whitehead, Bruce M., SLt
Zbarsky, Ralph, AB

SOURCES:

German, *The Sea Is At Our Gates,* pp. 180-182.
Hadley, *U-Boats Against Canada,* pp. 289-294.
Lenton, *German Submarines of WW II,* Vol I, p.48.
Macpherson, *Minesweepers of the RCN,* p. 62.
Macpherson & Burgess, *Ships of Canada's Naval Forces,* pp. 192, 200, 235.
Milner, *The U-Boat Hunters,* pp. 252-253.
NOAC, *Starshell,* Nov.'85, Feb.'86, May '86 and Oct.'86.
Paquette & Bainbridge, *Honours And Awards,* p. 353.
Rohwer, *Axis Submarine Successes.*
Schull, *Far Distant Ships,* pp. 397-398.
Tarrant, *The U-Boat Offensive, 1914-1945*, p.144.

CHAPTER 65

CANADIAN MERCHANT SHIPS LOST IN WORLD WAR II

This chronological listing includes only Canadian owned, registered and flagged ships lost directly due to enemy action. It does not include those lost due to marine accident. those salvaged later and re-employed, fishing vessels, or ex-enemy and ex-occupied Allied ships temporarily taken over by the Canadian Government. For these see Table 7. Casualties indicated are those obtained from various sources, and often vary slightly, particularly as to total crew numbers. The crews were quite often not all Canadian. The many Canadian merchant seamen lost serving in non-Canadian flagged ships are not included.

SHIP: *Magog* FATE: Torpedoed and shelled by *U 99*, SW of Ireland, 5 Jul 40
OWNER: Canada Steamship Lines, Montreal. 2,053 grt. Bulk canaller
BUILT: 1923, Fraser Brace, Trois Rivières, PQ, as *John C. Howard*

Magog, with a cargo of timber for Blyth, was sunk when Convoy HX-52 was attacked, but away from it somewhat. At 1025 (one source gives the time as mid-afternoon, but this is probably central European time kept by the U-boat) the surfaced ***U 99*** fired a shot from ***Magog's*** port quarter, one and a half miles off, which landed forty yards to starboard. The master, Capt. T.S. Doughty, as several more shots were fired, altered to follow them each time. He also ordered the wireless officer to send an SOS, which he reported as received. After about twelve rounds, a hit was scored on the port quarter of ***Magog***, destroying a lifeboat. Another shot brought down the foremast and aerials. In view of the hopeless situation, the engines were stopped, boats and rafts cleared away and confidential books thrown overboard in a weighted bag. ***U 99*** continued shelling, hitting the wireless office, masts and rafts. The crew abandoned the ship, with one man seriously injured, and lay half a mile astern in a heavy swell but moderate seas. ***U 99*** then fired one torpedo which hit between the engineroom and the main hatch. ***Magog*** sank by the stern, but with her bows still projecting about fifty feet vertically. The U-boat then fired several more shells into the bow, and came alongside the ship's boats. Captain Doughty reports that the CO, (KK Otto Kretschmer) "Asked what was my cargo, and when I told him it was timber he was rather disappointed.. Three or four of my men went over the side [of their boat] to try to dodge it [expected machine gunning as a U-boat petty officer had come up with a sub-machine gun] but the officer told them to get back in the boat." Kretschmer is reported to have ordered the petty officer below with considerable annoyance: "Go below. I don't want you up on deck again while we are here." Then, to Doughty, "You are not too far from the Irish coast. But don't let the wind take you too far south, or you'll end up in France..!" He had a bottle of brandy passed to the lifeboat. Captain Doughty was able to give a detailed description of ***U 99*** and the crew, including their clothing, accents and beards. The full crew was eventually rescued and reached England.[1]

1. From Master's interview, Shipping Casualty Section, Trade Division, located by Frank Redfern, Hampton, England in PRO, London. Hereinafter referred to as SCS Int. See also Terrence Robertson, *Night Raider of the Atlantic*.

SHIP: *Waterloo* FATE: Bombed by German aircraft, North Sea off Great Yarmouth, England, 10 Jul 40
OWNER: Canada Steamship Lines, Montreal. 1,905 grt. Bulk canaller
BUILT: 1923, Barclay, Curle Ltd., Glasgow, Scotland, as *Glenburnie.*

After involvement at Dunkirk, ***Waterloo*** was en route alone from Yarmouth to the Tyne in ballast, armed with a 3-inch gun and a single Lewis machine gun. At 1135, she was bombed from a considerable height, two of six bombs hitting No.1 hold, right behind the bridge. The hold thus filled with water. The plane flew off and ***Waterloo*** began to settle by the head. Engines were stopped and the boats got away with all the crew of twenty uninjured. They waited astern in case the interior bulkheads held but, fifteen minutes later, the bulkhead between No.1 and No.2 holds let go, blowing off the hatch covers. The ship sank by the head, hit bottom, and then disappeared entirely. All the crew reached shore safely.[2]

2. SCS Int.

SHIP: *Thorold* FATE: Bombed by German aircraft, South Irish Sea, off Milford Haven, Wales, 22 Aug 40

OWNER: Quebec & Ontario Transportation Ltd (Ontario Paper Co), Montreal. 1,689 grt. Bulk pulpwood carrier

BUILT: 1922, Swan Hunter, Newcastle, as *Chicago Tribune*

Bound from Cardiff for London with coal, off the SW Welsh coast, at 1130 ***Thorold*** was attacked by two Dornier 17 bombers and what the chief officer later described as "a fighter", but which may have been a Stuka dive bomber described in other reports. The latter aircraft first machine-gunned the decks from astern. The ship was unable to defend herself as the trigger was missing from her one Lewis gun. The bombers, seeing this lack of return fire, attacked with gunfire, and one aircraft dropped a salvo of bombs close alongside. This fractured the engine casings. The "fighter" continued the machine gun attacks while the Dorniers dropped four large bombs. The chief officer reported "One of them didn't explode and on my instructions Gunner J. Doucan, Royal Engineers [sic, but likely Royal Artillery], rolled it overboard... It must have been 200 pounds." One hit the bridge, killing seven there, seriously injuring the master. One dropped forward, blasting all six hatches and tearing up the deck, another bringing down the wireless aerial, although an SOS had been transmitted. The planes continued their attack for one and a half hours, until 1300, when they resorted to dropping incendiary bombs, most of which were hits. Some did not ignite and Doucan threw them overboard, as well as others he found burning below in the stokehold. The chief officer continued: "The whole ship was ablaze.. I broached the ship to the sea to put out the fires... tried zig-zagging to avoid the bombs, but that was not successful. Although he was badly injured, I went to the master for instructions. He asked if at all possible to make for Milford Haven. Knowing what damage she had sustained, I should have reasoned with him that we may not be able to reach [it] and should have advised launching of the lifeboats."

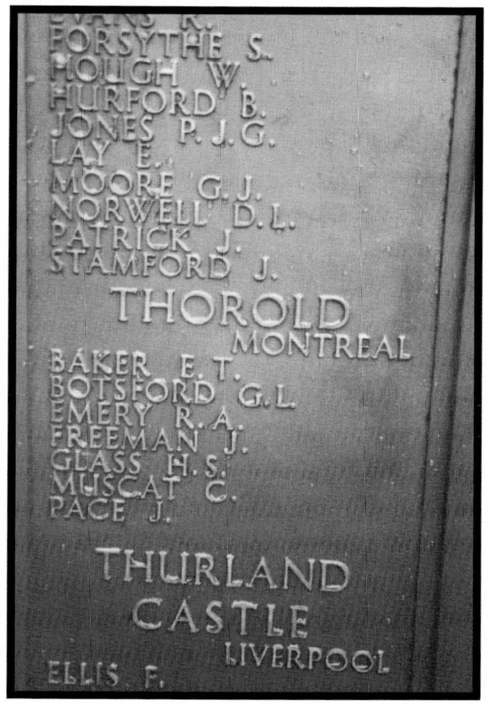

The names of those lost when the little laker *Thorold* was sunk by bombers off the Welsh coast. They are recorded on the Merchant Navy Memorial on the bank of the Thames, just east of Tower Bridge in London.

Thorold headed for shore in heavy seas and the fires eventually went out. A survey of damage indicated the ship was in serious danger of foundering. Life jackets were ordered put on and rafts cut loose from the shrouds and towed alongside. By now the ship's head was at the water-line and she was obviously sinking. The damaged lifeboats were ordered away and the injured carried to them. Then there was a terrific explosion, possibly from the boilers or a delayed action bomb, and the boats alongside were destroyed. Survivors were heaved onto the rafts, where they struggled for another three hours before a shore-based lifeboat appeared and took the survivors to a local town. In all, of the crew of twenty-three, ten died and five were injured including the master and the 2nd mate, who died on the way in. The chief engineer had been killed in the explosion on board. The valiant Gunner Doucan survived, but no record has been found that he received an award.[3]

3. SCS Int.

SHIP: *Kenordoc* FATE: Sunk by gunfire, possibly by *U 48*, mid-Atlantic, SE of Iceland, 15 Sep 40
OWNER: Paterson Steamships Ltd, Port Arthur. 1,780 grt. Bulk laker.
BUILT: 1926, Furness Shipbuilding, Haverton Hill-on-Tees, England, as the *George R. Donovan*

In Convoy SC-3, ***Kenordoc*** was bound from Sydney, Cape Breton for Bristol with a cargo of lumber. Due to engine problems brought on by heavy weather, ***Kenordoc*** straggled astern of the convoy. Although within sight of it again on 12 September, more bad weather caused her to carry on as an independent. At 0925 on the 15th, when west of the Hebrides, she sighted a surfaced submarine about five miles on their port beam. The ship's stern was presented to the U-boat and speed worked up from their normal six to seven knots. The U-boat overhauled her until only 200 to 300 yards off and opened fire with a deck gun. All hands were evacuated from the engineroom, and a shell hit the wheelhouse concrete shelter, injuring the helmsman. The 1st officer, Mr. D. Kerr, records the bravery of the wireless officer: "The next shell went through the wireless room but fortunately we had already got our SOS away. The wireless operator, G.T. Barker, who was only twenty-one years of age, proved very brave indeed. He got away all the messages and refused to leave his post until he had confirmation that they had been received. He was killed at his post by the second shell which destroyed the wireless room." The U-boat continued shelling steadily for ten minutes, and ***Kenordoc*** began to sink. One boat was wrecked and the other lowered with difficulty as shelling continued. Almost all the crew jumped overboard, some clinging to items thrown over such as the gangway and other debris. The 1st officer was in the water for about two and a half hours before the lifeboat picked him up. In the meantime, the U-boat approached it and asked the name of the ship and her cargo, and then motored away on the surface.

There were thirteen in the boat including six injured, the sea was rough and all were wet, so Mr. Kerr had the able men rowing to keep up their circulation.

At about 1630 the British destroyer HMS ***Amazon*** came across the boat and rescued the survivors. Then, as ***Kenordoc***'s bow was still visible, ***Amazon*** sank her by gunfire, later landing the crew at Greenock. The 1st officer particularly mentions the kindness of ***Amazon's*** crew in giving them dry clothing and tending the wounded in the officers' bunks.

There is some doubt, even after consulting German records, that ***U 48*** sank this ship. She may have been sunk by gunfire of another U-boat. Seven of her crew were lost and thirteen or fourteen rescued, six of them injured.[4]

4. J. Rohwer, *Axis Submarine Successes, 1939-1945*, and notes from Fr. Peter van der Linden, Detroit, hereinafter referred to as van der Linden notes. SCS Int.

Names of those lost from *Kenordoc* as recorded on the Merchant Navy memorial in London.

SHIP: *Trevisa* FATE: Torpedoed by *U 124*, mid-Atlantic, South of Iceland, 16 Oct 40
OWNER: Canadian Lake Carriers, Ltd. 1,813 grt. Bulk laker
BUILT: 1915, North of Ireland Shipbuilding Ltd, Londonderry.

Bound from Parrsborough, NS to Aberdeen with a cargo of timber, ***Trevisa*** was in Convoy SC-7. It included three little lakers, like ***Trevisa***, one of whom returned to Sydney with engine problems... maybe fortunately, for she had been built thirty-four years before. This unfortunate thirty-five-ship convoy was to suffer three horrendous nights of successive attacks by eight U-boats, with only three small escorts for defence. The attackers included the "aces" Endraß (***U 46***), Kretschmer (***U 99***) and Schepke (***U 100***). ***Trevisa*** was their first victim at about 1145, caught as a straggler astern with four other ships due to gale force winds from 10 to 15 October. The other laker in that group, the straggler ***Eaglescliffe Hall,*** picked up survivors of a torpedoed Greek ship, and made it all the way to Liverpool on her own. Able only to signal "SINKING", ***Trevisa*** lost seven of her crew before the rescue of the remainder by the corvette HMS ***Bluebell*** and the destroyer HMCS ***Ottawa***, coming up to join the too-meagre escort force. The convoy was to lose twenty ships, fifty-seven percent, of almost 80,000 tons before enough escorts could join to drive off the U-boats.[5]

5. van der Linden notes. See also an article by Lt Joe Marston, RCNR, in *Resolution* (Maritime Museum of BC, Fall 1994).

SHIP: *Maplecourt* FATE: Torpedoed by *U 107*, mid-Atlantic, West of N Ireland, 6 Feb 41
OWNER: United Towing & Salvage Co., Montreal 3,388 grt. 1-deck passenger freighter
BUILT: 1893, Globe Iron Works, Cleveland, Ohio as *North West* for Great Northern Railway. (Rebuilt in 1902 and 1920)

This ancient vessel was built for Great Lakes passenger service, Buffalo to Duluth. She partially burned and settled alongside a pier in 1911, was raised and laid up. In 1919 she was cut in half for passage through the old Soulanges Canal to Montreal but the bow section sank in Lake Ontario when under tow. Rebuilt and returned to the Lakes, she was owned by Canada Steamship Lines and then United Towing, who used her as a salvage vessel until pressed into war service.

Bound from Montreal to Preston, England, with general cargo, ***Maplecourt*** was sunk in Convoy SC-20 by ***U 107***, homed onto them by a *Condor* long range aircraft. The entire complement of thirty-seven were lost "in the terrible explosion and sinking." No other records have been found.[6]

6. van der Linden notes. See also J.J. Barry, *Ships of the Great Lakes* (California: Howell North Books, 1973).

SHIP: *Canadian Cruiser* FATE: Sunk by Armoured Ship *Admiral Scheer*, Western Indian Ocean, North of Mozambique Channel, 21 Feb 41
OWNER: Montreal Australia New Zealand Line Ltd, Montreal. 7,178 grt. Passenger freighter
BUILT: 1921, Halifax Shipyards Ltd., Halifax

Travelling alone in the Indian Ocean, bound for Durban with a cargo of iron ore, ***Canadian Cruiser*** was sighted at 0915 by ***Scheer's*** *Arado* scout aircraft. It took until late afternoon for the armoured ship to catch and stop ***Canadian Cruiser***, who pretended to be an American neutral. She got under way again at full speed, stern-on to ***Scheer***, sending delaying signals, and "R-R-R" indicating a raider, her name and position. ***Scheer*** opened fire with her smaller AA weapons, hitting ***Cruiser's*** bridge. The W/T operator continued, and his signals were picked up by many ships and stations. The master stopped the ship and ***Scheer***'s motor cutter crew boarded. The 1st officer and the captain still maintained they were Americans, but ship's papers proved otherwise. Five scuttling charges were placed, and ***Canadian Cruiser*** went to the bottom. The valiant captain had to be removed to ***Admiral Scheer*** by force.[7] The entire crew of thirty-six was taken prisoner. One ordinary seaman, W.H. McArthur, was later to escape from a prisoner-of-war camp near Bordeaux, made his way home via Spain, and reported what had happened to his ship.[8]

7. Adml T. Krancke and H.J. Brennecke, *Pocket Battleship: The Story of Admiral Scheer* (New York: Berkley Publishing Co, 1958).
8. SCS Interview with W.H. McArthur.

SHIP: *A.D. Huff* FATE: Sunk by battle cruiser *Gneisenau*, mid-Atlantic, 625 mi. E of Cape Race, 22 Feb 41

OWNER: Atlantic Transportation Ltd., Montreal. 6,219 grt. Freighter

BUILT: 1920, Ames Shipbuilding & Drydock Co, Seattle, as *West Jester*

The ***A.D. Huff*** was returning in ballast after taking a load of steel and newsprint to the UK, being damaged by bombing in the London blitz on that voyage. Her convoy dispersed east of Cape Race. ***Huff*** was located by ***Gneisenau*** and ***Scharnhorst*** during one of their raids against North Atlantic convoys. The two battle cruisers sank five unescorted merchant ships when they failed to locate an expected HX convoy, one being ***A.D. Huff***. The ships radioed that they were being attacked by raiders and scattered, despite warning shots from the two Germans. After each warship sinking two of the fleeing merchantmen, at 1244, ***Gneisenau*** caught up to the ***Huff*** and fired warning shots. The master tried to flee and make smoke, at about eight knots. To no avail, as ***Gneisenau*** then lowered her point-of-aim, hitting the forecastle windlass, then the bridge structure and the engineroom, killing the 4th engineer and an oiler. Some thirty-two shots were fired in all. As a result ***Huff*** began to list and the remaining crew took to the boats that had survived the shellfire. ***Gneisenau*** came closer, sank the ***Huff*** with smaller weapons, and picked up the surviving thirty-seven crew, who had started to row to Newfoundland. They joined the survivors of other sunken merchantmen and were sent to Germany in the supply ship ***Ernland***.[9]

9. A. Vulliez and J. Mordal, *Battleship Scharnhorst* (1958); SCS Int; Mike Parker, *Running the Gauntlet* (1994).

SHIP: *J.B. White* FATE: Torpedoed by *U 99*, North Atlantic, SW of Faeroes Islands, 17 Mar 41

OWNER: Atlantic Transportation Co. Ltd., Montreal. 7,375 grt. Freighter

BUILT: 1919, Skinner & Eddy Corp, Seattle, Washington as the *Jadden*

Bound from Mobile and Saint John, NB to Manchester with 2,500 tons of steel and 4,500 tons of newsprint, ***White*** sailed in Convoy HX-112. Six ships were sunk and two damaged but salvaged over two days. ***J.B. White*** was in a collision with another ship at 2330 on the 16th but continued slowly with her convoy, although astern of station, in moderate seas and light winds. At 2340, the master sighted a surfaced U-boat to starboard about 400 yards away and altered toward her. The U-boat dived and, at 0103, a torpedo struck ***White*** amidships, just behind her bridge. While most of the crew abandoned ship in one boat, the rafts could not be cleared. Fortunately a second boat fell into the sea the right way up and the final six crew were able to get into it. The ship did not sink at first but was given a *coup de grâce* by ***U 99*** (KK Otto Kretschmer). She sank in fifteen minutes. Kretschmer had sunk four tankers as well, and ***White*** was to be his last sinking. Captain Donald Macintyre in HMS ***Walker***, who picked up the ***White's*** thirty-eight survivors including the master, sank ***U 99*** within the next couple of hours, to the ***White's*** crew's considerable delight. Of ***J.B. White's*** crew of forty, two were killed.[10] This story was hard to trace because ***J.B. White*** had only transferred from American ownership some two months before, hence does not appear under her new name in any Lloyd's Register list.

10. Rohwer, *Axis Submarine Successes*; SCS Int; correspondence with Lloyd's Register.

SHIP: *Canadolite* FATE: Captured by raider *Kormoran*, Central Atlantic, Southeast of Freetown, 25 Mar 41

OWNER: Imperial Oil Ltd, Toronto. 11,309 grt. Tanker

BUILT: 1926, Frederick Krupp A.G., Kiel, Germany

Intercepted 600 miles southeast of Freetown, West Africa by the disguised merchant raider ***Kormoran***, ex-***Steiermark*** (Capt Theodore Detmers of the Kriegsmarine), ***Canadolite*** had carried naval fuel from Aruba, Netherlands Antilles to Freetown and was returning in ballast and alone when, at dawn on the third day, a suspicious ship, all lit up, appeared and closed her. Warned by the master, Captain Thomas Ferns, the wireless operator transmitted the raider warning "R-R-R." when ***Kormoran***, having passed, turned back, illuminating ***Canadolite*** by searchlight. When

Imperial Oil's tanker *Canadolite* in her wartime colours, and as she was captured by the raider *Kormoran.*

ordered to stop, Captain Ferns ignored the signal and steamed on at her maximum eight knots, slow due to her being a long time out of dry dock for cleaning. ***Kormoran*** fired a warning shot and, when ***Canadolite*** kept on, several more. At this, the master decided to abandon the ship, as he suspected that if a shell hit the empty tanker, filled with fuel fumes, she would explode anyway. He ordered the confidential books, the gun breech block and navigating instruments thrown overboard. The whole crew of forty-four took to the boats, rowing away, expecting the tanker to be shelled and explode. But Detmers sent a boat's crew to the abandoned tanker, and a large motor lifeboat after ***Canadolite***'s boats, towing them back to their own ship. The master, an engineer officer, the senior wireless officer and the DEMS gunner were taken aboard ***Kormoran***. A German prize crew of sixteen boarded ***Canadolite*** as, apart from capturing a valuable large tanker, Detmers wanted to return some sick crewmen to Germany. The two ships parted and Detmers set off south, to his eventual destruction in the Pacific by the cruiser HMAS ***Sydney*** on 19 November, although ***Sydney*** was destroyed as well. The four ***Canadolite*** officers had, in the meantime, been transferred to another support ship and joined the rest of the crew in captivity. ***Canadolite***, fitted by the German prize crew with scuttling charges to prevent her re-capture, reached the Gironde River uneventfully on 13 April, nineteen days after her capture. Renamed ***Sudetenland***, she served the Germans as a local tanker until sunk at Brest in an RAF raid in 1944. Although by mid-1941 it was known that the crew were interned "safely" in Germany at camp Milag und Marlag Nord, it was a long time before it was known that their ship had not been sunk but captured. All of the crew survived the war.[11]

11. Imperial Oil Ltd, *Esso Mariners*, and *Review* Magazine; Mike Parker, *Running the Gauntlet*.

SHIP: *Portadoc* FATE: Torpedoed by *U 124*, W of Sierra Leone, West Africa, 7 Apr 41

OWNER: Paterson Steamships Ltd., Port Arthur, ON. 1,746 grt. Bulk laker

BUILT: 1924, Cammell, Laird & Co, Birkenhead, as *Eugene C. Roberts*

En route from Saint John, NB to Freetown, Sierra Leone, ***Portadoc*** was sunk 150 miles west of her destination. Her crew abandoned ship safely and all were rescued. They were landed at French Guinea where they were held as prisoners (of the Vichy government) until exchanged for enemy prisoners six months later. One man died while incarcerated, the only seaman lost.[12] Patersons do not appear to have kept any records of their lost ships or seamen.

12. R. Fisher in CNRS *Northern Mariner* (Dept of National Defence records, July 1995). Hereinafter referred to as DND records.

SHIP: *Shinai* FATE: Captured by Japanese Forces, North Borneo, off Kuching, 12 Dec 41
OWNER: G.L.Shaw, Vancouver. 2,410 grt. 2-deck freighter
BUILT: 1920, Collingwood Shipbuilding, ON, ex-*Canadian Beaver*

Little is known about this loss, including the exact location of her capture or how it came about. Renamed ***Shinai Maru*** by the Japanese, she was sunk by US aircraft in the Gulf of Bône, Celebes on 16 September, 1944.

SHIP: *Lady Hawkins* FATE: Torpedoed by *U 66*, open Atlantic, East of Cape Hatteras, 19 Jan 42
OWNER: CN Steamships, Halifax, NS. 7,988 grt. 3-deck turbine passenger freighter
BUILT: 1928, Cammell, Laird & Co, Birkenhead

Southbound in her normal trade to the West Indies, ***Lady Hawkins*** stopped off in Boston to pick up a number of American and British passengers bound for West Indies bases. With 212 passengers and a crew of 109, ***Lady Hawkins***, under Captain Huntly Giffin, had no escort after leaving the entrance channel from New York. The precaution was taken of clearing away the lifeboats, as the radio operators had picked up distress calls from torpedoed vessels. Steaming a zig-zag course at fifteen knots, she was intercepted by the very successful Fregattenkapitän Richard Zapp in ***U 66***. He had already sunk six ships for a total of 33,000 tons on previous patrols, and was to sink another ten, including the ***Hawkins***, for 110,000 tons total. At 0105 local time, with no warning whatsoever, his first torpedo hit ***Lady Hawkins*** directly below the bridge. The explosion knocked the ship almost onto her beam ends, catapulted many on deck into the sea and brought down her mainmast. Another torpedo hit the engineroom, knocked out all electric power so no SOS was sent, and destroyed two lifeboats. Many passengers, unfamiliar with the ship in the dark, were trapped below, unable to find their way to the upper deck. Three boats were launched before the ***Hawkins*** rolled on her side and went down within twenty minutes. 1st Officer Percy A. Kelly took charge of one lifeboat, rigged a sail and within half an hour took in seventy-six survivors, so crowded they had to stand. Many were only in light night clothing.

U 66 examined the sinking ship by light and then came alongside one boat, looked at it by searchlight, then submerged. With the one boat crowded to the gunwales, Kelly had to haul clear, leaving another two boats and dozens of shouting swimmers to their fates. For five days Kelly's group survived, with a rising sea, cold with spray, often in water that had to be baled out, and only the most meagre rations of biscuits, tablespoons of canned milk and water for men, women and small children. Five that died gave up their clothes for the living. They were seen at midnight on their fifth day by the New York 7,100-ton passenger ship ***Coamo***, attracted by the boat's flares, who took in the seventy-one survivors and landed them at San Juan, Puerto Rico. ***Lady Hawkins'*** other two boats were never seen again. In the torpedoing and in those boats 250 died in total. Sadly, ***Coamo*** was herself torpedoed and sunk in December of that year, with no survivors. Percy Kelly was awarded a well-deserved MBE.[13] For the U-boats, this sinking marked the start of their second "Happy time" along the American east coast and in the Caribbean.

---

13. Gary Gentile, *Track of the Grey Wolf* (1989); Paquette & Bainbridge, *Honours and Awards*; CNS History.

SHIP: *Montrolite* FATE: Torpedoed by *U 109*, mid-Atlantic, NE of Bermuda, 4 Feb 42
OWNER: Imperial Oil Ltd, Toronto. 11,309 grt. Tanker
BUILT: 1926, Frederick Krupp A.G., Kiel, Germany.

Montrolite was carrying light diesel crude from Venezuela to Halifax, keeping well clear of the dangerous U-boat zone along the U.S. coast. Although neither escorted nor in convoy, the crew was not expecting trouble the night of 4 February because of rain and rough seas. The first torpedo hit amidships after dark at about 1945 with a crash and a bright flash. Her engines were stopped at once, either from the shock or because of orders. ***Montrolite's*** crew got the boats away and pulled away from the ship, anticipating another torpedo. This ***U 109*** put into the tanker's other side twenty minutes later, between the ship's fuel tank and the Venezuelan crude. This set her afire with a flash and ***Montrolite*** sank not long afterwards. One lifeboat had twenty in it, at least one a 16-year-old lad, and the 4th engineer and the electrician, the only surviving officers. The other two boats that supposedly got away had three men in one, and thus about twenty-five in the other, very crowded. Those two boats were never seen again. The weather turned rough, the surviving lifeboat being driven north in a gale, with sleet and rain. It was picked up after three days by a stray "old British merchantman", and the survivors taken to Halifax. Twenty-eight of the crew were lost, including the master, chief engineer and one DEMS gunner. There were, in all, twenty survivors.[14]

14. Imperial Oil Ltd, *Esso Mariners*; Parker, *Running the Gauntlet*; DND records.

SHIP: *Empress of Asia* FATE: Bombed by Japanese aircraft, off Singapore, 5 Feb 42
OWNER: CP Steamships, Montreal. 16,909 grt. 4-deck, coal-burning turbine passenger liner
BUILT: 1913, Fairfield Co, Glasgow.

Requisitioned by the British government as a troopship, ***Empress of Asia*** left Vancouver on 13 February, 1941 for conversion in the UK. ***Asia*** had been an armed merchant cruiser in World War I, and had 1,190 berths when running as a fast liner from Vancouver to the Orient. In her last role as a trooper, starting in April 1941 she eventually carried 7,923 troops and 3,495 tons of cargo in total. The liner was involved in the late 1941 last-ditch attempt to take supplies and troops into Singapore for its defence against the Japanese, already sweeping down the Malay Peninsula. There had been seven escorted convoys comprising forty-four ships, carrying 45,000 fighting men of all three Services, sent to the city to augment its defences. ***Empress of Asia*** was the only ship lost of that group, bombed and set afire. She was carrying 2,235 troops from Bombay and a crew of 416 including twenty-five Army and naval gunners. Their escort was two cruisers, two destroyers and two sloops.

Under Captain J.B. Smith, she was in last position in her small convoy of five ships heading for Singapore, with only a single 3-inch gun for anti-aircraft protection. They were sighted on 4 February at 1100 and bombed without success although some lifeboats were damaged. At the same time the next day, when only about fifteen miles northeast of the city, a large formation of Japanese aircraft attacked from all directions. Being the largest, the ***Asia*** was singled out. The first stick of bombs hit, one going through the ornate dome over the lounge, another destroying her radio equipment, others damaging the engineroom. By 1125 the 1st officer reported the fires aboard were uncontrollable. To prevent too great loss of life, the captain resolved to anchor just outside the swept channel, close to a lighthouse. After the Japanese flew off, a host of small vessels came out of Singapore, less than ten miles distant, to rescue survivors. Other ships in the convoy were able to send boats to her aid. The Australian sloop HMAS ***Yarra*** came alongside aft and took off over 1,000 troops and crew. Fifteen soldiers were later unaccounted for and only one crewman dead from injuries from the bombing. Two officers later re-boarded to toss overboard some depth charges but the fire reached other shells and ammunition which began exploding. The ***Asia*** eventually rolled on her side and settled in shallow water.

Most of the crew were able to escape from Singapore over the next two days in three small coastal steamers to Java and Australia, and 128 firemen to England. It was not until 8 February, three days after the ***Asia's*** loss, that it was decided it was useless to throw more men and supplies into the city. On 15 February Singapore, "Fortress of the East", surrendered to Japanese infantry. ***Empress of Asia's*** doctor, some medical staff and 132 of the catering staff who had volunteered to help in the local hospitals remained behind and were all taken prisoner. The wreck was sold after the war to a salvage company which eventually removed it. The master and Donald Smith, the chief engineer were awarded OBEs and the 1st officer, Leonard Johnson, an MBE for their services that day.[15]

15. George Musk, *Canadian Pacific Afloat, 1883-1968*; Capt S.W. Roskill, RN, *Official History*, Vol II; W. Kaye Lamb, *Empress to the Orient* (Toronto Marine Museum); SCS Int.

SHIP: *Victolite* FATE: Torpedoed by *U 564*, NW of Bermuda, 10 Feb 42
OWNER: Imperial Oil Ltd, Toronto. 11,410 grt. Tanker
BUILT: 1928, A. Stephen & Sons, Glasgow.

Victolite sailed in ballast from Halifax on 4 February, 1942 southbound for Las Piedras, Uruguay to load light diesel. She was sunk by gunfire and torpedo on the 10th, not far from where her sister-ship ***Montrolite*** had been sunk only six days before. Although she got away one brief submarine alarm signal, "S-S-S-S", she exploded when hit and none of her crew of forty-seven survived, including two DEMS gunners. The tankers were more vulnerable empty than loaded due to fumes remaining in their tanks and no time between sailings to air out those tanks.[16] A mountain in British Columbia has been named Mount Reid, after seaman Roy Reid, a twenty-four-year-old junior engineer lost in ***Victolite***.

16. Imperial Oil Ltd, *Esso Mariners*; Parker, *Running the Gauntlet*.

SHIP: *George L. Torian* FATE: Torpedoed by *U 129*, off British Guiana, 22 Feb 42
OWNER: Upper Lakes & St. Lawrence Transport Ltd, Toronto. 1,754 grt. Bulk laker
BUILT: 1926, Earle's Co Ltd, Hull, England.

En route from Paramaribo, Dutch Guiana for Trinidad with a cargo of bauxite for transhipment, ***Torian*** was torpedoed off the coast of British Guiana by ***U 129***. There was a violent explosion; one watchman, James Stillwell was blown into the water and clung to a hatch cover for twenty-four hours before rescue by a passing American vessel. In one record, two others from some other source joined Stillwell on his hatch cover. One report (DND) records the survivors picked up by a USN flying boat. ***U 129***, under Korvettenkapitän Nicolai Clausen, sank seven ships in the area in a period of two weeks, including the Canadian SS ***Lennox*** (see below). With his sinkings in 1941 and later in 1942, Clausen was one of the more successful U-boat commanders.[17]

17. Garnet Wilcox and Skip Gillham, *The Ships of Upper Lakes Shipping*; van der Linden notes; Rohwer, *Axis Submarine Successes*; DND records.

SHIP: *Lennox* FATE: Torpedoed by *U 129*, off British Guiana, 23 Feb 42
OWNER: Canada Steamship Lines, Montreal. 1,904 grt. Bulk canaller
BUILT: 1923, Swan Hunter & Wigham Richardson Ltd, Wallsend-on-Tyne, as *Glenlinnie*

Like the ***George L. Torian*** the day before, ***Lennox*** was taking a cargo of bauxite to Trinidad when also torpedoed by KK Clausen of ***U 129*** about 100 miles NE of the ***Torian's*** position. This time there was no explosion and only two of the crew of twenty were lost. The rest took to boats and were picked up by SS ***Athelrill***.[18]

18. van der Linden notes; DND records.

SHIP: *Sarniadoc* FATE: Torpedoed by *U 161*, Central Caribbean, 15 Mar 42
OWNER: Paterson Steamships Ltd, Port Arthur. 1,940 grt. Bulk laker.
BUILT: 1929, Barclay, Curle & Co., Glasgow

As there were no survivors of this torpedoing, there is little information on her loss. Canadian records say she was lost on 15 March, but Jürgen Rohwer's book records her as torpedoed at 0230 Central European Time on the 14th, which would have been about 2030 on the 13th in the Caribbean. ***Sarniadoc*** was by far the smallest of KL Albrecht Achilles' five sinkings and four vessels damaged on this patrol to the Caribbean. The best known to Canadians was his torpedoing of the CNSS ***Lady Nelson*** alongside the wharf at Port Castries, Santa Lucia four days before ***Sarniadoc's*** loss. Achilles was to become one of Germany's aces, with fourteen sinkings and seven ships damaged in his score.[19]

19. Rohwer, *Axis Submarine Successes*.

SHIP: *Robert W. Pomeroy* FATE: Mined, North Sea, off Cromer, Norfolk, 1 Apr 42
OWNER: Upper Lakes & St. Lawrence Transportation Co, Toronto 1,750 grt. Bulk laker
BUILT: 1923, Earle's Shipbuilding & Engineering, Hull, UK

Bound from London for Blyth in ballast, the ***Pomeroy*** sailed early on 31 March in Convoy FN-40. She was third ship in the starboard of two columns. She had been degaussed for protection against magnetic mines. On 1 April the master, Captain J.M. Fryett, reported the weather was fine with a slight breeze and a bright moon giving excellent visibility. At 0230, off Norfolk and in eleven fathoms, there was a muffled explosion in her bunkers amidships on the port side. Hatches and hatch-beams were blown off, the ship's side opened outward in a twelve- to fourteen-foot hole and her engines stopped, although ***Pomeroy*** carried way on for some time. About four minutes after, the master felt another dull thud and then almost at once there was another terrific explosion and a bright flash on the ship's port quarter and a huge column of water thrown up about thirty feet from the ship's side. After the first explosion thirteen of the ship's crew had jumped into the water. The escort trawler HMS ***Basset*** was going to their assistance when the second explosion enveloped her in spray and damaged her steering, preventing her from rescuing the men in the water. However they were able to scramble into the port boat which had been blown off its falls into the sea, but the second explosion capsized that boat. ***Basset*** later was able to reach and rescue them.

The master and seven men forward were unable to get aft due to the broken deck plating. But the ship's next astern in the convoy, the little Danish 1,260-ton SS ***Marx***, bravely closed the sinking ***Pomeroy***, lowered a boat and rescued those still aboard. One naval gunner was killed in the water by the second explosion, and two crew were injured, one when the ship's boiler exploded as she flooded. The master commended the action of one of the three naval gunners, John Butler, in rescuing one of his firemen, knocked unconscious by the boiler explosion, getting him off the ship and into a boat and to safety. The twenty-two survivors were taken to Blyth on 2 April.

Some records, including her owners', say ***Pomeroy*** broke her back in very heavy seas, then was intentionally sunk by an escorting RN destroyer to prevent her drifting eastward and falling into enemy hands. But the Admiralty considers she was mined as described.[20]

20. Wilcox & Gillham, *The Ships of Upper Lakes Shipping*; van der Linden notes; HMSO, *British Vessels Lost at Sea*; SCS Int.

SHIP: *Vineland* FATE: Torpedoed by *U 154*, Atlantic, N Windward Passage, 20 Apr 42
OWNER: Markland Shipping, Liverpool, NS 5,587 grt. Freighter
BUILT: 1919, American International Shipbuilding, Hog Island, PA as the Panamanian *Sapinero*

Operated for the Mersey Paper Company, the elderly ***Vineland*** had been taking newsprint to Australia and New Zealand before the war. In April of 1942 she was southbound, alone and in ballast, for St. Thomas, Virgin Islands to load bauxite for Portland, Maine. ***U 154***, surfaced and up sun, torpedoed ***Vineland*** by No.4 hatch, between the bridge and the DEMS gun aft. The crew promptly abandoned ship as a second torpedo missed the vessel. The third hit her amidships. This was followed by several rounds of gunfire at the bow of the sinking freighter, which went down in about twelve minutes. The ship's boats rowed about picking up survivors who had jumped into the sea, many of them covered with oil. One young crewman was killed, probably by falling debris. ***U 154*** came alongside the boats, and her CO, KK Walther Kölle, politely asked the master where they had been going, what their cargo was to have been and if they needed medical aid. His crew took pictures, passed the survivors cigarettes and told them the course for land, ninety miles to the west. The U-boat then motored off on the surface. The boats moved slowly west until picked up by fishermen from the Turks Islands four or five days later. They were moved to Grand Turk, then by Dutch supply ship to Curaçao where the thirty-six survivors were outfitted with new clothes, shaving gear and even given some money. Four days later they left for Halifax.[21]

21. Parker, *Running the Gauntlet.*

SHIP: *Lady Drake* FATE: Torpedoed by *U 106*, North of Bermuda, 5 May 42
OWNER: Canadian National Steamships, Montreal. 7,985 grt. Passenger freighter
BUILT: 1928, Cammell, Laird & Co, Birkenhead

Returning from her normal West Indies service, via St. Kitts and Bermuda, and with a large group of RN ratings returning to Britain, the ***Lady Drake*** was ordered to sail independently to Boston. She had hoped to pass through the dangerous U-boat zone northwest of Bermuda at night, but was delayed in discharging cargo, and found, when speed was urged on the engineroom, that inferior oil caused considerable smoke, even at her modest thirteen knots. Despite marked alterations of course, at 2100, about ninety miles north of Bermuda, a torpedo narrowly missed her stern and, before the DEMS gunners could alert the bridge, another hit her in No.3 hold, breaching the bulkhead into the engineroom. The ship was obviously doomed. Boats were quickly made ready, although No.4 was smashed against the ship due to the swells. In a well organised manner 260 survivors got away in the other five boats within ten minutes in the pitch dark. Six crew and six passengers had lost their lives in the initial explosions. No distress signal had been sent due to damage and static, and the ***Drake*** sank in twenty minutes. In charge of the small fleet of boats was the master, Captain P.A. Kelly, who had been the surviving 1st officer from the sinking of the CNSS's ***Lady Hawkins*** only three months earlier. The boats hoisted sail and made for Bermuda, suffering a dangerous storm the next day. They were passed at high speed on the 6th by the huge Cunard ship RMS ***Queen Mary*** on her way to New York who dared not stop in mid-ocean for them, nor even break radio silence on their behalf. However, on arrival in New York her master at once told the British consul of passing a group of five boats under sail with survivors. On the third day after the sinking a plane spotted them at 0630. The minesweeper USS ***Owl*** was directed to the boats, and took aboard all the survivors, delivering them back to Bermuda, including eight injured. The Canadian crew returned to Halifax in the CN's ***Lady Rodney*** this time escorted by an RCN corvette, and West Indian crewmen returned to their homes as well. Insurers paid $36,009 to crew and passengers for damages. Captain Kelly who had twice brought lifeboat survivors to safety was awarded an MBE and the Lloyds Medal for heroism.

SHIP: *Mont Louis* FATE: Torpedoed by *U 162*, off British Guiana, 8 May 42
OWNER: Hall Corporation, Montreal. 1,905 grt. Freighter
BUILT: 1927, Smith's Dock Co, Middlesborough, UK

On the "bauxite run", and the only Hall ship so employed, ***Mont Louis*** was ferrying a full cargo of heavy ore from Dutch Guiana northbound to the transhipment point of Port-of-Spain, Trinidad, when torpedoed late in the evening. She sank almost immediately, within half a minute as her master recalled. He saw no sign whatsoever of the U-boat that sank her. Thirteen of her crew were lost and there were eight survivors, all uninjured, including the master, Captain Walter Bowen and the chief engineer, Warren Covey. Captain Bowen went over the side as his ship foundered, seizing a plank while he kicked off his shoes. A life raft had floated clear and survivors on it pulled him on board. Just as dawn was breaking, around 0400, they were sighted by chance by a small Nova Scotia schooner that was trading to the Guianas, taken aboard and back to Georgetown, B.G. There the Red Cross looked after them, even providing new shoes. Captain Bowen, as soon as he reached home in Montreal, went back to sea with Hall Corporation.[22]

22. van der Linden notes; conversation with Mrs. Bowen.

SHIP: *Calgarolite* FATE: Torpedoed and shelled by *U 125*, NW Caribbean, near Grand Caymans, 9 May 42
OWNER: Imperial Oil Ltd, Toronto. 11,941 grt. Tanker.
BUILT: 1929, Furness Shipbuilding Co, Haverton Hill-On-Tees.

The master of the twin screw motor vessel ***Calgarolite***, Captain Tom Mountain, reported later that when his ship was torpedoed at 0215 on 9 May she was about 120 miles south of the Isle of Pines, Cuba, travelling at twelve knots, with the 1st officer on the bridge. She had left New York on 30 April, bound for Cartegena, Columbia for oil. Without warning the ship was hit on the starboard side by two torpedoes in quick succession, and began listing to starboard. While the starboard boats had been damaged, the two port boats were lowered, although with difficulty. All the crew embarked and they pulled away about three-quarters of a mile. At this time although the submarine was not seen, her periscope appeared and another torpedo was fired, hitting the ship close to the stern. The submarine then surfaced and shelled the tanker as she rolled onto her starboard beam and then sank by the stern, about an hour and thirty minutes after the first attack. The U-boat then motored away to the east without contacting the survivors.

Both boats raised sail and made for the Isle of Pines, Cuba, but became separated. The master's boat with twenty-two on board reached there at 1400 four days later, on 13 May, being towed the last forty miles by a fishing boat. The other boat had landed at Mujeres, Mexico on the 12th with the balance of the crew. All were saved.[23]

---

23. Imperial Oil Ltd, *Esso Mariners*; SCS Int.

SHIP: *Torondoc* FATE: Torpedoed by *U 69*, Caribbean off Martinique, 21 May 42
OWNER: Paterson Steamships Ltd, Port Arthur. 1,927 grt. Bulk laker
BUILT: 1927, Swan Hunter & Wigham Richardson, Newcastle, England

Torondoc was in the bauxite trade and en route from Trinidad to St. Thomas, Virgin Islands when she was torpedoed; there were no survivors from her crew of nineteen.[24]

---

24. van der Linden notes; DHist file.

SHIP: *Troisdoc* FATE: Torpedoed by *U 558*, Caribbean, West of Jamaica, 21 May 42
OWNER: Paterson Steamships Ltd, Port Arthur. 1,925 grt. Bulk laker
BUILT: 1925, Swan Hunter & Wigham Richardson, Newcastle, England

Troisdoc was sunk the same day as the company's ***Torondoc***, at 1100 about forty miles west of Jamaica. She was en route from St. Thomas to Georgetown, British Guiana in ballast for bauxite. The first torpedo hit but failed to explode, but a second doomed the small ship. The crew was able to launch at least one boat and some rafts. The U-boat approached them and asked about the cargo and destination "in fair English", reported the 2nd mate. Some even took photos. All eighteen of the crew reached lifeboats and were picked up five hours after the sinking.[25]

---

25. van der Linden notes; DHist file.

SHIP: *Frank B. Baird* FATE: Sunk by gunfire by *U 158*, Atlantic SE of Bermuda, 22 May 42
OWNER: Upper Lakes & St. Lawrence Transportation, Toronto. 1,748 grt. Bulk laker
BUILT: 1923, Napier & Miller Ltd, Glasgow

Employed in the bauxite trade, ***Frank B. Baird*** was bound from St. Lucia to Sydney, Cape Breton with 2,457 tons of bauxite. She left St. Lucia alone on 16 May, northbound at a slow five knots. Her master, Captain C.S. Tate, commented, "We were a lake boat and not meant for the open sea." At 2300 on 21 May her steering was damaged in severe weather, and the ship lay stopped until daylight would permit repairs. At 0815 a submarine surfaced about 200 feet away to starboard and immediately opened fire with her deck gun. One shot cut the whistle lanyard which flailed about and brought down all the aerials. Port and starboard boats were lowered and the crew abandoned ship, some very precipitately. The U-boat continued shelling aft to open the hull. The master, right forward, jumped over the bow, but the raft he made for had been damaged and sank. After he had spent considerable time in the water, the U-boat eased toward him, threw him a line and hauled him aboard. He commented that the boat and crew looked smart and the men were in uniform, but that the CO (KL Erich Rostin) was not. An English-speaking officer asked what they were doing so far from home and with such a little ship, adding "I am sorry I cannot take you along with me. We are sorry we have to sink your ship, but it is war." He then wished Captain Tate good luck and good weather, gave him some black bread, sausage, a packet of German cigarettes and French matches. They then put him in the port lifeboat and promptly submerged. The elderly chief engineer was in the starboard boat with the native West Indian crew, and pulling away rapidly. They were discovered later in the day by the Norwegian freighter SS ***Talisman*** bound for the Belgian Congo. When they were picked up, the engineer was so out of breath from his escape that he had trouble convincing the ship's master there was another boat. When this master found that the ***Baird*** had just been sunk, he was reluctant to search for the other boat, but was persuaded and they too were rescued. Captain Tate tried to have ***Talisman*** drop off the natives at Barbados; the ship's master refused when another submarine attack "S-S-S" signal was picked up. He set off for Africa at eighteen knots. After considerable travelling about the West African coast, all twenty-three of the crew arrived back safely.[26]

26. Wilcox & Gillham, *The Ships of Upper Lakes Shipping*; SCS Int.

SHIP: *Liverpool Packet* FATE: Torpedoed by ***U 432***, S of Yarmouth, Nova Scotia, 30 May 42
OWNER: Liverpool Shipping Co & Markland S.S. Co, Liverpool, NS. 1,188 grt. Coastal freighter
BUILT: (unknown)

The little ***Liverpool Packet*** was en route from New York to Halifax with a 1,945-ton cargo of "US government supplies" bound for their Newfoundland operations when intercepted twelve miles west of Cape Sable Island. She was steaming at seven and a half knots and not zig-zagging, in moderate weather and two mile visibility. With no warning she was torpedoed at 2045 in the starboard side of the engineroom. The ship broke in two and sank rapidly, in about two minutes. Most of the crew abandoned her in dories which floated clear as she went down. While she was fitted with wireless, it was destroyed in the explosion. The submarine was not seen until it surfaced fifteen minutes after the attack. Of the twenty-one crew, the master and eighteen others escaped, although two were wounded in the explosion. An oiler and a fireman were killed.

The U-boat, ***U 432***, KL Heinz-Otto Schultze, approached the captain's boat and asked questions about the ship's identity, cargo and where bound. When the master, N.E. Smith replied to the latter question "I don't know", his crew, with a machine gun on the U-boat trained on them, objected, so he told them "Halifax". As the U-boat turned away, the crew sang "There'll always be an England", but when the submarine seemed about to alter back toward them they abruptly stopped singing. When it submerged, the crew rowed to Sable Island and were rescued.

Schultze was one of the U-boat arm's aces, with twelve ships sunk of almost 50,000 tons by the time he sank ***Liverpool Packet.*** His final total was nineteen ships destroyed and one damaged. He himself was killed in the sinking of another U-boat in November, 1943.[27]

27. van der Linden notes; SCS Interview by N.C.S.O. Halifax.

SHIP: *Prescodoc* FATE: Torpedoed by ***U 160***, off British Guiana, 29 Jul 42
OWNER: Paterson Steamships Ltd, Port Arthur. 1,938 grt. Bulk laker
BUILT: 1929, Swan Hunter & Wigham Richardson, Sunderland, England

This was another ship lost to Patersons while in the bauxite trade in the West Indies. Bound from British Guiana for Trinidad at six knots under Captain J.C. Frowse and a crew of twenty, she was torpedoed at 0440 on 29 July. The three lookouts and the bridge watch did not see the U-boat until the torpedo hit the ship near the bow, but saw her immediately afterward, so she must have been on the surface when she fired. The ship sank very quickly bow first, and fifteen of her crew perished. Only five survivors reached a lifeboat that had floated clear. They were rescued by the small Yugoslav steamer ***Predsednik Kopatjic*** at about 0700 the same day.[28]

U 160 was commanded by KL Georg Lassen, another U-boat ace with twenty-five ships totalling over 145,000 tons eventually sunk to his credit and another five damaged, some of which were then sunk by other boats. He was the Kriegsmarine's seventh highest scoring ace.

28. van der Linden notes; SCS Int; Rohwer, *Axis Submarine Successes.*

SHIP: *Princess Marguerite* FATE: Torpedoed by *U 83,* Mediterranean, NW of Port Said, 17 Aug 42
OWNER: Canadian Pacific Railways, Montreal. 5,875 grt. 3-deck passenger liner.
BUILT: 1924, John Brown & Co, Clydebank, Scotland

Built for CPR's West Coast triangle service, ***Princess Marguerite*** was a fast geared turbine luxury liner, with an operating speed of fifteen knots. Requisitioned on behalf of the Admiralty at the end of her 1941 summer duties, she was sent to the Mediterranean after a refit at Esquimalt. Employed as a troopship and supply vessel she was en route to Cyprus on 17 August, 1942 with soldiers of the British 8th Army, screened by an armed merchant cruiser and three destroyers. At 1500, in calm seas and clear weather, she was hit by a torpedo fired by ***U 83***, the engineroom instantly filling with smoke and steam. Despite this, engineer officers E.E. Stewart and W.B. Harris stopped her engines at the throttles, for which they were later to receive MBEs. The torpedo had set fire to oil in her tanks and ***Princess Marguerite*** was soon burning fiercely. The fire reached her magazines and exploding ammunition added to the dangers. Her chief engineer, W. Neilson, received an OBE for his attempts to save the ship and those on board. CPR records simply state "The loss of life was remarkably small." In fact forty-nine died of over 1,000 on board in total. The destroyer HMS ***Hero*** picked up survivors and the liner sank in less than an hour. The U-boat CO, KL Hans-Werner Kraus, had sunk fourteen ships in 1941 and 1942 and another in 1943. His boat was itself sunk in 1943 by the RAF with no survivors.[29]

29. Norman R. Hacking and W. Kaye Lamb, *The Princess Story, A Century and a half of West Coast Shipping* (1974). See also R.D. Turner, *The Pacific Princesses* (1977).

SHIP: *Donald Stewart* FATE: Torpedoed by *U 517,* S of the Strait of Belle Isle, NFLD, 3 Sep 42
OWNER: Canada Steamship Lines, Montreal. 1,781 grt. Bulk canaller
BUILT: 1923, Smith's Dock Co, Middlesborough

The ***Stewart*** was in Convoy LN-7, just northwest of Newfoundland's Gros Mourne Park when she was hit. She was loaded with high octane aviation gasoline in forty-five-gallon drums and bulk cement for the new Air Force runways at Goose Bay, Labrador, needed to extend convoy protection. At 0130, the torpedo struck just forward of the engineroom. This ignited the gasoline in a huge pyre and the canaller sank in about seven minutes. Miraculously only three men died in this explosion, all in the engineroom. The rest were able to launch rafts and boats before the burning fuel on the water's surface surrounded the ship. The corvettes ***Weyburn*** and ***Shawinigan***, and in some reports ***Trail,*** tried to locate KL Paul Hartwig's elusive U-boat without success. The freighter's survivors were rescued by ***Shawinigan***, although her CO and ***Weyburn's*** were later criticised for not pursuing the U-boat contact rather than rescuing the seamen. One of ***Weyburn's*** crew saw a ***Donald Stewart*** crewman, trapped aboard, calmly turn to face the raging fire before it consumed him. It would have taken a more hard-hearted CO not to try to save as many as he could. This was an early sinking in that September's "Battle of the St. Lawrence" and significantly delayed the completion of the runways at Goose Bay.[30]

30. James W. Essex, Victory in the St. Lawrence; van der Linden notes; M.L. Hadley, U-Boats Against Canada; DND records.

Princess Marguerite burning furiously after being abandoned in the eastern Mediterranean on 17 August, 1942. Probably taken from HMS *Hero*.

SHIP: *Lord Strathcona* FATE: Torpedoed by *U 513*, at Wabana, Conception Bay, NFLD, 5 Sep 42
OWNER: Dominion Shipping Co (Dominion Coal Co), Montreal. 7,335 grt. Bulk ore carrier.
BUILT: 1915, W. Doxford & Sons, Sunderland, Scotland.

The ***Lord Strathcona*** was at anchor just off the pier at Wabana, waiting to load iron ore in her peace-time trade of hauling it in bulk to the mills in Cape Breton from Bell Island in Conception Bay. KK Rolf Rüggeberg first torpedoed the British ore carrier ***Saganaga***, also waiting off the island, with the loss of twenty-eight men of her crew. There was no local warship protection, and as crewman Gordon Hardy put it, "The 3rd mate of the ***Lord Strathcona*** gave orders to abandon ship when he saw this [***Saganaga*** torpedoed] because she was sitting there a target anyhow... As soon as they got in the lifeboats, [the U-boat] put two torpedoes into her." Fortunately, it took the U-boat thirty-one minutes to set up her next attack. As well, she fired at the Canadian ore ship ***Rose Castle*** alongside, but missed the ship, hitting and badly damaging the loading pier. ***Rose Castle*** was only to survive another two months, being torpedoed off Newfoundland later (see below).[31]

31. Parker, *Running the Gauntlet*; Rohwer, *Axis Submarine Successes*; Hadley, *U-Boats Against Canada*; SCS Int.

SHIP: *John A. Holloway* FATE: Torpedoed by *U 164*, Caribbean, NW of Netherlands Antilles, 6 Sep 42
OWNER: Upper Lakes & St. Lawrence Transportation, Toronto. 1,745 grt. Bulk laker
BUILT: 1925, Earle's Co, Hull, UK

Employed, like several other Upper Lakes vessels, in the West Indies bauxite trade for Alcoa, ***Holloway*** sailed from Guantanamo, Cuba on 3 September bound for Trinidad with a general cargo, mostly of construction materials. There she was to load bauxite. She was steaming southeast at five knots when, at 1645, she was torpedoed on the port side amidships. A bridge lookout saw the tracks just before the torpedo hit. Her holds rapidly flooded and, while two boats were lowered and rafts dropped, she sank in six or eight minutes. One boat capsized but was soon righted. There was one casualty, a fireman, presumably blown overboard. ***U 164***, KK Otto Fechner, then surfaced and questioned the twenty-three survivors as to the ship's identity, cargo and so forth in good English. The submarine then made off only fifteen minutes after the sinking and submerged. After stripping the rafts of any useful materials, the two boats headed west. The crew alternately rowed and sailed for six days, becoming separated. The first reached Sant Marta, Columbia at 1900 on 12 September and the second boat at midnight on the 13th. While the men were suffering from exposure, there were no serious cases and all survived.[32]

32. SCS Int.

SHIP: *Oakton* FATE: Torpedoed by *U 517*, off Cap Chat, Gaspé, 7 Sep 42
OWNER: Gulf & Lake Navigation Co, Montreal. 1,727 grt. Pulpwood carrier.
BUILT: 1923, A. McMillan & Son, Dumbarton, Scotland

Oakton was lost in Convoy QS-33 from Quebec to Sydney. This time she had a cargo of coal for delivery to Corner Brook, Newfoundland. Hit in the engineroom, the ship sank quickly, off Cap Chat in the Gulf of St. Lawrence. Three lives were lost, an oiler and two firemen, plus the ship's mascot, a large Saint Bernard dog. The Fairmile ***Q 083*** rescued seventeen survivors, plus another group from two Greek ships sunk within minutes of ***Oakton*** from the same convoy, seventy-eight in all. HMCS ***Raccoon*** was lost that night as well, plus more ships the next day. It was the most disastrous Gulf convoy of the war.[33]

33. J.W. Essex, *Victory in the St. Lawrence.*

SHIP: *Norfolk* FATE: Torpedoed by *U 175*, off British Guiana at Venezuelan border, 18 Sep 42

OWNER: Canada Steamship Lines, Montreal. 1,901 grt. Bulk laker

BUILT: 1923, Swan Hunter & Wigham Richardson, Wallsend-on-Tyne as *Glenbuckie*

Bound from Paramaribo, Surinam to Trinidad at a meagre six knots, with 3,055 tons of bauxite for Alcoa, ***Norfolk*** was hit by two torpedoes at 0700, with no warning whatsoever and sank within a minute. She had no armament fitted and never saw the submarine. She was hit on the starboard beam in the way of No.6 and No.7 holds which flooded, and then on the starboard bow which "blew up the bridge." The master, Captain Thomas Edge, was killed, as well as two firemen, the cook, and two seamen. The remaining thirteen reached four life rafts blown over the side by the explosions and were picked up by the Spanish 3,100-tonner ***Indauchu*** and taken to Port-of-Spain the next day. DND records indicate fourteen were saved of a crew of twenty.[34]

34. SCS Int.

SHIP: *Rose Castle* FATE: Torpedoed by *U 518*, off Bell Island, Conception Bay, NFLD, 2 Nov 42

OWNER: Rose Castle SS., Halifax (Dominion Steel & Coal Co.) 7,803 grt. Ore carrier.

BUILT: 1915, Short Brothers, Sunderland

After being near-missed alongside at Wabana in September, this time, fully loaded with iron ore for Sydney, Cape Breton, ***Rose Castle*** was at anchor with the French-owned ***PLM 27*** just off the port of Wabana, awaiting convoy. At 0210 she was hit by two torpedoes on her starboard side, the second in her engineroom, by the fully surfaced ***U 518***. Three minutes later, so was ***PLM 27***. A lot of the crew were lost, reports Pierre Simard, a crewman in the French ship, and later an RCN captain. The ship sank in less than a minute, with an underwater explosion, probably from her boilers, tossing swimmers about and probably killing some. This left the surviving members of the crews, including Simard, to swim toward shore in the freezing water, a distance of about three-quarters of a mile. Some were picked up by rafts cut loose from the rigging. Just before dawn a Fairmile came across one raft and took the survivors aboard. Of ***Rose Castle's*** crew, thirty-five were lost including the master, and between seven and eleven saved (reports vary). Thirty-three bodies were recovered. Records are very variable as to the total number of her crew and thus the number lost. KL Friedrich-Wilhelm Wissmann calmly watched the two ships sink before departing.[35]

35. Parker, *Running the Gauntlet*; Rohwer, *Axis Submarine Successes*; Hadley, *U-Boats Against Canada*; Max Reid, *DEMS at War!*

SHIP: *Jasper Park* FATE: Torpedoed by *U 177*, Indian Ocean, W South Africa, 6 Jul 43

OWNER: Canadian Government/Park SS Co. 7,129 grt. Freighter

BUILT: Sep 1942, by Davie Shipbuilding, Lauzon, PQ

Jasper Park was the first of the Canadian built and owned war emergency ships to be sunk. They were developed from a British standard freighter of J.L. Thomson & Sons' *North Sands* type. Owned by the Crown Corporation Park Steamships, formed in 1942, 176 *Parks* were built as freighters or tankers. The *Forts* were similar in design. Bound from Cochin, India, to Durban with a cargo of tea and jute, ***Jasper Park*** was torpedoed at 1005 on 6 July without warning, 1,150 miles east of Port Elizabeth, South Africa and south of Madagascar. She was alone, steaming at eleven and a half knots and not zig-zagging. The ship was struck by two torpedoes on the starboard side in No.2 hold and the stokehold or boiler room, which stopped the engines at once. The engineroom soon flooded and the ship's DEMS gun was disabled. An S-S-S alarm was transmitted by emergency set. While the starboard boats were destroyed, the port boats were lowered and the ship abandoned. The U-boat then surfaced north of the vessel and approached the lifeboats, one person asking questions as to her cargo, last port of call and destination. As the report on her loss in US Naval Operations files states, "Evasive and contradictory replies were given." The CO of the U-boat, KK Robert Gysae, expressed surprise that the ship had not streamed her anti-torpedo nets and said he had fired two torpedoes at the same ship the night before but had missed. Lookouts and the 3rd officer on ***Jasper Park*** had indeed reported what seemed to be a submarine's exhaust and what looked like torpedo tracks, her course had been temporarily altered, but nothing else was seen nor further precautions taken. The ship sank about three-quarters of an hour after being hit, and the U-boat moved off southwards after rescuing several boxes of tea that were floating about.

Forty-seven members of the crew of fifty-one, including DEMS gunners, survived, picked up twenty-seven hours later by the Australian destroyers HMAS ***Quiberon*** and ***Quickmatch***, who had sailed from Durban as soon as ***Jasper Park's*** report of being attacked was received. Four of the engineroom crew were killed, including the 4th engineer.

Gysae was a formidable opponent for, with ***Jasper Park***, he eventually had twenty-five vessels sunk to his credit, two of them 10,000-tonners, in two U-boat commands. Fourteen were sunk in two patrols in mid-1943 in the Indian Ocean. He was a contemporary of Endraß, Kretschmer and Lemp.[36]

36. SCS Int; Halford, *The Unknown Navy*, 233-234; notes from LCdr J. Butterfield, RCN, the ship's 2nd mate, courtesy Cmdre Jan Drent.

SHIP: *Watuka* FATE: Torpedoed by *U 802*, off Nova Scotia, SW of Halifax, 22 Mar 44
OWNER: Nova Scotia Steel & Coal Co, New Glasgow. 1,621 grt. Collier.
BUILT: 1918 by Nova Scotia Steel & Coal Co, New Glasgow, NS

This coastal vessel was in convoy SH-125 from Sydney to Halifax in an isolated attack not far off the Halifax headlands, according to the Canadian Press. One crewman was killed and twenty-five rescued by HMS ***Anticosti.***[37] No other history of the vessel or loss has been found.

37. DND records.

SHIP: *Albert C. Field* FATE: Torpedoed by German aircraft, English Channel, S of Bournemouth, 18 Jun 44
OWNER: Upper Lakes & St. Lawrence Transportation Co, Toronto. 1,764 grt. Laker.
BUILT: 1923, by Furness Shipbuilding Co, Haverton Hill-on-Tees

Bound from Penarth, Wales to the Normandy invasion beaches in the twelve-ship Convoy EBC-14 with 2,500 tons of ammunition and 130 bags of US mail, the ***Field*** sailed on 6 June. On the late evening of the 18th, steaming east at six knots off St. Catharine's Point, Portsmouth, as third ship in the starboard column, the 1st officer reported seeing a JU88 aircraft flying parallel to the convoy, but no-one firing at it. It then wheeled and released a torpedo, striking the ***Albert C. Field*** at 2340 on the starboard side amidships, on the bulkhead between her two holds. There was a thud, "like a very heavy depth charge" but no water thrown up and no flash. At first the ship listed slightly to starboard, and the mail stored in No.2 hold caught fire. Boats aft were blown into the water and many of the crew jumped overboard, some reaching rafts also blown over or released. The ship broke in two within three minutes and quickly sank, with some ammunition exploding. The seamen and others forward could not get aft, so either jumped or swam off as the ***Field*** sank. The Isles class trawler HMS ***Herschell*** promptly dropped her own boats and rescued those in the water, some clinging to scorched mail bags, and then others that had reached rafts. The rescue was much aided by the small red lights and the whistles on the life vests of those in the water. Three members of the crew were picked up by another vessel. Of the ship's crew of thirty-three, including ten Army and Navy gunners, the master, two able seamen and an Arab fireman were lost.

There are reports the ***Field*** was expended as a breakwater off Normandy, but this is probably a case of confusion with another ship.[38]

38. Wilcox & Gillham, *The Ships of Upper Lakes Shipping*; SCS Int.

SHIP: *Cornwallis* FATE: Torpedoed by *U 1230,* Gulf of Maine, off Portland Maine, 3 Dec 44
OWNER: Canadian Transporter Ltd (Canadian National Steamships), Montreal. 5,458 grt. Freighter.
BUILT: 1921, by J. Coughlan & Sons, Vancouver. Ex-Canadian Govt. Merchant Marine's *Canadian Transporter.*

Cornwallis had already been torpedoed once and survived: by ***U 514*** on 11 September, 1942, off Barbados when serving as a freighter in CNSS's West Indies trade. On this occasion she was again en route from Barbados to St. John, N.B. She left a convoy off New York and proceeded independently for St. John with a load of sugar and molasses. ***Cornwallis*** was torpedoed at about 0600, just before dawn, in calm but frigid sea. While her boats were swung out as was usual, she sank so rapidly that their crews didn't have time to lower them or cast off the falls. All those in the boats were drowned when ***Cornwallis*** rolled onto them on sinking. The Bos'n, anticipating this, knocked the pins off a raft's lashings on the stays, and jumped into the sea after it. He then pulled out the single seaman he came across and four of the black galley staff. The radio operator had only time to transmit "S-S-S - OFF DESERT..." before the ship went down. While this was received ashore, it was confusing, as there were several locations with Desert in their names within the larger area. Aircraft were sent out, but found nothing. Then at 1134 a fishing vessel came across bodies and other debris. Two USN destroyers and a Coast Guard cutter were diverted to the search but also missed the survivors. It was not until about 1400, some eight hours after the sinking, that the fishing vessel ***Notre Dame*** came across the raft with the six survivors. Thirty-five seamen, including the master and all his officers, plus seven DEMS gunners were lost.[39]

39. Gentile, *Track of the Grey Wolf*; Michael Gannon, *Operation Drumbeat*; Felicity Hannington, *The Lady Boats*; Hadley, *U-Boats Against Canada.*

SHIP: *Point Pleasant Park* FATE: Torpedoed by *U 510,* S Atlantic, NW of Cape Town, SA, 23 Feb 45
OWNER: Canadian Government/Park SS Co, Montreal. 7,136 grt. Coal-fired freighter.
BUILT: Nov. 1943, by Davie Shipbuilding, Lauzon, PQ

This ship sailed from Saint John, NB on 8 January for Trinidad and then Africa under Captain Owen Owen, leaving a southbound convoy on 11 February alone for South Africa. She was sighted by ***U 510*** (KL Alfred Eick) well off the usual U-boat routes, as the large Type IXC submarine was bound for Germany from the Far East with a cargo of tungsten. (At first it was recorded ***Point Pleasant Park*** had been sunk by ***U 532***, but in 1967 the latter's CO denied this.) The ship, steaming at ten and a half knots, was hit aft in the crew's quarters at 1355 by one of the two torpedoes fired, killing eight men. The explosion also flooded No.5 hold and the engineroom and blew off the ship's propellor. The ship settled slowly as the officers ordered her boats launched at 1420. They collected sextants, binoculars, jackets and cigarettes, and threw the CBs overboard. Three boats got away, pulling to the opposite side of the sinking ship as the submarine surfaced at 1430 and then shelled her forward in No.2 and No.3 holds. The U-boat lay off for a bit, then returned to fire several more rounds into the ship to hasten her demise. ***Point Pleasant Park*** finally sank about 1615. The S-S-S-S submarine alarm signal had been tried but no confirmation of its receipt was noted, as the dynamo failed just then, and the emergency radios did not work. The boats set sail for the coast of Africa, about 375 miles distant. One man who had suffered a broken back died on the way. Crews were divided equally between the boats under the master, and the 1st and 2nd officers. (Some with cameras even took pictures which appeared in a Readers Digest book.) While the boats were tied together for some time to help the slow sailers, they became separated by the eighth day in a storm. On the next day the 2nd officer's boat flashed a distant vessel by heliograph mirror, was picked up by the fishing vessel ***Boy Russel*** off the bleak Kalahari coast and taken to Luderitz. A search for the others was instigated by the South African Navy and Air Force and the other two boats picked up the next day by HMSAS ***Africana*** who towed them to Walvis Bay, all the crew suffering from exposure. There were nine lives lost and forty-two survivors.[40]

40. DHist file notes, Ottawa; SCS Int; *Readers Digest*, "The Canadians at War", Vol 2 (1969).

SHIP: *Taber Park* FATE: Torpedoed by *Seehund* midget submarine, North Sea, off Southwold, 13 Mar 45
OWNER: Canadian Government/Park SS Co, Montreal. 2,878 grt. Freighter.
BUILT: Aug 1944, by Foundation Maritime Ltd, Pictou, NS

Tabor Park was sunk when in coastal convoy FS-1753, Methil to the Thames. In March of 1945, in a last-ditch effort, the German Navy sent out two groups of these miniature *Seehund* 2-man-crew U-boats, designated Type XXVIIB. They were true U-boats, unlike many of their counterparts in the *Kleinkampfverbänd* that were little more than manned torpedoes. They were to sink nine merchantmen between January and 28 April, when their operations ceased.[41] ***Taber Park*** was one of these unfortunate nine. The crew was British, and twenty-four crew and four DEMS gunners were killed; only four were saved. Some sources indicate the ship was mined, but *Kleinkampferbänd* records are quite clear, for that crew reached home safely to report.

41. Whitley, *German Coastal Forces of World War Two.*

SHIP: *Avondale Park* FATE: Torpedoed by *U 2336*, Firth of Forth, Scotland, 7 May 45
OWNER: Canadian Government/Park SS Co, Montreal. 2,878 grt. Coal-fired freighter
BUILT: May, 1944, by Foundation Maritime Ltd, Pictou, NS

Avondale Park was the last British ship to be sunk in World War II, two miles southeast of May Island in the Firth of Forth. In Convoy EN-91, bound from Methil for Belfast, she sailed during the 7th and was torpedoed at 2240 that evening, sinking by the stern within ten minutes. Although fitted with a 4-inch gun and five Oerlikons, ***Avondale Park*** was unable to use them as the U-boat was not seen, nor her torpedo tracks. The torpedo hit on the starboard side between the engineroom and No.3 hold, destroying a starboard lifeboat. Rafts were released but some jammed in their rails. Of the thirty-four British crew, four RN DEMS gunners and three Maritime Regiment RA gunners, the chief engineer and one donkeyman were lost. Survivors were picked up by a convoy escort.[42]

42. SCS Int.

The last two British merchant seamen lost from a Canadian-owned ship in World War II. It is sad to realise that in another two days they would have been safe. Recorded on the Merchant Navy memorial on the Thames at London.

"The fog still stands on the long tide rips,
The gulls go wavering to and fro
But where are all the beautiful ships
I knew so long ago?"

Bliss Carmen

Typical of so many: HMCS *Chilliwack* in June, 1942

Halifax, September 23rd, 1945

PHOTO CREDITS

Admlty.	- originally an Admiralty photo
IWM	- from Imperial War Museum, London
KRM	- from K.R. Macpherson collection
NAC-	- from National Archives of Canada
RCAF	- from Royal Canadian Air Force wartime files
RCN	- from Royal Canadian Navy wartime files
US Naval Inst.	- United States Naval Institute, Annapolis, MD

CHAP.	CREDIT
Dust Jacket	D.W.Piers
	NAC/PA110924
1	NAC/E.35756
	KRM
2	NAC/CN.3804
	KRM
3	NAC/O.10962
4	KRM p
	KRM/Toronto Daily Star
5	KRM
6	NAC/O.915-1
7	NAC/H.1355
	NAC/H.2693
	NAC/A.1414
8	NAC/O.326-1
9	KRM
10	NAC/H.592
11	NAC/NP.348
12	NAC/PA104472
13	Peter Chance
	Robert Eakins
14	NAC/NF.785
	NAC/O.4443
15	Shiels/KRM
16	Port Arthur Shipbuilding
17	Montye McCrae
	KRM
18	NAC/CN.3636
19	KRM
	L.B.Jenson
20	NAC/H.1847
	NAC/O.1678
21	J. Allan
22	NAC/CN.3564
23	NAC/CN.6445
24	NAC/NP.543
	KRM
25	NAC/PA116956
26	NAC/UT.1554
	Robert Eakins

CHAP.	CREDIT
27	KRM/Admlty.
28	J. Hughes
29	RCAF
	KRM
	J.O.Bayford
30	RCAF
	KRM
31	KRM/Admlty.
	NAC/S.424
	KRM/Admlty.
32	NAC/GM.1159
	KRM/Admlty.
33	E.G.Giles
	Alan Arnold
34	KRM
	KRM
	NAC/SY.161-10
	KRM
	NAC/PA140824
	C.Rathgeb
35	KRM
	Pat Hardy
	NAC/PA107941
	KRM
	H. Frubrick
36	NAC/CN.3643
	US Naval Inst.
	US Naval Inst.
37	NAC/PA167315
38	NAC/GM.1463
	MARPAC-Pub.Affr. PL.15752
39	NAC/PA163952
40	NAC/R.1039
41	KRM
42	NAC/A.1115
44	George Mannix
46	NAC/PA136831
	NAC/C127034

CHAP.	CREDIT
47	NAC/NF.785
	NAC/L.4124
49	NAC/A.1003
50	RCAF
51	NAC/S.429
	LCdr R.Stacey
52	J.Hume
	NAC/A.389
53	KRM/Admlty.
	NAC/CN.3817
	KRM
54	C.Rathgeb
	KRM
55	KRM
56	NAC/GM.0362
57	Don Warren
	NAC/CN.6140
58	NAC/PA116484
59	LCdr R.Stacey
60	D.Trimingham
61	Bruce/KRM
	I.W.M.
	NAC/CN.3536
62	NAC/L.5281
63	NAC/F.2499
	NAC/HZ-2344
64	NAC/S.426
65	***Thorold*** - F. Redfern
	Kenordoc - F. Redfern
	Canadol. - Imperial Oil Ltd.
	Pr.Marg. - Cdn.Pacific Ltd.
	Avond.Pk. - F. Redfern
Epil.	NAC/H.2644
	KRM

TABLE 1 RCN LOSSES IN WW 2

	BY ENEMY ACTION							BY SEA HAZARD								
	TORPEDOED				MINED		AIR CR	COLLISION			FNDRD	FIRE		STRANDING		
LOCATION	Gulf St. Lwr	N. Atlan.	Off N.S.	Eng. Ch. Ir. Sea	Eng. Chnnl	Gibr.	Med	N. Atlan.	Biscay	Gulf St. Lwr	Gulf St. Lwr	Belgium	Off N.S.	Iceld	N.S.	TOTAL
1940								2	1		1					4
1941		1						1					1		1	4
1942	2	2														4
1943		1				1	1			1						4
1944		1	2	3	2									1		9
1945		1	1	1								5				8
TOTALS	2	6	3	4	2	1	1	3	1	1	1	5	1	1	1	33
	15				3		1	5			9					
	19							14								

Locations: Gulf of St. Lawrence, North Atlantic, Off Nova Scotia, English Channel & Irish Sea, Gibraltar area, Mediterranean, Biscay coast area, Belgium, Iceland

TABLE 2 RCN SUCCESSES OVER ENEMY WARSHIPS

	U-BOATS & SOMMERGIBILI							SURFACE SHIPS			
LOCATION	N. Atlan.	West Appr.	Eng. CH. Ir. Sea	Fr. Coast	Carib'n	Med	N. Sea	Destr.	Mine Swpr	E-Boat	TOTAL
1940		1									1
1941	1										1
1942	5				1						6
1943	4					3					7
1944	6	2	2	3			2	3	7	1	26
1945			1				2				3
TOTALS	16	3	3	3	1	3	4	3	7	1	44
	33							11			

Locations: North Atlantic, UK Western Approaches, English Channel & Irish Sea, Off French Coast, Caribbean, Mediterranean, North Sea

TABLE 3 COOPERATIVE METHODS OF DESTRUCTION

Units Cooperating to Sink Enemy Vessels

U-BOATS & SOMMERGIBILI				SURFACE SHIPS		
RCN ALONE		RCN & RN SHIPS	RCN & USN A/C	RCN ALONE	RCN & RN DESTROYERS & CRUISERS	TOTAL
SINGLE SHIP	2 OR MORE					
9	13	10	1	2	9	44

TABLE 4 U-BOAT SURVIVOR RATES

Number of U-boats Sunk and Men Lost

	NO SURVIVORS	FEW SURVIVORS	1/2 CREW OR MORE SURVIVED
BOATS	17	3	13
CREWS LOST:	901	122	173

This table presumes an average German submarine crew of 53, and 46 in Italian crews. Thus the total complement in the boats involved was about 1,735 men. Of these 1,196 did not survive, or 68.9% of those crewmen. This is about average for the whole German U-boat service losses in the boats that went on operations.

Of the 33 boats sunk, 20 had no or few survivors, a 60.6% loss rate of the boats. The astounding point in these statistics is that U-boats were still departing on operations until the last week of the war in May, 1945.

TABLE 5 SUCCESSES & LOSSES

+ = with other units involved. (59) = men lost

DATE		SUCCESSES	LOSSES
1940			
12	MAY		YPRES. Collision, REVENGE (0)
25	JUN		FRASER. Collision, CALCUTTA (59)
19	OCT		BRAS D'OR. Foundered (30)
22	OCT		MARGAREE. Collision,PT FAIRY (142)
6	NOV	S/M FAA' DI BRUNO. OTTAWA +	
1941			
26	MAR		OTTER. Fire (19)
10	SEP	U 501. CHAMBLY, MOOSE JAW	
19	SEP		LEVIS. Torpedoed, U 74. (18)
7	DEC		WINDFLOWER. Collision, ZYPENBERG (23)
20	DEC		ADVERSUS. Ran ashore (0)
1942			
10	FEB		SPIKENARD. Torpedoed, U 136. (57)
24	JUL	U 90. ST CROIX	
31	JUL	U 588. WETASKIWIN, SKEENA	
6	AUG	U 210. ASSINIBOINE +	
28	AUG	U 94. OAKVILLE +	
31	AUG	U 756. MORDEN	
7	SEP		RACCOON. Torpedoed, U 165. (37)
11	SEP		CHARLOTTETOWN. Torpedoed, U 517 (10)
13	SEP		OTTAWA (I). Torpedoed, U 92 (119)
27	DEC	U 356. ST LAURENT, CHILLIWACK, NAPANEE, BATTLEFORD	
1943			
13	JAN	U 224. VILLE DE QUEBEC	
19	JAN	S/M TRITONE. PORT ARTHUR +	
6	FEB		LOUISBURG. Italian Air Torpedo (42)
8	FEB	S/M AVORIO. REGINA	
22	FEB		WEYBURN. Mined, U 118. (9)
4	MAR	U 87. SHEDIAC, ST. CROIX	
13	MAR	U 163. PRESCOTT, NAPANEE	
13	MAY	U 753. DRUMHELLER +	
20	SEP		ST CROIX. Torpedoed, U 305. (148)
21	OCT		CHEDABUCTO. Collision,LORD KELVIN.(1)
20	NOV	U 536. CALGARY, SNOWBERRY, NENE	
1944			
8	JAN	4757. CAMROSE +	
24	FEB	U 257. WASKESIU	
5	MAR	U 744. ST CATHARINES, CHILLIWACK, FENNEL, CHAUDIERE, GATINEAU +	
10	MAR	U 845. ST LAURENT, SWANSEA, OWEN SOUND +	
13	MAR	U 575. PRINCE RUPERT +	
14	APR	U 448. SWANSEA +	
22	APR	U 311. SWANSEA, MATANE	
26	APR	DD T-29. HAIDA, HURON, ATHABASKAN +	
29	APR		ATHABASKAN. Torpedoed, DD T-24 (128)

DATE		SUCCESSES	LOSSES
29	APR	DD T-27. HAIDA	
6	MAY		VALLEYFIELD. Torpedoed, U 548. (125)
9	JUN	DD Z-32. HAIDA	
11	JUN	E-boat S 136. SIOUX +	
14	JUN	M/S M 133. MTB 748 +	
24	JUN	U 971. HAIDA +	
28	JUN	M 4611, Vp 213. HURON +	
2	JUL		MTB 460. Mined. (11)
6	JUL	U 678. OTTAWA, KOOTENAY +	
8	JUL		MTB 463. Mined. (0)
6	AUG	M/S M-486, M 263. HAIDA, IROQUOIS +	
8	AUG		REGINA. Torpedoed, U 677. (30)
15	AUG	M/S M 385. IROQUOIS +	
18	AUG	U 621. OTTAWA, KOOTENAY, CHAUDIÈRE	
20	AUG	U 984. OTTAWA, KOOTENAY, CHAUDIÈRE	
21	AUG		ALBERNI. Torpedoed U 480. (59)
1	SEP	U 247. SAINT JOHN, SWANSEA, PORT COLBORNE	
9	SEP	U 484. DUNVER, HESPELER +	
16	OCT	U 1006. ANNAN, LOCH ACHANALT	
25	OCT		SKEENA. Drove ashore. (15)
12	NOV	M 416, M 427. ALGONQUIN +	
24	NOV		SHAWINIGAN. Torpedoed, U 1228. (91)
24	DEC		CLAYOQUOT. Torpedoed,U 806. (8)
27	DEC	U 877. ST THOMAS, SEA CLIFF	
1945			
14	FEB		5 MTBs. Fire. (26)
16	FEB	U 309. SAINT JOHN	
22	FEB		TRENTONIAN. Torpedoed, U 1004. (6)
7	MAR	U 1302. LA HULLOISE, STRATHADAM, THETFORD MINES	
17	MAR		GUYSBOROUGH. Torpedoed, U 878. (51)
20	MAR	U 1003. NEW GLASGOW	
16	APR		ESQUIMALT. Torpedoed, U 190. (44)

TOTALS

Successes	Losses
30 German U-Boats	6 destroyers
3 Italian *sommergibili*	1 frigate
3 German destroyers	10 corvettes
7 German minesweepers	4 Bangor Minesweepers
1 German E-Boat *	3 auxiliary vessels
	2 armed yachts
	7 MTBs
44	33 vessels, 1,308 seamen, including RN, but excluding merchantmen survivors. It also does not include those killed in ships that were hit but salvaged, or killed in action by gunfire when enemy vessels were sunk

* This figure is highly suspect but the only one so far indicated in German records.

TABLE 6 SHIPS REMOVED FROM RCN SERVICE FOR OTHER REASONS

A. CTL: Constructive total loss:

1. *Chebogue*:
frigate; torpedoed by ***U 1227***, 4 Oct. 1944, 800 mi. west of Ireland. Towed east but was driven ashore in a gale. CTL at Port Talbot, Wales. Broken up 1948

2. *Magog*:
frigate; torpedoed by ***U 1223***, 14 Oct. 1944 near Pointe des Monts Light, Godbout Bay, St. Lawrence. CTL at Québec. Broken up 1947

3. HMS ***Nabob:***
aircraft carrier. While not strictly RCN, she was Canadian-manned. Torpedoed by ***U 354***, 22 Aug. 1944. 21 killed. CTL at Rosyth but rebuilt as the merchant ship ***Nabob*** post war. Broken up 1978.

4. ***Mulgrave***:
Bangor minesweeper; mined near Le Havre, 8 Oct. 1945 (post war minesweeping). CTL in UK. Broken up 1947

5. ***Teme:***
frigate; torpedoed by ***U 246***, 29 Mar. 1945 in English Channel near Landsend. CTL in UK. Broken up 1946.

B. Damaged beyond use; retained:

6. ***Saguenay:***
destroyer; torpedoed 1940; then rammed by SS ***Azra*** and damaged by own depth charges, 15 Nov. 1942. Made stationary training ship, HMCS ***Cornwallis***. Broken up 1946.

7. ***Columbia:***
Town class destroyer; ran into Newfoundland cliff 25 Feb. 1944. Made ammunition hulk, Liverpool, NS. Broken up 1945.

C. Worn out; removed from active service:

8. ***Buxton***:
Town class destroyer; made engineering training ship, ***Cornwallis*** in 1943. Broken up 1945

9. ***St Clair:***
Town class destroyer; made damage control and fire fighting training hulk, Halifax, 1944. Abandoned, 1950.

10. ***Lynx:***
Armed yacht; worn out, April, 1943, sold July, 1943.

11. ***Beaver:***
Armed yacht; worn out, Oct., 1944. Sold.

12. ***Grizzly:***
Armed yacht; worn out, May, 1944. Broken up.

13. ***Renard:***
Armed yacht; worn out, Aug., 1944. Broken up 1955.

14. ***Skidegate***:
training auxiliary; of no further use and paid off 18 Feb., 1942. Sold out commercially 1946.

D.

A late and last loss is worth recording in HMCS ***Ironbound***, a Western Isles A/S trawler. Returned to the RN at the war's end, she was eventually sunk by a drifting mine off Cape Mondego, Portugal on 5 Nov. 1957 when operating as the Finnish trawler ***Korsö.***

TABLE 7 MERCHANT SHIPS SUNK: NON-CANADIAN PREWAR, AND FISHING VESSELS

Supplement to Chapter 65

The following merchant ships were Canadian registered and flagged, but had not been Canadian-owned ships pre-war. Most were taken over by the Canadian government when their home countries were overrun by the Germans or Italians, or were captured ships. Also included are Canadian fishing vessels destroyed by German U-Boat gunfire. This latter list may not be complete, as records are scarce and sometimes conflicting.

Bic Island:
ex-Italian ***Capo Noli***, captured by HMCS ***Bras D'Or*** 10 Jun. 1940, 4,000 grt. freighter. Sunk 29 Oct. 1942, torpedoed by ***U 224*** when in convoy HX-212, mid-Atlantic south of Iceland. No survivors of her crew or survivors from other torpedoed ships she had rescued beforehand.[1]

Carolus:
ex-Finnish, 2,375 grt. freighter. Sunk 9 Oct. 1942, torpedoed by ***U 69*** in convoy NL-9 off Matane, Qué. in Gulf of St. Lawrence. 11 of crew lost, 19 survivors.

Chr.J. Kampmann:
ex-Danish, 2,260 grt. freighter. Sunk 3 Nov. 1942, when in convoy TAG-18, torpedoed by ***U 160***, in Caribbean, north of Venezuela. 19 lost, eight survivors.

Erik Boye:
Ex-Danish; 2,238 grt. freighter. Sunk 15 Jun. 1940, torpedoed by ***U 38*** in convoy HX-48, off Land's End, UK. No casualties.

Europa:
ex-Danish, 10,224 grt. passenger freighter/troopship. Sunk 3 May 1941 in dock at Liverpool during air-raid; raised, hit again a few days later in drydock. Left in situ, dock filled in.[2] No casualties.

Nereus:
Ex-USN collier, 10,650 grt. Saguenay Terminals, Montreal. Sunk 12 Dec. 1941, from unknown cause, but suspected sabotage, possibly in cargo, in Caribbean. No U-Boats or other enemy vessels in the area. No survivors of crew of 61 including some passengers.

Proteus:
Ex-USN collier, 10,650 grt. Saguenay Terminals, Montreal. Sunk 25 Nov. 1941, from unknown cause, but suspected sabotage. Same circumstances as for **Nereus**. No survivors from crew of 58.

St. Malo:
Ex-French, 5,779 grt. freighter. Sunk 12 Oct. 1940, torpedoed by ***U 101*** in convoy HX-77, mid-Atlantic south of Iceland. 28 lost.

Vancouver Island:
ex-German ***Weser***, 9,472 grt. freighter. Captured by HMCS ***Prince Robert*** off Mexico 25 Sep. 1940. Sunk 15 Oct. 1941, torpedoed by ***U 558*** in mid-North Atlantic while sailing independently. No survivors of 65 crew, 32 passengers, eight DEMS gunners.

---

1. Some added details in this list were obtained from an article by Rober C. Fisher in *Northern Mariner/Le Marin du Nord*, Canadian Nautical Research Society, July 1995.

2. See *Port in a Storm*, John Hughes, Liverpool, 1993.

CANADIAN FISHING VESSELS LOST DUE TO ENEMY ACTION

This list does not include schooners owned in Newfoundland, of which at least three were sunk by U-boat gunfire

Angelus:
255 grt., barquentine, owned by "Government of Canada", but ex-French. Sunk 19 May 1943, by gunfire of ***U 161*** in open Atlantic, north of Bermuda. Two survivors, seven lost.

James E. Newsom:
671 grt., owned by Zwicker & Co., Halifax. Sunk 1 May 1942, by gunfire of ***U 69***.[3]

Lucille M:
54 grt., owned by Frederick Sutherland. Sunk 25 Jul. 1942, by gunfire of ***U 89*** on George's Bank, south of Cape Sable Island, N.S.

Mildred Pauline:
300 grt., owned by R.T. Sainthill & Son, Sydney. Sunk 7 May 1942, by gunfire of ***U 136*** off Nova Scotia.

Mona Marie:
126 grt., owned by L. Ritcey, Lahave, N.S. Sunk 28 Jun. 1942 by gunfire of ***U 126*** in eastern Caribbean, southwest of Barbados.

NON-CANADIAN SHIPS

Apart from the details on previous pages of Canadian registered and flagged merchant vessels lost by enemy action, these are omitted:

1. These were British-registered although Canadian-owned ships when lost: 6 ***Fort*** ships: ***Fort Athabasca, Bellingham, Maisoneuve, Missanabie, Norfolk, St. Nicholas***

2. One was a US registered ship when lost: Paterson's ***Soreldoc***. Also 22 ***Fort*** class Canadian built but American owned and registered ships were leased to Great Britain and were lost due to enemy action, 19 of them to U-boats or Japanese submarines.

3. Eight (and more) Canadian registered ships were lost at sea due to marine accident, not enemy action:
Canadian Government's (ex-French) ***Lisieux*** (foundered): ***Watkins F. Nisbet*** (ran ashore, English Channel); Atlantic Transportation's ***R.J. Cullen*** (wrecked, Outer Hebrides); Canada Atlantic Transit's ***Canatco*** (ran ashore, Labrador); Paterson's ***Mondoc*** (struck submerged object, Caribbean); Paterson's ***Hamildoc*** (foundered, off British Guyana); ***Silver Star Park*** (collision off New York; salvaged, sold, repaired); ***Greenhill Park*** (explosion, Vancouver).

4. Salvaged ships: three: CN SS's ***Lady Nelson*** was salvaged at Port Castries when torpedoed alongside; repaired.
Nipiwan Park lost her bow section when torpedoed, but the rest was salvaged and a new section added. She is not counted as "lost".
Collingdoc, a Paterson laker, was mined and sunk in the Thames, 200 feet from Southend Pier, on 13 July 1940, with the loss of two lives. She was salvaged, and then sunk as a blockship in an entrance to the Orkney Islands. She can still be seen there.[4]

6. Most CPR ships sunk were British registered, not Canadian, except ***Empress of Asia*** and ***Princess Marguerite***. E.g. ***Empress of Britain*** and four "***Beaver..***" ships, etc. Also the A.M.C. HMS ***Forfar*** (ex-***Montrose***).

7. CN SS's ***Lady Somers*** was requisitioned by the Admiralty and lost as an RN ocean boarding ship on 15 July 1941.

8. Ships owned and registered in Newfoundland are not included, such as the Bowood's pulpwood-carrier ***Waterton***, sunk by ***U 106*** on 11 October 1942 in the Gulf of St. Lawrence; and the ferry S.S. ***Caribou***, sunk in October, 1942 off Port aux Basques.

3. See *Running the Gauntlet*, Mike Parker.

4. Van der Linden notes.

TABLE 8 RCAF SUCCESSES AGAINST U-BOATS. EASTERN AIR COMMAND, & RCAF SQUADRONS OF RAF COASTAL COMMAND[1]

DATE	U-BOAT	AIRCRAFT & SQUADRON	LOCATION	SHARE CREDIT WITH
31.07.42	U 754	L/113/Hudson (#625)	Off Yarmouth N.S.	Solo
30.10.42	U 520	X/10/Digby	115 mi. E of St. John's, Nfld.	Solo
30.10.42	U 658	Y/145/Hudson	290 mi. NE of Torbay, Nfld.	Solo
04.05.43	U 209*	W/5/Canso	270 mi. S of Cape Farewell,Greenland	Solo

* Previous records show ***U 630*** sunk in this attack. ButW/5 attacked ***U 209*** and damaged her; she sank about 7 May due to accident, "probably contributed to by damage in W/5's attack." ***U 630*** was sunk by HMS ***Vidette*** on 6 May.[2]

DATE	U-BOAT	AIRCRAFT & SQUADRON	LOCATION	SHARE CREDIT WITH
13.05.43	U 753*	G/423/Sunderland	Mid-Atlantic, off the Brittany penninsula	HMCS *Drumheller* & HMS *Lagan*

* Previous records show ***U 456*** sunk by G/423, ***Drumheller*** and ***Lagan***. But recent records now agree this was ***U 753. U 456*** was sunk by RAF 86 Sqn. on 13 May.[3]

DATE	U-BOAT	AIRCRAFT & SQUADRON	LOCATION	SHARE CREDIT WITH
02.08.43	U 706	A/415/Hampden	NW of Cape Ortegal Spain.	USAAF a/c *

* RCAF a/c strafed & bombed first; then US a/c came in. This one is not normally credited, as damage by RCAF not fully verified.

DATE	U-BOAT	AIRCRAFT & SQUADRON	LOCATION	SHARE CREDIT WITH
04.08.43	U 489	G/423/Sunderland	170 mi. SE of Iceland	Solo
19.09.43	U 341	A/10/Liberator*	500 mi. S of Iceland	Solo

* Earlier records credit J/423/Sunderland, but the above is now accepted as correct.[4]

DATE	U-BOAT	AIRCRAFT & SQUADRON	LOCATION	SHARE CREDIT WITH
08.10.43	U 610	J/423/Sunderland	Mid Atlantic	Solo
11.02.44	U 283	D/407/Wellington	SW of Faeroes	Solo
10.03.44	U 625	U/422/Sunderland	West of Ireland	Solo
17.04.44	U 342	S/162/Canso	SW of Iceland	Solo
04.05.44	U 846	M/407/Wellington	N of Cape Ortegal Spain, in Biscay	Solo
03.06.44	U 477	T/162/Canso	250 mi. N of Shetlands.	Solo
11.06.44	U 980	B/162/Canso	NW of Bergen, Norway	Solo
13.06.44	U 715	T/162/Canso	NE of Faeroes	Solo
24.06.44	U 971	L/407/Wellington*	SW of Scilly	HMCS *Haida*, HMS Eskimo & Czech OTU Sqn. RAF

* This attack damaged ***U 971*** which left for home base, and was caught and sunk on 24 June by the Czechs and the two ships which were following up the lead by L/407. (See Chapter 44)

DATE	U-BOAT	AIRCRAFT & SQUADRON	LOCATION	SHARE CREDIT WITH
24.06.44	U 1225	P/162/Canso *	120 mi. N of Shetlands	Solo

* F/L David Hornell, captain of this a/c, was awarded posthumous VC for this action

DATE	U-BOAT	AIRCRAFT & SQUADRON	LOCATION	SHARE CREDIT WITH
30.06.44	U 478	A/162/Canso*	N of Shetlands	RAF Liberator

* A/162's D/Cs hung up so she homed Liberator E/86 onto the U-boat who sank her.

DATE	U-BOAT	AIRCRAFT & SQUADRON	LOCATION	SHARE CREDIT WITH
30.12.44	U 772	L/407/Wellington	30 mi. S of Portland Bill	Solo
02.05.45	U 2359	-/404/Mosquitoes*	In Kattegat, E of Denmark	With 3 RAF Sqns & Norw. a/c

* 4 RCAF Mosquitoes acted as air cover for RAF Mosquitoes of 143 & 248 Sqns. and Mustangs, firing RPs. -/404 did not attack directly.

THREE FORMER CREDITS

FORMER DATE	U-BOAT CREDIT	AIRCRAFT & SQUADRON	COMMENTS
07.09.43	U 669	W/407/Wellington	Now known to have attacked ***U 584***, not damaged. Loss of ***U 669*** now assessed as "unknown", but likely she was mined between 29 Aug. and 8 Sept.
26.10.43	U 420	A/10/Liberator	Now known to have attacked ***U 91***, not damaged. Loss of ***U 420*** now assessed as "unknown", sometime between 20 Oct. and 17 Nov.
24.04.44	U 311	A/423/Sunderland	Now known to have attacked ***U 672***, extensively damaging her, although she reached base. ***U 311*** sunk by HMCS ***Matane*** and ***Swansea*** on the 22nd. (See Chapter 38)

1. Many RCAF crews served in RAF squadrons and sank U-boats. The most note worthy is F/L Kenneth O. Moore, RCAF, with RAF's 224 Liberator Squadron who sank ***U373*** and ***U629*** off Brest within 22 minutes of each other. But these are not recorded in this RCAF table.

2. R.M. Coppock (MOD, Navy, UK), notes to author, 1987, 1991 and March 1996 on reassessment of U-boat losses.

3. Ibid.

4. W.A.B. Douglas, *The Creation of a National Air Force; Official History*, U. of T. Press, p. 562.

5. Notes of R.M. Coppock, MOD Historical Section.

GLOSSARY & ABBREVIATIONS

AA Anti-aircraft. Guns, seamen gunners and/or gunfire.

AB Able-bodied seaman, the first step up from an ordinary seaman

Admiralty British Naval Headquarters in London, who had overall operational control and some administrative responsibilities for Allied navies in its area.

A/S Anti-Submarine, both equipment and tactics. Hence ASCO, the Anti Submarine Control Officer, in charge of the detecting equipment on board.

ASV Air-to-surface vessel radar in maritime patrol aircraft, to detect surfaced submarines, and ships.

Asdic The wartime name for the device used to detect and track submarines by sound waves under water. Now called by its American name SONAR. Despite the widely reported source, the letters did not stand for "the Anti Submarine Detection International Committee" of the 1930s. It was a term in use by the end of the 1st War.

B-Dienst The German naval cryptanalysis service, comparable with Britain's Bletchley Park (q.v.)

BdU *Befehlshaber der Unterseeboote*: U-Boat Headquarters in Lorient, then Paris, then near Berlin.

Bletchley Park The British Government Code and Cypher School where enemy radio signals were studied, their codes and cyphers broken, and the results, known as "ULTRA", sent secretly to Commanders-in-Chief.

Bos'n The senior rating in charge of the upper deck, and short for the ancient term boats' swain.

BR A Book of Reference - manuals and textbooks that were not "Secret".

Carley Floats Cork or other material large floats, about twelve by five feet, with a net inner liner and supply box. Provided in growing numbers to all warships, as their boats rarely survived a torpedoing.

CAT Gear Canadian anti-acoustic torpedo gear, streamed astern to deflect homing torpedoes targeted for ships' propellers.

CB A Confidential Book - very carefully accounted-for secret publications.

Cdr A rank abbreviation for Commander. Also LCdr, Lieutenant Commander; Lt, Lieutenant; and SLt, Sub-Lieutenant.

C-in-C Commander-in-Chief.

CO The Commanding Officer. His rank depended on seniority and size of the ship. Usually a Lieutenant, a Lieutenant Commander or a Commander. Often referred to as "the Captain".

Captain (D) The senior operational Captain on the staff, responsible for ships in a command or at a major port. Based ashore. Also Commodore (D) in larger headquarter bases.

Corvette A rather small specialist A/S vessel, the workhorse of the early years of the war. 107 were built in Canada for the RCN.

Cox'n The senior Petty Officer in the ship, at the wheel when in action or leaving harbour. The valuable link between the officer administration and the ship's crew. Short for the older term, coxswain, thus often called "Swain".

DEMS Defensively Equipped Merchant Ships, the term used to refer to their naval crews and armament.

DF Direction finding, by radio waves. Or, as in 10 DF, the 10th Destroyer Flotilla.

DHIST The Directorate of History in DND headquarters, Ottawa.

DND The Department of National Defence, Ottawa. Also NDHQ.

Doppler The difference in pitch of asdic transmissions and the returning echo, indicating target aspect - moving toward or away.

DSO, DSC Naval awards, by the Admiralty and the King, for unusual naval valour: the Distinguished Service Order, the Distinguished Service Cross.

Depth Charges: A 300-pound container of explosive, detonated by a depth-sensing "pistol", and dropped on submarines in clusters. Invented in 1915, they had not changed much by 1945. Made "heavy" by addition of iron or concrete weights.

Destroyer The larger, more powerful, faster class of ships, one being usually included as a senior officer's ship in most close escort groups. Except for the end-of-the-war cruisers and the landing ships, the RCN's largest warships. While good anti-submarine vessels, they were often not available for that job, designed around gun and torpedo armament.

EG Escort Group–EG-6, EG-9, etc. Groups of ships, used as roving Support Groups (and often referred to by that title) designated to come to the aid of the Close Escort Groups of the convoys, styled C-8 (Canadian), B-3 (British), A-5 (American), when danger threatened. The close escort became the corvettes' role.

ETA Estimated Time of Arrival at a destination.

1st Lieutenant The deputy commanding officer and second in command. Also called the Executive Officer or XO. His orders said he was "responsible for the fighting efficiency of the ship."

First Operator The asdic rating controlling the direction and pulse rate of the asdic set's beam under water. The others of the team were the range recorder operator, the bearing recorder operator, and, later in the war, the depth predictor operator. All coordinated by the ASCO.

Frigate The larger and later version of the corvette. Faster, with much enhanced asdic, three times as many depth charges and with better armament. Apart from the British sloops and the *Castle* class corvettes, they became debateably the war's most useful A/S vessels when destroyers could not be present.

German naval ranks (spelling and abbreviations taken from a 1939 German Navy List):

Kapitän zur See (KS)	Captain
Fregattenkapitän (FK)	(no RCN equivalent–junior captain)
Korvettenkapitän (KK)	Commander
Kapitänleutnant (KL)	Lieutenant Commander
Oberleutnant zur See (OL)	(Senior) Lieutenant
Leutnant zur See (LS)	(Junior) Sub-Lieutenant

HE Hydrophone effect - the noise on asdic of a submarine engine running, or of an incoming torpedo.

HF/DF High Frequency Direction Finding. A radio-locating device for detecting U-boats' radio transmissions.

Hedgehog By mid-war an ahead-throwing weapon development that allowed a ship attacking a submarine to fire a cluster of 24 60-pound "bombs" 200 yards ahead while asdic was still in contact, unlike the depth charges which were dropped as the ship passed over her target.

HSD A Higher Submarine Detector rating, usually a PO or L/S and in charge of the seamen in the A/S team

I.E. Corvette Increased Endurance corvettes, with additional fuel capacity built in.

Knot A unit of speed at sea, equal to 1.14 miles per hour.

Leading Hand: A seaman, storesman or other rating classed as Leading Seaman

Mid-Ocean Group Escort groups covering the mid-Atlantic, from about south of Greenland to west of Ireland. At either end were the Western Approaches Groups (west of the United Kingdom) and the Western Local Escort Force (from Greenland to North American ports).

NSHQ Canadian Naval Service Headquarters, in Ottawa.

Oerlikon	A Swiss-developed anti-aircraft and anti-submarine heavy machine gun, firing a 20mm explosive shell. Could be single, hand-operated mountings, or twin power-driven mountings. A very useful weapon, fitted in U-boats as well, and still in use.
PMO	A ship's Principal Medical Officer or doctor. Not every ship carried one, particularly the corvettes.
Primer	The canister inside a depth charge that provided the added necessary explosion to detonate the whole 235 lbs. Could be withdrawn for safety.
RCN, RCNR & RCNVR:	The RCN were regular Navy men and officers; the RCNR were ex-merchant seamen or fishermen with sea experience; the RCNVRs were wartime only recruits, usually with no previous naval experience, unless they had been one of 1,300 in the "Pre-war" RCNVR.
RN	The British Royal Navy, used here to include its Reserves as well as the regular force, and refers to the organization as well as the people and their ships.
R/T	Radio telephone. The transmission of voice commands and reports by radio, different from W/T.
Snowflake	An illuminating rocket fired by merchantmen to hopefully expose surfaced U-boats.
SO or SOE	The senior officer of an escort group, responsible for his group of ships' tactical actions. Usually the CO of one of the ships, and a Commander, often from the Royal Navy due to their extensive experience.
Sono-buoy	An air-dropped sonar listening canister that transmitted to the parent aircraft any underwater sounds detected.
Squid mortar	A late war weapon development that fired one or three depth charge-sized "bombs" ahead of the attacking ship, like the Hedgehog, only set to explode at the submarine's depth.
TBS	Talk Between Ships: a short range VHF radio for tactical communications, usually bridge-to-bridge.
UK	The United Kingdom, including operational areas in England, Scotland and Northern Ireland.
ULTRA	The information produced from Bletchley Park's decryption of German radio traffic, *very* secret, and only passed to senior Commanders-in-Chief.
VCNS	Vice Chief of the Naval Staff, Ottawa. The Second-in-Command of the Navy.
WA	Western Approaches Command, in England, at Liverpool: The administrative command responsible for almost all of the (western) approaches naval and Air Force Coastal Command operations, defensive and offensive, from mid-Atlantic to the United Kingdom area.
WLEF	Western Local Escort Force, operating out of Halifax and responsible for convoying and defence off the Canadian coast, out to east of Newfoundland.
W/T	Wireless Telegraphy, usually taken to mean non-voice communication by radio morse code.

BIBLIOGRAPHY

PUBLISHED WORKS

Admiralty. *Navy Lists*. Various editions and years. London: HMSO.

Admiralty. *Manual of Seamanship,* Vols. 1 & 2. London: HMSO, 1932, 1937.

Alden, John D. *Flush Decks and Four Pipes.* Sea Power Monograph No. 2. Annapolis, MD: United States Naval Institute, 1965.

Barry, J.J. *Ships of the Great Lakes.* California: Howell North Books, 1973.

Bishop, Arthur. *Courage At Sea, Canada's Military Heritage,* Volume 3. Toronto: McGraw-Hill Ryerson, 1995.

Borrett, William C. *An East Coast Port; Tales Told Under the Old Town Clock.* Halifax: Imperial Publishing Co.,1944.

Borthwick, J.B. *History of the 29th Canadian MTB Flotilla.* Winnipeg: Naval Museum, 1991.

Brice, Martin H. *The Tribals.* London: Ian Allan, 1971.

Burrow, Len & Emile Beaudoin. *Unlucky Lady, The Life & Death of HMCS* ***Athabaskan****, 1940-44.* Stittsville, ON: Canada's Wings, Inc., 1982.

Butcher, Alan D. *I Remember* ***Haida***. Hantsport, NS: Lancelot Press, 1985.

Chance, Peter G. "Last Days of ***Skeena.***" Bulletin of the Chiefs & Petty Officers Assn. (November, 1990).

Chatterton Dickson, W.W.F. *Seedie's List of Submarine Awards for World War II.* Tisbury, Wilts.: Ripley Registers, 1990.

Chatterton Dickson, W.W.F. *Seedie's List of Coastal Forces Awards for World War II.* Tisbury, Wilts.: Ripley Registers, 1992.

Chesneau, Roger, ed. *Conway's All the World's Fighting Ships; 1922-1946.* New York: Mayflower Books Inc., 1980 (reprint).

Clark, Joseph A.P. *HMCS* ***Loch Achanalt****, A Memoir.* King City: Highwoods Prospect Publishers (privately published), 1995.

Clarkson, Robert. *Headlong Into The Sea.* Edinburgh: The Pentland Press, 1991.

Cunningham, Viscount of Hyndhope. *A Sailor's Odyssey.* London: Hutchinson & Co., 1951.

Department of National Defence. *The Canadian Navy List.* Various editions, 1929-1945. Ottawa: The King's Printer.

Donaldson, R.L. "Jimmy Hibbard's War." *Wings (Canada's Navy* edition, 1985): p.40-43. Calgary: Corvus Publishing Group.

Douglas, W.A.B. and Jürgen Rohwer. "The Most Thankless Task Revisited." *The RCN in Retrospect, 1910-1968*, edited by James A. Boutillier (1982): p.187, Vancouver: UBC Press.

Douglas, W.A.B., ed. *The RCN In Transition 1910-1985.* Vancouver: UBC Press, 1988.

Douglas, W.A.B. *The Creation of a National Air Force. The Official History of the RCAF.* Vol. 2. Toronto: U of T Press & DND. 1986. Vancouver: UBC Press, 1982.

Easton, Alan. *50 North; An Atlantic Battleground.* Toronto: The Ryerson Press, 1963.

Edge, William A. *First, The Navy. A collection of reminiscences and short stories.* Privately published, 1994.

English, John I. *Amazon to Ivanhoe*. Kendal, Cumbria: The World Ship Society, 1993.

English, John I. *The Hunts*. Kendal, Cumbria: The World Ship Society, 1987.

Essex, James W. *Victory in the St. Lawrence, Canada's Unknown War.* Erin, ON: Boston Mills Press, 1984.

Fisher, Robert C. "Canadian Merchant Ship Losses, 1939-1945." *The Northern Mariner/Le Marin du Nord.* Vol. 5 No. 3, (July, 1995). St. Johns: C.N.R.S.

Fraccaroli, Aldo. *Italian Warships of World War II.* London: Ian Allan, 1978.

Gentile, Gary. *Track of the Gray Wolf; U-Boat Warfare on the U.S. Eastern Seabord 1942-1945.* New York: Avon Books, 1989.

German, Tony. *The Sea Is At Our Gates, The History of the Canadian Navy.* Toronto: McClelland & Stewart, 1990.

Gould, Grant A. "Thirty Were Missing" *The Journal of the Canadian Medical Services.* Vol. 3, No. 1, (November, 1945). Ottawa: Government of Canada Medical Services.

Greenhous, Brereton, S.J. Harris, W.C. Johnston and W.G.P. Rawling. *The Crucible of War 1939-1945; The Official History of the RCAF.* Vol. 3. Toronto: U of T Press and DND, 1994.

Gregory, Walter. *Memories of H.M.C.S.* ***Trentonian****, Alias K368; Trenton's Own Ship*. Trenton, Ont.: Branch 110 Trenton Royal Canadian Legion, ca. 1979.

Gröner, Erich; Revision Eds: Dieter Jung and Martin Maas. *German Warships, 1815-1945.* Vol. 1, *Major Surface Vessels.* Annapolis, MD.: US Naval Institute Press, 1990.

Gröner, Erich; Revision Eds: Dieter Jung and Martin Maas. *German Warships, 1815-1945.* Vol. 2, *U-Boats and Mine Warfare Vessels.* London: Conway Maritime Press, 1991.

HMSO. *British Vessels Lost At Sea 1939-45.* Cambridge: Patrick Stephens, 1976 (reprint).

Hacking, Norman R., and W. Kaye Lamb, *The Princess Story; A Century and a Half of West Coast Shipping.* Vancouver: Mitchell Press, 1974.

Hadley, Michael L. *U-Boats Against Canada, German Submarines in Canadian Waters.* Montreal and Kingston: McGill-Queens' University Press, 1985.

Hague, Arnold. *The Towns.* Kendal, Cumbria: The World Ship Society, 1988.

Halford, Robert G. *The Unknown Navy. Canada's World War II Merchant Navy.* St. Catharines, ON: Vanwell Publishing, 1995.

Harbron, John D. *The Longest Battle; The RCN in the Atlantic 1939-1945.* St. Catharines, ON: Vanwell Publishing, 1993.

Hennessy, R.L. "And All Our Joints Were Limber. Sub-Lieutenant to Commanding Officer - Same Ship." *Salty Dips*, Vol. 2, p. 1, edited by J.A.M. Lynch. Ottawa: NOAC Ottawa Branch, 1985.

Herzog, Bodo. *Deutsche U-Boote 1906-1966.* Erlangen, Germany: Karl Müller Verlag, 1993.

Hodges, Peter. *Tribal Class Destroyers.* London: Altmark Publications Co., 1971.

Hogan, Margaret. *Esso Mariners, A History of Imperial Oil's Fleet Operations From 1899-1980.* Toronto: Imperial Oil, 1980.

How, Douglas. *Night of the Caribou.* Hantsport, NS: Lancelot Press, 1988.

Hoyt, Edwin P. *The Death of the U-Boats.* Toronto: McGraw-Hill Book Co., 1988.

Jenson, L.B. "The Sinking of HMCS Ottawa." *This Was My War: Memories of the 1939-1945 Conflict,* edited by Ian Maxwell. Tantallon, NS: Defence Research and Education Centre, 1992.

Johnston, Mac. *Corvettes Canada, Convoy Veterans of WWII Tell Their True Stories.* Toronto and Montreal: McGraw-Hill Ryerson, 1994.

Jones, Basil. *And So To Battle; A Sailor's Story.* Privately published, ca. 1977.

Keatts, Henry. *Field Guide to Sunken U-Boats.* Kings Point, NY: American Merchant Marine Museum Press, 1987.

Keene, Tony. *The Ship That Voted No and Other Stories of Ships and the Sea.* Hantsport, NS: Lancelot Press, 1995.

Krancke, Theodore, and H.J. Brennecke. *Pocket Battleship; The story of the Admiral Scheer.* New York: Berkley Publishing Co., 1958.

Lamb, James B. *On The Triangle Run.* Toronto: Macmillan of Canada, 1986.

Lamb, James B. *The Corvette Navy; True Stories From Canada's Atlantic War.* Toronto: Macmillan of Canada, ca. 1977.

Lamb, W. Kaye. *Empress To The Orient.* Vancouver: Vancouver Maritime Museum Society, 1991.

Law, C. Anthony. *White Plumes Astern; The Short, Daring Life of Canada's MTB Flotilla.* Halifax: Nimbus Publishing, 1989.

Lawrence, H.E.T. (Hal). *A Bloody War; One Man's Memories of the Canadian Navy 1939-45.* Toronto: Macmillan of Canada, 1979.

Lawrence, H.E.T. (Hal). *Tales Of The North Atlantic.* Toronto: McClelland and Stewart, 1985.

Lawrence, H.E.T. (Hal). *Victory At Sea; Tales of His Majesty's Coastal Forces.* Toronto: McClelland and Stewart, 1989.

Lay, Horatio Nelson. *Memoirs of a Mariner.* Stittsville, Ont.: Privately published, 1982.

Lenton, H.T. *Navies of the Second World War, German Submarines.* Vols. 1 and 2. London: Macdonald & Co., 1965.

Lenton, H.T. *Navies of the Second World War, British Fleet and Escort Destroyers.* Vols. 1 and 2. London: Macdonald & Co., 1970.

Lenton, H.T. *German Surface Vessels.* Vols. 1 and 2. London: Macdonald & Co., 1966.

Lenton, H.T., and J.J. College. *Warships of WW II.* London: Ian Allan, 1973.

Lloyd's *Register of Merchant Shipping*. London. 1941-42.

MacBeth, Jack. *Ready, Aye, Ready; An Illustrated History of the Royal Canadian Navy.* Toronto: Key Porter Books, 1989.

MacFarlane, John. *Notes No.4.* Victoria: Maritime Museum, 1993.

MacIntyre, Donald. *The Battle of the Atlantic.* London: B.T. Batsford, 1961.

Macpherson, Ken R. *Frigates of the Royal Canadian Navy, 1943-1974.* St. Catharines, ON: Vanwell Publishing, 1989.

Macpherson, Ken R. *The River Class Destroyers of the Royal Canadian Navy.* Toronto: Charles J. Musson & Associates, 1985.

Macpherson, Ken R. *Minesweepers of the Royal Canadian Navy, 1938-1945.* St. Catharines, ON: Vanwell Publishing, 1990.

Macpherson, Ken R., and John Burgess. *The Ships of Canada's Naval Forces, 1910-1981, A Complete pictorial history of Canadian warships.* Toronto: Collins Publishers, 1981.

Macpherson, Ken R., and John Burgess. *The Ships of Canada's Naval Forces, 1910-1981, A Complete pictorial history of Canadian warships.* St. Catharines: Vanwell Publishing, 1983.

Macpherson, Ken R., and Marc Milner. *Corvettes of the Royal Canadian Navy, 1939-1945.* St. Catharines, ON: Vanwell Publishing, 1993.

McKee, Fraser M. *HMCS* ***Swansea****, The Life and Times of a Frigate.* St. Catharines, ON: Vanwell Publishing, 1994.

McKee, Fraser M. *The Armed Yachts of Canada.* Erin, ON: Boston Mills Press, 1983.

McMurtrie, Francis E., ed. *Jane's Fighting Ships.* 1939, 1941 editions. London: Samson Low Marston & Co. 1944-45 edition, Toronto Macmillan of Canada.

Metson, Graham. *An East Coast Port.* Toronto: McGraw-Hill Ryerson, 1981.

Milner, Marc. *North Atlantic Run, The Royal Canadian Navy and the Battle for the Convoys.* Toronto: University of Toronto Press, 1985.

Milner, Marc. *The U-Boat Hunters; The Royal Canadian Navy and the Offensive against Germany's Submarines.* Toronto: University of Toronto Press, 1994.

Musk, George. *Canadian Pacific Afloat, 1883-1968.* London: Canadian Pacific Steamships, 1968.

Starshell. Various editors and editions (1980-1995). Naval Officers Association of Canada.

Nolan, Brian, and Brian Jeffrey Street. *Champagne Navy; Canada's Small Boat Raiders of the Second World War.* Toronto: Random House, 1991.

Noli, Jean. *Les Loups de l'Amiral; Les sous-marins allemande dans la bataille de l'atlantique.* Paris: Fayard, 1970.

O'Connor, Edward. The Corvette Years, The Lower Deck Story. Vancouver: Cordillera Publishing Co., 1995.

Paquette, Edward R., and Charles G. Bainbridge, *Honours and Awards, Canadian Naval Forces, World War II.* Victoria: Project Gallantry, privately published, nd.

Parker, Mike. *Running the Gauntlet, An Oral History of Canadian Merchant Seamen in World War II.* Halifax: Nimbus Publishing, 1994.

Pollina, Paolo M., and Marcello Bertini, *I Sommergibili Italiani 1895-1968; Ufficio Storico Della Marina Militare.* Rome: Luglio,1968.

Parsons, Robert. *Stories of the Forgotten Coast.* Grand Bank: Robert Parsons, 1995.

Pullen, T.C. "Convoy ON-127 & The Loss of HMCS Ottawa, 13 September, 1942: A Personal Reminiscence." The Northern Mariner/Le Marin du Nord. Vol. 2, No.2. April 1992. St. John's: C.N.R.S.

Reader's Digest. *The Canadians at War 1939/45.* 3 Vols. Montreal. 1971.

Reid, Max. *DEMS At War!* Ottawa: Commoners' Publishing Society Inc., 1990.

Revely, Henry. *The Convoy That Nearly Died; The Story of ONS-154.* London: William Kimber, 1979.

Richards, S.T. *Operation Sick Bay. The Story of the Sick Berth & Medical Assistant Branch of the Royal Canadian Navy, 1910-1965.* Vancouver: Centaur Publishing, 1994.

Roberts, Leslie. *Canada And The War At Sea.* Vol. 2 of *Canada's War At Sea.* Montreal: Alvah M. Beatty, 1944.

Robertson, Terrence. *Walker, RN; The Story of Captain Frederic John Walker, CB, DSO & three Bars, RN.* London: Evans Brothers, 1956.

Rohwer, Jürgen. *Axis Submarine Successes, 1939-1945.* Cambridge: Patrick Stephens, 1983.

Roscoe, Theodore, and Thomas L. Wattles. *United States Destroyer Operations In World War II.* Annapolis, MD: United States Naval Institute, 1953.

Roskill, S.W. *The War At Sea 1939-1945.* Vols. 1 to 3. London: HMSO, 1954-1961.

Schull, Joseph. *The Far Distant Ships.* Ottawa: Minister of National Defence/The King's Printer, 1950.

Sclater, William. ***Haida.*** Toronto: Oxford University Press, ca. 1946.

Shawiningan Lake School, eds. *Shawiningan And The War.* Victoria, n.d.

Shelley, C.R. "HMCS ***Prince Robert***: The Career of an Armed Merchant Cruiser." *Canadian Military History* (Spring, 1995).

Showell, Jak P. Mallman. *U-Boat Command and the Battle of the Atlantic.* St. Catharines, ON: Vanwell Publishing, 1989.

Smith, Peter C. *Hold The Narrow Sea; Naval Warfare in the English Channel 1939-1945.* Ashbourne, Derbyshire: Moorland Publishing Co.; Annapolis: Naval Institute Press, 1984.

Smith, Peter C. *Pedestal.* London: Crecy Books, 1994.

Swettenham, John. *Canada's Atlantic War.* Toronto: Samuel-Stevens, 1979.

Tarrant, V.E. *The U-Boat Offensive, 1914-1945.* London: Arms & Armour Press, 1989.

Terraine, John. *The U-Boat Wars; 1916-1945.* New York: Putnam, 1989.

Tucker, Gilbert N. *The Naval Service of Canada.* Vols. 1 & 2. Ottawa: Minister of National Defence/The King's Printer, 1952.

Turner, Robert D. *The Pacific Princesses; An Illustrated History of Canadian Pacific Railway's Princess Fleet on the Canadian Northwest Coast.* Victoria: Sono Nis Press, 1977.

Unger, Issac. ***Skeena** Aground.* Privately published, 1992.

van der Vat, Dan. *The Atlantic Campaign; World War II's Great Struggle at Sea.* New York: Harper & Row, 1988.

Venier, Mark Richard. *Ready, The Brave; A Chronicle in the Wake of HMCS **Huron.*** Vol. 1 (1943-46). Woodstock, ON: The HMCS ***Huron*** Assn., 1989.

Vulliez, Albert, and Jacques Mordal. *Battleship **Scharnhorst**.* London: Hutchinson & Co., 1958.

Watt, Frederick B. *In All Respects Ready; The Merchant Navy and the Battle of the Atlantic, 1940-1945.* Scarborough, ON: Prentice-Hall Canada, 1985.

Whitby, Michael J. "Fooling Around The French Coast: The RCN Tribal Class Destroyers in Action - April 1944." *Canadian Defence Quarterly* (Dec. 1989).

Whitley, M.J. *Destroyer! German Destroyers In World War II.* London and Harrisburg, PA: Arms And Armour Press, 1983.

Whitley, M.J. *Destroyers of World War Two.* Annapolis, MD: Naval Institute Press, 1988.

Whitley, M.J. *German Coastal Forces of World War Two.* London: Arms And Armour Press, 1992.

Wilcox, Garnet, & Skip Gillham, *The Ships of Upper Lakes Shipping.* St. Catharines, ON: Riverbank Traders, 1994.

Williams, Jack. *They Led The Way, The Fleet Minesweepers at Normandy, June, 1944.* Blackpool, England: Privately published, 1994.

Winser, John de S. *The D-Day Ships.* Kendal, Cumbria: World Ship Society, 1994.

Winton, John. *Convoy; The Defence of Sea Trade, 1890-1990.* London: Michael Joseph, 1983.

Y'Blood, W.T. *Hunter Killer; U.S. Escort Carriers in the Battle of the Atlantic.* Annapolis, MD: Naval Institute Press, 1983.

Young, John. *A Dictionary of Ships of the Royal Navy of the Second World War.* Cambridge: Patrick Stephens, 1975.

UNPUBLISHED MATERIAL

Directorate of History, Department of National Defence. Research files for all RCN ships, plus some material on Canadian merchant ships, U-boats and open personal files.

Kew. Public Record Office. Shipping Casualty Section, Trade Division. Interviews of merchant ship survivors (SCS Int).

Ministry of Defence. Foreign Documents (History Department). R.M. Coppock research notes.

National Archives of Canada. Series RG 24. RCN ships; events (Collisions & groundings; Boards of Inquiry; COAC, FOAC, FONF, etc. files and reports).

RCMP Historical Branch and quarterly magazine.

PERSONAL PAPERS and INTERVIEWS

Material was obtained from research notes, diaries, collected personal recollections of more than a few pages, or from extensive interviews with the following:

Campbell, Craig
Chance, Peter G.
Charles,John A.
Davis, E.M.
Dickinson, Neville S.C.
Freeman, Cable
Goodeve, A.G.
Hanbury, Ross M.
Hennessy, Ralph L.
Manuel, Terence C.
Marston, Joseph C.
Nixon, Patrick C.
Quinn, Howard, L.
Tate, C. Ian P.
van der Linden, Fr. Peter

INDEX OF PERSONS

Ranks are those held at the time; with the shortage of staff in DHist it has not always been possible to determine or check the service (RCN, RCNR or RCNVR) of Canadian ratings. KM = Kriegsmarine

NAME	RANK	SERVICE	CHAPTER
Adams, John	LCdr	USN	36
Allan, J.A.R.	Lt	RCNVR	8,61
Angus, E.J.	LCdr	RCNR	51
Archer, E.R	Capt	RN	1
Arnold, Gordon	AB		33
Ashmore, George	AB	RCNVR	14
Astor, Vincent	Mr.		7
Atkins, .	SLt	RNVR	29
Atherton, .	LS		56
Aubrey, R.M.	Cdr	RN	63
Ayre, A.	LCdr	RNR	14
Bakker, Jan	Capt	MN	10
Balfry, C.P.	LCdr	RCNR	53
Barber, .	Lt	RN	1
Bark, Wilfred	S/Lt	RCNVR	25
Barr, Rudolph	KL	KM	29
Barrett, R.D.	LCdr	RCNR	41
Barriault, .	Stwd.		19
Bateman, Cecil	SBA	RCNVR	18
Bathurst, Jack	Lt	RN	37
Baulne, Emile	AB	RCNVR	41
Beadon, Richard	Capt	MN	30
Beament, Harold	LCdr	RCNVR	21
Beaudoin, Emile	Tel	RCNVR	9
Beck, G.A.	Lt	RCNVR	20
Bell, Ian H.	A/LCdr	RCNVR	50
Berger, Joachim	KL	KM	26
Bernays, M.L.	A/CPO	RCNR	14
Berry, Peter	S/Lt	RCNVR	47
Betts, Roy	AB		43
Birch, J.D.	Cdr	RNR	33
Black, .	AB	RN	1
Blanchard, Henry	Lt	RCNVR	51
Blische, Heinz	OL	KM	34
Boehmer, Wolfgang	OL	KM	36
Bonner, J. Willard	Lt	RCNR	18
Boulton, A.G.	LCdr	RCNVR	47, 49
Boyle, D.S.	S/Lt	RCN	34
Bradley, J.R.	Lt	RCNVR	51,59
Briggs, W.E.S.	A/Cdr	RCNR	8,53
Brock, John	LCdr	RCNVR	61
Brown, David	S/Lt	RCNVR	41
Brown, W.I.	Sto.1	RCN	8
Browne, V.	A/Cdr	RCNVR	61
Budge, Patrick D.	Lt	RCN	39
Burgess, .	CPO	RCN	14
Burnett, P.	Cdr	RN	34
Butchart, A.A.	PO	RCN	13
Byron, John	Cdr	RNR	35,41
Campbell A.C.	A/LCdr	RCNVR	56
Campbell, H.C.	Lt	RCNVR	56
Campbell, W.F.	LCdr	RCNVR	13,23
Candy, G.W.	CPO	RCN	47
Carey, T.C.	Seaman		7
Cassivi, A.H.	Lt	RCNR	1
Cavenaugh, Vernon	OS		24
Chaffey, Charles	Lt	RCNVR	46
Chance, P.G.	Lt	RCN	54,57
Chandler, W.	Sto.PO	RCNR	10
Chandler, W.R.	Skpr	RCNR	6
Charles, J.C.	Lt	RCN	23
Charrier, Joseph	LS	RCN	10
Churchill, Winston	PRIME MINISTER		12,14
Clark, Joe A.P.	Lt	RCNVR	53
Clark, N.V.	Cdr	RCNR	56
Clayton, J.E.	Lt	RCNR	20,26
Coates, Bill	AB	RCNVR	18
Coates, John	Lt		44
Coleman, A.R.E.	LCdr	RCNR	21
Collings, .	Lt		19
Coppock, Robert	Mr.	MoD	27
Costello, E.	LS	RCNVR	14
Coughlin, C.R.	LCdr	RCNVR	34
Cowan, Peter	Lt	RCNVR	22
Cramp, W.J.	Sto.PO		48
Creaser, S.K.	Skpr	RCNR	1
Creba, Glen	Lt	RCNVR	46
Creery, W.B.	Cdr	RCN	2,30
Culley, K.B.	Lt	RCNVR	15,28
Cumming, L.G.	A/LCdr	RCNVR	30
Cummings, W.D.	Sto.		40
Cunningham, A.B.	Adm	RN	21
Curteis, A.T.B.	VAdm	RN	2
Czygan, Werner	KK	KM	25
Dalison, John	Cdr	RN	37
Daly, C.F. PO	Cook	RCNVR	14
Danckworth, D.	LtzS	KM	21,22
Dauter, Helmut	OL	KM	37
Davenport, W.	LCdr	RCNR	52
Davies, Fred	AB	RCNVR	53
Davies. J.H.B.	Lt	RCNR	30
Davis, E.M.	Lt	RCNVR	62
Davis, James S.	LCdr	RCNVR	62
Dawson, A.E.	Sto		48
Dawson, Lloyd	Radar Mech.	RCNVR	61
Deetz, F.	KL	KM	32
Denny, L.P.	LCdr	RCNR	28,57
Dery, Stan	Lt	RCNVR	57
Dery, Mrs.			57
Devonshire, George	AB		33
DeWolf, H.G.	Cdr/Capt	RCN	40,42,43,44
Dickinson,N.S.C.	LCdr	RCNVR	52
Dicks, .	PO		62
Dill, Sir John	FM		21
Dobson, A.N.	LCdr	RCNR	12,26 29
Donald, C.D.	Cdr	RCN	19
Douty, R.P.J.	Lt	RCNVR	64
Draney, R.W.	LCdr	RCNR	36
Duchesne, Julien	CPO	RCN	10

NAME	RANK	SERVICE	CHAPTER
Dunn, J.A.	A/Cdr	RCNVR	31
Dunn, J.B.	Capt	USN	36
Dyer, K.L.	A/LCdr	RCN	13
Easton, A.H.	Lt/LCdr	RCNR	13,43
Egerton, W.de M.	VAdm	RN	20
Emberley, P.	ERA	RCNR	47
Englemann, K-E.	KK	KM	27
English, D.T.	LCdr	RCNR	41
Evans, .	Cdr	RN	29
Evans, P.R.C.	Surg Lt	RNVR	25
Fellows, F.G.	F/L	RCAF	38
Fiorentini, Leone	Lt	It.N.	24
Findeisen, .	KL	KM	57
Finlay, Paul	Lt	RCNVR	56
Fish, R.W.	Lt	USCG	30
Fisher, W.	Sto	RCNVR	29
Fitzgerald, J.L.	Surg Lt	RCNVR	53
Forster, H-J.	OL	KM	50
Forster, Hugo,	KK	KM	8
Fortune, M.J.T.	PO		33
Fox, Ed	AB	RCNVR	19
Foxall, L.L.	A/LCdr	RCNR	20
Fraser, G.G.	Lt	RCNVR	10
Fraser, James P.	LCdr	RCNR	33
Fraser, W.R.	L/SBA	RCNVR	58
Freeland, Harry	LCdr	RCNR	24
Freeman, Cable	AB	RCNVR	59
Frubrick, Hermann	MR/GEF	KM	35
Gall, R. F.	Seaman		52
Galpin, Dick	Surg Lt	RCNVR	53
Garland, John	AB	RCNVR	18
Garrard, W.A.B.	Lt	RCNVR	25
German, Barry	Cdr	RCN	18
Gilding, C.W.	Lt	RCNVR	9
Gillick, John	Coder	RCNVR	26
Gillis, D.E.	CPO	RNR	7
Glassco, C.S.	Lt	RCNVR	60
Golby, T.M.W.	LCdr	RCNR	25
Gosnell, Henry	L/S	RCN	39
Gough, A.E.	A/LCdr	RCNR	56
Gould, G.A.	Surg Lt	RCNVR	48
Grant, George	AB	RCNVR	46
Groos, David W.	A/LCdr/LCdr	RCN	2,43,49
Groos, H.V.W.	A/LCdr	RCN	2,34,47,49
Grubb, F.E.	Lt	RCN	8
Guilford, T.K.	AB	RCNVR	7
Haagenson, L.P.A.	L/S	RCNVR	51
Hadrill, P.G.	Lt	RCNVR	47
Hanbury, Ross M.	LCdr	RCNVR	63
Hanington, D.L.	S/Lt	RCNVR	13
Hannam, Jack	AB		32
Harrington, J.E.	LCdr	RCNVR	57
Harrison, W.E.	LCdr	RCNR	60
Harney, Klaus	KL	KM	16
Hart, R.W.	A/LCdr	RCNVR	53
Hartwig, Paul	KL	KM	17,18
Hatrick, R.G.	S/Lt	RCNVR	9,21
Heisil, P.	Herr	KM	57
Henderson, J.G.	L/Sig		30
Henderson, J.J.	Lt	RCNR	20
Hennessy, R.	Lt	RCN	14

NAME	RANK	SERVICE	CHAPTER
Herwatz, Wolfgang	KL	KM	61
Haywood, Stan	L/S		24
Hibbard, J.C.	LCdr	RCN	8,43
Hill, H.K.	A/LCdr	RCNVR	31
Hinz, Rudolph	OL	KM	60
Hird, Thomas	Coder	RCNVR	25
Hodgkinson, J.J.	Lt	RCNR	16
Hoffman, Eberhard	KL	KM	17,18
Hoffner, N.V.	L/S	RCNVR	59
Holman, V.H.	AB	RCN	4
Hornbostel, K.	KL	KM	56
Hornsby, C.H.	Lt	RCNR	3
Horton, Sir Max	Adm	RN	34,47,63
Howe, C.D.	Minister M&S		7
Howitt, David	Lt	RCNVR	53
Hubbard, J.W.	Mr.		7
Hughes, J.W.	AB	RCNVR	59
Hurst, Allen	C/ERA	RCNR	24
Hurtubise, A.J.	L/S	RCNVR	37
Irvine, C.E.	Surg Lt	RCNVR	41
Ites, Otto	KL	KM	15
19			
Jenkins, Ivor	Mr. & Mrs.		48
Jenson, L.B.	Lt	RCN	19
Johnson, K.L	LCdr	RCNVR	56
Jones, Basil	Cdr/A/Capt	RN	39,40,42,43
Jones, G.C.	Cmdr	RCN	1,30
Jones, L.T.	Gnr(T)	RCN	19
Jones, W.J.	Lt	RCNR	55
Kappen, Gert	OL	KM	56
Kazakoff, Mike	S/Lt	RCNVR	64
Kelbling, Gerd	KL	KM	14
Kelpin, Kenneth	AB	RCNVR	54
Kent, D.A.	A/CPO	RCN	21
Kentrat, E-F.	KL	KM	9
Kerwin, M.R.	AB	RCNVR	14
Kidd, W.M.	Lt	RCN	54
Killam, David	Lt	RCNVR	46
King, C.A.	Cdr	RCNR	15,35,37,38,57
Kinsman, Burnley	Lt	RCNVR	60
Kirkpatrick,J.R.H.	LCdr	RCNVR	43,46,58
Kohlauf, .	KK	KM	39
Kosbadt, H-C.	OL	KM	21
Kreschmer, Otto	KK	KM	8
Kruschka, Max	OL	KM	49
Lade, H.E.	Lt	RCNR	18
Landles, A.D.	Lt	RCNR	13
Lay, H.N.	LCdr	RCN	2
Landymore, W.M.	Lt	RCN	4
Lange, K-H.	KL	KM	48
Law, C.A.	A/LCdr	RCNVR	46,58
Lawrence, H.E.T.	S/Lt	RCNVR	15
Layard, A.F.C.	Cdr	RN	35,38,51,59
Lees, D.M.	Capt	RN	2
Lemcke, Rudolph	KL	KM	14
Leslie, W.L.	Surg Lt	RCNVR	58
Liabo, H.V.	C/ERA	RCNR	51
Lincoln, J.H.	Lt		33
Lipton, John	CPO		44
Loeder, .	OL	KM	59
Longbottom, A.	ERA	RCNVR	34

NAME	RANK	SERVICE	CHAPTER
MacAulay, Ray	AB	RCNVR	18
MacBeth, Jack	Lt	RCNVR	63
MacDonald, Ian	Lt	RCNVR	37
MacDonald, J.H.S.	A/LCdr	RCNR	10
MacDonald,R.M.	Surg Lt	RCNVR	53
MacKay, T.C.	Lt	RCN	35
MacMillan, R.C.	Lt	RCNVR	64
MacNeil, R.A.S.	LCdr	RCNR	11
MacRae, Montye	Mr.		17
MacRitchie, Peter	Lt(SB)	RCNVR	31
McCallum, Archie	SURG Capt	RCNVR	13
McClure, W.A.	L/S	RCN	40
McConnell, Russ	S/Lt	RCNVR	17
McFadyen, Bill	Sto	RCNVR	18
McGaw, Dorn	AB	RCNVR	25
McIntosh, Chas.	Lt	RCNR	30,59
McIsaac, Wilfred	LCdr	RCNVR	27
McKillop, A.M.	Cdr	RN	43
McLaren, Joe	AB	RCNVR	59
McLean, Donald	OS	RCNVR	22
McLean, T.B.	Surg Lt	RCN	4
McMullin, T.A.	AB	RCNVR	51
McWhinnie, A.J.	Mr.		26
Mainguy, D.N.	VAdm	RCN	5
Mainguy, E.R.	Capt	RCN	5,10
Malone, T.D.H.	AB	RCNVR	48
Mannix, George	Sig(TO)	RCNVR	42
Marienfeld, F-W.	OL	KM	55
Marr, F.B.	Lt	RCNVR	24
Marshall, Barney	Lt	RCNVR	46
Marshall, J.	OS	RCNVR	30
Marston, J.C.	S/Lt	RCNR	11
Martin, Gerald	Tel.	RCNVR	18
Martin, Trevor	AB	RCNVR	24
Matschulat, G.	OL	KM	51
Maxwell, W.W.	C/ERA	RCNR	20,26
Meyrick, K.W.M.	Lt	RN	7
Miles, G.R.	Capt	RCN	40
Miller, D.L.	Lt	RCNVR	21
Miller, S.F.	AB	RCN	21
Mills, L.	ERA	RCN	13
Milsom, P.S.	Lt	RCNVR	25
Mitchell, John	ERA	RCNR	21
Monechi, Paolo	LCdr	It.N.	22
Montgomery, Joe	AB	RCNVR	18
Moors, G.M.	Lt	RCNVR	18
Morgan, F. J.	L.Sig	RCNR	10
Morrison, J.R.	S/Lt	RCNVR	30
Mortimer, Henry	AB	RCNVR	24
Mossman, D.S.	Lt	RCNR	7
Mountbatten, Lord L.	VAdm	RN	21
Munro, William	S/Lt	RCNVR	56
Murray, H.P.	PO	RCN	40
Murray, L.W.	RAdm	RCN	1,8, 9,11,30
Murray, L.W.	L.Sig	RCNVR	25
Musgrave, John	F/L	RCAF	28
Nares, G.P.	Lt	RCNVR	33
Nickel, Waldemar	LtzS	KM	33
Nixon, C.P.	A/LCdr	RCN	34,47,49,54
Noble, Sir Percy	Adm	RN	5
O'Brien, J.B.	LCdr	RCNVR	31

NAME	RANK	SERVICE	CHAPTER
O'Hara, I.W.	OS	RCNVR	7
Oldorp, .	KK	KM	12
Oneschuk, Wm.	L/SBA	RCNVR	48
Osborne, F.V.	Lt	RAN	11
Otto, P-F.	KL	KM	29
Paddon, Richard	Lt	RCNVR	46
Palmer, P.E.	L/Sig.		2
Pattie, Donald	Lt	USN	36
Pavillard, L.R.	Lt	RCNR	32
Percy, J.L.	Lt	RCNVR	20
Petersen, Charles	LCdr	RCNR	41
Petrie, W.	L/Coder	RCNVR	56
Phillips, .	PO		1
Pickard, A.F.	A/LCdr	RCNR	34
Piers, D.W.	LCdr	RCN	43,64
Portree, Donald	C/ERA	RCN	14
Powell, A.J.	Sto.PO	RCN	15
Prentice. J.D.	Cdr	RCN	3, 6, 8, 47, 49, 54
Price, John	Lt	RCNR	10
Pullen, H.F.	A/Cdr	RCN	9
Pullen, T.C.	Lt	RCN	19
Quinn, H.L.	LCdr	RCNVR	61,63
Racker, Lionel	ERA	RCNVR	48
Radford, Jack	Lt	RCNR	48
Rahe, K-H.	KL	KM	33
Rathbone, J.G.M.	SA	RCNVR	48
Rathgeb, C.I.	Lt	RCNVR	34
Rayner, H.S.	LCdr	RCN	10,39,42,45
Read, L.G.	S/Lt	RNVR	48
Reid, J.W.	AB	RCNVR	21
Reith, Edwin	OL	KM	64
Renaud, R.	ERA	RCNR	13
Rickard, J.H.	AB		33
Rodig, Johannes	KL	KM	62
Roosevelt, F.D.	President	USA	14
Ross, Phillip S.	Mr.		7
Roy, J.W.R.	Cdr	RCN	7
Rowe, Gordon	L/S	RCNVR	43
Royds, Wm.	L/S	RCNVR	51,59
Rumpel, Oscar	Lt	RCNVR	62
Ruppelt, Gunther	OL	KM	20
Rush, Fred	AB	RCNVR	18
Russ, .	AB	RCNVR	41
Russell, B.T.R.	Lt	RCNR	62
Russell, P.F.X.	A/LCdr/LCdr	RCN	4,54,43
Rutherford, C.A.	LCdr	RCN	19
Salsiccioli, P.P.	C/ERA	RCN	47
Saulnier, Joe	AB	RCNVR	24,48
Schaefer, W.A.	KK	KM	52
Schauenburg, Rolf	KL	KM	31
Schroeteler, H.	KL	KM	48
Schuneman, Horst	KL	KM	49
Scott, Graham	S/Lt	RCNVR	15
Seymour, E.P.	Sto PO	RCNR	59
Shadforth, H.G.	LCdr	RCNR	11
Sharpe, J.A.	AB	RCN	10
Shelley, Wm.	AB	RCNVR	25
Sheppard, Louis	Lt	RNR	7
Sieder, Heinz	OL	KM	49
Sigurdsson, Einar	Mr.		54

NAME	RANK	SERVICE	CHAPTER
Simmons, E.T.	Lt	RCNVR	8,22,63
Simpson, G.W.G.	Cmdr	RN	47,63
Sinclair, E.N.	LCdr	RN	45
Skillen, Rod	AB	RCNVR	19
Skinner, E.G.	Cdr	RCNR	17
Skinner, Jack	L/S	RCNVR	22
Slavin, J.V.	OS	RCNVR	7
Smith, J.N.	LCdr	RCNR	17
Smith, Percy	L/S	RCN	14
Spence, Wm.	C/ERA	RCNVR	8
Stacey, W.R.	A/LCdr	RCNR	51,59
Stannard, L.A.	AB	RCNVR	59
Starr, John	Sig	RCNVR	34
Stephen, George	LCdr	RCNR	9,35,52
Stephenson, Thomas	AB		33
Stoner, B.M.	AB		33
Storey, John	Lt(E)	RCNVR	41
Struckmann, H.	OL	KM	49
Struebing, .	OL	KM	63
Stubbs, J.H.	LCdr	RCN	14,39,40
Styles, G.M.	L/Sto	RCNVR	59
Tate, C.Ian P.	Lt	RCNVR	41
Taylor, T.	A/Cdr	RN	12
Terrabassi, Terry	AB	RCNVR	19
Terry, .	Sto.PO		26
Thomas, Roddick	Lt	RCNVR	24
Thorne, Charles	Mr.	USA	17
Timbrell, R.W.	S/Lt/Lt	RCN	4,47,49
Tingley, Hall W.	Lt	RCNVR	23
Tobin, H.E.	Sig	RCNVR	8
Todeus, .	AB	RCN	2
Tucker, Gilbert	Dr.	DND	14
Tuke, D.W.	S/Lt(E)	RCNVR	30
Turner, S.A.	Tel	RCNVR	40
Tyrwhitt, St. J.	Cdr	RN	39

NAME	RANK	SERVICE	CHAPTER
Van Clief, Ray	Mr.	USA	17
Vogel, Victor	KL	KM	13
Voigt, H.	OL	KM	53
von Mannstein, M.	KK	KM	28
Vyse, Donald	AB		31
Walker, F.J.	Capt	RN	14,37
Walkerling, H.	KL	KM	19
Wallace, D.C.	A/Cdr	RCNR	13
Warburton, R.W.	A/CPO	RCNR	51
Warren, Jake	Lt	RCNVR	41
Watson, Alan	Lt	RCNVR	39
Watson, J.M.	A/LCdr	RCNR	35
Watson, K.W.	OS	RCN	14
Weber, Werner	KL	KM	35
Whittemore, T.W.	ERA	RCNVR	59
Wilkinson, W.A.	LCdr	RCNVR	61
Willett, J.A.	L.Sto.		23
Williams, B.E.	AB	RCNVR	56
Williams, F.R.	A/Lt	RCNVR	50
Willson, W.H.	A/LCdr	RCN	47,49
Wilson, .	S/Lt	RCNVR	19
Wilson, David	Sto PO	RCN	15
Wilson, Norman	AB	RCN	19
Windeyer, Guy	LCdr	RCN	10,13,20
Winn, J.W.	A/CPO	RCNR	24
Wood, Tom	Mr.		28
Wurtele, Alfred	A/Cdr	RCN	10
Zander, Joachim	KL	KM	38
Zeplien, Walter	OL	KM	44
Zimmermann, E.	KL	KM	41
Zimmermann, H.	KL	KM	11

INDEX OF PERSONS FOR CHAPTER 65

Magog:
- Doughty, T.S. Master
- Kretchmer, Otto, KK KM
- Redfern, Frank Mr.

Thorold:
- Doucan, J. Gunner RA

Kenordoc:
- Kerr, D. 1st Officer
- Barker, E.T. Wireless Op

Trevisa:
- Endrass, E. KL KM
- Kretschmer, KK KM
- Schepke, J. KL KM

Canadian Cruiser:
- McArthur, W.H. OS

J.B. White:
- Kretschmer, KK KM
- Macintyre, Donald Capt RN

Canadolite:
- Detmers, Theo. Capt KM
- Ferns, Thomas Master

Lady Hawkins:
- Giffin, Huntly Master
- Kelly, Percy, 1st Officer
- Zapp, Richard KK KM

Lady Drake:
- Kelly, Percy Master

Empress of Asia:
- Smith, J.B. Master
- Smith, Donald Chief Eng.
- Johnson, Leonard 1st Officer

Victolite:
- Reid, Roy Eng. Officer

George L. Torian:
- Stillwell, James Watchman
- Clausen, N. KK KM

Lennox:
- Achilles, A. KK KM
- Clausen, N. KK KM

Robert. W. Pomeroy:
- Freyett, J.M. Master
- Butler, John Gunner RA

Vineland:
- Kolle, W. KK KM

Mont Louis:
- Bowen, Walter Master
- Covey, Warren Chief Eng.

Calgarolite:
- Mountain, Tom Master

Frank. B. Baird:
- Tate, C.S. Master
- Rostin, Erich KL KM

Liverpool Packet:
- Schultze, H-O. KL KM
- Smith, N.E. Master

Prescodoc:
- Frowse, J.C. Master
- Lassen, Georg KL KM

Princess Marguerite:
- Harris, W.B. Eng. Officer
- Neilson, W. Chief Eng.
- Stewart, E.E. Eng. Officer
- Krauss, H-W. KL KM

Donald Stewart:
- Hartwig, Paul KL KM

Lord Strathcona:
- Hardy, Gordon, Merch. Navy
- Ruggeberg, Rolf KL KM

John A. Holloway:
- Fechner, Otto KK KM

Norfolk:
- Edge, Thomas Master

Rose Castle:
- Simard, Pierre Seaman
- Wissmann, F-W. KL KM

Jasper Park:
- Gysae, R. KK KM

Point Pleasant Park:
- Eick, Alfred KL KM

INDEX OF SHIPS

All are HMCS unless indicated otherwise. SS = steamship, including motor ships, trawlers. KrM = Kriegsmarine, the German Navy. USS = United States Navy. USCG = US Coast Guard.

A.A. TREUTLAN, SS Ch. 49
ACCIAIO, Ital. Navy Ch. 23
ACHILLES, HMS Ch. 31
A.D. HUFF, SS Ch. 65
ADMIRAL SCHEER, KrM Ch. 56, 65
ADVERSUS Ch. 10
AEAS, SS Ch. 17, 18
AFRICANA, HMSAS Ch. 65
AGASSIZ Ch. 8, 13, 41
AJAX, HMS Ch. 31
ALACHASSE Ch. 10
ALBERNI Ch. 7, 50
ALBERT C. FIELD, SS Ch. 65
ALBRIGHTON, HMS Ch. 43
ALEXANDER KENNEDY, SS Ch. 60
ALFRED III, SS Ch. 43
ALGOMA Ch. 25
ALGONQUIN Ch. 43, 64
AMAKURA, SS Ch. 15
AMAZON, HMS Ch. 65
AMBLER, yacht Ch. 6
ANGELUS, barquent. Tbl. 7
ANNAN Ch. 53
ANNAPOLIS Ch. 19
ANNEBURG, SS Ch. 14
ANTELOPE, HMS Ch. 22
ANTICOSTI, HMS Ch. 55, 65
ANTONIA, SS Ch. 1
AQUHARAZA, SS Ch. 10
ARBUTUS, HMS Ch. 11
ARGONAUT, SS Ch. 26
ARLEUX Ch. 1
ARLYN, SS Ch. 18
ARVIDA Ch. 5, 19
ARROWHEAD Ch. 17
ASCANIUS, SS Ch. 49
ASHANTI, HMS Ch. 39, 40, 42, 43
ASPHODEL, HMS Ch. 36
ASSINIBOINE Ch. 14, 35, 41, 43, 51
ATHABASKAN Preface, Ch. 8, 39, 40, 42
ATHELRILL, SS Ch. 65
AUDACITY, HMS Ch. 14
AVONDALE PARK, SS Ch. 65
AVORIO, Ital. Navy Ch. 23, 24, 48
AZRA, SS Tbl. 6

BADDECK Ch. 35
BARHAM, HMS Ch. 4
BARON KINAIRD, SS Ch. 49
BASSET, HMS Ch. 65
BATTLEFORD Ch. 14, 20, 26
BAYNTUN, HMS Ch. 32
BEACON HILL Forward, Ch. 63
BEAVER ships Tbl. 7
BELLONA, HMS Ch. 40, 43
BIC ISLAND, SS Ch. 3, 21, Tbl. 7
BITER, HMS Ch. 28, 37
BLACK PRINCE, HMS Ch. 39, 40, 44
BLACK SWAN, HMS Ch. 25
BLAIRNEVIS, SS Ch. 61
BLIGH, HMS Ch. 49
BLUEBELL, HMS Ch. 65
BLUEBIRD, schooner, Ch. 3
BLYSKAWICA, Pol. Navy Ch. 39, 40, 42
BOGUE, USS Ch. 25, 36
BOY RUSSELL, SS Ch. 65
BRANDON Ch. 12
BRAS D'OR Ch. 3, 10, 21, Tbl. 6
BRINKBURN, SS Ch. 24
BROADWAY, HMS Ch. 28
BROKE, HMS Ch. 59
BUCTOUCHE Ch. 9
BURGEO, SS Ch. 55
BURLINGTON Ch. 56
BURNHAM, HMS Ch. 12
BURWELL, HMS Ch. 20
BUTTONWOOD, USCG Ch. 30
BUXTON Ch. 12, Tbl. 6

CALCUTTA, HMS Ch. 2, 4
CALGAROLITE, SS Ch. 65
CALGARY Ch. 31, 60
CALPE, HMS Ch. 14
CAMOSUN, SS Ch. 57
CAMROSE Ch. 31, 32
CANADIAN BEAVER, SS Ch. 65
CANADIAN CRUISER, SS Ch. 65
CANADIAN TRANSPORTER, SS Ch. 65
CANADOLITE, SS Ch. 65
CANATCO, SS Tbl. 7
CAPO NOLI, SS Ch. 3, 21, Tbl. 7
CAPRI, SS Ch. 52
CARDITA, SS Ch. 26
CARIBOU, SS Ch. 55, Tbl. 7
CARL ROVER, SS Ch. 45
CAROLUS, SS Tbl. 7
CELANDINE, HMS Ch. 5, 19
CHAMBLY Ch. 7, 8, 22, 29, 47, 50, 61
CHARLOTTE SCHLIEMANN, SS Ch. 33
CHARLOTTETOWN, cvt. Ch. 17, 18, 56
CHARLOTTETOWN, frgt. Ch. 55
CHATHAM, SS Ch. 18
CHAUDIÈRE Ch. 34, 47, 49, 54
CHEBOGUE Tbl. 6
CHEDABUCTO Ch. 17, 30
CHESHIRE, HMS Ch. 13
CHESTERFIELD, HMS Ch. 8
CHICAGO TRIBUNE, SS Ch. 65
CHILCOTIN, SS Ch. 52, 57
CHILLIWACK Ch. 11, 14, 20, 34
CHR. J. KAMPMANN, SS Tbl. 7
CITADELLE, tug Ch. 30
CITY OF CHRISTCHURCH, SS Ch 16
CLAUS BOLTEN, SS Ch. 45
CLAYOQUOT Ch. 11, 18, 56, 64
CLEOPATRA, HMS Ch. 62

COAMO, SS Ch. 65
COLLINGDOC, SS Tbl. 7
COLUMBIA Tbl. 6
COMET, HMS Ch. 49
COMMANDANTE FAA' DI BRUNO See FAA' DI BRUNO
COMOSUN, SS Ch. 57
CONSECO, yacht Ch. 6
CORIOLANUS, HMS Ch. 24
CORNCRAKE, HMS Ch. 24
CORNWALLIS, SS Ch. 65
CORY, USS Ch. 34
COVADONGA, Chilean Navy Ch. 57
CRESCENT, HMS Ch. 2
CRUSADER, HMS Ch. 5
CYGNET, HMS Ch. 20

DAUPHIN Ch. 11, 12
DECOY, HMS Ch. 47, 49
DIANA, HMS Ch. 4
DIANTHUS, HMS Ch. 14
DIRKJE, Dutch Navy Ch. 62
DONALD STEWART, SS Ch. 18, 25, 65
DRUMHELLER Ch. 9, 12, 28, 50, 57, Tbl. 8
DUCHESS, HMS Ch. 4
DUCHESS OF BEDFORD, SS Ch. 1
DUCKWORTH, HMS Ch. 50
DUFF, HMS Ch. 43
DUNDEE, SS Ch. 35
DUNEDIN, HMS Ch. 14
DUNVER Ch. 52

EAGLESCLIFFE HALL, SS Ch. 65
EDMUNDSTON Ch. 31, 32, 41, 57
E.M. HOUSE, SS Ch. 49
EMPIRE AUDACITY, SS Ch. 14
EMPIRE BOND, SS Ch. 14
EMPIRE HERITAGE, SS Ch. 52
EMPIRE HOUSMAN, SS Ch. 34
EMPIRE LAKELAND, SS Ch. 64
EMPIRE OIL, SS Ch. 19
EMPIRE SHACKLETON, SS Ch. 20
EMPIRE TURNSTONE, SS Ch. 49
EMPIRE UNION, SS Ch. 20
EMPRESS OF ASIA, SS Ch. 65, Tbl. 7
EMPRESS OF BRITAIN, SS Tbl. 6
ERIK BOYE, SS Tbl. 7
ERNLAND, SS Ch. 65
ESKIMO, HMS Ch. 39, 40, 42, 44, 45, Tbl. 8
ESPERANZA Ch. 56
ESQUIMALT Ch. 62, 64
ESSO ARUBA, SS Ch. 15
ETIENNE RIMBERT, SS Ch. 45
EUGENE C. ROBERTS, SS Ch. 65
EUROPA, SS Tbl. 7
EXE, HMS Ch. 31
EXETER, HMS Ch. 31
EXPRESS, HMS Ch. 34
EYEBRIGHT, Forward, Ch. 61
EZRA WESTON, SS Ch. 48

FAA' DI BRUNO, Ital.Navy Ch. 5, Ch. 7, 12, 19
FAME, HMS Ch. 42
FENNEL Ch. 34, 56
FESTUBERT Ch. 1
FIDELITY, HMS Ch. 20
FORESTER, HMS Ch. 35, 47
FORFAR, HMS Tbl. 7
FORTS, The, SS Tbl. 7
FRANK B. BAIRD, SS Ch. 65
FRASER Ch. 2, 3, 4
FREDERICK DOUGLAS, SS Ch. 29
FREDERICTON Ch. 35, 41
FRONTENAC Ch. 35, 41

GALT Ch. 13
GANANOQUE Ch. 55
GATINEAU Ch. 34, 47, 49
GENTIAN, HMS Ch. 11
GEORGE L. TORIAN, SS Ch. 65
GEORGE R. DONOVAN, SS Ch. 65
GEORGIAN Ch. 62
GERARD CALLENBURGH, Dutch Navy Ch. 42
GLENARM, HMS Ch. 29
GLENBUCKIE, SS Ch. 65
GLENBURNIE, SS Ch. 65
GLENLINNIE, SS Ch. 65
GIFFARD Ch. 35, 41
GNEISENAU, KrM Ch. 65
GOODSON, HMS Ch. 49
GORGO, Ital. Navy Ch. 24
GRAF SPEE, KrM Ch. 31
GREENHILL PARK SS Tbl. 7
GRIFFIN, HMS Ch. 47, 49
GRIZZLY Tbl. 6
GROVE, HMS Ch. 23
GUILDFORD CASTLE, HMS Ch. 52
GUYSBOROUGH Ch. 62

HAIDA Ch. 14, 39, 40, 42, 43, 44, 64, Tbl. 8
HALIFAX Ch. 15, 35, 41
HALONIA, yacht. Ch. 17
HAMILDOC, SS Tbl. 7
HAMILTON Ch. 12, 13
HANOVER, SS Ch. 14
HARVESTER, HMS Ch. 5
HAVELOCK, HMS Ch. 5
HAVERFIELD, USS Ch. 36
HEINA, SS Ch. 11
HELIOTROPE, HMS Ch. 52
HELMSDALE, HMS Ch. 52
HEPATICA Ch. 9, 17
HERSCHELL, HMS Ch. 65
HERO, HMS Ch. 5, 34, 49, 65
HERRING, USS Ch. 27
HESPELER Ch. 52
H.G. BLASDELL, SS Ch. 49
HIGHLANDER, HMS Ch. 5
HOBSON, USS Ch. 36
HOHER WEG, SS Ch. 43
HONEYSUCKLE, HMS Ch. 8
HOOGHLY, SS Ch. 33
HURON Ch. 39, 40, 42, 45

ICARUS, HMS Ch. 34
INCONSTANT, HMS Ch. 42
INDAUCHU, SS Ch. 65
INDEPENDENCE HALL, SS Ch. 30
INGENER N. VLASSOPOL, SS Ch. 3
INGER ELISABETH, SS Ch. 18
INGLIS, HMS Ch. 62
IRONBOUND Tbl. 6
IROQUOIS Ch. 39, 40, 43
ITCHEN, HMS Ch. 16, 29

J.A. FARRELL, SS Ch. 49
JADDEN, SS Ch. 65
JAMAICA PLANTER, SS Ch. 4
JANSEN, USS Ch. 36
JAN VAN BRAKEL, Dut.Navy Ch. 15
JACQUES MORGAND, HMS Ch. 48
JAMES E. NEWMAN, schnr. Tbl. 7
JASPER PARK, SS Ch. 65
JAUNTY, HMS Ch. 24
JAVELIN, HMS Ch. 40, 42, 45
J.B. WHITE, SS Ch. 65
JERVIS BAY, HMS Ch. 56
JOHN A. HOLLOWAY, SS Ch. 65
JOHN C. HOWARD, SS Ch. 65
JOOSKE W. WINKE, SS Ch. 20, 26

KAIMOKU, SS Ch. 14
KAMSACK Ch. 9
KELSO, SS Ch. 14
KEMPENFELT, HMS Ch. 14
KENILWORTH CASTLE, HMS Ch. 34
KENOGAMI Ch. 7, 20, 26
KENORA Ch. 62
KENORDOC, SS Ch. 65
KENT, HMS Ch. 43
KEPPEL, HMS Ch. 29
KING EDWARD, SS Ch. 20
KIRKLAND LAKE Ch. 56
KOOTENAY Ch. 13, 47, 49
KORMORAN, KrM Ch. 65
KORSÖ, SS Tbl. 6
KRAKOWIAK, Pol. Navy Ch. 43

LACONIA, HMS Ch. 4
LADY DRAKE, SS Ch. 65
LADY ELIZABETH, yacht Ch. 6
LADY HAWKINS, SS Ch. 65
LADY NELSON, SS Ch. 65, Tbl. 7
LADY RODNEY, SS Ch. 56, 65
LADY SOMERS, SS Tbl. 7
LAFOREY, HMS Ch. 23
LAGAN, HMS Ch. 28, 29, Tbl. 8
LA HULLOISE Ch. 61, 63
LAMERTON, HMS Ch. 23
LCI(L) 99, HM Ch. 48
LCT 644, HM Ch. 48
LEA, USS Ch. 15
LEAMINGTON, HMS Ch. 57
LENNOX, SS Ch. 65
LEOPARD, Fr. Navy Ch. 11
LETHBRIDGE Ch. 11
LEVIS Ch. 8
LIBERTAD, Venez.Navy Ch. 20
LISEUX, schnr. Tbl. 7
LIVERPOOL PACKET, SS Ch. 65
LOCH ACHANAULT Ch. 53
LOCH ALVIE Ch. 59
LOOKOUT, HMS Ch. 23
LORING, HMS Ch. 62
LORD KELVIN, SS Ch. 30
LORD STRATHCONA, SS Ch. 65
LOUISBURG Ch. 11, 13, 23, 24
LOYALTY, HMS Ch. 50
LST 362, HM Ch. 34
LST 921, USS Ch. 48
LUCILLE M., schnr. Tbl. 7
LUNENBURG Ch. 31
LYCAON, SS Ch. 21
LYNX Ch. 10, Tbl. 6

M 133, KrM Ch. 43
M 263, KrM Ch. 43
M 304, KrM Ch. 43
M 385, KrM Ch. 43
M 416, KrM Ch. 43
M 427, KrM Ch. 43
M 486, KrM Ch. 43
M4260 KrM Ch. 45
M 4611, KrM Ch. 45
MAGNIFICENT Ch. 44
MAGOG Tbl. 6
MAGOG, SS Ch. 65
MAHONE Ch. 30
MALPEQUE Ch. 51
MAPLECOURT, SS Ch. 65
MARCONI, Ital. Navy Ch. 5
MARGAREE Ch. 2, 4, 47
MARIE SIMONE, SS Ch. 43
MARX, SS Ch. 65
MATANE Ch. 35, 38, 51, 59, Tbl. 8
MAURITIUS, HMS Ch. 43
MAYFLOWER Ch. 8, 61
McCOOK, USS Ch. 12, 26, 29
MELROSE ABBEY, SS Ch. 5, 20
MEMEL, SS Ch. 43
MEON Ch. 51
METEOR, HMS Ch. 20
MICHEL FRANCOIS, SS Ch. 43
MILDRED PAULINE, schnr. Ch. 11, Tbl. 7
MILNE, HMS Ch. 20
MISGAV, Israel Navy Ch. 61
ML 600, HM Ch. 60
MONA MARIE, schnr. Tbl. 7
MONARCH, SS Ch. 60
MONDOC, SS Tbl. 7
MONNOW Ch. 51, 59
MONT LOUIS, SS Ch. 65
MONTREAL Ch. 61
MONTROLITE, SS Ch. 65
MONTROSE, SS Tbl. 7
MOOSE JAW Ch. 7, 8, 9, 15, 22, 47, 50
MORDEN Ch. 16, 29
MOUNT KAISSON, SS Ch. 14
MOUNT PINDUS, SS Ch. 18
MOUNT TAYGETUS, SS Ch. 18
MTB 105, HM Ch. 20
MTB 459 Ch. 46
MTBs 460, 463 Ch. 46
MTB 465 Ch. 46
MTB 466 Ch. 46
MTB 469, HM Ch. 50
MTB 470, HM Ch. 50
MTB 485 Ch. 46
MTB 735 Ch. 43
MTB 736 Ch. 43
MTB 743 Ch. 43
MTB 748 Ch. 43
MTBs, other Ch. 46, 58
MULGRAVE Tbl. 6
MUNERIC, SS Ch. 7
MYNGS, HMS Ch. 43
NABOB, HMS Ch. 43, Tbl. 6

NAPANEE Ch. 20, 26, 27
NARCISSUS, HMS Ch. 29
NASTURTIUM, HMS Ch. 9, 14
NATCHEZ, USS Ch. 41
NENE Ch. 31, 32, 33, 51, 59
NEREUS, SS Tbl. 7
NEW GLASGOW Ch. 53, 61, 63
NEW LISKEARD Ch. 64
NEW WATERFORD Ch. 53
NIELS EBBESEN, Dan.Navy Ch. 53
NIPIWAN PARK, SS Tbl. 7
NOOTKA Ch. 64
NOREEN MARY, SS Ch. 51
NORFOLK, SS Ch. 65
NORTH BAY Ch. 35, 56
NORTH WEST, SS Ch. 65
NOTRE DAME, SS Ch. 65
NOURMAHAL, yacht Ch. 6
NUBIAN, HMS Ch. 40
NYASSA, SS Ch. 24

OAKTON, SS Ch. 65
OAKVILLE Ch. 15, 28, 35, 38, 57
OCEAN EAGLE, tug Ch. 10
ORILLIA Ch. 7, 14
ORKNEY Ch. 61
OTINA, SS Ch. 49
OTTAWA 1st Ch. 5, 7, 8, 12, 19, 65
OTTAWA 2nd Ch. 33, 47, 49
OTTER Ch. 6, 10
OUTREMONT Ch. 53
OWEN SOUND Ch. 35, 38, 51
OWL, USS Ch. 65

PASTEUR, SS Ch. 56
PATRIA, Venez. Navy Ch. 15
PELICAN, HMS Ch. 11, 14, 37
PICTOU Ch. 9
PIORUN, Pol. Navy Ch. 39, 40, 42
PLATINO, Ital. Navy Ch. 24
PLM 27, SS Ch. 65
POINT PLEASANT PARK, SS Ch. 65
POLYANTHUS, HMS Ch. 12, 16, 28, 29
PORTADOC, SS Ch. 65
PORT ARTHUR Ch. 21, 22
PORT COLBORNE Ch. 51, 59
PORT FAIRY, SS Ch. 4
PORTCHESTER CASTLE, HMS Ch. 52
PREDSEDNIK KOPATJIC, SS Ch. 65
PRESCODOC, SS Ch. 65
PRESCOTT Ch. 27
PRIMROSE, HMS Ch. 14
PRINCE HENRY Preface
PRINCE LEOPOLD, HMS Ch. 49
PRINCE OF WALES, HMS Ch.14
PRINCE ROBERT Ch. 31, Tbl. 7
PRINCE RUPERT Ch. 36
PRINCESS MARGUERITE, SS Ch. 65, Tbl. 7
PRINCESS MARY, R.N.L.I. Ch. 48
PROTEUS, SS Tbl. 7
PUGWASH, tug Ch. 1
PUKAKI, HMNZS Ch. 53

Q 065 Ch. 17
Q 083 Ch. 17, 65
Q 090 Ch. 56
Q 091 Ch. 64
Q 099 Ch. 64
QU'APPELLE Ch. 43, 54
QUEBEC, HMS Ch. 21
QUEEN MARY, SS Ch. 1, 65
QUEEN WILHELMINA, Dut.Navy Ch. 62
QUIBERON, HMS Ch. 65
QUICKMATCH, HMS Ch. 65

RACCOON Ch. 17, 65
REGENSBURG, SS Ch. 27
REGINA Ch. 22, 23, 24, 35, 48, 50
RENARD Tbl. 6
RESTIGOUCHE Ch. 2, 43, 49
REVENGE, HMS Ch. 1
RHYL, HMS Ch. 24
RIBBLE Ch. 63
RICHTHOFEN, KrM Ch. 43
R.J. CULLEN, SS Tbl. 7
ROBERT W. POMEROY, SS Ch. 65
ROSE CASTLE, SS Ch. 65
ROWLEY, HMS Ch. 50
ROYALMOUNT Ch. 62
ROYAL ROADS Ch. 7

S 136, KrM Ch. 43
SACKVILLE Ch. 13, 29, 34
SAGANAGA, SS Ch. 65
SAGUENAY Ch. 13, Tbl. 6
ST ALBANS, HMS Ch. 11
ST CATHARINES Ch. 34
ST CLAIR Tbl. 6
ST CROIX Ch. 5, 12, 16, 19, 26, 28, 29
ST FRANCIS Ch. 29
ST LAURENT Ch. 2, 13, 20, 35, 47, 49, 54
ST MALO, SS Tbl. 7
ST PIERRE Ch. 59
ST THOMAS Ch. 28, 30, 57
STE THERESE Ch. 56
SAINT JOHN Ch. 51, 59
SAMNEVA, SS Ch. 59
SAMTUCKY, SS Ch. 56
SANDGATE CASTLE, HMS Ch. 57
SANDOWN CASTLE, HMS Ch. 57
SAN FRANCISCO, SS Ch. 35
SANS PEUR, yacht Ch. 6
SAPINERO, SS Ch. 65
SARNIA Ch. 64
SARNIADOC, SS Ch. 65
SASKATCHEWAN Ch. 43, 49
SASSAFRAS, USCG Ch. 55
SATURNUS, SS Ch. 18
SCHARNHORST, KrM Ch. 65
SCOTTISH HEATHER, SS Ch. 20
SEA CLIFF Ch. 28, 57
SG 3, KrM Ch. 43
SHAWINIGAN Ch. 9, 55, 65
SHEDIAC Ch. 11, 20, 26
SHINAI, SS Ch. 65
SHINAI MARU, SS Ch. 65
SILVER STAR PARK, SS Tbl. 7
SIOUX Ch. 43
SIR WILLIAM HILLARY, R.A.F. Ch. 48
SKEENA Ch. 7, 10, 13, 43, 54
SKIDEGATE Tbl. 6
SKUDD III, HMS Ch. 64
SNOWBERRY Ch. 15, 31, 32
SOEKABOEMI, SS Ch. 20

SONJA VINKE, SS	Ch. 7
SORELDOC, SS	Tbl. 7
SPAR, SS	Ch. 14
SPEY, HMS	Ch. 11
SPIKENARD	Ch. 11, 26
SPRINGHILL	Ch. 55
STADACONA	Ch. 17
STAD AMSTERDAM, SS	Ch. 15
STARLING, HMS	Ch. 37
STATICE, HMS	Ch. 47
STEIERMARK, SS	Ch. 65
STELLA MARIA, SS	Ch. 52
STORK, HMS	Ch. 37
STORMONT	Ch. 38, 51, 59
STRATHADAM	Forward, Ch. 61, 63
SUDETENLAND, SS	Ch. 65
SUMMERSIDE	Ch. 9
SUSSEXVALE	Ch. 63
SWANSEA	Ch. 15, 35, 37, 38, 51, 57, Tbl. 8
SWENNING, USS	Ch. 36
SWIFT CURRENT	Ch. 30
SYDNEY, HMAS	Ch. 65
T 24, KrM	Ch. 39, 40, 42
T 27, KrM	Ch. 39, 40, 42
T 29, KrM	Ch. 39
TABER PARK, SS	Ch. 65
TACONITE, yacht	Ch. 51
TAHCHEE, SS	Ch. 7
TALISMAN, HM S/M	Ch. 6
TALISMAN, SS	Ch. 65
TARTAR, HMS	Ch. 39, 40, 42, 43
TEME	Tbl. 6
TERRA NOVA	Ch. 12 (note)
TERVANI, HMS	Ch. 23
TETRARCH, HM S/M	Ch. 6
THEODORE DWIGHT WELD, SS	Ch. 29
THETFORD MINES	Ch. 61, 63
THORLOCK	Ch. 64
THOROLD, SS	Ch. 65
THORSHOLM, SS	Ch. 25
THUNDER	Ch. 9
TIMMINS	Ch. 41
TINTAGEL CASTLE, HMS	Ch. 62
TIRPITZ, KrM	Ch. 43
TORONDOC, SS	Ch. 65
TOWARD, SS	Ch. 20
TRAIL	Ch. 9, 65
TRANSCONA	Ch. 56
TRENTONIAN	Ch. 34, 60
TREHATA, SS	Ch. 14
TREVISA, SS	Ch. 65
TRITONE, Ital. Navy	Ch. 22
TROISDOC, SS	Ch. 65
TRONGATE, SS	Ch. 30
TRURO	Ch. 17, 55
TWEED, HMS	Ch. 29, 31, 32
URSA, HMS	Ch. 43
V 414, KrM	Ch. 43
V 702, KrM	Ch. 43
V 717, KrM	Ch. 43
V 720, KrM	Ch. 43
V 729, KrM	Ch. 43
V 730, KrM	Ch. 43
VALLEYFIELD	Ch. 35, 41
VANCOUVER ISLAND, SS	Tbl. 7
VANQUISHER, HMS	Ch. 62
VEGREVILLE	Ch. 17, 62
VENTURE	Ch. 10
VERULAM, HMS	Ch. 43
VICTOLITE, SS	Ch. 65
VICTORIA, Venez. Navy	Ch. 13
VICTORIAVILLE	Ch. 64
VICTORIOUS, HMS	Ch. 18
VIDETTE, HMS	Tbl. 8
VILLE DE QUEBEC	Ch. 21, 22, 33, 50
VINELAND, SS	Ch. 65
Vp 203, KrM	Ch. 45
Vp 213, KrM	Ch. 45
WAINWRIGHT, USS	Ch. 14
WALEHA, SS	Ch. 29
WALKER, HMS	Ch. 65
WANDERER, HMS	Ch. 29
WASKESIU	Ch. 32, 33
WASP, USS	Ch. 36
WATERLOO, SS	Ch. 65
WATERTON, SS	Tbl. 7
WATKINS F. NISBET, SS	Tbl. 7
WATUKA, SS	Ch. 65
WESER, SS	Tbl. 7
WEST JESTER, SS	Ch. 65
WETASKIWIN	Ch. 13, 20
WEYBURN	Ch. 17, 18, 25, 65
WHEATLAND, HMS	Ch. 23
WILLIS, USS	Ch. 36
WINDFLOWER	Ch. 9
WINNIPEG, SS	Ch. 16
WISHART, HMS	Ch. 8
WISLA, SS	Ch. 6
WITCH, HMS	Ch. 13, 19
WIVERN, HMS	Ch. 25
WOODSTOCK	Ch. 20, 25
WRESTLER, HMS	Ch. 8
YARRA, HMAS	Ch. 65
YORKTOWN, USS	Ch. 61
YPRES	Ch. 1
YUKON STAR, SS	Ch. 57
Z 24, KrM	Ch. 42
Z 32, KrM	Ch. 42
ZH 1, KrM	Ch. 42
ZAMBEZI, HMS	Ch. 43
ZYPENBERG, SS	Ch. 9